CORPORATE ROMANTICISM

Sara Guyer and Brian McGrath, series editors

Lit Z embraces models of criticism uncontained by conventional notions of history, periodicity, and culture, and committed to the work of reading. Books in the series may seem untimely, anachronistic, or out of touch with contemporary trends because they have arrived too early or too late. Lit Z creates a space for books that exceed and challenge the tendencies of our field and in doing so reflect on the concerns of literary studies here and abroad.

At least since Friedrich Schlegel, thinking that affirms literature's own untimeliness has been named romanticism. Recalling this history, Lit Z exemplifies the survival of romanticism as a mode of contemporary criticism, as well as forms of contemporary criticism that demonstrate the unfulfilled possibilities of romanticism. Whether or not they focus on the romantic period, books in this series epitomize romanticism as a way of thinking that compels another relation to the present. Lit Z is the first book series to take seriously this capacious sense of romanticism.

In 1977, Paul de Man and Geoffrey Hartman, two scholars of romanticism, team-taught a course called Literature Z that aimed to make an intervention into the fundamentals of literary study. Hartman and de Man invited students to read a series of increasingly difficult texts and through attention to language and rhetoric compelled them to encounter "the bewildering variety of ways such texts could be read." The series' conceptual resonances with that class register the importance of recollection, reinvention, and reading to contemporary criticism. Its books explore the creative potential of reading's untimeliness and history's enigmatic force.

CORPORATE ROMANTICISM

Liberalism, Justice, and the Novel

Daniel M. Stout

Fordham University Press

New York 2017

This book's publication was supported by the University of Mississippi's Department of English.

Visit us online at www.fordhampress.com.

Library of Congress Cataloging-in-Publication Data available online at catalog.loc.gov.

Printed in the United States of America

19 18 17   5 4 3 2 1

First edition

Contents

Anaximander, son of Praxiades, a Milesian, who was a successor and pupil of Thales, said that the infinite [*aperion*] is principle and element of the things that exist. . . . And the things from which existing things come into being are also the things into which they are destroyed, in accordance with what must be. For they give justice and reparation to one another for their injustice in accordance with the arrangement of time (he speaks of them in this way in somewhat poetical words).

      —Simplicius, *Commentary on the Physics*, 24.13

The immortal but soulless corporation with her wealth of accurate records would yield no inch, would enfranchise no serf, would enfranchise no tenement. In practice the secular lord was more humane, because he was more human, because he was careless, because he wanted ready money, because he would die.

      —Sir Frederick Pollock and Frederic William Maitland,
    The History of the English Law Before the Time of Edward I

Introduction: Personification and Its Discontents

> No man, if he had his choice, would be the angel Gabriel
> to-morrow! ... He might as well have an ambition to be turned
> into a bright cloud or a particular star.... He would rather
> remain a little longer in this mansion of clay, which, with all its
> flaws, inconveniences, and perplexities, contains all that he has
> any real knowledge of or any affection for.
> —William Hazlitt, "On Personal Identity"

> What are we? Personified *all-powerful points.*
> —Novalis, *Logological Fragments* §55

It has come to seem axiomatic that modernity and individuation are essentially synonymous processes, the twin faces of what we know variously as the history of liberalism, secularism, bourgeois capitalism, or, sometimes, just "the Enlightenment."[1] Virtually every major account of modernity contains a version of the story Charles Taylor has recently called "the great disembedding," the process by which individuals are extracted (or abstracted) from some earlier, more integrated form of collective life. For Taylor, writing on secularism and modernity, the historical break occurs within religion: when the "collective" and "often cosmos-related rituals of whole societies" are supplanted by an "individuated religion" organized around "individual responsibility" and "rationally understood virtue." But the basic shape of this story—in which "whole societies," as Taylor says, are "reconceived as made up of individuals"—remains more or less the same, regardless of which aspect of modernity one emphasizes.[2] We can see it, for instance, in Foucault's account of the individuating, disciplinary regimes of modern power; Habermas's account of the bourgeois public sphere as a meeting of rational minds; Ian Watt's account of the realist novel as the literary inheritance of rational individualism; and in the seminal histories of Lawrence Stone, E. P. Thompson, and Eric Hobsbawm, all of whom chart, in their various ways, the decline of a collective imagination. Depending on the history you are writing, the inflection point might be Gutenberg, Locke, Defoe, or Bentham, but the trajectory remains the same: wholes (groups, communities, families, aristocracies, collectives, etc.) are disaggregated into the single, universal currency of the individual.

Corporate Romanticism draws our attention to some of the limits of this narrative by revealing a surprising scarcity of individuals in a historical period—the early nineteenth century—and a literary form—the novel—in which the dominance of individualism is frequently taken for granted. We have typically understood the decades between the French Revolution (in 1789) and England's Second Reform Act (in 1867) to be crucial for consolidating liberalism as a political formation and confirming the ideological preeminence of contract more generally. As such, our common narrative sees the nineteenth century as both a microcosm and the apotheosis of modernity's atomizing sweep. The seeds of the liberal individual, we think, may have been germinating in English life and letters for some time, but it is in the nineteenth century's drive toward an expanded franchise and the ascent of market rationality that we see it finally emerge as an exceptionless rule. What, after all, still stood in its way? Chartism's economic resistance to what Marx and Engels called "the icy waters of egotistical calculation" had come to an abrupt, disappointing end in the 1840s, by which point romanticism's aestheticized resistance to "the business of getting and spending" (as Wordsworth put it way back in 1802) was already more a memory than a cause.[3] The decline of those practices and cultures of resistance, along with the proindividualist legislative changes that took place between the 1820s and 1860s—including lightened restrictions on political representation (for example, Catholic emancipation) and financial contract (for example, repealing usury laws)—led Henry Sumner Maine to conclude, from the none-too-distant vantage of 1861, that the great social metamorphosis from "status" to "contract" was complete.[4] Maine's famous claim would be replayed in a minor key a century later by Marxist historians, who saw in midcentury England the final faltering of a collective tradition that extended back through Chartism, the Swing Riots, romanticism, and the working-class radicalism of the later eighteenth century. Thompson's seminal account of working-class consciousness ends, accordingly, in the 1830s, with the collapse of the last viable holdouts against "Utilitarianism [and] the exploitative and oppressive relationships intrinsic to industrial capitalism"; for Hobsbawm, similarly, the decades between 1789 and 1848 are defined not by "the emergence" of an "individualist, secularist, rationalist" ideology but by "its triumph."[5]

Beneath such bright lights it may appear merely perverse to argue that the individual was in these decades something less than a given. But, as we will see, however individualist it may be in theory, liberalism does not, once deployed, simply reduce the social field to a set of isolated actors subjecting one another to the instrumental logic of atomic self-interest. The larger, more complicated story I bring out here centers on two interlinked developments within the history of liberalism, both of which, separately and together, undermined the most basic assumption of liberalism and justice alike: that individual human persons might be meaningfully correlated with particular actions.

The first complicating development is the rise of corporate persons. The specific legal fiction of the business corporation—now the *sine qua non* of modern capitalism but relegalized in England only in 1825 and not fully widespread until the 1860s—is certainly one part of this story. But the business corporation is, as we will see, only one element in the broader history of corporate persons I offer here. Under my broader construal this history also includes the various conceptions of persons and minds as material assemblages developed in later eighteenth-century natural philosophy; political visions like the French Revolution's theory of a "national will," which refer agency to larger (and perhaps imaginary or only abstract) bodies; and a number of ideas that emerge within and are especially identified with romantic writing—"the spirit of the age," the "One Life within us and abroad," the symbol. Clearly, there are basic differences here: sometimes the corporate person is a product of nature, or nation, or legal stipulation. But what links them all, and what justifies thinking of all of them as corporate persons, is that in each case agency is understood to be first and foremost (and possibly strictly and finally) the property of the corporate group—the nation, the assemblage, the age, etc.—and not the human individual. Like the "veil" that, in the theory of the modern business corporation, separates shareholders and employees from the actions of the company itself, these corporate persons create conditions in which the agency and responsibility of human individuals is obscured or, more fully, mooted by the attribution of agency and responsibility to a transcendent, suprapersonal entity.

The second complicating development involves not the corporateness, exactly, but the collectivity of action itself. Unlike the incorporation of the person—which, after all, still posits a singular (if nonhuman) agent—the problem that emerges at the level of action involves its inherent multiplicity, its tendency to expand or spill over, to collect more effects and, thereby, to redefine itself as it goes. The problem the corporate person poses for liberalism involves identifying *who* is to blame for an action; the problem of action's collectivity involves specifying *what* constitutes "an action" in the first place. To acknowledge action's collectivity is to initiate a crisis of confidence about the scale at which we read the world. As a matter of philosophy, this question does not begin in 1800; one can trace versions of it back to the earliest metaphysical inquiries into the static versus always-unfolding nature of Being. But in the early nineteenth century the industrialized expansion of life turned a perennial topic of philosophical speculation into a highly pressurized question about the nature of legal liability in a scaled-up world. Like any causal narrative, legal cases and verdicts rely on the possibility of dividing the world into discrete sets of actions and effects. But denser living conditions and the amplified actions of industrialism made these divisions seem extraordinarily dubious. Courts became confused about how to calculate liability in light of downstream effects. Public health officials struggled to trace systemic problems (for example, pollution) back to individual actors. Liberal philosophers like John Stuart Mill worried often and at length about the logical shortcuts needed to frame an "event," "action," or "crime" out of a theoretically infinite set of ancillary causes and effects. As John Plotz has argued, new forms of agglomeration "arrived in Britain as nowhere else in the first half of the nineteenth century." One effect, as many scholars have shown, was a new awareness of the networks of affect, information, and opinion that stitch individuals into what Mary Poovey calls "a social body."[6] But more than this—more, that is, than how it is that we feel, think, or believe together—agglomeration also changed the shape of action itself.[7] So while we often see the industrial landscape as a monument to ruthless self-interest, industrialization also—and conversely—lit up action's stubborn refusal to fit the forms of first-person accountability. It may be that all action can be said to begin in self-interest; the problem we encounter here is that no action can be said to stay that way.

Both of these significant developments—the broad rise of corporate persons and the increasingly perspicuous social life of action—steer us away from a view of the period as one in which a monolithic individualism replaced the older forms of a collective England. Certain forms of collectivity (for example, Chartism, the aristocracy) were undoubtedly in or on the brink of decline in the early nineteenth century, but other forms of collectivity were also appearing in the period, revived, like the business corporation or the romantic nation, where they weren't brought into being by what some nervous Lancashire magistrates called "a general spirit of combination."[8] Our view of the early nineteenth century is not complete without a fuller understanding of how these collective dynamics informed both its literature and the political formation we know as liberalism.

One payoff of revising our assumptions about the history of individualism in the early nineteenth century is a new perspective on a complicated stretch in the history of the novel. It has not always been easy to think about "the novel" during the romantic period, when the grandest aesthetic claims were often made on behalf of poetry (and, in one famous instance, *against* "story") and when the novel itself seems to fracture into a variety of subgenres as it shifts toward romance and reflects a rapidly changing social landscape.[9] It has been hard to fit this generic instability, both epitomized and oversimplified by the dichotomy of Jane Austen versus Sir Walter Scott, into a linear history that begins with the invention of novelistic realism in the eighteenth century and proceeds in an orderly fashion toward its apogee in the Victorian period. When Coleridge complained about how "the multitudinous Public, shaped into personal unity by the magic of abstraction sits nominal despot on the throne of criticism," he was identifying only one of the mass personalities— the reading public—brought into being by "the magic of abstraction" (a magic Coleridge, it should be said, had in spades).[10] At the turn of the nine-teenth century, social forms multiplied in theory (the mob, the crowd, the multitude, the combination) as well as practice (new political groups, corre-sponding societies, and worker's collectives), ideological options merged and diverged (genteel radicalism, working-class radicalism, democratic popu-lism),[11] questions about the relation of the local to the national sharpened as society-level dynamics were debated (the Condition of England, the spirit of the age, Godwin's reason, Malthus's scarcity),[12] and fundamental political ideals like "democracy" and "liberty" underwent thorough redefinition.[13] Within the genre of the novel, these social reorganizations produced the "exceptional turbulen[ce]" many critics have charted.[14] The sheer scale of historical change demanded new genres—like the gothic or historical novel—that could reflect the power of transgenerational dynamics.[15] Geo-graphic upheavals (rural–urban migration, colonialism, war) yielded new prose genres like the "national tale" or the "village tale" and hybrid cultural formations like "metropolitan romanticism," "global romanticism," or the "colonial gothic."[16] And an increase in various forms of political and religious factionalism produced highly specialized and often short-lived microgenres like the "Jacobin novel," the "Chartist novel," "the anti-Jacobin novel," the "evangelical novel," and so on.[17]

Much important critical and bibliographic work has gone into mapping this thematic pluralism. Without at all wanting to discount any of that work or the texts and traditions it has called to our attention, my project here aims at identifying at least one source of formal consistency within the roman-tic novel: a persistent concern about how corporate persons and collective action obscure justice and accountability. This concern is formal in the sense that it is less interested in the specific nature—the ideological glue—of the corporate person (which might be an aristocratic family, a national culture, a predestined elect, or a human body) than it is in the philosophical problems corporateness as such creates, and it is formal—or at least properly generic— in the sense that the constant question of whether actions can be assigned to human individuals amounts to skepticism about one of the novel's most consistent operating premises. My study, as I see it, returns to a version of the problem Robert Kiely adduced several decades ago as a primary source of embarrassment in the generally "embarrassing subject" of the romantic novel: that romantic novelists "tried to introduce the unnamable into a genre which derived much of its strength from an insistence on naming names."[18] My version of that problem is equally formalist but runs the other way around: not what happens when the unnamable (Kiely is thinking about extreme psychological states and sublime aesthetics) is introduced into an insistently nominalist genre but how it is that an insistently nominalist genre reckons with the ways in which modern life had, in its incorporated complexity, already made individual names seem like only the most figurative of flags. The claim is not, then, that we have been wrong to see the novel as a genre closely tied to the liberal individual or "an insistence on naming names" but that we have understood that connection in terms that were too narrow in large part because we have understood liberalism to be a more monolithic ideological contender than it actually was. We have tended to speak as if the individualism of liberalism went without saying and as if novels, therefore, could only either play conscriptedly along (in the mainline realist tradition) or support some other losing, if not in fact already lost cause ("the hereditary faith of Sir Everard in High-Church and in the house of Stuart" we see in *Waverley,* for instance).[19] But things loosen up for the novel when we recognize that liberalism was beset by very basic questions—what does it mean to be "a person" and what defines "an action"?—and they loosen up even more when we realize that these fundamental doubts appeared not because some actively antiliberal ideology suggested them but because they grew out of the conditions—the representative structures, corporate forms, and self-ramifying dynamics—that liberalism itself creates. Once we have this constitutive (and still running) contradiction between the individualism of liberal ideology and the corporatism of the liberal world in mind, the odd contradictions of the novels I've gathered here—which are something like arguments for individualism after anyone has stopped believing in individuals—begin to fall into place: innocence you don't have to earn, virtue you cannot deserve, guilt that never ends, action that never stops, character without innerness, many persons speaking through a single human, a single creature who is also a species, a man who is not himself because he is his double, a man who is neither himself nor his double. These confusions of personhood and action are not exceptions to the law of liberal individualism; they are the confusions that are its only history.

—+—

The bourgeoisie, Marx and Engels write in their famous description, "has put an end to," "has pitilessly torn," "has left remaining no other nexus," "has drowned," "substituted," "stripped," "torn," and "swept away." Theirs is an extraordinarily vivid account of a revolution whose sudden and wholesale violence Edmund Burke had, though writing from a rather different disposition, tried to bring home almost sixty years before. It's hard not to hear Burke's exercised rhetoric—the "delightful vision" of a "queen glittering like the star of the morning" dissolved by "this new conquering empire of light and reason"—ringing, at least half sardonically, through the *Manifesto*'s prose.[20] The "idyllic relations" of feudalism, gone; "chivalrous enthusiasm," ended; patriarchy, dead; "heavenly ecstasies of religious fervour," also dead.[21] A bad world replaced by an even worse one.

Relieved of the manifesto form, more recent views have described this transformation in less upheaving but equally teleological terms. Eugenio Biagini and Jonathan Parry, for instance, have recently done important work charting the ideological consolidation required to establish the broad individualist ethos that gave the Liberal Party its political dominance under Gladstone. Similarly, literary and cultural scholars such as Elaine Hadley, Lauren Goodlad, David Wayne Thomas, and Amanda Anderson have offered us new and highly nuanced perspectives on what it was like to *live* liberalism, as Hadley's title puts it, during this time of transition.[22] What, these studies have asked, were the promises and burdens of being an individual in an age that was, as Biagini and Parry argue, figuring out how to be individualist? In these more recent views, liberalism is less a destroying flood than a product of long development. At the level of the political party, ideological coalitions needed building, and at the level of the individual, inner resources (reflection, detached judgment, sympathy, etc.) needed to be cultivated and the tensions between them managed. But even across these longer timelines, the one-point perspective that is the rise of the individual emerges. "Most of the ingredients of Gladstonian Liberalism were," Biagini argues, "already present in previously existing movements: independence, anti-State attitudes, free trade, anti-clericalism."[23] Burke's sacking hordes are thus replaced by more gradual social hegemony, but we don't really lose the narrative arc. Parry's liberalism, compared with Burke's, is decidedly more sober but, in its apparent monopoly on good sense, no less dominant: "If nineteenth-century Liberalism meant anything," he writes, "it meant a political system in which a large number of potentially incompatible interests—whether nationalities, classes, or sects—were mature enough to accept an over-arching code of law which guaranteed each a wide variety of liberties."[24] A lot less drowning and sweeping away, then, but a convincing victory for individualism nonetheless: who doesn't want "a wide variety of liberties"?

For my part, I am interested in what can sometimes feel like the backside of this historical narrative. My study doesn't contest—indeed, it presumes—the plausibility of these historical narratives, and its conclusions aren't greatly affected by the relative speed with which liberal ideology rose to dominance. What I am interested in are the many ways that persons (and the cultural forms that traditionally deal in persons, like novels and the law) found themselves strangely, surprisingly, and often anxiously unable to get a clear view of the very individuality on which they are premised. The project's claim, most simply, is just that the units of Hobsbawm's "individualist, secularist, rationalist" ideology were hardly self-evident, even in their moment of ostensible triumph. Beyond this, what I mean to show is that the self-possessed persons and discrete actions liberalism presumes were often obscured by the very economic entities (the corporation), political forms (the democratic nation), social conditions (crowded industrialism), and epistemological perspectives (empirical science) we most associate with liberal modernity. What we are seeing, in short, is a contradiction between theory and practice: that while modernity may be liberal-individualist in theory or on paper, many of its key features—freedom of contract, representative government, urban life, scientific empiricism—serve rather to point up the fragility and fictionality of the atomic units on which its image of itself relies. The twentieth-century critique of liberalism—which suggested that liberalism's abstract units denied thickly lived reality, historical and cultural specificity, etc.—was, from this perspective, a second pass at a basic intuition already alive in the early 1800s: that things are more complicated than liberalism's pointillist doctrine of "to each his own" can admit.[25] The history of liberalism is in this sense a history of anxiety about its own capacities.

As I show in Chapter 1, two very basic anxieties—what, exactly, is a person? and where, exactly, does an action end?—were the objects of highly self-conscious debates within what may look, from the outside, like a confident monolith of liberal ideology. The debate over the business corporation, for instance, went on for three decades (from its relegalization in 1825 until the Companies Act in 1856), with both pro- and anticorporate sides arguing that their position was enjoined by their larger commitment to individualist liberty. That, for me, is a useful fact because it reveals a persistent uncertainty about how to put individualism into practice even and especially within an ideologically individualist dispensation. As we will see, similar difficulties—not about whether one should "do individualism" but about whether one even can—turned up in the courts of law and the laboratories of empirical science, where operations premised on the possibility of matching *this* cause with *that* effect foundered in the face of the complex collectivities in or across which action takes place. In light of these wide-ranging debates and difficulties, I present liberal individualism not as an ideology that projected itself as if into a placeless void or rose up in external opposition to some prior collective. Instead, liberal individualism here is a persistently (and perhaps constitutively) ironic formation. It is, we will see, an individualism that carries its collectives along with it, sometimes producing them knowingly (as with the corporation) and sometimes discovering them, like Victor Frankenstein, at the end of a chain it hadn't, or hadn't exactly, meant to be forging.

In this revised perspective, liberal individualism looks less like a self-sufficient, hegemonic doctrine that rolls out against all alternatives than it does a political formation trying to assert meaningful order over the collective and recombinatory world its own agents and agencies keep putting into motion. And in this regard my view is happy to share its basic intuition with the one animating Edmund Fawcett's recently published history of liberalism. Liberalism, for Fawcett, is less the name of a coherent and monolithic doctrine than a linked series of attempts to solve the "predicament" of "a masterless world."[26] Liberalism, that is, is as much the response to a highly collectivized and densely packed modernity as it is that modernity's origin point. This makeshift or, as I sometimes think of it, *flailing liberalism* has not been much highlighted in our views of the period. We have focused more on the dissolving power that produced, in Engels's oft-quoted phrase, "a world of atoms" and much less on the "colossal centralization" Engels also identified (only a few sentences away) as a defining feature of modern life.[27] But what I'm doing here is trying to hold both of these countervailing movements together, to respect both dimensions as, in fact, part of the same story. The goal is to watch how the move toward atoms ends up centralizing and how, on the other hand, even the most centralized world continues to demand that we understand it (if we are to understand it at all) in atomic terms. The story of this internal struggle is a little awkward to tell because, inconveniently and unsurprisingly, no one wins, and no one could have. But it belongs, I think, within our picture of modernity, of what it means to be modern. And it would be important even if it had never made itself felt as a warping within the aesthetic history of the novel, although it did that, too.

One might—as Chapter 1 does—compile an archive of individualism's ideological crisis from legal decisions, philosophical treatises, and newspaper editorials. But the genre of the novel was a cultural form particularly, and perhaps supremely, sensitive to the abiding friction between the grammar of liberal justice and the unshapely agencies of the early 1800s. Though it sounds slightly strange to say, part of what made the novel so sensitive to the problems of justice posed by group persons and group actions was that it had not, at least as it emerged out of its eighteenth-century development, been particularly prone to thinking about them. Like the broadsheet confessions alongside which they grow, novels do best, or at least seem to work the most smoothly, when they can see a character's ending as a plausible outcome of her actions.[28] *Robinson Crusoe* is smooth: "We have seen him work like no other character in fiction," writes Franco Moretti: "How can he not deserve what he has?"[29] *Pride and Prejudice* might be smoother still, a novel able not only to score an individual against a fixed field of value (the abstract ledgers of Robinson's double-entry books) but to adjust the systems of social evaluation *even as* Elizabeth changes her own mind or pauses to recalibrate her perspectives. For Nancy Armstrong, it is this ability to coordinate and synthesize two separate developmental movements that defines the novel as a genre. "To be a novel," she has argued, "is to be a story in which "two conditions are met: (1) the protagonist acquires a position commensurate with his or her worth, and (2) the entire field of possible human identities changes to provide such a place for that individual."[30] Armstrong might not be thinking of *Pride and Prejudice* in particular, but it doesn't matter: her point is that these evaluative operations belong to a literary machine that bourgeois England was busily mass producing. But aren't there, we might pause to ask, many novels in which punishment seems to fall on the wrong head or credit seems in unfairly short supply? What about Hardy's *Tess*; or the "relentless brutality" to which Clarissa is subjected; or the serial subjugation of Sade's *Justine*; or the enormous disproportion between the "harsh destinies" assigned to "poor wandering Hetty, poor Mr. Casaubon, poor Gwendolyn" and their original sins?[31] Our first thought may be that such plots ought to make us skeptical about an assessment like Armstrong's: tons of novels fail to give protagonists "positions commensurate with [their] worth." But we can just as soon see how much our objection and the novels on which it is premised, in fact, confirm Armstrong's position: the perception of injustice, like the perception of irony, to which it is closely related, involves our being able to compare how things went with how things should have gone. Novels can present us with brutality or the far subtler slights of attention that plague someone like *Persuasion*'s Anne Elliot in the full faith that we will recognize them for what they are—in full faith, that is, that we have kept a very minute and steadily updated tally of who is owed what by whom.[32] The refusal of justice, in this sense, assumes accountability quite as much as the happier, or at least commensurating, alternative. So sometimes, as in *Pride and Prejudice*, verdicts click home with the satisfaction of a couplet. Other times, the alignment feels off: sentences seem too light, or the judge is in a punishing mood. But its ability to go wrong requires the liberal machinery to be up and running: the novel is counting, even when it is counting wrong, and it knows that we are, too.

The version of injustice I am interested in here is quite different. I am not interested in stories where individuals get more or less than they deserve. I am, instead, interested in stories where the very units that deserving requires are unavailable: where it is populations or processes that need to be brought to account; where corporate ontologies moot individual responsibility; where the prospect of valuing an action is undercut by its tendency to drift, so that a local kindness becomes a distant harm. I am not, then, interested in cases where justice goes wrong for reasons of prejudice or class interest, although it was undoubtedly the case that women and the poor were greatly disadvantaged before and disproportionately harmed by the English penal system.[33] Nor am I interested in a whole set of epistemological problems whose roots lie essentially in individual psychology—the fact that vision fails, for instance, or that memory is unreliable, or that the intentions of other minds are hard to gauge. These are all reasonable subjects to explore. But because they appear only in systems that already understand themselves to be composed of individual persons and discrete actions, they are not my focus, and I have tried to keep my focus from sliding toward them. This project is about the conflict between the individualism of justice and the corporateness of both actors and actions. The question corporateness poses for justice isn't about vision or bias or error. It's about whether justice's most basic units have any defensible purchase, any legitimately ordering force.

In the chapters that follow, I track this problem—not injustice, exactly, but something more like the deformations of justice in a world without definite individuals or discrete actions—through a set of important novels: *Caleb Williams* (1794), *Mansfield Park* (1814), *Frankenstein* (1818), *The Private Memoirs and Confessions of a Justified Sinner* (1824), and *A Tale of Two Cities* (1859). The goal of these readings is not to replace our most common narrative about the novel's connection to individualism but to construct a more nuanced, self-reflexive version of that story. The novel, here, does not act as a mouthpiece for liberal ideology. It confronts the philosophical difficulty (and maybe the impossibility) of thinking about individual accountability in a collective world.[34]

Although I've just listed them chronologically, this project's chapters do not proceed according to the publication date of their major examples, and I should say something about why that is here. As a matter of philosophy, both the groupness of persons and the hazy boundaries of action date back

well before the early 1800s: the legal form of the *universitas* (the legal fore-
runner of our modern corporation) reaches back to Roman law; materialist
conceptions of the person go back at least to Lucretius; and, for someone like
Hannah Arendt, action just is always-already networked and expansive—the
"constant establishment of new relationships within a web of relations."[35]
So we are dealing with problems that are sometimes very old and, in certain
cases, properly timeless. The question of origin, accordingly, seems either
very difficult to answer or a little misguided. For this reason, the following
discussions will talk about an *intensification* of certain problems within the
early nineteenth century, but I do not pretend to offer a complete history
of any of the major intellectual-historical threads that I take up here. As it
goes for the make-believe of a beginning, so too, the end: as I will suggest
in the final chapter, which looks at the crisis of universal responsibility in
Frankenstein and some recent theoretical work on environments and systems,
many of the questions I chart here remain with us today. It's clear from any
newspaper that we continue to struggle to fit the individualizing grammars
of justice onto complicated and mutually ramifying circumstances (oil spills,
climate treaties, class actions, etc.). Given this persistence, it doesn't seem
sensible to argue that Dickens in 1859 just closes up the box Godwin opened
in 1794. We may worry a lot less today about the inherent indeterminacy of
an idea like "proximate cause" than we did in 1840. But that's less because the
conceptual strain has disappeared than the fact that proximate cause, like a
number of the other fictions we use to manage the strained relations between
individuated justice and an interrelated modernity, has weathered into more
or less comfortable conventionality.

Thus absent clear beginnings or endings, I have organized the literary
chapters of this project not according to the date of their central example
but according to the kind of corporate problem they engage. The arc of
the main literary cases begins with two texts—*Mansfield Park* and *Justified
Sinner*—both of which understand the existence of corporate personality to
have a negative or muting effect on the prospect of individual action. Because
these novels imagine the corporate person as a timeless structure into which
individuals are slotted, individual action and the determinations that we
might make on its basis (virtue, blame, guilt, credit) disappear from view. In
these novels, doing is replaced by being. In the final two novels I treat, *Caleb
Williams* and *Frankenstein*, the situation is very nearly reversed: doing—the
autonomous, self-propagating nature of action itself—is preeminent, but,
again, the determinations of justice falter, now because action itself ripples
forever out into new effects and/or is nothing more than the present face of
an incalculable fan of causality that extends into the past. *A Tale of Two Cities*,
historically the most recent text, plays a central role in linking these two ver-

sions of the problem. Like *Mansfield Park* and *Justified Sinner*, it finds a form of being that action can't alter in the naturalized memberships of birth (as aristocrat or citizen) that underwrite the French Revolution's political logic. Like *Caleb Williams* and *Frankenstein*, it sees both the Terror and the distributed, transhistorical oppression it seeks to avenge as a product of national or aristocratic, rather than personal, will. Perfectly capital punishment in a world without persons: the famous equivocations of its opening aside, Dickens's novel really offers us something like the worst of both worlds.

To begin a project about the problems of justice and action with Austen's *Mansfield Park* (Chapter 2) may seem either too easy, given the novel's famously passive heroine, or very odd, given the novel's reputation for depicting an incessantly scrutinizing, punishing patriarchy.[36] But our two most common thoughts about the novel—that it both is programmatically against action and offers a detailed code for how individuals should act—obviously present an important and underelaborated contradiction about what we mean by conservative morality. The case I present here seeks to clarify that contradiction, by reading against the common view that sees *Mansfield Park* as a novelization of Burke's conservative morality and arguing, instead, that the novel reaches back not to Burke but to the even older legal form of the manor for a notion of corporate personhood that is not a way of evaluating individual action at all. Unlike a legal code, which can tell you where you've gone wrong, or a utilitarian classroom, which can tell you how you've done relative to others, the manor is a set of preestablished, noncontractual obligations into which persons (including the lord, who is himself "held of" the manor) are slotted. Within this structure, individuals appear not as actors whose potentially wayward impulses need to be controlled (à la Burke) or whose freedom needs to be honored (à la Paine) but as entities who either will or will not meet the scripted, predetermined requirements. The logic of the manor is, in this sense, something like the opposite of the logic of contract; it does not solicit certain types of behavior (obey your father, say) or sentimental attachment (filial piety), and it does not address itself, like the law, to rational self-interest. Operating according to a binary logic of obligation met or obligation missed, the manor can't be understood as a code of moral values; one cannot pay one's rent well or badly, and the credit of filling one's role does not accrue to anyone's personal account. It is, I will argue, thus a mistake to read the perplexingly meek character of Fanny Price as an icon of conservative morality, as if she were a model for hedonistic liberty well curtailed. She is not a model for liberty at all. She is, instead, the center of a legitimately radical aesthetic experiment: to write a novel in which personality, if it exists at all, exists at the level of the institution rather than the human person.

Mansfield Park has an ending that seems happy—or at least happy enough that one feels Austen is willing to give the formal perfection of institutional personality a kind of credit. The mooting of individual action we see in *Mansfield Park* does not, at the end of the day, seem to have disordered much beyond readerly expectation. In *The Private Memoirs and Confessions of a Justified Sinner*, by contrast, James Hogg imagines the psychological deformations that might plausibly come from taking formal completion personally. As I read it in Chapter 3, Hogg's best-known novel turns on a parallel between the Calvinist belief in predestination (which it decries) and romantic nationalism (which many critics have understood it to vindicate). As I show, what Calvinism and romantic nationalism share is their commitment to a form of collective identity defined by its permanence, its immunity to change. The "death in life" advocated by Calvinist theologians and literalized in the Justified Sinner's sense that he lives under a form of diplomatic immunity is thus redoubled in romantic nationalism's allegiance to an antiquated authenticity it can preach but never practice.

One way to understand these two problematic novels together is to see both *Mansfield Park* and *Justified Sinner* as suspicious assessments of the fantastic proposition in romantic aesthetics that each might represent the all and that the all might represent each, without either form of representation coming at the expense of the other. Examples of this faith in costless figuration abound: in the "translucence" with which Coleridge imagined the general might show through the special and the universal through the general; in Wordsworthian personification, which treated individual persons as mediums for what Coleridge called a "living and acting power"; in Shelley's claim, in his fragmentary essay "On Life," that "the words *I, you, they*, are not signs of any actual difference" but "merely marks employed to denote the different modifications of the one mind."[37] As a political and ethical move, romanticism's claim for a thoroughly figurative ontology in which every part stands for the whole and vice versa strikes a powerful blow against the arbitrary distinctions that restricted representative significance to a narrow band of aristocrats and kings.[38] But its costs become clearer when we see that the elimination of certain distinctions is achieved by the elimination of all distinction: that nothing is or ever could be the "sign of any actual difference." Representativeness, in this view, is a fact, not a capacity. Persons are not just potentially representative; they are *nothing but* representative: "not signs," "merely marks." And action, accordingly, changes from something that persons do in or add to the world to become simply a modification or flux within the total order of Being for which every particular speaks. It is against this backdrop of romantic figuration that we can start to understand some of the contemporary force of *Mansfield Park*'s and *Justified Sinner*'s

interest in the way even an ostensibly utopian holism obviates the very individual persons we might expect it to protect. As novels, then, these texts
expose the basic failing of romantic politics: that it routes its claims on behalf
of the person through the claim of the person's representativeness.[39] Totality,
wholeness, or what Schelling calls "allness" are not, Austen and Hogg see,
routes to justice.[40] Caring about justice means believing that not all ways
of framing the world are equal, that some signs *are*, in fact, "signs of actual
difference." Because universal personification makes thinking in this way
impossible, it is hostile to justice. And because romanticism made universal
personification central to both its aesthetics and its politics, justice and romanticism don't go together either.

If Austen and Hogg thus offer one analysis of how romantic holism
causes words like "*I, you, they*" to lose their meaning, Dickens's description
of the French Revolution in *A Tale of Two Cities* (Chapter 4) offers another.
The claim in The Declaration of the Rights of Man that "the principle of all
sovereignty rests essentially in the nation" sets up an entire country on the
principle of romantic personification and funds a novel obsessed with the
question of what it would mean to take seriously the idea that individuals
are avatars of a transcendent agency. The considerable interest and insight
of *A Tale of Two Cities* involves its resistance to the standard view in which
modernity trades representativeness for individual action—the "nobleman,"
says Habermas, "was what he represented"; "the bourgeois, what he produced." Instead, *A Tale* sees how the forms of representativeness we associate
with aristocratic personhood—in which the lord is, as Habermas puts it, "an
embodiment of a higher power"—are not only conserved but in fact universalized by the democratic state.[41] "It was nothing to her, that an innocent man
was to die for the sins of his forefathers," says the novel of its revolutionary
Madame Defarge; "she saw, not him, but them."[42] By operating according to
a logic in which the claims of both nobility and national citizenship are premised on birth, on "forefathers," the French Revolution sets up a situation
in which both agency and liability are inherited rather than inherent. The
result is not a conflict between democratic individualism and aristocracy but
a collision between two forms of corporatized agency. This is why reports of
the actions of the novel's well-intentioned noble, Charles Darnay, who has
gone to some lengths to redress the brutality of his ancestors, fall on deaf ears
whether he's talking to his aristocratic uncle (who can't think in any terms
other than family) or Madame Defarge (who can't either).

The problem that focuses *A Tale of Two Cities*, then, is the idea at the
heart of political economy or what we now often refer to as the biopolitical:
the structural incommensurability between the individualized agency that
belongs to persons and the socialized agency that belongs to nations, "fore-

fathers," populations.[43] It seems, on one view, entirely reasonable to imagine that the two levels—the personal and the popular—bear on each other. We need bad nobles to have a bad nobility, and you can determine a bad nobility only by its real-time effects on real-live persons. At the same time, however, we can see the analytical problem of structural conditions emerging: that social conditions are not simply the sum total of individual ones and cannot necessarily be disaggregated accordingly. The badness of a nobility is not really a sum total of all the individual bad actions of individual nobles, and still less is it a warrant for moving inductively from the general badness of a group to the guilt of a particular person. Like the equally mysterious and conceptually identical aggregations that yield us our sense of character—how often does one have to do generous deeds to be a generous person?—the perspective of political economy is founded on the nonidentity between the species and the instance.[44] In this way the massified democratic nation that, for Lukács, made both historical consciousness and Scott's historical novel possible produces a moral crisis: a situation in which agency and responsibility exist only in distributed or aggregated form and can, therefore, only ever be partially or figuratively bodied forth by any particular human.[45] The materialism of the areas with which political economy concerns itself (bodies, health, energy, etc.) and, even more bluntly, the physicality of action itself thus light up a problem—the disconnect between population and person—that can remain muted when we think of the individual-aggregate relation in the speculative terms of consciousness.[46] Thinking or feeling like a class or a culture is one thing. But how does one prosecute an amorphous and fundamentally plural *them*? One answer is that one doesn't, that it doesn't make sense to treat population-level dynamics as if they yielded an account of individual action.[47] But if one is going to do it—to hold a "them" legally accountable—one can only do it serially, going after "them" by executing him, him, him. This is, of course, the very feat the guillotine makes possible. Dickens sees the serial executions of the Terror neither, with Burke, as a proof of mass irrationality, nor, with someone like the early Wordsworth, as the tragic perversion of otherwise admirable political ideals, but as a perfectly logical follow-though on the distributed agency the democratic nation imagines. One hundred and fifty years before German *Einsatzgruppen* devised a gas van to reduce the occupational fatigue of death squads, the guillotine marks the birth of what we now know as the biopolitical: a way to punish at the level of the population rather than the individual, a way to behead thems rather than hims.[48]

If there's something illogical about the Terror, then, it is its refusal to honor the categorical gulf that separates those forms of power that are proper to populations from those forms of agency that are proper to persons; it keeps treating biopolitics as if it were, after all, just the sum total of politics. The Terror treats individuals as if they were derivable from populations, and the guillotine, in this sense, functions as a kind of prosthetic technology for bridging the philosophical gap between the popular and the personal.[49] As such, we might see ourselves enjoined by Dickens's novel to draw sharper distinctions between the two fields. As we will see in the final two chapters, however, the idea of a bright line that could separate the corporate from the individual is itself a fiction. Both *Caleb Williams* and *Frankenstein* (Chapter 5 and the Epilogue) are horror stories about the impossibility of maintaining a sense of individual responsibility within the crowded, networked relations of the modern world. What we are dealing with here are not the confusions of agency introduced by the corporate person but the confusions of agency produced by action's own seemingly autonomous capacity to spread itself. In these retooled gothics, the problem comes not from the past—as in *The Castle of Otranto*'s idea that "the sins of fathers are visited on their children to the third and fourth generation"—but from the hopelessly intermixed present and the constantly unfolding, limitless list of liabilities that is the future.[50] Their closest fictional relatives, in this sense, are not behind but ahead of them, in fundamentally epidemiological gothics like *Dracula* or the *Alien* franchise.

Godwin's stringently individualist *Enquiry Concerning Political Justice* had insisted that "no man must encroach upon my province nor I upon his."[51] Only a year later, however, he published a novel fundamentally concerned with the impossibility of disentangling the province (or provenance) of any one person's story from any other's. What *Caleb Williams* calls out for is not, as we have often thought, a less prejudiced justice system—one in which the rich and powerful were prevented from tyrannizing over the poor and weak—but a theory of easement law: a way to negotiate and give form to the inevitable ways we share the world with others. Similarly, I read *Frankenstein* not as a novel that studies the moral failings of its characters—the failures of sympathy, the refusals to take responsibility, etc.—but as one interested in the way an interpenetrated and mutually ramified material world produces conditions that, by making actors everywhere, can't see justice anywhere.[52] Well before the twentieth-century shift away from the rational actor of classical economics and toward theories of social cost and externality, both Godwin's and Shelley's novels treat action as inherently networked and, therefore, fundamentally unpredictable. In *Caleb Williams* the fact that an action has positive effects locally is no bar to its having deleterious ones somewhere down the line. And *Frankenstein*, with a similar perversity, reveals how a natural philosophy premised on tracing effects to their causes not only fails to give us reliable law but produces situations in which it is impossible to speak meaningfully about "an individual action" at all. The problem is not that the famous flash of Enlightenment enables overreaching action but that it obliterates the concept of action itself, yielding a world in which the agency of persons has no special weight.

This, then, is the shape of this book's overall narrative. The goal is to see how the corporate and the collective appeared as an analytical problem for individualism—a problem for moral philosophy, justice, accountability—but was also itself a product of the romantic, revolutionary, and modernizing dynamics that frequently understood themselves to be operating in the individual's name. It is in formulating this doubled, counterintuitive position—a liberalism without individualism, or an individualism without persons—that we can most clearly see the intellectual contribution of these novels. They show us that we might be the most perfectly liberal individuals *as individuals* but that we would still be neighbors to one another, that we might sign contracts but that we do so frequently in order to delegate authority in ways that both extend and attenuate our own responsibility, that we act as self-interested animals even though we live in a world that functions as an unpredictably interconnected system of systems, and that we take our liberal feet to the polls to vote for a representative whose relation to us has all of the ambiguity and existential complication Hannah Pitkin so importantly described.[53] What does it mean to represent another person? To act on another's behalf? To see one's actions as part of a larger collective enterprise? To stand there at the head of a collective body or the tail end of a chain of events and say, *Yes, that was all me*? These are the questions. In asking them I seek to continue the work of scholars like Sandra Macpherson and Jonathan Kramnick, who have offered strong revisions of intentionalism in the eighteenth-century novel, but also to show some of the ways confusion about individualism persisted even in (and often just because of) an era increasingly organized around the assumptions of contract and representative government.[54] These confusions persist because, as these novels saw, all the liberal personhood in the world won't help you establish justice in a world where a good action today grows into a bad one tomorrow or where actors are simply the delegates of some larger agency. We are, these novels show, always costs to one another, and we can be costs to one another even at a great distance. So whether action is (or ever could be) intentional is only one version of the problem. Even in a system of intentional actions someone will be paying prices (and someone will be reaping benefits)—living with consequences—that no one had, and maybe no one could have, written into the contract.

Before the externalities of the economists, then, there was the novel: a fictional form uniquely suited not just to mark the value of individual actions, as we have often said, but to mark the uncertainty of the individuality of both persons and actions. In offering this revision I do not understand myself to be correcting some broadly mistaken view of the novel; the argument is not that a genre we have taken to be individualistic was, in fact, working in favor of the collective. Nor am I suggesting, like David Kurnick's interesting and subtle account of the Victorian novel's relation to the theater, that we can glean from these texts the last flickers of an absent or suppressed collective imagination.[55] In these texts, the collective emerges not as a utopic horizon but as an always-available way of construing a given situation.[56] These are novels that remain deeply aware of the thinness of the margins and the fictions of phrasing that separate self-presentation from representative selves. As such, they are animated not by the competition between the inner life of character and the external frameworks of the social world in the ways that Alex Woloch and others have described but by a never-settled question about whether to read persons and actions closely or from a distance. Individualism, they know, is a question—which is also to say an answer about, a determination of scale.

My interest in justice and collectivity returns us to a problem—liberalism's insistence on individualized verdicts—that was at the center of its extensive and decades-long ideological critique. That critique did the important work of making us all aware of liberalism's insufficiencies as a theoretical entity: we all are now capable of reminding ourselves, for instance, that cultural praxis matters; that issues of embodiment and locality complicate liberalism's putatively abstract universalism; that liberalism may not give us a very useful or accurate framework for action if we really are, as virtually every branch of empirical science is busily confirming, complex bundles of mutually imbricated materials. But we are, I think, perhaps also now in a position to see that unbinding the individual in order to turn it loose in a system of infinite connections can only count as a correction for so long before it begins to deteriorate our ability to say why it seems better to us to have things—property, punishment, regard—distributed one way rather than another. Indeed, to the degree that we want to make an argument for widening our perspectives to admit the fact of our systemic interconnection, it cannot possibly be just the *fact* of interconnection that drives us. Interconnection is, in and of itself, not a value, and we do not get kinder or better or more just or less globally warm simply by belonging more extensively. We may seek, as everyone from Coleridge to the most recent object-oriented ontologist has sought, to liberate ourselves from the human categories that organize our perception. But the freer we get, the more difficult it will be to say why we ever wanted that freedom (if we could even still think of it as that) in the first place. In the end it seems entirely possible that we will have been right to lodge our complaints against the antisocial tendencies of the liberal subject—its rigid closure, its instrumentalizing logic, its balefully thin metrics for human flourishing, its tendency to reduce persons into what E. P. Thomson condemns as "Acquisitive Man."[57] But it does not follow from this dissatisfaction that the unfettered transactions of Being carrying itself out ought to be preferable—or that there would, in this flattened ontology, be anyone there to do the preferring. The pressing question, that is, is not *whether* we are, as M. H. Abrams put it in his famous essay on the romantic lyric, "intervolved with the outer scene"; the pressing question is about how the fact of "intervolvement" impacts the moral frameworks that depend on intervolvement having hard, specifiable limits.[58]

For a quick, closing snapshot of this problem, take Thomas Carlyle's description of the 1819 "Peterloo" uprising in Manchester. His reading of the event does not, as it might have, focus on the heroism of the peacefully resisting crowd or the tense cruelty of the troops sent to disperse it. Instead, Carlyle sees the event as a dramatic demonstration of the difficulty of perceiving (or pursuing) justice in a systemically interconnected world. The spirit of the age, we might say, now rerecognized as an analytical crisis. Could, Carlyle wondered, even the most carefully intentioned intervention avoid coming up either empty handed or fatally arbitrary? Perhaps not:

> A million of hungry operative men, rose all up, came all out into the streets, and—stood there. What other could they do? Their wrongs and griefs were bitter, unsupportable, but who are they that cause these wrongs, who that will honestly make effort to redress them? Our enemies are we know not who or what; our friends are we know not where! How shall we attack any one, shoot or be shot by any one? O, if the accursed invisible Nightmare, that is crushing out the life of us and ours, would take a shape . . . any shape that we could see, and fasten on![59]

What these men need, but can't have, Carlyle sees, is the handhold of a meaningful sense of individual agency. What they need is a shape, "any shape to see and fasten on," something to personify "the accursed invisible Nightmare," something to make it susceptible to address and, thereby, redress. A shape might have been found, perhaps. We could hope so. But we'd also have to find ourselves hoping—for the particular sake of whichever body bore the brunt of it—perhaps not. What follows is a literary history of this ambivalence.

1. The Pursuit of Guilty Things

Corporate Actors, Collective Actions, and Romantic Abstraction

> The other shape
> (If shape it might be called that shape had none
> Distinguishable in member, joint, or limb,
> Or substance might be called that shadow seemed,
> For each seemed either)
>
> —Milton
>
> Methinks, a less equivocal word than *Person* ought to have been
> adopted.
>
> —Coleridge

If only "the accursed invisible Nightmare, that is crushing out the life of us and ours, would take a shape ... any shape that we could see, and fasten on!"[1] As we said at the end of the Introduction, the problem Carlyle saw facing the men of Manchester—the Manchester predicament, we could call it—was how to convert what we would now call structural conditions—the aggregate motives and massed effects of a social body—into the terms of individual action and accountability. This chapter argues that the Manchester predicament was, in fact, much more general across the late eighteenth and early nineteenth centuries, decades that were caught—in a historically new way—between the crushingly palpable (because real) but bafflingly obscure (because incorporated, distributed, collectivized) nature of modern agency.

What the men of Manchester are recognizing is the peculiar semitranscendence of modern agency. On the one hand, who could deny its force as it "crush[es] out the life of us"? On the other, where are the bodies doing the acting—"how," Carlyle's men ask, "shall we attack any one"? If this combination of force and facelessness is a modern given by the time we get to, say, the interminable bureaucracy of Kafka's *The Trial* (Der Process), Carlyle's men and the early nineteenth century more broadly register its contradictions with suffocated and plaintive immediacy. Justice, in its necessarily particularizing way, keeps asking who's responsible for this, keeps asking where all this began. But it does so now in a world that can no longer supply an answer. The Manchester predicament: at the moment when we most need "substance," we find "shadow." The sublime obscurity Burke found modeled in Milton's famous image of Death—a shape without one—might thus be said to take up a life in the romantic era beyond the strictly aesthetic realm.

Coleridge admired Milton's image for compelling the mind "to reconcile opposites and qualify contradictions" by leaving it "unfixed and wavering" between images, "attaching itself permanently to none."[2] As we will see in the final section of this chapter, Coleridge's thought here—that the poetic image as *image* might manage the contradiction between the abstract and the individual or between the "unfixed" and the "attach[ed]"—was characteristic of his aesthetic theory more generally. But outside of poems—in, for instance, the streets of Manchester or the courts of law—speculative suspense was in short supply and the "contradictions" and "opposites" far less easily inhabited. Either someone is to blame (substance), or, because no one did it or everyone did it together, someone isn't (shadow). As a matter of justice, both cannot be true even if, as a matter of fact, both are.

To make the case for the pervasiveness of these contradictions—agency without agents, effects without causes—this chapter strings together three distinct but conceptually interrelated minihistories. The first section looks at the history of the corporation and follows its much debated and far-from-inevitable rise in nineteenth-century England. Our contemporary tendency is to see the corporation as synonymous with the acquisitive self-interest of liberal individualism. But the matter is more complicated. Because the defining feature of the corporation is that it possesses a legal personhood distinct from the identities of its shareholders—a body, as Milton might say, "not distinguishable in member"—the corporation is ontologically duplicitous: at once made up of contracts and, at the same time, not reducible to those individual agreements. As the first legal treatise dedicated to the subject (published 1793) put it, the corporation is like the river Thames: a corporation stays itself despite having different members just as "the river Thames is still the same river, though the parts which compose it are continually changing."[3] In the corporation, then, we see a quotidian, widely available transcendence. Where it used to be only special entities—Death or kings or the "stationary blasts" of Wordsworth's waterfalls or the "frozen floods" of "Mont Blanc"—that might exist in two ontological realms simultaneously, by 1862 any seven or more people could, by simply "subscribing their names to a memorandum of association," create an immortal being.[4] "Of woods decaying," as Wordsworth put it, "never to be decayed."[5]

This metaphysical perplexity about the identity of a corporate agent was, as we will see in the second section, paralleled by uncertainty about the nature of action itself. Although the law had, well before 1800, begun to expand its basic forms of direct, intentional, red-handed action (assault, trespass, etc.) in order to comprehend less immediate or less intentional forms of harm, England's industrialization challenged concepts like negligence, nuisance, and vicarious liability in new ways. As public health authorities, courtrooms, and various governmental commissions noted, the vast scale of industrial action made it possible for a single action to harm thousands of people at once or to do damage many miles away. This increased capacity for harm went hand in hand with an increasing density of action that made it difficult to trace a condition (smog, a polluted river) back to a finite number of actors. Under industrialism, actions seemed, like Deleuze's Alice, to get bigger and smaller at once.[6] The obvious limit-case version of the thought— the whole world imagined as one action for which everyone is responsible (an idea we will later see taken up in *Caleb Williams* and *Frankenstein*)—lit up, for both practicing judges and liberal philosophers like J. S. Mill, the arbitrary boundaries that make a case a case and the nonce determinations that allow us to recognize an action as such.

Such legal and industrial contexts may seem far from the green fields of romanticism, but in the third and final section I am going to demonstrate how the part-whole problems we see in the corporation and the law inter-sect with both late eighteenth-century empiricism and romantic aesthetics. Although we frequently oppose them, the promise of both the empirical method and the romantic symbol as Coleridge theorized it was a perspective in which parts and wholes, members and bodies, could be made intelligible simultaneously. Both the empirical method and the symbol can be thought of, in this sense, as answers (or as the promise of answers) to the problem of corporate identity and amorphous action alike: a way to see the parts that make something what it is without, therefore, losing focus on the unified field. As we will see, though, both answers had their weaknesses. Empiricism tended either to multiply particles beyond count or to drift off into content-less abstraction. And the symbol, which offered a solution to this problem of focus by insisting on the essential unity of part and whole, could do so only by deleting action from the equation entirely. Romantic unity, in a thought we will see taken up in both *Mansfield Park* and *The Private Memoirs of a Justi-fied Sinner*, comes at the expense of action; the unity of being is secured, but only at the expense of doing.

Corporate Actors

> Whoever saw a public body in tears?
>
> William Hazlitt, "On Corporate Bodies"

Despite our tendency to think of the nineteenth century as an ostentatiously laissez-faire period and of the corporation as more or less synonymous with capitalism as such, the rise of the corporation as a business entity in nineteenth-century England was a long, uneven, and debate-ridden process.[7] Starting in 1720, those corporations not already in possession of a royal charter (that is, all but relatively few of the operations that had been issuing transferable shares) were outlawed under the Bubble Act. That act was Parliament's hurried response to a financial crisis that had developed when the value of shares in the South Sea Company (less a trading company than a scheme to finance the national debt) dropped precipitously. In the wake of the South Sea crash, both government and law took a pious stance against allowing joint-stock companies to avail themselves of the privileges of incorporated status. These privileges included the right to issue freely transferrable shares; to sign documents with a corporate seal; and, although there are debates about this, to the protections of an early form of limited liability.[8] There are some indications that actual enforcement of these restrictions was light and that even under the Bubble Act companies operating without royal imprimatur were able to transfer shares or even to sell entire corporate charters.[9] Officially, though, it would not be until 1825, when Parliament repealed the Bubble Act, that associated investors could petition Parliament for corporate status. Even then, though, incorporation was not unanimously endorsed. After 1825, incorporation still required a private act of Parliament (and therefore a time-consuming and expensive petition process), and England's courts in the first decades of the century sent enough mixed signals that, as B. C. Hunt put it in his classic history of the business corporation, "confusing litigation and the ghosts of 1720, harried the course of the unincorporated joint-stock company until the middle of the [nineteenth] century."[10]

This hesitation was not caused by litigation alone; incorporation came up periodically for intense public and legislative debate well into midcentury. In 1837 Parliament commissioned Bellenden Ker to produce a lengthy *Report on the Law of Partnership*, and in 1850 and again in 1851 Robert Slaney convened two separate Select Committees to discuss ways in which the laws of partnership might be adjusted to allow for greater participation from the working and middle classes. Still, Parliament hardly rushed to unfetter contract or generalize limited liability. In 1844 Gladstone decided, under significant pressure, to remove from the Factory Acts provisions that would have established general limited liability. In his assessment of this midcentury landscape, the historian Ron Harris finds a "complex and mixed picture" in which laissez-faire stances alternated with regulatory ones.[11] Eventually, thanks to the Companies Acts of 1856 and 1862, incorporation became a standard, easily invoked status, but basic questions about the form persisted. *Salomon v. Salomon and Co., Ltd.*—an 1897 case involving the debts of a company set up by one Salomon (with 20,001 shares) and his wife and five eldest children (one share each)—is frequently cited as a resounding affirmation of the distinction the 1862 Companies Act made between the personality of the corporation and the personality of its shareholders. But the case's existence in the first place—that Salomon Co.'s creditors were still trying to sue Salomon the man—and the fact that the final verdict arrived only when the House of Lords reversed a series of lower court decisions suggests that uncertainties lingered even at the end of the century.

From our current vantage, the rise of incorporation seems inevitable, and it has become entirely commonplace to assert that industrialization would have been impossible without it. But what seems most remarkable about the shape of the midcentury debate is that much of the resistance to incorporation came from people who saw it as a threat to (rather than an extension of) individualism. When the Mercantile Laws Commission convened in 1854 to inquire into "what Alterations and Amendments should be made in the Law of Partnership as regards the Question of limited or unlimited Responsibility of Partners," one William Entwhistle, a banker (!) from Manchester, offered the following view: "It seems to me that we deal, and ought to deal with men as individuals, not with an abstraction called capital, which we are thus called upon to recognise as possessing a separate and independent existence."[12] If our tendency today is to read neoliberal corporatism as an extension of liberalism's contractual individualism, views like Entwhistle's (held, no less, at the height of industrial expansion) not only distinguish individualism from capitalist abstraction but far more pointedly understand individualism as abstraction's antithesis.[13] What we can see in Entwhistle's comment, then, is an intimation of a larger rift within liberalism. Does one's allegiance to contractual individualism entail a commitment to free and unrestricted rights of incorporation? Or should one's allegiance to individuals, as Entwhistle suggests, entail hostility to the mysterious abstractions of incorporation as such?

Across the nineteenth century this difficult either/or remained unresolved as both pro- and anticorporate views presented themselves as positions derived from a fundamental commitment to "men as individuals." In 1825, for instance, a procorporate editorial in *The Morning Chronicle* argued that repealing the Bubble Act was in keeping with a more general trend in which England was "happily now beginning to shake off those restraints which 'the wisdom of our ancestors' thought beneficial to encumber us." "We have," the editorial observed, "ceased to fetter the public press."[14] And in an age of such liberality, what could be the argument against permitting individuals to "employ, or even squander their money" in whatever way they might choose? In basic form, these liberalizing arguments run backward—to Bentham's *Defense of Usury* (1787) and to Wollstonecraft's and Paine's arguments against "the rust of antiquity" and "the tyranny of the dead." And they run forward as well: In his 1851 testimony before the Select Committee on the Law of Partnership, John Stuart Mill wrote that "the liberty of entering into partnerships of limited liability appears to me an important element in the general freedom of commercial transactions." Prohibiting that liberty was, he argued, "only tenable on the principles of the usury laws, and may reasonably be abandoned since those principles have been given up."[15] For *The Morning Chronicle* as for Mill, the right to incorporate—the freedom to assemble *financially*, as it were—was, like the right to a free press, just a principle reasonably deduced from an overarching commitment to individual liberty. Absent some other consideration, the only legitimate position is one of regulatory noninterference.

This clever hitching of the freedom to squander money to the freedom of the press gives incorporation an attractive philosophical pedigree. But to other commentators it was by no means clear that one's allegiance to contractual individualism required supporting incorporation. In fact, because corporations had enjoyed special trading privileges for much of their early history and because they inevitably entailed a structure in which a manager oversees capital belonging to others, many took the Entwhistle position to argue that corporations were not a logical outcome of contractualism but its antithesis. No less an advocate for contract than Adam Smith had argued forcefully that corporations were bastions of protectionism and lethargic management. "If you would have your work tolerably executed," Smith wrote in *The Wealth of Nations*, "it must be done in the suburbs, where the workmen, having no exclusive privilege, have nothing but their character to depend upon."[16] Because the directors of incorporated companies are "the managers rather of other people's money than their own," Smith warned, they are without the "anxious vigilance" we would see if their own money were on the line. Several decades later, Mathias Attwood, a liberal Tory and a banker, expressed his admiration for the ability of unincorporated companies to work "honourably, profitably, [and] usefully to the country" even while being "without the pale or protection of, the law" since "the parties were a law for themselves, their character was their law."[17] Even Marx (not, to say the least, a regular fan of the Smithian line) pointed out that the corporation allowed managers to "proceed quite unlike owners who, when they function themselves, anxiously weigh the limits of their private capital." To Marx, the corporation, which he called "private production unchecked by private ownership," was uniquely bad: it preserved the fundamental injustice of capitalism (private production) without the one thing (private responsibility) that might have operated as a check on its exercise.[18] An 1836 editorial in *The Times* made this Smithian-Marxian point forcefully: "Let shareholders be pronounced only partially liable, and they will scarcely remember the existence of the bank, except when they occasionally receive some interest for their investment." Limit the shareholder's "liability, and the bank becomes a delusion."[19] The problem with the corporation is not, in these views, its self-interested contractualism; the problem with the corporation is that it's not private *enough*.

One thing this debate reveals is the inadequacy of describing the nineteenth century as a period in which individualism simply replaced collectivism. In one sense, the governing thought behind this commonplace—that there was in the nineteenth century a pervasive commitment to individualism—is entirely borne out by what we have seen so far: everyone, even Marx, is trying to preserve a notion of individual responsibility. But we can also see that the "commitment to individualism" does not, in fact, say much about how a world that reflects that commitment ought to be set up. When we think of the century as a debate between liberal individualists and anti-individualists who stand somehow outside of liberalism, we risk missing the substantial contest taking place within liberalism itself: not about whether to be individualist, but how.

It's no accident that the corporation reflected so intensely this uncertainty about how to put individualism into practice since from the very beginning the corporation had been a profoundly ambiguous entity, at once an individual capable of real action and an ungraspable, disembodied abstraction. The legal innovation of the corporation's *persona ficta* is usually attributed to Pope Innocent IV,[20] but the basic notion reaches back to the *universitas* of Roman law and filters into English life very early as the legal structure for decidedly nonprofit entities such as guilds, vills, boroughs, universities, and parishes.[21] The point of the corporation was to convene an entity that would be able to function in certain legal senses like a natural person but that would also be immune to some of the fragility to which natural persons are prone: that we are careless, lose interest, die. As Blackstone explains, the corporation can "sue or be sued, implead or be impleaded, grant or receive, by its corporate name, and do all other acts as natural persons may." But it does so in ways that a "mere voluntary assembly" of natural persons never could. Towns, universities, and the like cannot do their work well if the "rights and immunities" they enjoy are, upon the death or removal of a member, "utterly lost and extinct."[22] The usefulness of the corporation thus inheres in its *non*contractual and transpersonal nature, its ability to persist over and above the changing, local configurations of human bodies. The impersonal abstraction Smith and others decried in the corporation was—at least originally—precisely the point.

Society's need to think in timelines longer than a human lifetime gives what Blackstone calls the corporation's "perpetual succession" an obvious utility. But useful as it is for running towns and building cathedrals, perpetual succession also creates a crisis for our understanding of corporate action since it prevents our seeing a clear connection between the actions of the corporation and the actions of its members. Blackstone clearly marks this divide between "private consent" and corporate action: if, he says, "particular members . . . express their private consents to any act, by words, or by signing their names, yet this does not bind the corporation." Even, we might ask, if all the "private consents" are unanimous? Still no, explains Frederick Pollock: when "the assembled Fellows of a College resolve to grant a lease of certain college land, their resolution, whether unanimous or by the suitable majority, would seem to be the act not of agents but of the College itself." Although clearly some internal procedures—board meetings, motions, votes, etc.—lie "behind" the action, the legal fiction is that the actions of the corporation, once enacted and signed by the corporate seal, belong entirely to the corporation as corporation and not at all to the members as persons. The corporation is, Pollock says, under rights and duties that "as against the world at large are wholly distinct from the rights and duties of the particular persons immediately concerned in the transactions." The members just work here, "and it is not to their personal responsibility that third parties dealing with [the corporation] are accustomed to look."[23]

The obvious difficulties this legal fiction poses for notions of responsibility lay dormant during the corporation's preindustrial life, and they did so because corporations were relatively inactive "as against the world at large." Most early corporations functioned on timelines that feel, by today's standards, practically geologic. Early corporations would have had transferrable shares ("perpetual succession") by definition, but the shares were not typically vendible commodities. Indeed, because corporations were often oriented toward things like municipal maintenance, charity (for example, Christ's Hospital, incorporated 1552), and the advancement of religion or professional knowledge, it would have seemed strange to think of one's membership as having any monetary value at all. Pursuing these various civic aims did, of course, require the corporation to engage in various kinds of contractual action—institutions need to acquire property, libraries to buy books, towns to rent land—but those actions were in service of the corporation's essentially nonprofit aim. The early corporate person was, we might say, capable of acquisition, but it was not what E. P. Thompson calls an "Acquisitive Man"; it was not the relentlessly transactional machine for maximizing shareholder value we know today.

In writing about the corporation, the conversion from a primarily non-profit entity to primarily for-profit one does not receive the attention one might expect. Mankind has always been a social creature, the usual thought runs, and now we just pool our money. But insofar as there is something inherently curtailed about the timelines of shareholder value (since a share is only worth something to me if *I* am the one who can transfer it), the monetization of the corporation amounts to a wholesale reversal of the reason for ever wanting corporations in the first place, namely, that society needs some interests that last longer than individual lives. This perhaps explains why the corporation's public orientation was surprisingly slow to die out: Blackstone, even though he is writing well after the share-driven panic of the Bubble Act (and some two hundred years after the Crown's first mercantile efforts), insists that corporations exist because it was "found necessary . . . for the *advantage of the public* to have any particular rights kept on foot and continued," and the idea that a commitment to the common good was part of what entitled one to corporate status persists into the nineteenth century.[24] This is not to say that all corporations had to be strictly charitable but that even at the end of the eighteenth century the form is still understood as best suited for long-term and essentially open-ended aims. (Blackstone's list of corporation-appropriate projects includes "the furtherance of religion," "the good government of a particular town," and "the improvement of the medical science.") Because the operative assumption is that a corporation will be directed at projects that are essentially never ending (furthering religion, improving science), the corporation is animated by something like the opposite of self-interest. It is a creature capable of contract but aimed at undertakings from which there is for all intents and purposes no cashing out.

It is not really, then, until well into the nineteenth century that it becomes an assumption in need of no explication that corporations are primarily devoted to advancing their own financial interests and, thereby, the financial interests of their shareholders. This increasingly self-interested corporation became, predictably, increasingly active. As Harris explains, because early corporations "held most of their assets in immoveable land [and] did not aim at profit, transact commercially, or have joint stock capital," their "tort liabilities were not expected to be considerable."[25] But in the busily industrializing nineteenth century, the situation reversed, and the development put great strain on a legal tradition that not only was without any developed theory of corporate liability but that remained unsure about whether corporations, long thought of as "invisible beings," could perform any substantial, physical actions at all. In his famous decision in *Sutton's Hospital* (1612), Sir Edward Coke laid out some of the limitations of these invisible beings: corporations "may not commit treason, nor be outlawed, nor excommunicated, for they have no souls"; "a corporation cannot do fealty, for an invisible body cannot be in person, nor swear."[26] The idea that corporations are depthless and cannot be said to have intentions like natural persons (they can't pledge allegiance or neglect their pledges) lingered well into the period when corporations were fast becoming the most obviously capable actors in the economic landscape. In their monumental history of the common law, published at the end of the nineteenth century, Pollock and Maitland recapitulated and even extended Coke's list of what invisible bodies can't do: "The corporation is invisible, incorporeal, immortal; it can not be assaulted, or beaten, or imprisoned; it can not commit treason; a doubt has occurred as to whether it can commit a trespass, but this doubt (though it will give trouble so late as the year 1842) has been rejected by practice, if not removed by any consistent theory."[27]

But it is difficult to square this view of the corporation as paper tiger with any more detailed look at the legal history of the nineteenth century. Despite Pollock and Maitland's chipper tone, the very basic question of whether a corporation "can commit a trespass" was not an odd, malingering doubt. Because corporations, prior to 1856, required statutory approval from Parliament, many held that the idea of a corporate wrong was, *prima facie*, impossible, tantamount to legally sanctioned crime.[28] And beyond the statutory hurdles, any number of lingering complexities remained. Are corporations liable for wrongs committed by their employees? Are employees exempt from prosecution if operating under instructions from their corporate employer? Can an employee be harmed by his corporate employer? None of these questions had settled answers circa 1800, and a century later, in 1895, Thomas Beven's important treatise on negligence described corporate liability as a "difficult question"—which is what it remains today.[29] It is, thus, a little disingenuous to insinuate, with Pollock and Maitland, that we have simply failed to develop a "consistent theory," as if corporate tort were a legal curio we had yet to blend into an otherwise coherent body of thought. It's disingenuous because the problem corporate tort presents is not a historical one. It's a theoretical problem, which no amount of waiting is going to soften into unobtrusiveness. The theoretical problem, as I've been arguing, is that a perfectly coherent theory of corporate ontology—the notion of a separate legal personhood that English law inherits from the *universitas*—produces a theory of corporate liability that is fraught with difficulties. The liability problem can be solved by holding employees and/or shareholders criminally responsible—but that is also to cancel the distinction between corporation

and member that is the *sine qua non* of the form. So: the law can solve liability by killing the corporation, or it can keep the corporation and continue
to face the "difficult question" of liability. But the law cannot develop a
"coherent theory" of corporate liability. Corporateness and justice are, by
definition and not by history, incompatible grammars.

Indeed, there is no more eloquent an example of this incompatibility
than the hesitation and inconclusiveness that riddles the late lecture in
which Maitland promised to resolve it. Much of "Moral Personality and
Legal Personality," delivered in 1903 as the Sidgwick Lecture at Newnham
College, Cambridge, argues for the legal personality—what Maitland calls
the "phenomenal reality"—of the form. Even if the corporation lacks strict
philosophical coherence, Maitland urges, it has a long history and remains
a manifestly functional and inarguably ubiquitous form. The corporation is
so obviously a part of modern reality that it seems to Maitland that there's
something misguided about any effort to write it off as a *mere* fiction. We
might, he says, "impound the minute-book," but there would remain something quibbling and perverse in the protest.[30] Despite moral personality's lead
position in the title, then, it's not until the final pages of the lecture that
Maitland turns to the subject. And despite the ambitious title of the final
section ("The Ultimate Moral Unit"), the discussion of the corporation
as moral person trails off in intelligent but somewhat surprising hesitancy.
"Perhaps," Maitland writes, "I have not succeeded in raising just the question
I want to ask. . . . It is a moral question." Let's say, he continues, that there is
a place called Nusquamia and it,

> like many other sovereign states . . . owes money, and . . . you are one of its
> creditors. You are not receiving the expected interest and there is talk of
> repudiation. That being so, I believe that you will be, and indeed I think that
> you ought to be, indignant, morally, righteously indignant. Now the question
> that I want to raise is this: Who is it that really owes you money? Nusquamia.
> Granted, but can you convert the proposition that Nusquamia owes you money
> into a series of propositions imposing duties on certain human beings that are
> now in existence? The task will not be easy. Clearly you do not think that every
> Nusquamian owes you some aliquot share of the debt. No one thinks in that
> way. . . . Nor shall we get much good out of the word "collectively," which is
> the smudgiest word in the English language. . . . I do not wish to say that I have
> suggested an impossible task, and that the right-and-duty-bearing group must
> be for the philosopher an ultimate and unanalysable moral unit. . . . Still, . . .[31]

Or better: "But still. . . ." In the lecture's final paragraph, the apparently
not-"impossible task" (*but is it?*) remains unaccomplished, and the originally
promising ultimacy of that "ultimate moral unit" has been revised into the

never-ending problem of "an ultimate and unanalysable" one. The elaborate story problem of Nusquamia's national debt and its attendant questions—can you "convert the proposition that Nusquamia owes you money into a series of propositions imposing duties on certain human beings"? Is it true that "no one thinks" you can? Is there any other way to think of it?—trail off into an uncertain future Maitland resigns to the philosophers. That division of labor seems like a relief—the practical-minded historian and lawyer leaving the big questions to someone else—but it's not clear the law really can afford to leave the moral nature of the group personality to some other discipline. Maitland's good-humored prose portrays the law as a homely, unassuming institution. The philosophers may quibble, but the law, in its commitment to "phenomenal reality," is happy in its "sound instincts" to "muddle along with semi-personality or demi-semi-personality toward convenient conclusions."[32] But unless the law really is content to count oil spills, or train wrecks, or institutionalized forms of fraud and malpractice as just demiactions or demisemi-actions, it's hard to see how the law could seriously adopt Maitland's genially plodding attitude. As Hazlitt had put the problem in his essay "On Corporate Bodies," published nearly a century before Maitland, the basic problem with corporate bodies lies not in the fictitiousness of their personhood but in the fundamental asymmetry they create at the level of action: "corporate bodies have more power to do mischief and are less amenable to disgrace or punishment."[33] For Hazlitt, as for Maitland, as for us today, this is the irresolvable, properly Frankensteinian problem: that the corporation is—which is to say that it remains—both a child of the law and a creature beyond it.

Corporate Actions

> Everyone is more or less responsible but no one will admit it.
>
> Rene Girard, *The Scapegoat*

The corporation is proof that contractualism, however individual in theory, does nothing in and of itself to ensure that our enterprises will remain human scaled or reducible to the terms of human morality.[34] As we will see in this section, the problem the corporation introduced at the level of agent was paralleled in the nineteenth century by a problem at the level of action itself. Compared to the murky psychological reaches of intention and motive, action can seem reassuringly palpable and perceptible: it either happens or it doesn't. In the nineteenth century, though, the apparently inbuilt legibility of action wavered. A single, discrete action could suddenly become visible as simply one link in a much longer chain; many separate actions could combine in one effect; consequences, like prodigal sons, could wander back after many months and many miles to surprise their fathers with terrible news.

One doesn't need industrialism to see how fragile the boundaries are that separate one action from another, but it helps. As the ominously titled study of England's smoke problem, *The Destruction of Daylight*, put it in 1907: "Before the days of modern cities smoke could be sent up into the clean air without harm. The sky was relatively so vast that the atmosphere was not seriously dirtied before the carbon and the sulphur acids descended along with the rain harmlessly again to earth."[35] For the prior hundred years, that relative vastness had been a thing of the past. In the thirteenth century, one legal historian writes, "the worst nuisance in a town might be a brick kiln or a chandler." But in the nineteenth, "when whole towns could be built, demographic patterns altered, occupations eliminated, and skies blackened," a single action could prove "disastrous for hundreds or even thousands of people."[36] We may see this ambient harmfulness—nicely epitomized in *The Destruction of Daylight* by the thought that even rain is no longer benign—as a distinctly postmodern condition (compare *White Noise*'s airborne toxins). But the situation did not go unnoticed in its nineteenth-century beginnings. In the 1850s, William Farr, one of history's first medical statisticians, took on the task of trying to measure the cost of these massive new agencies in human lives. "The progress of science," he wrote,

> has created new forces, often fatal, and has produced new substances, of which our forefathers had no knowledge. Machinery is organized on a large scale, so that the lives of numbers of men are liable to be destroyed, not by malicious intent, but by the negligence of other men who have their lives in charge. Thus, great numbers die by railway accidents; many perish in mining operations; children are suffocated in bed or are burnt by "their clothes taking fire."[37]

One change was that agents—these "new forces"—were just bigger in the nineteenth century. But Farr's emphasis on "the negligence of other men" also makes clear that the issue was not just the "large scale" of industrial action that made it possible to bring harm to the "hundred or even thousands" but the increasing density of modern life.[38] Increasingly compressed settlement patterns meant that everyone effectively had their lives in someone else's charge and that it was, therefore, only a matter of time before one found oneself, with the weird impersonality Farr's quotation marks stress in the phrase about "clothes taking fire," collaterally damaged.

To comprehend this situation, nineteenth-century law needed to solidify a trio of concepts—proximate cause, negligence, and nuisance—whose primary function was to corral a world of unintended or vaporously rhizomatic action into something like the first-hand directness of contract.[39] These three ideas are now familiar, relatively stable concepts of modern law. But one can see the depth of their philosophical innovation by putting them up against what may seem like the most basic or intuitive understanding of the law—famously articulated by Oliver Wendell Holmes Jr. in his 1881 history of the common law—as "a system of private liability [that] started from the notion of actual intent and actual personal culpability."[40] The law, Holmes thought, shouldn't tarry with shadowy notions like unintended consequences, accidents, or harms that occur over significant chronological or physical distance. Even though he is writing in the thick of transatlantic industrialization, Holmes continues to argue that the law is not a "mutual insurance company against accidents." Such "universal insurance" might, Holmes allows, be a reasonable project for a state to undertake—"there might be a pension for paralytics, and state aid for those who suffered in person or estate from tempest or wild beasts"—but it is not, he thinks, an appropriate role for the law. "Unless my act is of a nature to threaten others, unless under the circumstances a prudent man would have foreseen the possibility of harm," Holmes writes, "it is no more justifiable to make me indemnify my neighbor against the consequences, than . . . to compel me to insure him against lightning."[41] Holmes allows for negligence—he's written the foreseeability of harm into the law's proper purview—but just barely, and it's not clear that nuisance or zoning law have any place under this description. Holmes divides the world into action and luck, insists on their difference, and argues that only the former is the object of law.

Holmes's position is, in theory, reasonable. But the real world frequently generates situations in which acting or not acting do not feel like the only, or the right, options. One of the best-known illustrations of the ambiguity of action comes from the 1773 case *Scott v. Shepherd*. Now a law school classic fondly known as "the Squib Case," the incident in question began when Shepherd threw a firecracker (or squib) into a crowded market-house in Somersetshire.[42] The squib (as described by William Selwyn in a survey of cases published in 1806) then fell "upon the stall or standing of B.," such that "C, in order to protect himself and the wares of B. from injury, took up the squib, and threw it across the market-house, when it fell upon the standing of D., who to save his wares, threw the squib to another part of the market-place." In the course of this final flight, the squib struck "the plaintiff in the face" and, the "combustible matter bursting," put out one of Scott's eyes.

Beyond illustrating just how much slapstick and tragedy share, the case is important to legal history for raising a crucial question about the distinction between direct action or trespass and what English law knows as action or trespass *on the case*. The distinction between simple trespass or action and "action on the case" is one of immediacy: action on the case is a way to factor in extenuating or circumstantial considerations. Standard action or trespass, sometimes given in its full form of trespass *vi et armis* ("with force and arms"), dates back to very early years when the common law relies on a relatively restricted set of rote pleadings. You could assault someone with force and arms or violate their property, but, if a situation didn't fit one of the few formal options, the law had no response to it. As the common law developed, though, it began to rely on the notion of "case" as a special form of pleading, a way to treat situations in which injury or offense arose in ways less immediate than the law's basic forms imply. Selwyn explains: "If the injury be occasioned by the act of the defendant at the time, or the defendant be the immediate cause of the injury, trespass *vi et armis* is the proper remedy; but where the injury is not direct and immediate on the act done, but consequential only, there the remedy is by action on the case, sometimes termed an action on the case for consequential damages."[43] The reliance on case allowed the law to graft situations of indirect harm or extenuated circumstances onto its basic form of direct harm, to make amorphous or attenuated circumstances function, as Holmes put it, like "actual intent and actual personal culpability."

The interest of *Scott v. Shepherd* lies in the challenge it presents to the clarity of this distinction. Read as strict trespass (as Blackstone did) the event is actually composed of several distinct, intentional actions: Shepherd's toss, followed by two more volitional acts carried out (Selwyn reports) by "two rational agents successively." Trespass *vi et armis* ought, Blackstone reasoned, "in strictness of the law [to] lie against D., . . . [who] had not used sufficient circumspection in the act of removing the danger from himself."[44] This is, however, not how the majority saw things. They viewed the case—as perhaps we, too, are most prone to do—as an initial volitional act (Shepherd's) followed by a series of actions that were really the "continuation of the first force, and the first act, which would continue until the squib was spent by bursting." "The several acts of throwing," Selwyn writes, "must be considered as one single act, namely, the act of the defendant."[45] The majority's ruling was, essentially, that Shepherd had, *for all intents and purposes*, firecracked Scott in the eye. Shepherd did something either malicious or idiotic, Scott got hurt, so Shepherd pays Scott some damages. That "for all intents and purposes"—the sense that one has landed on an inexact but intuitively or morally satisfying description—is the hallmark of action on the case.

Holmes, for his part, seems to have agreed with the majority's ruling, taking the majority's willingness to read over "even human agencies"—provided the actor can be got at "through a comparatively short train of intervening causes"—as further proof of the primacy of vengeance in the legal mind.[46] Clearly, though, the majority's ruling also works against Holmes's insistence on "actual intent" and "actual personal culpability" since it converts the actual intentional agents who are C and D into something like inanimate matter. C and D are, Holmes says, "treated as more or less nearly automatic."[47] The point *Scott v. Shepherd* makes, then, is not exactly that Holmes is wrong about what the law should do (punish "actual" action) but that, starting from what Holmes thinks the law should do, there's *no way to determine* how to handle a situation like the one in *Scott v. Shepherd*. Reminding oneself of the law's fundamental object—the pursuit of vengeance for intentional acts—does not tell one how to proceed. And it fails us not because it's wrong to punish action but because the world does not divide itself neatly into action and accident, law and "lightning." The real lesson of *Scott v. Shepherd* is that lots of our circumstances are people, too.

In seeing even persons as "more or less nearly automatic," action on the case manages both to think beyond the liberal model (which emphasizes the discrete agency of every individual) and to preserve that same fiction (that Shepherd was the real actor). Action on the case opens the door to seeing action as something that can flow through objects and persons as much as originate from them, but because its logic remains finite (no one, for example, suggested that the person who sold Shepherd the squib ought to be included in the case), it remains committed to a world in which responsibility can be parceled up and distributed to discrete sets of actors. Action on the case is, in short, law for an amorphous world, but it is still law. As such, we can see its continuity with a much older legal notion, the concept of the deodand. Deodand deals with cases in which fatal harm seems to originate in objects that (like animals and stones) are understood to be incapable of intention. The history of deodand reaches back at least into Anglo-Saxon law and, possibly, to the bit in Exodus about what to do in case "an ox gore a man or woman: that they die." Exodus's answer—"the ox shall be surely stoned, and his flesh shall not be eaten" (21:28)—installs sacrifice as the appropriate response to fatal accidents involving animals or inanimate things (wagon wheels, falling anvils, etc.), an idea preserved in the term deodand ("given to God"). English law replaced stoning with a system in which the owner of the object or animal that had moved *ad mortem* forfeited the value of the object (so, if an ox, the value of an ox) not to God but to His representative—the monarch, by way of the Exchequer. Doing so allowed the deodand to act as an early, informal form of tort law, with the general custom being for the fines assessed by coroner's juries to be paid to the victim's family. And it was to this tort-law end that juries in the late eighteenth and early nineteenth centuries revived the deodand, a law that had been on the books for something like one thousand years and asleep for most of the recent ones. What this seemingly arcane concept offered was a way to deal with an industrial age in which, thanks to industrial accidents, harm was entirely evident but no one in particular seemed to be responsible. The large sums awarded by coroner's juries made the deodand a fast enemy of the industrial interest,[48] but it would not be repealed until it had been replaced by the 1846 Fatal Accidents Act, the first provision in England (though not in Scotland) to allow family members of a victim of a fatal accident to sue for damages.

Most discussions of the deodand, then and now, treat it from a sardonic distance, noting its sacrificial logic and its seemingly premodern, apparently animist foundations. In the parliamentary sessions working toward the deodand's abolition and replacement, Lord Denman called it the "remnant of a barbarous and absurd law."[49] Still, it's hard not to admire the ingenuity of these coroner's juries reaching so far into the bag of legal tricks to address the blossoming violence of industrialized life. But even this view—deodand as a plucky anachronism—probably still underrates the audacity of its legal intelligence. For the concept is, in many ways, an answer to the problems presented by the promiscuous, distended shape of action in a densely settled world: if you have to go after something, go after what's nearest to hand. In one sense, it's perfectly Holmesian—something moved *ad mortem*, so take your revenge there—but in another sense it's a staunchly illiberal form of legal recourse: it doesn't depend on psychological notions like intention, forseeability, or personality, and it doesn't stop to measure the proximity of a cause or the contributory value of extenuating circumstance.[50] In this sense, the deodand is less the child of an animistic world that sees intelligence and motive everywhere than a form of law that can survive in a world in which intelligence and motive have disappeared altogether.[51] The deodand doesn't claim that, "in some special sense, the tree meant to do it," and it doesn't get bogged down in apportioning blame to the wind that blew the tree or the drought that came before and loosened the soil. The deodand is, rather, a form of law of whose commitment to responsibility goes well beyond its commitment to, or its need for, individuals.

One can see the usefulness of such stark simplifications in an age where everyone seemed to be involved with everything.[52] In 1888, the Royal Commission on Noxious Vapours described the difficulty it was having coming up with an account of the pollution they had been commissioned to measure and correct. There is, the commissioners complained, an "almost insuperable difficulty of separating the consequences specially due to [certain] works from those which are common to all works generating dust, smoke and dirt, and surrounded by a dense population, and of deciding what proportion of mischief can justly be attributed to the noxious vapours with which we are dealing."[53] In the twentieth century, economics formalized such problems as social costs or negative externality, largely through Arthur Pigou's *Economics of Welfare* (1920) and Ronald Coase's extremely famous (and anti-Pigovian) paper "The Problem of Social Cost" (1960). Both Pigou and Coase were thinking about cases in which action undertaken for private purposes or self-interested ends has social costs/benefits not priced into the contractual form: a well-lit house on the seaside guides ships who don't pay for its upkeep; the pollution from a factory harms another man's trees. People are, Pigou and Coase saw, constantly paying for one another in all kinds of incidental ways.

As a development within economics, the significance of social cost can hardly be overstated (Coase's article is one of the most cited works of scholarship in history, and he won the Nobel Prize in 1991 for his work on the question), but this twentieth-century effort is in many ways a second pass on a question that plagued nineteenth-century courts, which struggled to find a coherent way to handle situations in which one person's lawful use of his property seemed to impinge on another's lawful use of his own. *Gerard v. Muspratt* (1846) involved damage done to some valuable timber by a chemical factory; *Hole v. Barlow* (1858) involved a brickmaking operation; in *Stockport Waterworks Co. v. Potter and Another* (1861) the plaintiffs, whose waterworks relied on the river Mersey, sued a cotton-printing operation for polluting it; *Bamford v. Turnley* (1862) was brickmaking (again); and *Tipping v. St Helen's Smelting Company* (1865) was another case of ruined timber on account, the plaintiff alleged, of a nearby smelting operation.

Nineteenth-century courts, of course, had no trouble enforcing contracts between parties, but they had trouble with situations in which there was no contract and/or in which the very idea of contract (for example, dividing the Mersey) seems inappropriate. The absence of established convention for such questions is visible in the swings between verdicts and the wide variety of factors the courts used in their decisions.[54] But beyond the institutional growing pains, we can glimpse a much more fundamental philosophical danger for the law in a notion like nuisance. In *Hole* (which upheld the defendant's right to continue making bricks since it was "a lawful trade in a convenient and proper place") and *Bamford* (which reversed course to argue that even actions otherwise in the public interest—like making bricks—need to be conducted in ways that do not interfere with the rights of other individuals), the legality of an action is a feature not of the action itself but of its place in space and time.[55] Nuisance law thus marks a crucial step towards a slippery—that is, potentially infinite—slope of circumstantial or contextual considerations (public good, inconvenience, tolerability) that are impossible to formalize once and for all. As the legal historian A. W. Brian Simpson writes, the judicial system's inability to "make up its mind as to what ought to be done about the problem of social cost was intimately connected" to the problem of whether the "law of nuisance can be encapsulated in precise rules." It was a worry the dissenting judge in *Bamford v. Turley* put clearly: "The nuisance for which an action will lie is not capable of any legal definition which would be applicable to all actions and useful in deciding them, for that question depended entirely upon surrounding circumstances . . . so as to make it impossible to lay down any rule applicable to every case."[56] Nuisance law's hostility to form is a result of its consequentialism, of thinking of actions as having value only so far as they intersect with a social field of other actions.[57] As with action on the case, which both recognizes and controls the amorphousness of action, nuisance is underpinned by a far more radical intuition than its legal deployment in fact brings about. For in seeing the character of an action as relative rather than intrinsic, nuisance opens the door to philosophically unanswerable questions about the limits of that relational field. A nuisance complaint brought by A against B is a vastly oversimplified construal of the basic fact of mutuality that nuisance itself acknowledges. In its heart of hearts, nuisance law recognizes not only that, as Coase puts it, "the cost of exercising a right . . . is always the loss which is suffered elsewhere in consequence of the exercise of that right" but that there are no clear boundaries to that "elsewhere."[58] Nothing more than the law's procedural insistence that complaints be made in binary form ($X v. Y$) and our self-generated conventions about how to draw lines around a field of action keep nuisance's antinomian intuitions safely in the service of the law.

As John Stuart Mill saw in his 1843 *System of Logic*, the "real Cause" of an event "is the whole of [its] antecedents, and we have, philosophically speaking, no right to give the name of cause to one of them, exclusively of the others." When "a person eats of a particular dish, and dies," we are "apt to say that eating of that dish was the cause of his death." But the scrupulous philosopher sees that the dying in question involved a whole constellation of facts: "the act of eating the dish"—sure—but also "a particular bodily constitution, a particular state of present health, and perhaps even a certain state of the atmosphere." A philosophically defensible account of cause would be a list of all of the relevant conditions, "and the statement of the cause is incomplete, unless in some shape or other we introduce them all."[59] But for the same reason, we can also see that a philosophically defensible account would, in its essential limitlessness, not be much of an account at all. Because our sentences cannot go on all day before getting to the verb, we resort to what Mill called "logical fictions." We "dignif[y] with the name of cause . . . the condition which came last into existence," or we choose "from among the conditions" in "some other capricious manner" a single item on which to hang the whole.[60]

Like the difficulty facing the Royal Commission on Noxious Vapours, who found more vapors than they could count and more polluters than they could blame, the problem Mill is locating involves the simultaneous necessity and "insuperable difficulty" of distilling a set of generalized conditions into something with the immediate transitivity of action. And faced with this problem, we can see that the corporate personhood we looked at in the first section is only one side of a larger problem about how to make legal (or grammatical) sense of multiplicity—how to talk about the agency of collectives and the collectivity of agency. Just as we require the fiction of corporate personhood to make our social bodies capable of something like individual action, we need conventions like action on the case, the deodand, and nuisance law to make the lived reality of an interconnected, unintention-ally harmful, and constitutively shared world susceptible to the individualist assumptions of justice. The skeptical take on these strategies, strategies that allow the law to look, Perseus-like, at the tangle of reality without turning to stone, is that they can only ever be figures. We talk about how X caused Y or how A caused a nuisance to B, knowing all the while that an infinity of culprits—"ancillary" effects and "nonproximate" causes—waits in the wings. The less skeptical take just involves recognizing that, without the technology of these legal or logical fictions, we don't have justice at all. In its willingness to speak so pragmatically, Mill's *System of Logic* knows something that his *On Liberty* is, for obvious reasons, less eager to admit: that self-regarding actions (as opposed to actions that concern others) are not naturally occurring but conventionally established kinds. It's not a happy thought. If our first impulse is to discard *mere* convention as so much arbitrary static, we can also see that the only actions and justice that there are in the world are the actions and justice that our frames have put upon it.

Figuring the End of Number: Romantic Empiricism / Romantic Abstraction

> The favourite illustration of our old lawyers, in speaking of the identity of corporations is,—"Just as the river Thames is still the same river, though the parts which compose it are changing every instant;" and had the discoveries of modern science been known to them, they might have chosen a more striking

parallel, and have said,—"just as the body of a man is the same body, though it be ascertained that every particle thereof is changed within a limited space of time."

The Law Magazine, 1850

The men of Manchester longing for "a shape to fasten on," J. S. Mill's "logical fictions," the rise of action on the case, nuisance law's attempt to formalize social cost, the fiction of the corporate person: all are attempts to make the ontological reality of collective agency responsive (or at least nonlethal) to a legal system, a common sense, and a language in which actions continue to be conceived of as singularized events undertaken by discrete actors and attached to stipulable effects.[61] In this final section, I turn back toward topics that will be more familiar to students of literature to argue that the romantic symbol, in its insistence on the identity of part and whole, ought to be understood as aesthetic philosophy's answer to the Manchester predicament—a way to distill an actually existing plurality into a singular—and therefore *perceptible*—form.

Passages like Coleridge's showstopping diatribe against the classificatory imagination in *The Statesman's Manual* ("Man of understanding—canst thou bid the stone to lie, canst thou bid the flower to bloom, where thou hast placed it in thy classification? ... [D]o not far rather all things spread out before thee in glad confusion [and] promiscuous harmony?") prime us to see romantic aesthetics primarily as a corrective to the dissecting rationality of empiricism.[62] As it turns out, though, the symbol as Coleridge would develop it is not only concerned with the central problem of late eighteenth-century empiricism—the relation of the part and whole—but was directed toward a similarly phantasmal ambition: the achievement of a perspective in which collectives and wholes (or aggregation, complexity, glad confusion, allness) would be no bar to particularity (or objectivity, singularity, graspability, individuality). The symbol is the promise that one does not have to choose between the One as the all and the one as one.

In the second half of the eighteenth century, this promise was at the heart of the empirical method's appeal more generally: that one could work from the smallest units to an understanding of the whole and that one could, at the same time, disaggregate any complex whole into its basic parts. At the center of this vast, Lockean legacy was David Hartley's 1749 masterwork of associationist psychology, *Observations on Man, his Frame, his Duty, and his Expectations,* which insisted that "many of our intellectual ideas, such as those that belong to the heads of beauty, honor, moral qualities, etc. are in fact ... composed of parts."[63] The lure of Hartley's project—compelling enough that James Mill, in his 1829 *Analysis of the Phenomena of the Human Mind*, sought to update and reintroduce Hartley's ideas in a volume that would again be reissued (with extensive commentary by John Stuart Mill, Alexander Bain, Andrew Findlater, and George Grote) in 1867 and 1879—was its promise that the gauzy tissues of thought and hazy-seeming ideas like beauty or honor were in fact composed of empirically discernible constituents. One could know the parts, and by knowing the parts, one could know the whole—an idea appealing not only to a romanticism committed to the formative power of nature (as very many passages in Wordsworth attest: "But Nature then was sovereign in my mind, / And mighty forms, seizing a youthful fancy, / Had given a charter to irregular hopes.") but also to materialists like Joseph Priestley who were working in the last decades of the eighteenth century to establish all things human (including the soul) on a material footing.[64] When Coleridge dismisses the classificatory schemes of "the man of understanding," he does so out of the conviction that no static enumeration of the parts could ever grasp the buzzing harmony of the whole. But it was not really the case that empiricists like Hartley and Priestley were only interested in murdering to dissect, for the real goal of the empirical method was a perspective in which one would not have to choose between part and whole, a perspective that could comprehend in one motion how it is that things are built up into wholes as well as how even very complex or abstract phenomena might be broken down into "their simple compounding parts," the way a prism resolves, as Hartley put it, "the colours of the sun's light" or, for that matter, the way an Aeolian harp makes the One Life perceptible as a series of "sequacious notes."[65]

One place we can clearly see the prismatic promise of empiricism intersect with the more particular problem of language (and thus enter the intellectual canon of literary romanticism) is in the ambitious and idiosyncratic etymological project undertaken by John Horne Tooke, published in two, widely spaced volumes (1786 and 1805) as *Epea Pteroenta*. The title, which is taken from Homer and means "Winged Words," alludes to Tooke's belief that words are primarily abbreviative in function. "Abbreviations," says Tooke's avatar in the Socratic dialogue that is *Epea Pteroenta*, "are the wheels of language, the wings of Mercury. And though we might be dragged along without them, it would be with much difficulty, very heavily, and tediously."[66] This view of words as ways to capture groups too large to enumerate severally was not exclusive to Tooke. Both James Mill and Priestley, for instance, understood the usefulness of words to lie in their ability to bundle empirical sensation. If we were to apply the rigid particularism that we see in our systems of number (where each quantity has its own name) to all of language, Priestley argued, we would "increase our written characters to a most enormous and unmanageable quantity."[67] Tooke, likewise, argued that many of our common terms are useful primarily to "save time in our discourse."[68]

Even as he stressed this aggregative function, however, it was crucial to Tooke's project that what convenience had joined, etymology could always put asunder. An earlier pamphlet, written during a stint in prison (and written to argue, no less, that his imprisonment was based on a philosophically mistaken understanding of the word "that"), made it clear that abbreviation, though useful, isn't exactly benign: "Abbreviation and Corruption," he wrote, "are always busiest with the words which are most frequently in use."[69] The point of etymology, then, was to strip away the corruption that use introduces. Our vision thus cleared, Tooke argued, we would see that there is never "any such fluctuation whatever" in the meaning of words and that, while our understandings are winging their way haphazardly around, "the words themselves continue faithfully and steadily attached, each to the standard under which it was originally enlisted."[70] Tooke's belief in the groundedness of the "simple" and "necessary" parts of language goes hand in hand with his frequent reliance on metaphors of transportation (sledges, wheels, wings, etc.) to model language, or what he often calls (with an emphasis, one assumes, on the running-ness of its root) "discourse." There is some ground to be covered and, however winged, words remain responsive (and responsible) to that empirical fundament. Abbreviation is, in this sense, not a form of abstraction but actually opposed to it since abbreviation implies a *condensation of* but not a *drawing away from* substance. At one point in the second volume of *Epea Pteroenta*, the Socratic interlocutor asks Tooke's dialogic stand-in how he would "account for what is called Abstraction, and for abstract ideas, whose existence you deny." "If it must have a name," Tooke's avatar H responds, "it should rather be called subaudition than abstraction; though I mean not to quarrel about a title."[71] H is making a mistake, I think, in shrugging off the disagreement, since what "subaudition" preserves and "abstraction" does not is the idea that the terrain words enable us to cover efficiently is still present within them. Flying to New York, as opposed to walking there, *abbreviates* the journey but is not more *abstract* than getting there on foot—the ground you're covering's the same; you're just moving faster.

Tooke's belief that the "simple" or the "necessary" forms of language are still subaudible within even a very abstract term like "Right" or "Fate" allows him to move in two directions at once: he can, in one commentator's description, "emphasize that language is fundamentally metaphorical" even as he can, at the same time, believe in an etymology that was essentially antimetaphorical—capable, as he said, of "dissipat[ing] a metaphysical jargon and false morality" that prompted us to believe in "sham deities [like] Fate and Destiny." Such grand notions, he argued, were "merely Participles poetically embodied."[72] Tooke lists twenty or so metaphysical commonplaces (including Luck, Accident, Innocence, Desert, and two etceteras) in order to argue such entities aren't, properly understood, metaphysical at all. Behind each of them is an ordinary verb—an actual, material action. This action has, by the exigencies of use, been turned into an abstraction, but it might, by a kind of reverse sublimation, be converted back to substance.[73] Tooke didn't think we should stop using terms like Accident or Fate, exactly, but he did think, like any good empiricist, that we needed to be reminded of the substances out of which they were composed. We need to be reminded that behind our metaphysics is something like physics—or, as Hazlitt put it in an admiring comment on Tooke's work, chemistry. Tooke's great insight, Hazlitt wrote, was to treat "words as the chemists do substances . . . to separate those which are compounded from those which are not decompoundable [and to explain] the difficult by the plain, the complex by the simple. This alone is proceeding on the true principles of science."[74] Just as the chemical constituents of an object are present whether or not a chemist is bothering to analyze them, so too could Tooke argue that the "simple" and "necessary" elements persist—"continue faithfully and steadily attached"—beneath the obscuring "jargon" of indoctrinated thought. And just as Wordsworth believed the language of common men preserved a form of life that was true and stable by virtue of being close to the ground (in "low and rustic life," he wrote, "the essential passions of the heart find a better soil"), Tooke believed he could excavate at his convenience an original standard that was in and of itself substantial and immune to change (what Wordsworth called "the beautiful and permanent forms of nature").[75] "Proceeding on the true principles of science" and proceeding on the principles of romanticism are thus linked by the insistence that truth is whatever is "not decompoundable" and that complex abstraction and arbitrary jargon can always be resolved into some ultimate and permanent set of essences.

For all its vaunted interest in the infinite, unbounded, or sublime, then, we can also see that there was a wide strain of romantic thought committed to the finite, simple, and grounded. The idea that one might decompound the complex into the "simple and necessary" and strip off the abstractions that use and fancy talking have laid over the "beautiful and permanent forms" entails believing that the world is composed of a finite set of ultimate units— that there is, at bottom, a bottom. Without this fundamental and finite substratum, there would be no scale according to which something could be more arbitrary, abstract, complex, compounded, or jargony than something else. So even as one standard romantic move involves pointing out the inadequacy of our classificatory schemes in the face of reality's multiplicity (as when Wordsworth's "Ode: Intimations of Immortality" derides the "little plan or chart" on which we rely), equally romantic is a commitment to substance: to the low, basic, permanent, and finite. Romanticism may feel most itself, most dramatic, most revolutionary when engaged in powerful acts of divestment—throwing off an unnatural self, departing a dim city, rising beyond the fetters of custom. But these moments in which some arbitrary and engrained structure of order is transcended exist alongside—and, in fact, have their felicity guaranteed by—a belief in the unity and, therefore, the essential finitude of the real life (a natural self, nature, truth, etc.) the structures otherwise conceal. Being glad about something like Coleridge's "glad confusion and promiscuous harmony," for example—like giving our blessing to the sea snakes—involves being able to see all mutation as permutation, to understand the world as an extremely (and perhaps infinitely) recombinatory process carried out across a set of One. The appeal of such a view, one that can offer the order of harmony and the freedom of promiscuity, is the promise that we might be both the infinite and the grounded. As with Tooke's etymological schemes, which revel in the wingedness of words even as they seek to "remain steadily and faithfully attached" to what Hazlitt called "the plain" and "the simple," the goal is a perspective that retains all the substance of particularity (the ability, as Wordsworth says, to "grasp a wall or tree") but without its bad limitations ("plan or chart") and that, at the same, launches us into all the freedom of infinity, but does so this time for real.

This dialectical balance is fragile. When it falters in the pages of eighteenth-century empiricism, we get something that eerily resembles the corporation: the paradox of a composite body without identifiable members. Not even a hundred pages into his *Observations*, for instance, Hartley admits that the decompounding methods of empiricism—on which its claims to authority and knowledge absolutely rest—frequently find themselves bedeviled by unsortable complexity. "If the number of simple ideas which compose the complex one be very great," he writes,

> it may happen that the complex idea shall not appear to bear any relation to these its compounding ideas. . . . The reason of this is that, each single idea is overpowered by the sum of all the rest, as soon as they are all intimately united together. Thus, in very compound medicines, the several tastes and flavours of the separate ingredients are lost and over-powered by the complex one of the

whole mass: so that this has a taste and flavor of its own, which appears to be simple and original, and like that of a natural body.[76]

Hartley's paragraph confronts the categorical gulf between totality and particularity that the empirical method is otherwise committed to bridging. So multiple and so "intimately united" are these particulars that the composite entity takes on an undecompoundable identity of its own. If these "separate ingredients" were people rather than various medicines, we'd be talking about the difference between the legal form of partnership, which can always be devolved to the persons of its members, and the corporation, which, as we saw in the first section, never can. But the important point, here, has to do not with the specific terms in which the problem appears (corporations, chemicals, etc.) but with the extraordinarily wide purchase the formal problem of part-whole identity has as a *problem*. So while we often gloss romanticism as advocating togetherness, as underlining the essentially joint or collective nature of existence, a wider view allows us to see corporateness less as a position we are for than the name for the problem—a composite but nondecomposable body—that appears once collectivity (assembledness) is understood to be a feature of reality.

When the particulars vanish, we're left with what Hartley calls a "symbol" (and what Mill called a "logical fiction"). "When a variety of ideas are associated together," Hartley says, "the visible idea, being more glaring and distinct than the rest, performs the office of a symbol to all the rest, suggests them, and connects them together. In this it somewhat resembles the first letter of a word, or the first word of a sentence, which are made use of to bring all the rest to mind."[77] "Rose" or "beauty" in this way of thinking are not really objects in and of themselves; they're just placeholders "performing the office" for a whole set of vibratory associations that do not and cannot speak their names directly. Hartley's description of this symbolizing process—which moves from seeing the symbol as the thing that "connects them" to the much more allusive operation of suggesting them in the way the "first letter" suggests "a word" or a "first word" suggests "a sentence"—tails off into increasingly tenuous acts of extrapolation. Even if we're on board with the general idea that "rose" is the "visible idea" for "a variety of ideas associated together," it seems highly unlikely that we could confidently say what word *r* represents or how, *pace* Shakespeare and Stein, the sentence that begins "a rose" goes. Hartley's shift to the semiotic register—the move from the direct impressment of vibrations to the referential signification of symbols—ushers arbitrariness and approximation into a system whose whole aim had been a direct—because material—connection between elements. The empirical mode always starts out fine: as James Mill says, "we give the name wood to a particular cluster of sensations, the name canvas to another, the name rope to another," and "to these clusters, and many others, joined together in one great cluster, we give the name ship." But it quickly tips into abstraction: "How great a number of clusters are united in the term House?" Mill asks. "And how many more in the term City?"[78] The questions go unanswered. "How infinitely complex," Joseph Priestley asks, "must be the vibration of the air a little above the streets of such a city as London[?]" No telling. "And yet," he adds, "there can be no doubt but that each sound has its proper effect, and might be attended to separately, by an ear sufficiently exquisite."[79] Individuation remains a theoretical possibility. Given less bungling ears we might be able to line up "each sound" with "its proper effect"; empiricism as a form of knowledge (and not just experience) remains theoretically possible, but we can now see with Blake that framing it would require something like an immortal ear or eye.

It would require, in other words, what Coleridge would have called—as if in direct contradiction to Hartley's deployment of the term—a symbol: a means by which we might perceive the whole without losing our sense of any particular. For Hartley, symbols appear when empiricism's telescopic vision turns figurative; for Coleridge, the symbol is not a figure (something that stands for something else) at all but, quite the opposite, a phenomenon of copresence. Coleridge's famous account of the symbol's revelatory power makes this clear. The symbol, he writes, shows us the "translucence of the Special in the Individual," "of the General in the Especial," "of the Universal in the General," and, most importantly, "of the Eternal through and in the Temporal."[80] Clearly, this is not a description that rejects the taxonomies (or even the hierarchies) we associate with Enlightenment thought. Rather, it points toward the possibility (signaled by Coleridge's careful choice of "translucence") that one *unit* might shine through another—and do so in a way that would be revealing rather than falsifying. It is, in this light, profoundly important that Coleridge's scrolling up the scale of existence comes back to the notion of the singularly perceptible unit. The symbol, his next sentence reads, "always partakes of the Reality it renders intelligible; and while it enunciates the whole, abides itself as a living part in that Unity, of which it is the representative." This is the real promise of the symbol: a perpetual peace between units and unity.

The "inspired writings" of the Bible, which for *The Statesman's Manual* are the primary example of the symbol in action, are thus less a monolithic alternative to an uninspired empiricism than—like the corporation—a way to serve two disputatious masters (the unit and the unity, the temporal and the eternal) simultaneously.[81] Where the "human understanding" gets bogged down by multiplicity, "musing on many things" and "frustrated and disheartened by the fluctuating nature of its objects," the symbol projects what Coleridge calls "absolute science," an all-comprehending perspective that offers an "enlargement and elevation of the soul" and "the intuition of ultimate principles."[82] And—moving the other way, now—where such all-comprehending ambitions drift toward vaporous abstraction, the symbol continually regrounds itself in the necessarily immediate stuff of emotion. Principles disjoined, Coleridge writes, "from the emotions that inevitably accompany the actual intuition of their truth . . . are like arms without hearts, muscles without nerves."[83] The symbol is Coleridge's name for this double move: to "the fleeting *chaos of facts*" the symbol (or Scripture) adds unity, functions as the "realizing principle" without which this chaos of particulars would "no more form experience, than the dust of the grave can of itself make a living man."[84] And to the "unenlivened generalizing Understanding," the Scripture/symbol adds life and substance, establishing "its freedom from the hollowness of abstractions" and rejecting the "shadow-fight of Things and Quantities."[85] The symbol thus negotiates an unstable middle ground stretched between the dispirited leadenness of particularity—"the fleeting chaos of facts"—and the groundlessness of "hollow abstractions." Coleridge described this balancing as a way to achieve "clearness" without losing "fulness": "To know God," he wrote, "is to acknowledge Him as the Infinite Clearness in the Incomprehensible Fulness, and Fulness Incomprehensible with Infinite Clearness." Like a legal fiction that combines "finite being with the essentials of infinity" ("above all," Coleridge has said, "the Eternal through and in the Temporal"), the symbol is a kind of poetic fiction designed to allay what Coleridge described as one of "the miseries of the present age": that "it recognizes no medium between *Literal* and *Metaphorical*."[86]

For these reasons it makes sense to think of the symbol, as Nicholas Halmi's recent reexamination of the concept puts it, as working to "redeem representation" by responding to "an anxiety" that, Halmi argues, "Enlightenment semiotics bequeathed to Romanticism."[87] But if the symbol's promise of a lossless mode of representation—an image that takes no shortcuts with the infinite exquisiteness of reality yet remains perceptible as an image—refuses empiricism's hard bargain, we can also see that it purchases this reassurance at some rather significant cost. For while the symbol corrects what had seemed a tragic flaw in the structure of knowledge—of the part's relation to the whole—this same representational perfection makes it impossible for the scheme of the symbol to understand change or action. If, this is to say, the flaw in Enlightenment knowledge is understood to lie in the gaps that linger in its representational structures, the symbol drives that flaw away. In doing so, however, the symbol also rules out the possibility of being able to say that X *in particular* is responsible for Y *in particular*. The doctrine by which we recognize, as Coleridge put it, "the actual immanence of the ALL in EACH" reduces us to being able to say only that the whole is responsible for the whole—a claim that may well be true by the identity property but that does nothing to admit a system of justice or form of knowledge that depends on the inequality or nonidentity of one thing with another. The perfect distribution of significance achieved by fusing the countable particular and the uncountable, because singular, One means that the only action of which a part can be conceived capable is a representative one: an essentially intransitive standing for, rather than an acting in one's own name. If justice means correcting an inequality of representativeness, then the symbol announces a millennial peace. But if justice means allocating inequality—distributing responsibility, reward, or blame here rather than there—the symbol does not merely leave the question of justice unanswered but actively dissolves the grounds on which we might ask it in the first place.

How big a problem this is depends on what one wants from one's millennium. If the establishment of the final, once-and-for-all recognition of unity is what we're after, the symbol is all we need. If, however, one remains committed, as Joseph Priestley did, to what he called "the great doctrine of future retribution," in which, quoting from the Book of John, "all that are in the graves shall hear the voice of the son of man, and shall arise; *some to the resurrection of life, and others to the resurrection of condemnation*" (my emphasis), one needs to secure a meaningful (that is, nonsymbolic, nonuniversal) notion of individuality in the face of the infinite exchangeability of part and whole.[88] As a devout materialist and an equally devout Christian, Priestley was particularly concerned to find a way to square the two perspectives, and he published his major philosophical work, *Disquisitions Relating to Matter and Spirit* (1777), in hopes that he might make "*materialism*, obnoxious as the term has hitherto been . . . the favourite tenet of *rational Christians*; being perfectly consonant to the appearances of nature, and giving a peculiar value to the scheme of revelation."[89] That "peculiar value" is putting it a little optimistically. Priestley's insistence on materialism entailed, first and foremost, rejecting the dualist doctrine of an immaterial soul that is separate (or separable) from the material body in favor of a view that understood the soul to be a property of the body's physical composition. Priestley was pleased about the anti-Catholic implications of the premise—there could be no Purgatory where souls wait out the remainder of secular time—but he also saw that his materialism created severe difficulties for imagining how "the great doctrine of future retribution" was supposed to work. If "after death the body putrefies, and the parts that composed it are dispersed, and form other bodies, which have an equal claim to resurrection," then where "can be the propriety of rewards and punishments, if the man that rises again be not identically the same with the man that acted and died?"[90]

It was a reasonable concern, one also lodged, for instance, by the anonymous author of *Letters on Materialism* (1776), who argued that for the promise of the resurrection to mean anything it was required not only that the soul "remain united to an organized body" but that the body "be the same, or a body similar to that he had upon earth."[91] Richard Price, in a published set of exchanges with Priestley largely devoted to this question, was even stricter in his phrasing. Price scrapped the *Letters'* hedging clause about "the same or similar" and insisted that only sameness would do it. If all we are, on the materialist view, is an "order or relation of parts," then "any change" would convert us "into some other figure, so would any change in that order of parts which constitutes myself, destroy me, and convert me into some other person."[92] What Priestley kept talking about as a resurrection was, in Price's view, an impossibility on the materialist view: assembling even a really, really similar being out of recycled materials amounts not to the resurrection of an earlier being but the "creation of a new set of beings."[93] If, as the author of the *Letter on Materialism* put it, our "fate[s] be equal, to be mingled for ever with the dust;—then are justice and goodness words without meaning; vice and virtue are airy bubbles; [and] the world is left to the dominion of chance, or fate, or confusion."[94]

Priestley responded to these difficulties in the only way he could: with an assertion of faith. "It is," he wrote, "my own opinion, that we shall be identically the same beings after the resurrection that we are at present," but he couldn't say how that was supposed to happen and fell back on the softer position of similarity. The idea that we will be *similar* at the resurrection to what "we are at present" ought, he thought, to be "sufficient for the regulation of our conduct here." To make the argument that similarity, and not just identity, would be sufficient, Priestley introduced a new distinction between "the identity of the man" and "the identity of the person" and claimed that, although the identity of the man—his material being—might be altered, the identity of the person would be continuous. "Ask any person to shew you the river Thames," he wrote, heading in direction that will now feel familiar,

and he will point to water flowing in a certain channel. . . . And yet, though the water be continually and visible changing so as not to be the same any one day with the preceding, the use of language proves, that there is a sense in which it may be called, to a very real purpose, the same river that it was a thousand years ago. . . . In the same manner forests, which consist of trees growing in certain places, preserve their identity, though all of the trees of which they consist decay, and others should grow up in their places.

As it goes for rivers and forests, Priestley argued, so it goes for persons. For even as we recognize the material reality according to which

in the course of nutrition, digestion and egestion, every particle of the body, and even of the brain . . . [is] entirely changed, we manage to still retain the idea of a real identity, and such a one as would be the proper foundation for approbation, or self reproach, with respect to the past, and for home and fear with respect to the future. A man would claim his wife, and a woman her husband, after more than a year's absence, debts of a year's standing would not be considered cancelled, and the villain who absconded for a year would not escape punishment.[95]

Priestley is arguing that human persons have what, as we saw in the first section, Frederic Maitland's corporate persons do: "a phenomenal reality"—an identity guaranteed not by fact or philosophy but by practice ("a man would claim his wife"), convention (debts would not be cancelled), and common sense ("the use of language proves . . ."). As with action on the case, we might accordingly say that identity for Priestley is a matter of being for all intents and purposes ourselves. Maybe this looseness is freeing: Priestley claims he would not feel "any concern" in being told that "the particles of matter" that "compose the table on which I write" should "instantly, and without any painful sensation to myself . . . change places" with "those particles of matter which compose my body."[96] But if he really is unconcerned it can only be because he holds a notion of identity that is, if not fully immaterial like the soul, somehow metamaterial—a form of personality that is not simply an epiphenomenon of the material body but properly transcendent in the sense that it persists over and above its material components and allows us to still think of ourselves as *our* selves even after we've traded all our atoms with our writing tables.

The logic on which Priestley's defense of the personality—if no longer the individuality exactly—of retribution is, we can now see, corporate in the full and legal-technical sense. It's no accident that Priestley, like Kyd and a host of other writers on the corporation, turns to the Thames to establish a precedent for an identity that exists as a logical fiction or a phenomenal reality—a symbol, we could say, but not a Symbol. Priestley's interest in retribution and punishment, quite against the tendency of his extraordinary commitments to materialism, pushes him to contend that it is to the phenomenal reality, and not to the material facts, that spouses, creditors, and prosecutors both secular and divine should look. The irony, here, is that the corporate status that, in the case of an Exxon or a Nusquamia, prevents our locating a culpable agent is the same corporateness that, for Priestley, ensures that we—or someone very much like us—will get our due. Persons, for Priestley, are corporations, too. And justice, or the only kind of justice there is, is always a matter of "impound[ing] the minute book." In the largest sense, then, we are left with two options: continue to mete out exact sentences to figurative entities (not good) or insist on the unity of anything and everything and stop talking forever about what X did to Y (not good either). There aren't two ways to have it: it's one or the other, and neither is just. It is this double bind that the novels I take up in this study recognize and that the following chapters explore.

2. The One and the Manor

On Being, Doing, and Deserving in Mansfield Park

> One way of being solid, simple, and sincere is to be a vegetable.
> —Lionel Trilling, *The Opposing Self*

Status as a State

As virtually every one of its readers has noted, *Mansfield Park* (1814) is a difficult novel.[1] Or, perhaps better to say, it is a *problematic* novel—one about which it feels difficult, as Philip Larkin said about another marriage plot, to find words that will be "both true and kind / Or not untrue and not un-kind."[2] In the modern critical literature, the trouble with *Mansfield* goes back at least to Kinsgley Amis's 1957 piece in the *Spectator,* "What Became of Jane Austen?," an essay whose working premise is more or less that the person who wrote *Pride and Prejudice* (1813) could not also be the one who, a year later, published *Mansfield Park*.[3] Any attempt to explain *Mansfield Park*'s puzzling bleakness by positing an authorial identity crisis—depression? religious conversion? financial instability? spinsterhood?—is bound to run up against the fact that, as Janet Todd points out, Austen was likely still revising *Pride and Prejudice* even as she was composing *Mansfield Park*: polishing the "too light, bright and sparkling" thing we all love, then, even as she overdarkened the one we keep trying to like.[4] In fairness to the aesthetic impressions that lie behind the biographical reaching, though, it's worth noting that Austen herself seemed to understand that the likability of her most recent novel was not a given. She extensively charted the "gradations of liking" evinced by her first and most familiar readers, carefully and, one hopes, wryly compiling the results in a document called "Opinions on *Mansfield Park*."[5] They would, in an interesting twist, be the only contemporary reviews the novel received.[6] A number of them find things to admire, but many sound more like her mother:"My mother—not liked it so well as P. & P. Thought Fanny insipid."[7]

As I will be explaining more fully throughout this chapter, it's a mistake to think of insipidness as a personal failing of Fanny Price, the novel's famously meek heroine. For one thing, given that Mary Crawford, the novel's antihero, is banished from the eponymous estate by novel's end for being what D. A. Miller calls a "stylist," it's not clear that a glossier, more assertive character would have been able to liven things up without our also, as they say in zoning law, having to change the character of the neighborhood.[8] For it is really that question—a question about the character of a neighborhood rather than the character of a heroine—that is on the table in *Mansfield Park*, a novel ceaselessly interested in the way characters are circumscribed by and identified with (and the one because the other) the circumstances in which they happen to fall.[9]

Mansfield Park's willingness to put the claims of circumstance over and above the claims of persons is, right from the beginning, one of the deepest sources of the difference between it and the novel against which, for Cassandra Leigh Austen as so many others, it comes up wanting. As if knowing (and how could she not?) which sentence would still be ringing in her readers' ears, the fourth sentence of *Mansfield Park* responds with a disappointed echo to *Pride and Prejudice*'s ultrafamous opening. "It is a truth universally acknowledged," says the first, "that a single man in possession of a good fortune, must be in want of a wife." "But there are not certainly so many men of large fortune in the world," answers the other, "as there are pretty women to deserve them."[10] The sad redux makes clear how much the ironic loft of the earlier novel depends on a sense of surplus possibility that the regimented landscapes of *Mansfield Park* will never assume. *Pride and Prejudice* is, as Claudia Johnson puts it, a "categorically happy novel" in the sense that "felicity is not merely incidental, something that happens at the end of the novel," but operates as a kind of formal principle: happiness is "at once its premise and its prize."[11] *Pride and Prejudice*, entails and all, is a novel that unfurls under the sign of "good fortune." The capacity of that first sentence to sail us up and over a field of social forms in the full promise that we will be able, should we desire it, to touch back down in an arrangement of our own choosing has, by the start of the next novel, disappeared. There already isn't enough to go around, and you'll be lucky to get a gouty parson whose death (third chapter, first sentence) will be made easier by the thought of the money you'll be saving (third chapter, second sentence). The question of desire, the question of what it is that, at least in one reading of the phrase, you are *in want of*, seems beyond the pale of the given world. In *Mansfield Park*, circumstances circumscribe, and that's that.

It's this pressure of circumstances that causes *Mansfield Park* to open not on the question of wanting, the question of desire, but on the question or, more precisely, the irrelevance of deserving. In 1814 the prior novel's "good fortune" is bluntly monetized into a "large" one. And fortune, thus shorn of its promissory halo, reappears as the merely arbitrary and amoral allocation of *fortuna*—her blind sorting manifested, first, in the "good luck" by which one "Miss Maria Ward, of Huntingdon," although "three thousand pounds short of any equitable claim," nevertheless manages "to captivate Sir Thomas Bertram, of Mansfield Park" and then, again, in the worse luck that lands her younger but "quite as handsome" sisters considerably down the ladder. The second sister wags around the title of Miss Ward for six years before finally finding "herself obliged to be attached to the Rev. Mr. Norris," the clergyman who takes over the Mansfield living (*M*, 3). And by the time we get to the third and youngest sister, Fanny's mother seems to be marrying not for love or for money but as a sort of social exit strategy—a pattern her wealthy niece Maria Bertram will repeat when, no longer "able to endure the restraint her father imposed" (*M*, 236), she presses ahead with an engagement to a man she doesn't love. "Miss Frances," the novel says, "married, in the common phrase, to disoblige her family" (*M*, 3). The "common phrase" efficiently captures both the idea of "giving offense" as well as its more material consequence: putting one's self beyond the obligations (the interest, the patronage) of those who might otherwise have understood your fate to be bound up with their own. Miss Frances achieves both "very thoroughly" (*M*, 4): "her husband's profession was such as no interest could reach," and the marriage puts "an end to all intercourse" between Mrs. Price and her sisters "for a considerable period" (*M*, 4). But if Frances would thus seem to have secured the one good to be had in falling off the social map—getting to be alone—she quickly learns that the only game outside the range of "interest" is no game at all. Halfway through the second paragraph of the novel, Mrs. Price, who "could no longer afford to cherish pride or resentment," writes a letter full of "contrition and despondence" to mollify her most fortunate sister (*M*, 5). That "no longer afford" is brutally material: to be "in want," now, is not a condition of possibility but a description of real need. Along with the more aristocratic fare of "advice and professions," forms of help so material and ungentle that a different Austen might forbear to mention them—"money and baby-linen" (*M*, 5)—begin to arrive.

This compressed prehistory positions the plot as one that picks up after the end of some other, demythologized *Pride and Prejudice*. *Mansfield Park* begins not in the social harmony that marriages in novels are supposed to confirm but in the disunification and disparities that a marriage—that "origin of change," as Mr. Woodhouse calls it—has already produced.[12] As such, the opening offers a decidedly unvarnished case study of the marriage market's massively consequential contingency—its scattering of equally marriageable (that is, "handsome") daughters across vastly unequal settlements. The small prospects of individualism and justice that appear in certain of its phrases—the fantasy about pretty women getting what they deserve, Miss Fanny's equally brief fantasy that "disobligation" might mean independence, the narrative's conclusion that all of this is "the natural result of the conduct of each party"—are quickly locked down into permanent features of a social geography that is as much a brute fact as the 125 miles that separate Northampton from Portsmouth. "Their homes," the narrative tells us, "were so distant, and the circles in which they moved so distinct, as almost to preclude the means of ever hearing of each other's existence during the eleven following years, or at least to make it very wonderful to Sir Thomas, that Mrs. Norris should ever have it in her power to tell them, as she now and then did in an angry voice, that Fanny had got another child" (*M*, 4–5). In this novel, even recent developments seem, by a process of accelerated time, to have aged prematurely into permanent conditions. The quick congealing of process into status that we see in the Bertram daughters—who, at the wise ages of twelve and thirteen, already "cannot remember the time when [they] did not know a great deal [about] the chronological order of the kings of England, with the dates of their accession, and most of the principal events of their reigns" (*M*, 20–21)—operates as general principle. History comes, here, already completed, and five years ago might as well be time immemorial; "very wonderful," then, that anyone can even remember when it wasn't always thus.

In one sense these early depictions of the social world in *Mansfield Park* are just what we expect as readers of Austen: the grounds for a critique of a status quo that takes its good luck and large fortunes too much to heart (think, for instance, of *Persuasion*'s Sir Elliot soothing his considerable and injured pride with the *Baronetage*, or of "the real evils" of *Emma*'s too-perfect transcendence, or of the less-moneyed myopia that keeps Mrs. Bennet "solace[d]" by "visiting and news").[13] But already things feel more difficult. For where in these other texts we read under the implicit promise that the opening assumption will be rethought—that the "evils" will be corrected and the superficial "solace" will be replaced by some more substantial notion of the good—here we are offered no clear hints of an alternative system. The mistakes people seem to be making in treating status as if it were the law of the land do not seem on the brink of being corrected and, worse still, reflect a blunt facticity that belongs as much to the novel itself as to any of the characters it describes. The plot, after all, works *forward from* (rather than subjecting to further scrutiny) the arbitrary disparity its first sentences establish. Sir Thomas's interest may not be able to help Mr. Price, but his money can reach Portsmouth, and he's not unwilling to take over the wardship of a surplus child. The question whether Mrs. Fanny Price deserves her precarity is thus lost in the patronage arrangements that ameliorate the sting of the structure but do not change (and only confirm) the structure itself. And even the narrative perspective, our reliable angel of extraterritoriality, remains stubbornly intrinsic to the world it is describing. The determination that "the absolute breach is the natural result of the conduct of each party" feels, in its self-satisfaction, like something that could belong to the trivial mind of a minor character, but there is nothing here to signal it as a moment of ironic ventriloquism or tell us at whose regrettable feet we might lay the thought. It is possible, and sort of disturbingly plausible, to go back and reread the first paragraphs of *Mansfield Park* as if they were a radically free and indirect discoursing of the character we will come to know as Mrs. Norris. Maybe, we'll say, we should call it free indirect narrative (a novel narrated in an unmarked way by a character) or an act of ventriloquism so extended that it only *seems* nonironic? Maybe. But these far-flung interpretive options, and the relief with which we might meet them, measure the degree of our conscription more than they serve as setup, as Austen has herself taught us to think they might, for our eventual freedom. We are trained to begin an Austen novel ready to share the thought that nothing this complacent can stand. But there are precious few openings in the closures of this beginning for thinking that it won't.

From the beginning, then, we can see that the difference between *Pride and Prejudice* and the more open-ended, promissory plots we have come to love is formal rather than thematic. We feel it as a fact of the world before we know, really, anything very specific about the persons who populate it—that, say, Sir Thomas is an especially intimidating man (while Mr. Bennet is obliging), or that Fanny is insipid or intimidated (while Elizabeth is flashing and fearless), or that Edmund is sympathetic but flat (while Darcy is unsympathetic but passionate). And we can feel it before we know these things because, on some level, the content of character doesn't matter here; personalities and personal claims still flicker on the edges in *Mansfield Park*— it's not that the individual characters don't have feelings, or habits, or hopes, or dreams—but they seem immaterial up against the impersonal relations of structure. Sir Thomas has "interest," "a general wish of doing right, and a desire of seeing all that [are] connected with him in situations of respectability" (*M*, 4), and these general wishes and boilerplate formulations for standard desires ("situations of respectability") are motivation enough; when he approves the plan to adopt young Fanny, it's not because, on second thought, her mother was rather harshly treated but because doing so is "so consistent with the relative situations of each" (*M*, 7). If *Mansfield Park* is a dispiriting novel, it is dispiriting not because of how the characters are (looming, indolent, trivial, trivial, trivial, weak, dissipated, flat, etc.) but because it doesn't really matter how they are. Though critics have debated the import of Austen's comment that she had decided to "write on something else;—it shall be a complete change of subject—Ordination," the remark seems borne out by these opening paragraphs, which map a structure of connections that slots people into places (provided they aren't "such as no interest can reach") that determine virtually everything and seem determined by almost nothing.[14] Much later on in the novel, for instance, Fanny will feel grieved "to the heart—to think of the contrast between [her aunt and her mother]—to think that where nature had made so little difference, circumstances should have made so much" (*M*, 473). Where in other novels (for example, *Great Expectations* or even, in its odd way, *Daniel Deronda*) contingency opens the door to fairer prospects or the possibility of self-recognition, there seems no possibility here that some combination of luck and fortitude will reorder "circumstance" in such a way that its inhabitants can, as Nancy Armstrong has put it, "acquire a position commensurate with his or her worth" or see themselves meaningfully reflected as individuals by the social matrix. The fact that anyone's life could have gone otherwise—that it might as well have been one of her sisters who got "thereby raised"—doesn't mean that it should have been. The fact of contingency carries no counterfactual force.

It is on these grounds that a reading of the novel like William Galperin's seems to me particularly convincing. Galperin, whose recent book-length study reads Austen's broader project as a "possibilistic" enterprise resisting domestic fiction's commitments to closure and probabilistic plots, finds in *Mansfield Park* a futureless outlier. It is, Galperin argues, a "dead end" text that documents—like a scuttled ship or the green baize curtain left over from the "systematically discredited" opposition the novel's amateur theatricals sought to mount—a lost battle fought against a conservative future "from which there is increasingly no turning back."[15] Where other Austen novels sought to acknowledge and activate all the latent potentials within her famously narrow lens—showing us "not just that all politics are local" but that they are "sufficiently local that anyone, from Jane Bennet to Catherine Morland, may have made a genuine difference"—*Mansfield Park* turns away (already!) from the "relatively new" idea that history is something "ordinary agents [are] capable of making."[16] *Mansfield Park* is, in Galperin's reading, not a historical novel about the bad old days of status (aristocracy, family interest, structure) that came before these liberating ones of contract (and merit, individualism, and possibility). It's a historical novel that marks how narrow, or even illusory, was individualism's window—a brief and possibly hypothetical heaven between the end of the aristocracy and the rise of the corporate and suprapersonal agencies that replaced it. What is problematic about this novel, then, is not that its main character doesn't speak her mind more forcefully or make something happen but that it has ceased to believe in the importance of individual action, the possibility that a person might make something happen.

There are, as we will see, many odd consequences—thematic, political, narratological—that come from an attempt to write a novel that seems somehow after action. That the novel will, at the end of the day, opt for the contingent determinations of status and stasis rather than the individualist grammar of merit and desert is a well-known feature of what, critics have agreed, is Austen's most conservative novel (Clara Tuite, for instance, calls it "a formidable conservative masterpiece").[17] But in what follows I am going to argue that our readings of *Mansfield Park* as a conservative novel in support of the status quo have, however strange it seems to say so, underrated the conservativism of status as the novel imagines it. The critical line on the novel's conservatism, most prominently exemplified by the key place Marilyn Butler and Alistair Duckworth give *Mansfield Park* in their overall evaluation of Austen's oeuvre, has involved attaching it to the thought of Edmund Burke. Both Burke and Austen's novel, Duckworth argues, recommend moderate, cautious forms of "improvement" rather than the more assertive and disruptive changes that, for Burke and his age, fell under the fearful heading of "innovations."[18] Individuals and individualism need, the Burkean thought goes, to be held in check. But because conservativism is, in this sense, a guide to individual action, there's something fundamentally mistaken (as I show in this chapter's second section) in reading Burkean conservatism as truly anti-individualist. Even as it clothes itself in the guise of timeless principles and moral absolutes, late eighteenth-century conservatism was, as we will see, as fully pragmatic (and therefore as consequentialist) as the contractualism it seeks to oppose.[19] But *Mansfield Park*, I am arguing, is doing something both more radical and more conservative in showing what it would mean to take status seriously—to take status, that is, not as a recommendation for highly moderated individualism but as necessarily above and indifferent to individual action.

To see how *Mansfield Park* understands status's independence from individual action, it is helpful (as I argue in this chapter's third section) to think about the feudal ethos of manorial title to which the novel frequently turns—sometimes subtly and sometimes more overtly (as when the narrative makes special note during a visit to a neighboring estate of the "ancient manorial residence of the family, with all its rights of Court-Leet and Court-Baron" [*M*, 95–96]). The usefulness of the manor, as I will explain, lies in its decidedly nonindividualist conceptions of persons; it starts not from an idea of persons as idiosyncratic bundles of desire, will, and reason that need to be fettered to a greater (Burke) or a lesser (Paine, J. S. Mill) degree but from a view in which persons are placeholders within an essentially corporate system of rights and obligations. In good corporate fashion, it is the manor itself that is the true bearer of personality; the human bodies that are the lords, freemen, or villeins at any given moment have a role to play, but what they want as individuals or how they feel about their roles are matters to which the manor is, in a strict sense, indifferent.

It is with this understanding in mind that we can (as I show in this chapter's fourth section) start to make sense of some of the more perplexing features of Austen's novel: at the level of plot it gives us, for instance, a new way of understanding the much-discussed question of the thwarted theatricals or the notably odd fact that an Austen heroine might be described at the height of her independence as a "renter" rather than an owner;[20] at the level of form, it helps account for the novel's extraordinarily uneven handling of time, the narrative's glancing (at most) interest in interior life, and the self-professed and rather dramatic arbitrariness of its ending. The goal of my reading here is, in short, to take the novel at something like its initial words: to read it as a novel governed by the grammar of status (and therefore not by the question of merit and action). We might, in this light, continue to think of it as conservative. But we will want to avoid misleading ourselves with the thought that status is something that we renegotiate our relationship to; like fate or fortune, status either is or isn't, and it doesn't make sense to think of yourself as a "cautiously improving" or "radically innovative" fatalist. We might do better, then, just to think of it in the absolutist and nonrelative term the novel's final sentence provides us: not as conservative but as "thoroughly perfect" (*M*, 548).

Beyond (or Before) Happiness

> Filial and conjugal ties are no remnants of feudal barbarisms, but happy institutions, calculated to promote domestic peace.
>
> Jane West, *A Tale of the Times*

Status's antithetical relation to action presents a serious challenge to any attempt to read *Mansfield Park*'s as if a commitment to status (which, I am arguing, the novel has) could be easily equated (which, I am arguing, it cannot) with a plan for conservative action.[21] Be quiet, listen to dad, wrap that libido up tight, and love your country—these are (some of) the predictable recommendations of a conservative morality (as thin in 1814 as they are two hundred years later). But while conservative morality's preference for hierarchy (flags and fathers) and privative commands (shalt nots) makes it seem like a set of absolute and inviolable principles, it is, very clearly, a code of individual action. It addresses itself to agents who are (all-too) free, and it argues its case at the level of consequence. Do this, or things will get worse. . . . Conservative morality thus adopts the style of absolutism without the structure to back it: at heart, it is a variety of pragmatism, one as committed to the claims of happiness as the liberal individualism it opposes. The one may value personal ambition and the other respect for one's elders—or expression versus passivity, or innovation versus caution, or abstract reason versus family feeling, and so on—but both systems are fundamentally utilitarian in their implicit promise that we will have a recognizably better world if we conduct ourselves according to their terms. What, both liberals and conservatives concede, would be the point of a good that wasn't happy?

Austen's early, unfinished fragment *Catherine, or the Bower* (begun in 1792) captures the conservative penchant for consequentialist thinking (otherwise known as "threats") perfectly and then sticks it in the mouth of a scolding aunt: "The welfare of every Nation," says Mrs. Percival, "depends on the virtue of its individuals and any one who offends . . . is certainly hastening its ruin."[22] The conservative position, in its panicked sense that national virtue is the sum of individual virtuousness, is as thoroughly individualistic as the liberality it opposes. "The force of [the conservative] argument," as Kevin Gilmartin writes in his study of literary conservatism in the romantic period, "lay precisely in its warning that any compromises in matters of domesticity, manners, and taste would precipitate the fall of governments and 'universal confusion.'"[23] Every time you let a weird boy just up and kiss your hand while you're in the middle of a discussion about "the character of Richard the Third" (the events that prompt Mrs. Percival's diatribe), England gets a little worse.[24] In its backhanded way, then, Mrs. Percival's scandalized hyperbole—"I bought you Blair's *Sermons*, and *Coelebs in Search of a Wife*," she protests, and now this?[25]—points out the mistake in thinking that what's conservative about conservative morality is that it deals in abstract rights or absolute wrongs while progressive morality is concerned with the (merely) self-serving, pragmatic, or hedonistic. Via a feedback loop Bentham could only dream of, every time you get kissed, France wins.

So while it's true that both Burke and his romantic opponents will take frequent recourse to the absolutist distinction between what is natural (and therefore is right whether we acknowledge its claims or not) and what is unnatural or arbitrary (and therefore has no claim to exist at all), claims for the happy-making power of "filial and conjugal ties" like the one we find in Jane West's antijacobin *A Tale of the Times* in fact testify to a gap that has already appeared between a code of conservative morals and a notion of truly transcendent right.

Feeling, at the end of the eighteenth century, is both the source and the barometer of morality. The French Revolution is, Burke argues, a perversion of feeling: people used to have respect, admiration, and love for the very nobles they now are happy to see humiliated, naked, and dead. And because the revolution is a perversion of feeling, the counterrevolution has to take place within the hearts and minds (but especially the hearts) of individual citizens. It is on these grounds that it seems so perfect for Claudia Johnson to describe Burke's *Reflections* as "a fearsome novel of manners" aimed at shoring up a sentimental network of "fond solicitude, unselfish benevolence, and grateful submission."[26] Action, for Burke, is determined by an appeal to a necessarily individualized, because sentimentally determined, notion of the good. If you're ashamed that your queen has been driven from her palace in her nightgown, let her back in. If you're horrified by the blood in your streets, stop the beheadings. But when the citizens aren't killing the nobles just because they don't feel like it, you're already in a liberal, contractual world in which getting the guillotine back out just doesn't seem *worth it*.

What's true of Burke's "novel of manners" is true of those (other) conservative novels, such as those published by people like West and Hannah More, whose didactic plots repackaged the blossoming eighteenth-century genre of conduct literature and sermons in order to direct them, increasingly, to young women.[27] These didactic fictions—like Mrs. Norris's "loud angry letter" pointing out "the folly of her [sister's] conduct, and threaten[ing] her with all its possible ill-consequences" (*M*, 6)—do their instructing via threats to our self-interest (you'll end up unhappy, your nation will collapse, etc.) or our self-image (would you be so unfeeling as to disobey?). As such, they are in fact already playing an incentivizing game that belongs to a system of individual action rather than natural status. The longer timelines of Burkean conservatism—that it deals in decades rather than days and therefore seems to offer more disinterested objects of concern (the good of your family or nation or culture)—may attenuate the immediacy of the self-interest we can see at work. But such ends are, in this sense, only as un-self-interested as a life insurance policy (that is, not very). Conservative individualism is, at the end of the day, an individualism, too. And if this was the "war of ideas" Austen was joining—if, as Joseph Litvak puts it, the question is "whether the presiding genius of *Mansfield Park* is Edmund Burke or Mary Wollstonecraft"—it's not really much of a war: whichever side comes out on top will involve a fundamentally liberal framework that takes individual persons as its essential units and seeks to give them accurate reflections of the value of their actions.[28]

Thus while we may agree with Marilyn Butler that Austen's novels recommend "a strenuous critical code which preaches self-understanding, self-mastery, and, ultimately, subordination," we would have no call for thinking of that code as anti-individualist.[29] Self-mastery, as Foucault's later and William Flesch's more recent work make clear, is no less a practice of the self than self-expression, and the decision to subordinate oneself is no less first-personal than the decision to rebel.[30] Indeed, the fact that Butler's ideal of the self-subordinating individual requires a deep well of inner resources makes it seem like one of the more maximal individualisms on offer. Among Anne Elliot's exemplarily conservative characteristics, for example, Butler lists "fortitude" and "self-control" but also "the ability to act"; one must be able to reject the ego's demands but also to support "an intense, withdrawn inner life."[31] Passive but active, detached but sympathetic, nonegotistical but deeply reflective, oriented toward the greater good and completely "intense": it is an interesting fact, although not one Butler could have anticipated in 1974, that the inner resources that are the hallmarks of her conservatism have now reappeared virtually verbatim as the set of disinterested, cultivated, reflective practices that, for Elaine Hadley and others, constitute the "life" of (or, as we sometimes used to say, under) liberalism.[32] So while Butler argues that Austen's "critical code" does not "give special value to the individual," that's true only in the rather limited sense that the individual's most short-term gratification is not (in Austen or ever) the only operative version of the good.[33] Actions that are cautious or less than immediately gratifying may be rarer or require more thinking than those that bring immediate pleasure, but they aren't any less individual—a fact made perfectly, almost embarrassingly clear in the conservative novel's commitment to the marriage plot as the delivery system for its rewards and demerits. For Butler, it is Austen's willingness to use "fiction's chief tool, its fable, with complete conviction" that made her the period's most successful channel for conservative ideology. Unlike Sir Walter Scott, who sometimes entertained the possibility that duty might kill and therefore seems, to Butler, less orthodox, the "marriages which end [Austen's] novels . . . carr[y] her partisan meaning further than it could be carried in reasoned argument, even by Burke."[34] We should think, then, of the marriages that end Austen novels as a kind of emotionally charged neoclassicism: a set of couplets that not only rhyme on paper but actually feel *happy*.

That's a powerful sales tool. But the larger point is that there is, or ought to be, something disappointing—or, worse, fallen and self-cancelling—to the antirelativist about the need to be selling in the first place. What was antiliberal about the Burkean line was its insistence on the distinction between what was really right and what was merely rational (right in the arid and abstract of the natural-rights theories he decries) or merely pleasure seeking (like the drunken sans culottes that appall his decorum). The point was to protest the age of "sophisters, oeconomists, and calculators."[35] But it's hard to win that battle against the oeconomists and calculators by compiling an ever more extensive account of the wages of sin.

So what we have in the conservative rhetoric of the late 1700s is the paradox of a moral order that wants to think of itself as absolute but, nevertheless, finds itself compelled to pitch itself to the interests and actions of individuals. One might think of it as a version of the problem of value Anne-Lise François sees as central to *Mansfield Park*: "How do we reward the good," she asks, "without making hypocrites of them, if being good means showing oneself ready to go without reward?"[36] Behind that question about the willingness to go without reward is, clearly, a more general question about how to orient oneself in relation to a system (status, the good, etc.) that not only doesn't reward action but, in fact, cannot reward it without turning itself into something else (merit, *this particular* good, etc.). In romantic aesthetics, as we saw at the end of Chapter 1, this conundrum appears as the mutual exclusion between getting the all down to earth via the symbol and, at the same time, imagining the all as actually doing something (besides just being) in the world; totality, there, entailed intransitivity. In *Mansfield Park*, the question is about the possibility of seeing persons as inhabiters rather than earners, of a conception of character in which occupancy or "just being" are more important than—where they can overwrite—action.

Surprisingly, given his otherwise firmly liberal commitments to hard work and the virtues of moral struggle, the estranging prospect of a world of status and stasis appears, just briefly, at the end of Lionel Trilling's famous reading of *Mansfield Park*. As readers will remember, Trilling's account is mostly committed to reading the novel as a testament to the humanist ideal of individual sincerity versus insincere acting, a dichotomy that has been, as David Marshall points out, crucial to much of the criticism on the novel.[37] But in the closing paragraph Trilling offers the deeply countervailing and basically unpursued possibility that the sated and somnolent Lady Bertram ("I was not asleep." "Oh dear, no, ma'am, nobody suspected you!" [*M*, 118]) might, in fact, represent an "ideal existence." "One way of being solid, simple, and sincere," Trilling writes, "is to be a vegetable." I'm not sure we should go that far, but it does at least seem right to say that being a vegetable is one way to be beyond the suspicion of being anything else—that it doesn't make sense to think of rocks and carrots as dissembling or, via a virtuous duplicity, being willing to go without the prize today in order to get the bigger prize tomorrow. But what would a system of order that addressed itself to vegetables look like? And can you—the great experiment of *Mansfield Park*—write a novel about it? Those two questions are the subject of the remaining two sections of this chapter.

The Manor

> Our land law has been vastly more important than our law of ranks. And so it is at an early time; we read much more in the law-books of tenants by knight's service, serjeanty, burgage, socage, than of knights, serjeants, burgesses and sokemen; nay, even the great distinction between bond and free is apt to appear in practice rather as a distinction between tenures than as a distinction between persons.
>
> Pollock and Maitland, *History of the English Law*

I have been suggesting that the problem with seeing *Mansfield Park* as a novel that looks back only as far the Burkean conservatism of its immediate setting—it begins "about 30 years ago" (*M*, 5), in the early or mid-1780s—is that it commits us to a conservatism that functions primarily as a code for individual action (No play acting! No adultery!) and therefore stops short of the more thoroughgoing, blanket aversion to change that Fanny formulates as the refusal of "any addition" (*M*, 182).[38] Burkean conservatism, as we've seen, presumes individuals as its essential units and emerges, therefore, as a strange hybrid: a sentimentalized absolutism, a categorical imperative that, for some reason, needs its daughter to love it. For writers like Burke and West, the social order is not a transcendent system that exists independently of the hearts and minds of the people that occupy it. That's the difference for West between the "filial and conjugal ties" of the domestic present and "the feudal barbarisms" of the past. The latter really were indifferent structures, and that's what, to West, seems barbaric about them—they don't care how you feel. If that's true, the feudal barbarisms should give us a good model for the kind of deindividualized conservatism we have already seen budding in the first pages of *Mansfield Park*—where conditions seem to have replaced action and where the claims of feeling seem to have been overwritten by the claims of structure. It's as though we've been cast back, in *Mansfield Park*, to an earlier moment (or cast forward to a later one) in which the patronage of corporate interest cannot be confused with paternalism, in which we would be fools to confuse the "interest" corporations take in us or the "advice" and "professions" they offer for love.

West is right: the feudal manor is a system in which the fact of individual persons is a working assumption but not much beyond that. It is an estranging thought, coming from our modern conception of property, but as Pollock and Maitland explain in the passage cited at the top of this section, early English land law doesn't imagine that its function is to define and protect the spheres in which individuals might exert their personal wills or pursue their private interests. Quite the contrary: what English land law offers is an abstract set of formal positions, each of which is understood not as a space or zone of freedom but as a specific set of obligations within a structure of other obligations. Status (being a knight or serjeant or burgess, for example) has no reality independent of the services it entails, and virtually all land is held on the condition of some kind of service. The familiar scene in an Austen novel in which the income of some aristocrat or another goes circulating through the room—"What is his property?" "Four thousand a year." (*M*, 139)—thus represents the middle-class inversion, the gentry-fication (downward this time) of a system organized around obligation into one centered in private income. The question of what you make is the liberalization, the individuation, of the feudal question of what you owe.[39]

This isn't to say that money was never at issue: all along there were profits on manors.[40] But it was not primarily in terms of profit and ownership that the English land law organized itself. Indeed, because the working assumption is that the king owns everything (one could call it a legal fiction, but it's more like the only legal reality), no one else in England owns any land at all. It's for this reason that an important seventeenth-century treatise on the manor to which I will return begins by announcing itself to be "written for the good of Lords and Tenants, and *by consequence of all men.*"[41] Everyone, that is, is either a lord or a tenant—and many are both. The king is a lord but not a tenant, and at the bottom the villeins are tenants but not lords. In between, though, it's mixed: people are under obligation to you, and you are under obligation to someone else. Ownership doesn't come into it. Everyone is simply inhabiting or "holding"—they are in possession of certain rights over a certain parcel. Properties, like the statuses according to which they are organized, are situations that are occupied rather than owned.

Take, for instance, the description Pollock and Maitland supply of Sir Robert de Aguilon. When he died in 1286 his situation (slightly abbreviated) looked like this:

He held lands at Greatham in Hampshire of the king at a rent of 18s; he held
lands at Hoo in Kent of the Abbot of Reading at a money rent; he held lands
at Crofton in Buckinghamshire of William de Say by some service that the
jurors did not know; he held a manor in Norfolk of the Bishop of Norwich
by the service of a sixth part of a knight's fee and by castle-guard ... he held
tenements in London of the king in chief by socage and could bequeath them
as chattels.[42]

Sir Robert, clearly, was doing rather well. But whatever wealth these holdings yielded, none of them, in and of themselves, count as private property.
The closest item we see to our modern conception of property is in the
exception of the final item in the list, the London tenements that Sir Robert can bequeath "as chattels"—that is, that he can direct in his will as he
pleases.[43] But even this prerogative seems, here, exercisable only *in extremis*. In
life he is entirely, if rather extensively, a renter ("socage" can refer to a broad
array of payments and services). The partial and time-limited connotations
of terms like "holding" and "tenant" have, then, a legal reality. In Sir Robert,
we have a wealthy man whose relation to land is primarily one of owing
(different rents, assorted services) rather than owning.

The emphasis I'm putting on indebtedness as a constitutive condition
may seem to underrate the not inconsiderable power a lord of the manor
possessed. He would have been in charge of the Court Leet (dealing with
intramanor disputes among copyholders) and the Court Baron (in which
business pertaining to the freeholders took place). In addition to the annual
rents, his coffers would have benefited from a bevy of tolls that turned the
mundane facts of life (death, marriage, a change of one tenant for another)
into sources of income.[44] And it was into the lord's hands that the land re-
verted when a tenant died without heirs. This last fact, Pollock and Maitland
argue, implies a sort of silent assumption of absolute ownership: "In the
background," they write, "but ever ready to become prominent stands the
lord's rights to escheats. This forms, as it were, a basis for all his other rights,"
and "the superiority which he always has over the land may at any time
become once more a full ownership of it."[45] But even if there can be a lord
with no tenants, the lord himself would have had obligations that went *up*
the ladder—the manor is his as long as (and only as long as) he meets those
obligations. So what Pollock and Maitland are noticing isn't really the lord's
"absolute ownership" but the complete indifference any higher title has to
where the rents the lower title is paying are coming from.[46] As Pollock and
Maitland write in a comment that might (but doesn't seem to) have pushed

them in this direction:"The tenant in demesne, the tenant on the lowest step of the feudal scale, obviously has right in the land, amounting to a general, indefinite right of using it as he pleases."[47] The right of doing what you please belongs to even the "lowest step"—but not because it is understood as a space of positive freedom. You can use the land however you want as long as the accounts continue good. The structure wants exactly what it wants, and, so long as it gets it, the rest is up to you.

I want to pause here to cast forward, for just a moment, to one of the points where this discussion intersects with some of the literary issues found in *Mansfield Park*. We are now in a good position to see how the manorial structure's odd combination of absolutism and indifference lines up with one way of thinking about the character of Fanny Price. One of the problems Fanny Price presents to literary criticism (and to readers of *Mansfield* more generally) has to do with the way she seems to refuse the convenient dichotomy of flat versus deep (or round) that we often use to talk about novelistic character.[48] It is one of Austen's truly remarkable aesthetic achievements (though not one that has tended to please readers) that in Fanny she manages to create a character who seems to have a sensible, palpable innerness without much needing to treat the contents of that innerness as direct objects of narrative description. There are, of course, sentences that provide us information on Fanny's inner state ("Fanny thought it a bold measure" [*M*, 18], "Fanny grew more comfortable" [*M*, 19], "Fanny was often mortified" [*M*, 22–23], etc.), but what we tend to get fewer of are depictions of the living contours of whatever inner monologue and mental representations are getting summarized by predicates like "grew more comfortable" or "was often mortified." The descriptions of Fanny present cumulative effects or habitual states rather than impressions mapped in the moment. Even moments that signpost themselves as psychological insights don't follow through in the ways we might expect. "And Fanny," the narrative asks, rendering reader rather than character by free indirect discourse, "what was *she* doing and thinking all this while? and what was *her* opinion of the newcomers" (*M*, 56)? The answer:"In a quiet way, very little attended to, she paid her tribute of admiration to Miss Crawford's beauty; but as she still continued to think Mr. Crawford very plain, in spite of her two cousins having repeatedly proved the contrary, she never mentioned *him*" (*M*, 56). The rhetorical question seems to promise an account of Fanny's real-time thinking (although how much duration does "all this while" comprehend?). But in fulfillment it tells us only one thing that she's barely mentioned and that everyone knows (Mary Crawford is beautiful) and another (that her brother is plain) that she hasn't mentioned at all. As if to confirm this turn away from the innerness it seemed to promise, the narrative's very next sentence reverses view entirely, describing not what Fanny is thinking about but—"The notice, which she excited herself, was to this effect . . ." (*M*, 56)—what others are thinking about Fanny.

Compare this, for example, to Anne Elliot, another character who, like Fanny, is what Nina Auerbach calls a "fixed point of knowledge" around which the social world happens rather than a direct actor in its economy.[49] Anne Elliot, readers will remember, spends much of *Persuasion* listening rather than speaking, but the reticence is not, it is made abundantly clear, for lack of things to say: "How eloquent could Anne Elliot have been,—how eloquent, at least, were her wishes on the side of early warm attachment, and a cheerful confidence in future, against that overanxious caution which seems to insult exertion and distrust Providence!"[50] Fanny's "quiet way" is, by contrast, not (or not even) presented as eloquence withheld (*M*, 56). And while it's true that other moments in the novel will enable us to spend more time in the direct presence of Fanny's thoughts and impressions, it is, nevertheless, one of the narrative's characteristic practices that it often holds back, in a way that it doesn't with Anne, from providing Fanny with an alternative or surrogate venue for self-expression. There is nothing to stop us from seeing Fanny's "quiet way" as a feature of her character—it's just the behavior we'd expect from what Trilling calls a "terrified little stranger"—but in a moment like this one the quietness does not really belong to Fanny.[51] It is, instead, the effect of a narrative that, as Anne-Lise François points out, seems to allow Fanny her space, one that doesn't confuse indifference or non-narration with denial or repression. "Lacking the means to cover herself," François says, Fanny "is also spared the kind of attention from others"—and from the narrative—"that would require concealment."[52] Where in other novels the narrator takes up what cannot be said (either because social pressure forbids saying it or the thought seems too compressed, in process, or multifaceted to fit a direct form of discourse), *Mansfield Park* seems conspicuously manorial in its narrative strategies. There is an inner life there—who would deny it?—but it is registered as kind of low-level white noise rather than the detailed transcript of a score. Fanny has a mind and, like everyone else, the "indefinite right of using it as [s]he pleases"—but so what?

Mind, for Fanny and for François, thus becomes the name of an extraterritorial space that is not, as it was for Milton's Satan, defined by its aggressive contradiction of some hierarchical structure. Instead, it appears in more interstitial and less oppositional ways—like a Bartleby who wouldn't bother even to voice his negative preference—as what is simply left outside or beyond some scheme of value or the modern political demand that all virtues show themselves in action. What François's reading of the novel opens up is a way of understanding Fanny's odd quietness as something other than what Trilling personalizes as Fanny's "debilitated condition" (or what Cassandra Austen personalized as "insipid[ness]"); it appears instead as whatever might (or not) be happening outside of a structure that can, like the manor, organize persons without concerning itself about their inner states.[53] Fanny, this is to say, has a "debility" only under a certain set of liberal assumptions that define the bourgeois novel: namely, that the social world is a structure in which (a) individuals need to be given an opportunity to demonstrate themselves because (b) they will be assessed according to their demonstrated merits in order to (c) be positioned in a social structure accordingly.

But that's not how the manor proceeds. The manor doesn't try to match preexisting individuals with positions. It starts with preexisting positions and derives whatever it needs of individuals from there. Indeed, the manor's strength as an institution and its usefulness as the primary module of feudal governance lay in its ability to minimize its dependence on individual decisions—that it could be a self-sustaining and self-resupplying set of forms.[54] As such, we have in the self-sustaining formal structure of the manor something similar (though not quite identical) to the early versions of the corporate persons whose history we examined in the prior chapter. "The 'community of the vill,'" write Pollock and Maitland, "is generally a body of men whom the lawyers call serfs and these men, who must be treated as the normal shareholders in the village, form a community, a commune, something that might not unfairly be called a corporation."[55] There are some important technical differences, most saliently the fact that manors, unlike corporations, had no institutional resources separate from the resources of their assembled holders.[56] Still, the broader similarities are significant and worth noting: the manor, like the early corporation, represents a fixed and theoretically immortal framework to be inhabited by one generation after another, and the manor, like the early corporation, is oriented primarily toward its own continuance rather than toward the accumulation of profit. Indeed, if there's a distinction to be drawn between the corporation and the manor, it's that the corporation is more individual than the manor. As Frederick Pollock writes, the reason "that the corporate or quasi-corporate unit of archaic property law, the family, or house or village community, is not like a modern corporation" is because the modern corporation is set up on the assumptions of individualism: "The modern law first assumes individual *dominium*, and then by a fiction treats the corporation as a single person and invests it with capacities of dominion, obligation, and so forth." But "the archaic family or community is not a *dominus* or a person in the modern legal sense at all."[57] Like the early corporation, then, and unlike the modern one, the manor is a subsistence-level institution: it's set up to be a repeating and repeatable form—which doesn't mean that people won't have lives outside of that repeating, or that there won't be economic surpluses, or that those surpluses won't eventually drive the manor toward privatization and individualism—only that if these things happen, they do so in the substantial space of existence with which the manor does not, at least in theory, concern itself.

"In theory," because the perfect repetition of a social form is impossible. In actual practice, the manor bore traces of the different historical moments through which it lived: the personal service and military protection of early tenures were converted into money rents or the obligation to supply a post; the Black Death produced a massive oversupply of land vis-à-vis the number of people available to work it, forcing lords to cede power to attract new copyholders; the Reformation and Henry VIII's confiscation of church lands did away with the substantial manorial holdings of the church and centralized both tax collection and patronage; inflation in the 1600s caused lords to seek rent increases and manor courts (typically limited to cases regarding sums less than 40s) to hear fewer cases.[58] The historian Richard Lachmann estimates that while "at no point before 1567 did more than an eighth of English peasants lack personal bonds to land," 40 percent of English peasants were "proletarianized" between 1570 to 1640, and, by 1688, "a majority, 56 percent, of English rural laborers were proletarians."[59] England, in short, modernized, and the manor changed accordingly.

No surprise, then, that we find in 1641 a treatise titled *The Compleat Copy-Holder* lamenting that "copyholder" no longer means what it used to.[60] "The time," our author complains, "hath bred such an alteration, that in the point of service a man can scarce discern any difference between Freehold-lands and copyhold-lands" and "men of all sorts of conditions, promiscuously, turn both freeholders and copyholders."[61] But in a slightly paradoxical way, the promiscuity of current practice becomes the grounds for idealizing the manor as a structure whose essence is its immunity to change. Thus *The Compleat Copy-Holder* tells us: "The efficient cause of a manor is expressed in these words, *of long continuance*: for indeed time is the mother, or rather the nurse, of manors, time is the soul that giveth life unto every manor, without which a manor decayeth."[62] Time makes manors because custom makes manors, and only time makes custom. "Time," the treatise says, "is the soul that giveth life unto every manor."

Beginning with *The Compleat Copy-Holder*, an essay Wolfram Schmidgen holds up as "the central event in the legal recognition of the manor as a distinct communal form," the next two centuries of legal talk about the manor would consolidate the idea that the manor is defined by its unchangingness.[63]

As such, the discussion of the manor increasingly centers on how to preserve the entity, on all the limitations unchangingness implies. It goes virtually without saying, for instance, that an ordinary citizen cannot *start* a manor. But neither, any longer, can the king: "The king himself," the *Compleat Copy-Holder* says, "cannot create a perfect manor at this day; for such things as receive their perfection by the continuance of time come not within the compass of the king's prerogative."[64] The lord can't change the rents or terms according to which the copyholders hold. Because the lord, Blackstone writes, "is bound to observe the ancient custom precisely in every point," he can "neither in tenure nor estate introduce any kind of alteration"; he "can neither add to nor diminish the ancient rent, nor make any the minutest variation in other respects."[65] And if the lord sells some manor lands, their manorial "character," as John Scriven put it in an important *Treatise on the Law of Copyholds* (originally published in 1821), disappears: "If the demesne lands of a manor are treated by conveyance as a distinct property, they cease to form part of the manor." If the lord buys the parcel back the next day, he does so not as a returning lord but as just another "fee simple owner of it."[66]

In a way that, I hope, already speaks to the quiet passivity of *Mansfield Park* and argues the relevance of the manor (as opposed to the more general form of the "estate"), the manor as it emerges from this legal history is an entity defined by its antithetical relation to action and the change that any action would introduce. If the point of the early corporation was to create an entity that could be relatively immune to change (because its existence wasn't tied to the lifespans of its members), the manor radicalizes that position and suffers a new kind of fragility as a result: not relatively immune to change but so perfectly timeless that it is absolutely, fatally allergic to "any the minutest variation." Being "compleat," being what *Copy-Holder* calls "a perfect manor," means being majestically separate from the mundane transpiring of plot and human doing. To the degree that the manor intersects with this plodding realm, it becomes something else (fee simple property or what the law refers to as merely "a manor by reputation").[67] To the degree that the manor can be said to exist at all, it does so in its transcendence—sitting, like a more famous romantic form, "far, far above . . . still, snowy, serene." Put less loftily: the manor's way of "being solid, simple, and sincere is to be a vegetable."

Because the manor is such an old formation, it can feel like Austen is reaching way back, much further than Scott's "sixty years." But we can also see in the manor the land law's version of the transcendent logics that animate romantic aesthetics. Thought of as "a fortress island of Franco-Norman feudalism strangely blended with ancient local custom," the manor in 1814 is an anachronism.[68] But seen as a way to talk about the especially romantic problem of totality, the manor is entirely of its moment—as romantic as the "allness" of Schelling's unrepresentable divinity or the romantic nationalisms that emphasize the unchanging identity of a culture (see Chapter 3). In his important study on the manor and eighteenth-century fiction, Schmidgen argues that "the ideological and imaginative value" of the manor remained "extremely high" even as "the manor as an actual community was on the decline."[69] It did so, I would argue, because the manor answered to the romantic demand for a form of community that could, as *The Compleat Copy-Holder* puts it, have "all its members knit together in compleat order" in spite of, as Fanny puts it, "all the changes of opinion and sentiment, which the progress of time and variation of circumstances occasion in this world of changes" (*M*, 431).[70]

But as with the romantic symbol or the romantic nation, the "compleat order" promised by the manor's transcendent timelessness comes at the expense of individual action. It is the primary force of the manor to counter the forms of belonging that rest on contract and the forms of doing that rest on will. The manor, as Sir Paul Vinogradoff writes, "is not based on agreement"; "it is the holdings in their unconscious and unwilling combination which form the group and define its aims." The manor is defined in terms of being rather than doing—as something that *is* rather than something that *does*. If it can be said to change at all, those changes are understood to take place at the level of being, in "conscious and unwilling combination." The manor thus arrives as an entity that is, even through its changes, "as thoroughly perfect in [Fanny's] eyes as everything else within the view and patronage of Mansfield Park had long been" (*M*, 548).

How to Marry a Manor

> *Frederick.* Good friend, look at that poor woman. She is perishing in the public road! It is my mother; Will you give her a small corner in your hut? I beg for mercy's sake; Heaven will reward you.
>
> *Cottager.* [. . .] Why could not you say all this in fewer words? Why such a long preamble? Why for *mercy's sake*, and *Heaven's reward*? Why talk about *reward* for such trifles as these? Come . . . lead her in.
>
> *Frederick.* Ten thousand thanks, and blessings on you!
>
> *Wife.* Thanks and blessings! Here's a piece of work indeed about nothing!
>
> *Lovers' Vows*

"As thoroughly perfect in her eyes as everything else within the view and patronage of Mansfield Park had long been": in the conflated sightlines of the novel's final sentence we have, it would appear, the identification of a character's perspective (Fanny's eyes) with a perspective that seems to belong to a place ("the view . . . of Mansfield Park").[71] Reading quickly, we might take it as a repetition of the famously felicitous alignment of eyes and windows (and person with place) we see when Elizabeth Bennet goes up "to a window to enjoy its prospect" and finds not only that "the hill, crowned with wood," is "a beautiful object" but that "every disposition of the ground" (the river, the trees, the winding valley) is "good" and full of "delight." Except that, here, the addition of that third term—"patronage"—is jarring, disrupting the happy parallelism of "eyes" and "view." Appearing at the end of the novel, the word "patronage" reaches all the way back to the beginning, to the questions of "interest" and inequality raised, as we saw, in its opening paragraphs. Its appearance thus marks the continuity or sameness of this conclusion rather than the accomplished difference of a social world reordered. Tonally, the term feels insistently aristocratic, remote, and institutional—subtly but substantially shifting us from thinking of Mansfield Park as a place we might possess ("And of this place," says Elizabeth of Pemberley, "I might have been mistress!") to seeing it as a field of social power that is, in the long tradition of the manor, only contingently and temporarily identified with particular persons.[72]

From this vantage we can better see what's wrong with—what's antimanorial about—the vocabulary of improvement the novel criticizes. The fashionably improved estate is wrong not, or not primarily, as Duckworth argues, because of the scale of the change it introduces but because it belongs to a mindset that wants to take property personally. "You may raise it into a *place*," Mary Crawford says of Edmund's prospective parsonage, "the residence of a man of education, taste, modern manners, good connexions" (*M*, 283). The house, in Mary's middle-class mind as in Elizabeth's swooning trip to Pemberley, bespeaks the man. But not so Mansfield or the manor: patronage accrues to the patron not as an accomplishment—as an effect of "education" attained, "taste" achieved, or "modern manners" demonstrated—but as a structural fact. There is, on the manor, no way to conflate the "disposition of the ground" for the disposition of the person—no way to read from place to placeholder—and so the pleasures of the modern gentry, not the least of which is the self-congratulation of taking your house personally, are impossible in this institutionally scaled scene. Fanny's eyes can, presumably, share the *views* of Mansfield Park—she can look out its windows and see what it "sees," and she may even applaud, like a later Richard Dalloway looking at Buckingham Palace, the work the place does as an institutional symbol. But Fanny can't see the *patronage* of Mansfield Park as a personal possession—and, in fact, no one can. Fanny, like everyone else in the world, falls either within the radius of its protection and influence or she falls, like her mother in paragraph one, beyond the "reach" of it, but the patronage belongs to and is a function of the place, not the person.

None of this, again, is to say that the anti-individualism of either manors or Mansfield makes them egalitarian. The current lord of Mansfield, like the lord of any manor, is the one most able to guide the direction and shape of patronage's field. That said, though, it's also true that whatever considerable sway this lends the master, it is sway based on position and not on private property, a point nicely made by the final pages of the novel, which, after casting us an unknown distance into the future, don't bother to tell us who the current lord is. It might be the man we've known as Sir Thomas for most of the novel, but it might be his eldest son. And we might, inspired by that thought, find ourselves foreseeing that it will soon be Fanny's husband, Edmund Bertram (hasn't the young Tom been ill?). But if we do, we would be wise to remember that this is precisely the thought whose utterance signs the writ for Mary Crawford's excommunication:"Poor young man!" she says of Tom's illness, "—If [Tom] is to die, there will be *two* poor young men less in the world; [though] would I say to anyone, that wealth and consequence could fall into no hands more deserving" (*M*, 502). Although it's never polite to wish death on the heir so that you might marry his brother, Mary's dream is at least as deeply sociopathic in its insistence—almost heroic in its refusal to countenance all the evidence to the contrary—that she's in a novel that cares about which hands are most "deserving" of "wealth and consequence." Mary keeps talking like someone who's wandered out of *Pride and Prejudice*, but in a novel governed by patronage (and not private property), it's the manor that matters and not the master—whoever he is.

Mansfield Park is, therefore, mostly misunderstood when we describe it, as Trilling says we all do, as a story in which "the terrified little stranger in Mansfield Park grows up to be virtually its mistress."[73] What's wrong about that view is that it assumes for the novel a standardly bourgeois machinery of individual acquisition and accomplishment from which the novel pointedly and repeatedly distances itself. Fanny is not oriented toward rewards and deserts, and neither is the novel. In fact, the response Trilling imagines for us already admits as much in the vague terms—*"virtually* its mistress"—in which it is compelled to register its dissatisfaction. What's the value of being "virtually" the mistress?—a lot, too much, not enough? Has "the terrified little stranger" been overpaid, underpaid, or merely, as Claudia Johnson contends, all too easily bought off? Whatever it is, we just, Trilling says, "do not like it."[74] Behind our peevish imprecision is not the injustice of the outcome, that Fanny has gotten something she didn't deserve, but the fact that the novel isn't abiding by our assumption that endings are rewards. Indeed, it's only under some duress that our readings have been able to maintain that standard novelistic assumption. For Johnson's progressive reading—which sees the novel laying bare the grim reality of conservative paternalism—the ending is a problem because it seems to reward the victim; it can only thus be understood as another, particularly deflating turn of the screw. Readings in the Burkean line are, unsurprisingly, eager to see this as a case of virtue rewarded—"after dispossession, comes possession" is how Duckworth summarizes the Austenian view—which might work if Fanny had actually taken possession of anything.[75] What she has done is married a man, and what her man has is not a property but a living that is attached to the estate and whose next disposition will not (minus the death of his brother, perish the thought) be up to him. It is this shiftier state of affairs—an ending that looks like a prize or a reward but that we know isn't one—that "virtually mistress" really captures. What "we do not like" isn't the verdict (that so-and-so got such-and-such) but the much more general and programmatic refusal to think in terms of verdicts.

Where we expect a meritocracy, then, we get a manor—or, in its less anachronistic formulation—luck. "Miss Maria Ward," as we have seen, "had the good luck to captivate . . . and thereby be raised." But Fanny's selection, however much we might like to imagine it has to do with her particular virtue, is no less arbitrary—"Mrs. Price seemed rather surprised that a girl should be fixed on, when she had so many fine boys" (M, 12)—and neither is the adoption with which the novel concludes. In the penultimate paragraph, Fanny's sister Susan arrives "first as a comfort to Fanny, then as an auxiliary, and last as her substitute" (M, 438). According to the bourgeois logic the novel refuses, this doesn't sound like a particularly happy fate: to be the substitute for the person whose role has been to be something like a universal substitute ("Fanny's consequence increased on the departure of her cousins" [M, 190]). But according to the manorial logic the novel accepts, good fortune is good fortune and should be accepted as such: "Susan remained to supply [Fanny's] place—Susan became the stationary niece—delighted to be so!" (M, 546–547).

It's a little hard to know what our position on this kind of persistent contingency should be (if it even makes sense to have a position on contingency). On the one hand, we may find ourselves wanting back the old, bourgeois novel—even with all its reifying marriage markets, surveilling appraisals, and alienating individuation—if it means being free of a system that imagines itself only as a succession of substitutes and can never, therefore, go forward. On the other hand, though, we can also see that what feels like the confining because unappealable force of these "station[ings]" has, as its flipside, an ethic hard to tell from Samaritanship—a code in which you accept whatever obligations befall you in, as *Lovers' Vows* puts it in the section epigraph above, "the public road." In that short scene (the one, it's worth noting, that would have been Fanny's had she been pressed into playing the Cottager's Wife), the Cottager asks Frederick, the young hero begging the cottagers to help his sick mother, why he keeps talking about rewards and payments and gratitude. "Why for mercy's sake, and Heaven's reward?" the Cottager asks. "Why talk about reward for such trifles as these?" "Ten thousand thanks, and blessings on you!" replies Frederick, who, like Mary Crawford, can't seem to take the point. "Thanks and blessings!" the Cottager's Wife makes clear, are not relevant, and they're not relevant because this is not a system of merit; it's a system of duty: "Do you think husband and I have lived to these years, and don't know our duty?" This talk of reward is, she says, "a piece of work indeed about nothing!"[76] So, on the one hand, the manorial logic we see here is arbitrary, unequal, and tyrannical, and it presents itself as a set of duties and obligations, not as a set of promises and rights. On the other hand, it also underwrites an ethic of unpaid caretaking, in which charity doesn't have to be deserved and "comfort" (the term in which *Mansfield Park* often understands the good) doesn't have to be earned.

It feels, in this light, misleading to describe *Mansfield Park* as conservative, as if the parameters of that definition went without saying. It's true that it is deeply anti-individualistic, but in being so it not only depicts the way individuals might be made unfree ("coerce[d] and mislead," says Johnson) but gestures to a set of more compelling objections to a world in which even trivial forms of aid (helping strangers, chatting with a boring aunt) are done only on the understanding that the check is in the mail. To the degree that the politics of *Mansfield Park* seem grim to me, they seem grim not because they are conservative rather than progressive but because the novel sees clearly a possibility we might prefer to skip over: that there is no easy fit between our self-interested selves and our social bodies. What the corporate system of the manor costs is the forsaking of one's individual claims ("she thought too lowly of her own claims to feel injured by it" [*M*, 23]), but what it gains you is the possibility of a pure, because unrewarded, charity. What the liberal system of individualism gains you is the opportunity for a particular value (the chance, as Mary Crawford puts it, to "rise to distinction" [*M*, 249]), but what it costs you is the impossibility of ever really ruling out mercenary speculation or the worry that, at bottom, even our best deeds are just ways to amass reward. Both our modern liberalisms and conservatisms try to broker this impasse: well-behaved liberalism pushes a mandatory individualism tempered by a healthy respect for our place in the whole, and incentivized conservatism (à la Burke) purchases a mandatory respect for our place in the whole on the promise of future health and stability. *Pride and Prejudice*, Johnson argues, is almost "shamelessly wish fulfilling" in its suggestion that we might find a way to bridge this gap. But whatever "fantasies" Austen "satisfies" there, she is not satisfying them here.[77] Instead, the novel unashamedly asks difficult questions: what absolute forms of virtue do we sacrifice to live in a world of justice? And what kinds of justice must we sacrifice to live in a world defined by absolute virtue? To ask those questions is to refuse either of the attractive but oversimplifying promises: that, from the free-market maven, the greater good entails every individual doing better according to their own lights or, from a Burke or a West, that you can have your good fortune and earn it, too.

Whatever we do about this ideological impasse, reading this novel fairly does require that we at least be open to seeing Fanny (and her replacement, Susan) not as characters who are never permitted to own anything but as the fullest instantiations of the manorial ideal in which no one does. Take, for instance, the brilliant passage that describes Fanny's living quarters. "The little white attic," the novel tells us, "had continued her sleeping room ever since her first entering the family." But Fanny also had, the passage continues:

> recourse . . . to another apartment, more spacious and more meet for walking about in, and thinking, and of which she had now for some time been almost equally mistress. It had been their school-room; so called till the Miss Bertrams would not allow it to be called so any longer, and inhabited as such to a later period. There Miss Lee had lived, and there they had read and written, and talked and laughed, till within the last three years, when she had quitted them.—The room had then become useless, and for some time was quite deserted, except by Fanny, when she visited her plants, or wanted one of the books, which she was still glad to keep there, from the deficiency of space and accommodation in her little chamber above;—but gradually, as her value for the comforts of it increased, she had added to her possessions, and spent more of her time there; and having nothing to oppose her, had so naturally and so artlessly worked herself into it, that it was now generally admitted to be hers. The East room as it had been called, ever since Maria Bertram was sixteen, was now considered Fanny's . . . and Mrs. Norris having stipulated for there never being a fire in it on Fanny's account, was tolerably resigned to her having the use of what nobody else wanted. (*M*, 176–177)

What begins as a grant (and what Mrs. Norris is not entirely wrong to consider a gift) becomes not ownership but a kind of tenure Fanny has acquired according to what *The Compleat Copy-Holder* calls "the continuance of time." In modern property law this kind of property would fall under the dubious heading of adverse possession—a conception with which this description flirts—a notion that writes a common-law flexibility into the rigidity of contractual ownership. But on a manor it looks perfectly regular since there's no ownership to be "adverse" to.[78] With "nothing to oppose her" and no one else to want them, the rooms and the objects become hers by virtue of duration and remain for her use on a kind of permanent loan. The language of private possession, it is true, does not quite disappear: the passage goes on to describe Fanny as a "collector" and to suggest that the pleasures she derives from "her plants, her books" have something like the privilege of privacy. But those intimations of individuality seem to appear, like Mary Crawford's occasional arguments for the meritocracy, largely in order to be replaced. The next stretch of narrative converts what leans toward a survey of her possessions—"her plant, her books"—into the signs of a constitutive indebtedness that someone like Sir Robert de Aguilon would certainly recognize. "Every thing," Fanny thinks,

> was a friend, or bore her thoughts of a friend; and though there had been sometimes much of suffering to her—though her motives had often been misunderstood, her feelings disregarded, and her comprehension under valued; though she had known the pains of ridicule, and neglect, yet almost every recurrence of either had led to something consolatory . . . and the whole was now so blended together, so harmonized by distance, that every former affliction had its charm. The room was most dear to her, and she would not have changed its furniture for the handsomest in the house, though what had been originally plain, had suffered all the ill-usage of children . . . as she looked around her, the claims of her cousins . . . were strengthened by the sight of present upon present that she had received from them . . . and she grew bewildered as to the amount of the debt which all these kind remembrances produced. (*M*, 178)

Fanny's "nest of comforts" (*M*, 178) is also a nest of hand-me-downs, a nexus not of contracts but of debts and obligations: a record of inhabitation and "intervolvement" whose duration and distance "harmonize" torts into charms. The closest Fanny will ever come to owning anything occurs during her visit to Portsmouth—the period when the novel comes the closest to switching gears and becoming a liberal marriage plot defined by money and merit—and is marked with some Latin legalese. "Wealth is luxurious and daring," the narrative says, "and some of hers found its way to a circulating library. She became a subscriber—amazed at being anything in *propria persona*, amazed at her own doings in every way; to be a renter, a chuser of books!" (*M*, 461). Even at its most luxurious and daring, then, Fanny's acquisitive power gets figured in decidedly manorial terms—she's bought herself a right to borrow (and so, too, an obligation to return) books; she's not bought the books themselves. No longer simply patronage's ward, she is now a patron—which is to say (only) a renter.

It's tempting to read the scene as a moment of self-assertion, and the exuberance of the narrative phrasing here may encourage us to feel that we have, after a long journey over manorial plains, finally arrived in an oasis of the personal. At the same time, however, the recourse to that technical phrase (in *propria persona*) holds us back in the world of impersonal forms. That Fanny signs herself by what is, in effect, the mark of a name rather than the name itself preserves for the scene a sense of unreality or, more exactly, of legal-fictionality. We are presented not with a situation in which Fanny finally finds herself self-identical but with a situation in which Fanny is able to hold her ostensibly *pro se* identity up as a role to be wondered at ("amazed at being anything in *propria persona*"). The personhood of the choosy renter, here, remains nearly as formal and impersonal as the personhood of the patiently accepting debtor who takes for her use only whatever is left over or happens to fall in her way.

Seen in this light the valences of the moment are more complicated—the exclamation points stepping Fanny forward in her own name but the italics stepping her back behind the form for one's own name. David Marshall's terrific exposition of the in *propria persona* that marks Fanny's subscription helps capture the contradictions involved in this "ambiguous act."[79] Especially ambiguous, Marshall observes, is the fact that self-assertion takes place via a phrase entered into the rolls of literary theory by Aristotle's praise for Homer's ability precisely *not* to show up in his own person, to keep himself behind the scenes in the role of an imitator.[80] Through this connection Marshall suggests that we can see in Fanny's impersonal person (or her personalized impersonality) a reflection of the there-not-there-ness that defines the personality of omniscient narration, "an ambivalent self-portrait of the absent author: the supervising author who would not speak *in propria persona*."[81] In Fanny, who can see even her own personality for the role that it is, we have a character whose relationship to herself is structured like an author's relationship to her characters: a relationship defined by deep identification and, at the same time, a categorical antithesis (between person/role, author/narrator) that no amount of identification can surmount.

This "self-portrait" of self-portraiture is, thus, ambivalent in both a formal sense—bridging a categorical gap between the impersonal supervisor and the properly personal—and an affective one, merging significant authority with something hard to tell from self-suppression, a refusal to come forward that may be as painful as it is principled.[82] It's this psychic conflict that structures D. A. Miller's account of "Austen Style" more generally. Austen Style, for Miller, is defined above all by the renunciation of "the desire *to be a Person*."[83] As with the bright star that Keats first does and then doesn't want to be, the freedom, autonomy, and omniscience of the narrative perspective can only be achieved by means of a stoic relinquishment of the charms, warmth, and personality that come from being a character. For this reason Miller describes Austen Style as an aesthetic accomplishment shot through with a "divine melancholy [that] unceasingly contemplates the Person that is its own absolutely forgone possibility." The "stylothete," Miller writes, "harbors a hidden wish—of whose impossible fulfillment she has made an absolute refusal—to renounce the renunciation that makes her one."[84] The psychic drama in Miller's moving account arises from the tragic antithesis he sets up between persons who really are authentically themselves—who suffer no haziness in their peripheral vision—and the "ceaseless" or sleepless melancholy of those dissonant nonpersons who are artists, spinsters, queer. "Like the Unheterosexual," writes Miller, "the Spinster too resorts to Style, the utopia of those with almost no place to go."[85] The implication of the claim is that these figures might turn away from style if personhood were truly in the offing—if there *were* some "place to go"—such that the history of Style appears written largely by the ways society has deferred the dream of personhood for any number of minoritized positions. The stylothete, for Miller, is always in *propria persona* because they find themselves forever barred from being properly personal.

Following this set of thoughts through in relation to *Mansfield Park* has some useful consequences. On the particular question of how to understand "in *propria persona*" we are left with the enticing idea that the phrase might function as something like Austen's name for the free indirect style with which she (or her narration?) has come to be identified. And on a broader level it offers us a way to revalue (if not reverse) the long tradition of seeing Fanny as simply an unaccountably insipid or oddly conservative character. Instead, we could start to think of her and the novel she leads (precisely by refusing to lead it) as a statement in which Austen recognizes the parameters—both the affordances and the relinquishments—of her own art. If style is the province of those nonpersons who are left with "no place to go," we can start to think of Fanny—a no one who owns nothing of her own—as something like the incarnation of Austen Style itself. Free indirect style, for Miller, is prose's way of bringing "the two antithetical terms" of "character and narration" asymptotically together ("as close as possible," Miller says, "to the bar . . . that separates them"), and Fanny, in this light, would just be Austen working that asymptote from the other side, through character this time rather than narration. In free indirect style we watch the narration arc closer and closer to the warmth of character—and in the free indirect person that is Fanny Price we watch character arc close and closer to the impersonality of narration. In Fanny we have the novel's version of the "depersonification" M. H. Abrams saw in Wordsworth's poetry (according to which "single and solitary human figures transform themselves into something which is both less and more than human").[86] To the degree that we have latched more readily onto the first version of the phenomenon—in which the godlike voice takes on human form—than the second—where the human takes on a godlike but also cold impersonality—it's because we have an eye for the face on the forest floor.[87] We are quick to pick out what's personlike about even those things we know to be the product of formal procedures and the abstracting operations of style. But the question Fanny raises is not about our capacity to see something that is not a person (because it's language, or dirt, or a corporation) as if it were one; it's a question about our capacity to see something that is a person (because it's Fanny Price) as if it were, in fact, "both less and more than human"—a structure of debts, obligations, duties. If the drama of Austen Style as Miller has given it to us is the sight of a form that arrives trailing memories of the person that it was, in Fanny Price we have the drama (though that may seem exactly the wrong term) of a character who arrives seemingly preprogrammed to operate as a placeholder's placeholder, the abstract form for where a person (for example, her sister) might go rather than a unique personality.

Take, for instance, the famous scene in which Fanny watches Edmund helping Mary ride the pony Fanny shares rather than owns ("As the horse continued in name, as well as fact, the property of Edmund, Mrs. Norris could tolerate its being for Fanny's use" [*M*, 43]):

The houses, though scarcely half a mile apart, were not within sight of each other; but by walking fifty yards from the hall door, she could look down the park and command a view of the parsonage and all its demesnes, gently rising beyond the village road; and in Dr. Grant's meadow she immediately saw the group—Edmund and Miss Crawford both on horseback, riding side by side, Dr. and Mrs. Grant, and Mr. Crawford, with two or three grooms, standing about and looking on. A happy party it appeared to her—all interested in one object—cheerful beyond a doubt, for the sound of merriment ascended even to her. It was a sound which did not make her cheerful; she wondered that Edmund should forget her, and felt a pang. She could not turn her eyes from the meadow, she could not help watching all that passed. . . . After a few minutes, [Edmund and Mary] stopt entirely, Edmund was close to her, he was speaking to her, he was evidently directing her management of the bridle, he had hold of her hand; she saw it, or the imagination supplied what the eye could not reach. . . . She began to think it rather hard upon the mare to have such double duty; if she were forgotten the poor mare should be remembered. (*M*, 78–79)

The scene, it's clear, establishes Fanny as a particularly important point of vision. Claudia Johnson calls this moment "a *tour de force* of free indirect discourse," and she's right to do so—pointing not only to the value Fanny's imagination is accorded as the thing that makes the scene possible (supplying "what the eye could not reach") but to the way the most obviously interesting feature of the passage, that "sequence of run-ons" (she could not turn . . . she could not help . . . Edmund was close to her . . . he was speaking to her . . . he was directing her), captures the oppressive compounding of Fanny's recognition.[88] We might, on these grounds, see this as a virtuoso but fundamentally standard-issue example of the phenomenon, in which the impersonality of style veers close enough to be overrun by the run-on rhythm of its person's thoughts. The passage is, though, equally clear in its assertion that the conditions of Fanny's perception involve her precisely *not* being part of, not being a person in, the scene. So while it's true that we are, here, particularly close to what's personal about Fanny—her psychic pain strong enough to disrupt the surface that renders it—the scene also strenuously underlines how far Fanny is from everyone else: "the sounds of merriment ascended *even* to her," her lordly perch only enough in earshot to pick up the tone but not the content of "a happy party." And lordly it is: that explicitly manorial anachronism—"demesnes"—is not an accident. "Demesne," in the explanation Maitland wrote for entry 1a. in the *OED is* "applied either to the absolute ownership of the king, or to the tenure of the person who held land to his own use, mediately or immediately from the king. Opposed to 'to hold in service' (*tenere in servitio*)." Unlike, then, the final scene of the novel, which, as we saw, disarticulates Fanny's gaze from the "view and patronage" of Mansfield Park, this scene seems to hold them together in a moment of lordly possession: "she could look down the park and command a view of the parsonage and all its demesnes, gently rising beyond the village road." Fanny, lord of these demesnes, doesn't owe anyone anything. Except, just as forecast in the previous section and as the concluding claim of Maitland's explanation makes clear, the independence Fanny's isolation provides and the power it implies (to see a place better than it can see itself ["The houses, though scarcely half a mile apart, were not within sight of each other"]) are strangely coupled to a kind of social abandonment: "In every case, the ultimate (free) holder, 'the person who stands *at the bottom of the scale*, who seems most like an owner of the land, and who has a general right of doing what he pleases with it, is said to hold the land in demesne.'"[89] "Demesnes," thus, like in *propria persona*, captures the odd symmetry between freedom—being the ultimate free holder—and minority—the person who stands at the bottom of the scale, between being someone and being no one. It is thus in Fanny, a character who is nothing but that flicker, that we see the doubled ontology of style's de/personifications. Where a character like Emma offers up "the most perfect *and* the most melancholy" example of style's "impossible desire to possess the perfection of a Person who has, who is, everything," Fanny runs style's melancholy vector in the other direction: a person shifted toward the perfect emptiness of style precisely by having, by being almost nothing.[90] Like the human version of Robert Ferrar's nearly empty toothpick case that kicks off Miller's account of style, Fanny, as Leo Bersani says, "almost *is not.*"[91] What Austen's amazing scene offers us, then, is not just an example of free indirect style but an example that is also a theorization of the manorial, depersonifying dynamics free indirect style entails, in which a person is edged free of their personality by becoming an occasion for an impersonal structure to appear as such.

The novel, like everyone in it ("My Fanny—my only sister—my only comfort now" [*M*, 515]; "Dear Fanny! Now I shall be comfortable." [*M*, 517]), thus needs Fanny, but it is only in a limited sense *about* her. Such thoughts help explain why it is that the novel itself seems so little exercised by the restraint and silence that has vexed so many of its readers, from Cassandra Austen to Kinsgley Amis. It's true that Fanny, when a newly arrived seven-year-old at Mansfield Park, finds "something to fear in every person and place" and is "equally forlorn" whether "in the school-room, the drawing room, or the shrubbery" (*M*, 16). But things settle down rather quickly after that: a few pages later we find "her appearance and sprits improved" (*M*, 20) and a couple more see her "learning to transfer" to her new home "much of her attachment to her former home." Fanny, "with all her faults of ignorance and timidity, was fixed at Mansfield [and] grew up there not unhappily among her cousins" (*M*, 22). Perhaps, we think, Fanny should ask for more than "not unhappy," but Fanny doesn't seem to think so: for although "often mortified by their treatment of her, she thought too lowly of her own claims to feel injured by it" (*M*, 23).

Clearly, it is not entirely wrong to think that Fanny is mistreated—she is mortified; Mrs. Norris frequently says horrible things to her; Sir Thomas will try to force her into a marriage—but she is not *only* or even consistently mistreated: "Edmund was uniformly kind himself, and he had nothing worse to endure on the part of Tom, than that sort of merriment which a young man of seventeen will always think fair with a child of ten. He was just entering into life, full of spirits, and with all the liberal dispositions of an eldest son. . . . His kindness to his little cousin was consistent with his situation and rights; he made her some very pretty presents, and laughed at her" (M, 19–20). It is, in light of these descriptions, difficult to find a strong moral position: Fanny is not, or not only, "the terrified little stranger," but she's also not exactly the heroine, either. She could be treated better (or worse), but really she is treated "uniformly," "consistent with . . . situation and rights"; she is treated, that is, about how one would expect.

If that seems in itself like a form of mistreatment, a refusal of the structures of recognition that other characters might benefit from, it's worth noting that many passages confirm Fanny's preference for this impersonal, because pro forma, status. "Fanny had no share in the festivities of the season, but she enjoyed being avowedly useful as her aunt's companion. . . . As to her cousins' gaieties, she loved to hear an account of them, especially of the balls, and whom Edmund had danced with; but thought too lowly of her own situation to imagine she should ever be admitted to the same, and listened therefore without an idea of any nearer concern in them. Upon the whole, it was a comfortable winter to her" (M, 40). Time and again, the pattern repeats: what looks on a standard (that is, bourgeois) view like neglect and exclusion looks, on another, like a kind of freedom: "She was not often invited to join in the conversations of others," the narrative tells us, but "nor did she desire it" (M, 94). Crowded parties are valuable for the space they leave: "every addition to the party must rather forward her favourite indulgence of being suffered to sit silent and unattended to," and "though she must submit . . . to being the principal lady in company . . . she found while they were at table, such a happy flow of conversation prevailing in which she was not required to take any part" (M, 260). We might, of course, chalk all this up to an idiosyncratic preference for self-denial. But it's hard, at the same time, to find a language to criticize a self-denial that doesn't, at the end of the day, seem to deny the self anything it wants. Happiness seems like the wrong word for whatever Fanny is getting out of this—"not unhappy" gets closer, but it is hard to find a positive term.

If we have trouble coming up with terms to summarize a cost/benefit analysis of Fanny's condition, we should perhaps feel consoled that the narrative itself is notably unconcerned to do so. In speaking in the prior section of the manorial behavior of the narrative, I compared Fanny with *Persuasion*'s Anne Eliot. Both characters, it is true, seem consistently slighted and under-acknowledged by the social worlds in which they live. But in *Persuasion* the narrative voice offers Anne Eliot an alternative system of recognition; her potential eloquence gets counted even as her actual eloquence is withheld. In *Mansfield Park*, by contrast, the narrative seems largely unconcerned to offer itself as an alternative venue. And I want to extend that earlier observation here by showing how that lack of concern for personal representation is a kind of structural fact or operating principle of the narrative itself: it is something far more, that is, than the sorts of slights or inattentions that Fanny experiences at the level of plot.

We might think that, by taking the unconventional (for her) step of beginning her novel with a child, that Austen is setting off on what will be a minutely detailed bildungsroman, with all the intelligent perception of free indirect discourse deployed to track a child's growing awareness of her world. But this is not what happens. "The little girl," a genre before she is a name, arrives at the beginning of the second chapter: "The little girl performed her long journey in safety . . . Fanny Price was at this time just ten years old" (*M*, 13). The third chapter begins in this way: "The first event of any importance in the family was the death of Mr. Norris, which happened when Fanny was about fifteen" (*M*, 26). So what we have in chapter 2 is an immensely compressed rendition of five years—about a year every two pages—that could hardly seem more consequential for the person who feels like our main character. The chronological signposts in the second chapter are few and notably general; its characteristic procedure is to follow the narration of a specific moment—"The young people were all at home, and sustained their share in the introduction very well" (*M*, 13)—with a generalized sweep of time—"It required a longer time, however, than Mrs. Norris was inclined to allow, to reconcile Fanny to the novelty of Mansfield Park, and the separation from everybody she had been used to" (*M*, 15). That sweep of reconciliation over "a longer time" contains innumerable mental adjustments that are hypothesized but not described: we can only imagine ourselves back to them from some already established fact ("reconciled to the novelty"). The result is that even the more pointillist moments, where Fanny actually appears rather than simply being the subject of a report, take on the feeling of typicality: not "this happened at this time" but "things like this generally happened" or "imagine that events of the sort that might plausibly lead to reconciliation took place." Like the description of the two Miss Bertrams, who "adjourned to whatever might be the favourite holiday-sport of the moment, making artificial flowers or wasting gold paper" (*M*, 16), or like the dinnertime chatter made up of "pleasant anecdotes about any former haunch" or an "entertaining story about 'my friend such a one'" (*M*, 61), we are presented with a duration that we are invited to fill in with examples of general talk—the Georgian yadda yadda yadda—but whose particular specifics seem without value.

The procedure feels decidedly un-Austenian. Where others of her novels give themselves over to minute descriptions of very recent and minor events—"That the Miss Lucases and the Miss Bennets should meet to talk over a ball was absolutely necessary; and the morning after the assembly brought the former to Longbourn to hear and to communicate"—*Mansfield Park* passes over seasons and years in the blink of a sentence.[92] The "alterations and novelties" (*M*, 26) produced by the death of Mr. Norris turn out mostly to involve several months of speculation about the expensive culinary tastes of his replacement—"These opinions had been hardly canvassed a year . . ."—only to be left off in favor of a new nonevent. Sir Thomas's trip to Antigua, where his plantation is somewhere between unprofitable and outright rebellion, promises some narrative, and "Mrs. Norris had been indulging in very dreadful fears." But no: "The winter came and passed without [her 'very dreadful fears'] being called for; their accounts continued perfectly good" (*M*, 39). Perfectly good, that is, and perfectly unspecific. A few pages and a full year later, Mrs. Norris's meditations in an emergency are, again, washed away: "The return of winter engagements, however, was not without its effect; and in the course of their progress, her mind became so pleasantly occupied in superintending the fortunes of her eldest niece, as tolerably to quiet her nerves" (*M*, 44).

It's hard to know what to make of this. Sometimes, as in the sarcasm of "opinions that had been hardly canvassed a year" and the critique of Mrs. Norris's ability to lose herself in "winter engagements," the narrative voice seems to hate the tedium it's creating; even Lady Bertram "listened without much interest" (*M*, 36). More often, though, it adopts this generalizing (or harmonizing?) distance as its proper mode. On at least two separate occasions, the narrative seems to announce the typicality of its presentations and to do so nonironically. When Henry and Mary Crawford first arrive, a series of local sightseeing adventures are described in terms that suggest that life itself is already as generic as its Merchant Ivory reproduction: "There were many other views to be shewn, and though the weather was hot, there were shady lanes wherever they wanted to go. A young party is always provided with a shady lane. Four fine mornings successively were spent in this manner" (*M*, 82).[93] And when Edmund starts to fall for Mary's charms, it is similarly represented as the carrying forward of a routine already established and ready to roll in the stock footage of domestic romance: "A young woman, pretty, lively, with a harp as elegant as herself; and both placed near a window, cut down to the ground, and opening on a little lawn, surrounded by shrubs in the rich foliage of summer, was enough to catch any man's heart. The season, the scene, the air were all favourable to tenderness and sentiment ... and as every thing will turn to account when love is once set going, even the sandwich tray [was] worth looking at" (M, 76). It's true that some moments treat this kind of automatism with a more familiar critical distance—"Miss Bertram's engagement made [Henry Crawford] in equity the property of Julia ... and before he had been at Mansfield a week, she was quite ready to be fallen in love with" (M, 52). In those moments, our old expectations come rushing back: that the goal will be to carve out a personality from the generic machinery of romance ("You make me laugh, Charlotte," says Elizabeth, "but it is not sound. You know it is not sound, and that you would never act in this way yourself").[94] But our expectations of a personality, as familiar as they are, are hard to maintain; it's as if the novel is training both us and itself out of them every time it supplies a young party with what young parties are always supplied and young lovers with young love's standard props (a harp, a certain kind of window, shrubs, summer). The narrative seems entirely willing to let the generic stand forward as an impersonal repertoire of tropes.

What I'm suggesting, then, is that the narrative's commitment to the generic registers as an indifference to *bildung*. Look how much time is passing: Fanny, ten years old on page 13, is fifteen on page 26 and by page 46 has "just reached her eighteenth year," by which point Sir Thomas has been gone at least a year and a half and Maria Bertram has gotten engaged: "such," the novel summarizes, "was the state of affairs in the month of July" (M, 46) of seventeen-ninety- or eighteen-hundred-and-something. It would be one thing, that is, if Fanny were simply ignored by her rich and entitled relatives who don't have time to pull her forward. But the narrative itself seems to turn away. Sometime in Fanny's first five years at Mansfield, for example, she is paid a visit from the person she loves most in the world, her brother William, just before he embarks on a new and very dangerous life at sea. "Once and only once in the course of many years had she the happiness of being with William," the narrative rolls its drum. (M, 23). How does the visit go? "Their eager affection in meeting, their exquisite delight in being together, their hours of happy mirth and moments of serious conference *may be imagined;* as well as the sanguine views and spirits of the boy even to the last, and the misery of the girl when he left her" (M, 24, my emphasis). Even where, as here, the narrative seems to set itself an opportunity to show us Fanny rather than tell, to represent rather than conjecture, it doesn't follow through. Indeed, at one point the muting effect of narrative happens not in synch with but over the top of Edmund's attempts to bring Fanny forward. The opportunity opened up by Edmund at the level of plot—"Fanny would rather have had Edmund tell the story, but his determined silence obliged her to relate her brother's situation"—is closed at the level of form by a narrative that notes the tone of Fanny's voice but omits the content of her speech: "her voice was animated in speaking of his profession, and the foreign stations he had been on, but she could not mention the number of years that he had been absent without tears in her eyes" (*M*, 70). When, a bit later, Mary has rudely taken up Fanny's time on the pony they share, she offers the setup for a classic Austen clinic in self-incrimination. "Selfishness must always be forgiven you know, because there is no hope for a cure," Mary says. All Fanny has to do is reply in a way whose graciousness reverses the brash spin. Maybe she does. "Fanny's reply was very civil" (*M*, 80) is all we are told. You have, Austen seems to say, read this book before.

But have we? We can of course fill in the gaps from our cultural repertoire, imagining the sort of thing that gets said in commemoration of a particularly good haunch or the depth of Fanny's sorrow on the departure of her brother. So maybe there's nothing lost. But it is an expensive thought since thinking it means that there is, in a sense, nothing gained by the novels (Austen's included) that do it differently by allowing characters to speak for themselves. And even if these costs could be somehow minimized, one might still want to assert the importance of the difference between a novel and a plan for a novel, between the life of a life and the shape of a life, the personality of person and the mere persona of one. It is by opting consistently for the latter that we get what I am suggesting we think of as a novel oriented toward the manor rather than the market, a novel that we read expecting the story of person but that repeatedly gives us—as if "in *propria*" meant "in place of"—the story of a "such a one."

The negative move—the reduction of person to form, or the supplanting of the personal by the scripted—is odd and alienating, but it is not without its satisfactions. Much of the first part of the novel spends its time rather contentedly not only defeating our readerly expectations but picking off, one by one, the characters who, mistaking this for some other kind of novel, are out to squirrel away what they can for themselves. Dismissive parodies of individualist acquisition begin early and sustain the minor moral scandal of Tom's spendthrift heirdom and the equal and opposite running joke of Mrs. Norris's attempts to save up a nest egg out of the allowance provided her by the Mansfield living in order, she seems to think, to leave something for her nieces and nephews, Mansfield's much more significant beneficiaries ("My object," she tells Lady Bertram, "is to be of use to those that come after me. It is for your children's good that I wish to be richer" [*M*, 34]). Other moments, though, suggest a greater strain. The claims of individualism are not always so disposably expressed. Mary Crawford, for instance, the character whom D.A. Miller, and not incorrectly, lists as the "heroine," sets herself up as the clear-eyed critic of the manorial model, in which individual inclination gets no traction. "It is fortunate," she tells Edmund, who is set to inherit "a very good living" as a clergyman nearby, "that your inclination and your father's convenience should accord so well" (*M*, 127). Edmund has just tried to assure Mary that he wants to accept the local clergyman's living that's been designed for him from birth—"My taking orders I assure you is quite as voluntary as Maria's marrying" (*M*, 127)—but the picture we get of Maria's romance hasn't lent Edmund's argument much weight ("Maria Bertram was beginning to think matrimony a duty; and as a marriage with Mr. Rushworth would give her the enjoyment of a larger income than her father's . . . it became by the same rule of moral obligation her evident duty to marry Mr. Rushworth" [*M*, 44]). Mary is not, at least before the end disqualifies her from credit by reshaping her into an entirely mercenary character, a flippant or conceited Wickham. She has a fully developed, meritocratic social theory that prioritizes professional careers, "lines [where] distinction may be gained" (*M*, 107). "I do look down upon it," she says, "if it might have been higher. I must look down upon anything contented with obscurity when it might rise to distinction" (*M*, 249). Mary, in moments like these, is less a character than an advocate for a certain version of a character, the avatar of the novel in which she happens to have had the bad luck not to find herself.

But in this novel the rule toward which its curve continually pushes is that no one must rise to distinction. Thus the amateur theatricals are quashed not because of the immorality of the action depicted in *Lovers' Vows*—a play whose action generally involves everyone acting better than they "actually" do in *Mansfield Park* (illegitimate sons are acknowledged, and a father considers forcing his daughter to marry a man for money and decides not to)—and still less because of the insincerity acting involves. The problem that really plagues the theatricals is that the players can't seem to avoid taking the roles personally, to avoid thinking that what accrues to the characters they represent somehow also accrues to them as persons. Edmund initially parodies the desire for distinction that governs the enterprise—"If we do not out do Ecclesford, we do nothing" (*M*, 145)—but shortly thereafter is himself caught "between his theatrical and his real part" (*M*, 191), and as he talks himself into participating his language slides into the vocabulary of credit and gain that are the theater's most powerful and pernicious attractions: "if I can be the means of restraining the publicity . . . I shall be well repaid . . . This will be a material gain" (*M*, 182). The problem the play presents is thus not, as many have argued, the problem of insincerity but that no one seems to be able to take the script in any way *except* sincerely, to take the script *as a script*. "I should not have thought it the sort of play," Edmund says, "to be so easily filled up, with *us*" (*M*, 164). But all along this prospect of what the novel and Marshall call "true acting"—the fantasy that one might really be saying personally the lines of a script that has been presented to you—is precisely the appeal of the event: "Consider what it would be to act Amelia with a stranger," Edmund pleads to the naysaying Fanny (*M*, 181).[95] But it can only matter who plays a part if the part is not a role—it only matters who plays a part if one thinks that the words an actor says are the words of the actor rather than the words of the play.

One common interpretation is that, in dismissing the theater from its pages, the novel dismisses a potentially rampant individualism in favor of a Burkean paternalism. But it would be more correct to say that what the novel is dismissing in dismissing the theater is the incoherence of Burkean paternalism—in which one somehow has to take the absolutism of a script personally—in favor of an even more conservative notion of script that seems studiously rinsed of personality. When the specter of the dramatic arts reappears, it does so as the voice of a culture rather than a person: "And sure enough," the narrative says, as if surprised to find itself returning to the idea, "there was a book on the table which had the air of being very recently closed: a volume of Shakespeare" (*M*, 389). When Henry Crawford picks up the book, he does so not to select a speech that will set him forward but in order to continue where Fanny left off reading to Lady Bertram. "Let me," he says, "have the pleasure of finishing that speech to your ladyship," and he finds his place "by carefully giving way to the inclination of the leaves." The self-opening book is also, it turns out, something like a self-reading one: "In Mr. Crawford's reading there was a variety of excellence beyond what she had ever met with. The King, the Queen, Buckingham, Wolsey, Cromwell, all were given in turn; for with the happiest knack, the happiest power of jumping and guessing, he could always alight at will on the best scene, or the best speeches of each; and whether it were dignity, or pride, or tenderness, or remorse, or whatever were to be expressed, he could do it with equal beauty. It was truly dramatic" (*M*, 389–390). Henry, the lesson is, is conspicuously good at disappearing into roles. "But Shakespeare," he says, protesting his own remarkability, "one gets acquainted with without knowing how. It is a part of an Englishman's constitution. His thoughts and beauties are so spread abroad that one touches them everywhere; one is intimate with him by instinct. No man of any brain can open at a good part of one of his plays without falling into the flow of his meaning immediately" (*M*, 390–391). Indeed, confirms Edmund, "we all talk Shakespeare" (*M*, 391).

So, in this adjusted typology, the drama in *Mansfield Park* is not about the sincerity or insincerity of individuals; it's about the nature of scriptedness: on the one hand, the manorial, constitutional, automatic set of impersonal options that is the Shakespeare we all talk just by talking English and, on the other hand, the incoherent Burkean mix of absolutism (the script isn't yours to write . . .) and individualism (. . . but you have to *feel* it) in the *Lovers' Vows* episode. Still, Henry's argument for the transcendent givenness of Shakespeare ("one touches [him] everywhere") is not without its contradictions—and they bear on the broader, generic question of whether the novel can bring itself to a conclusion *as a novel*. For while the claims of individuality can, it seems, be muted in any given moment, they have a way of reappearing in the next. Homer was not, after all, so committed to keeping himself in the role of the imitator that Aristotle didn't know whom to praise. And Edmund is quick to insist that the "talking Shakespeare" that everyone does is "totally distinct from giving his sense as you gave it." "To hear him read well aloud is no everyday talent." The "bow of mock gravity" (*M*, 391) with which Henry meets Edmund's praise is particularly ingenious (a nod to the possibility of credit without exactly taking it), but it can only momentarily defuse (and not resolve) the paradox of having a particular talent for impersonality. This is, in miniature, the paradox the novel itself has solicited by virtue of its very premise: a novel with a nonperson for its main character. On any given page, it's not too big a problem to suggest that Fanny exists somehow outside of the usual economy of reward and desert that structure standard novelistic plots. But it is also not hard to see why, on a larger scale, the prospect of an ending would entail a set of rather severe complications. These complications, it should be said, will exist for the other novels in this study—all of which, in their absence of individuals or their absence of action (or both), face significant problems concluding. One popular strategy, perhaps predictably, is the death, dissolution, or disappearance of the main character (Robert Wringhim, Sydney Carton, Victor Frankenstein, Victor's creature); *Caleb Williams* doesn't kill Caleb, but Godwin's first ending almost does, and the second one leaves Caleb half-wishing he could have the original one back. Austen alone among these postpersonal novels remains committed to the marriage plot, and the third volume of *Mansfield Park* represents something like a real-time experiment in whether it's possible to marry a manor. How, that is, can a novel make marriage, the classic emblem of novelistic achievement, into something that counts for nothing? How can our narrative establish a marriage for Fanny without seeming to have rendered a judgment on her performance, without its seeming, to adjust Fanny's favorite line from Cowper, like a fate that she has merited?

Fanny's first marriage plot involves Henry Crawford, and because it is so overshadowed by Sir Thomas's "medicinal project" (*M*, 425) to force Fanny to recognize the benefits of marriage to a wealthy man, it seems

easy to take her refusal of his proposal, especially in light of her abiding
affection for Edmund, as a given. But it is, I think, important to recognize
that—whatever we think—the novel doesn't treat his rejection as quite so
automatic. Indeed, in what feels like a reversal but is in fact a continuation
of his suit's inauspicious beginnings, it turns out to be a harder call than
anyone, perhaps even Fanny, was likely to expect. When Henry makes up
his mind to marry Fanny, it looks bad—like nothing more than a version of
that activity the handsome, clever, and rich use to fill up afternoons when
there is no other hunting to be done ("And how do you think I mean to
amuse myself," he asks his sister, "on the days that I do not hunt? . . . [M]y
plan is to make Fanny Price in love with me" [*M*, 267]). It is, to be sure, a
not particularly promising opening. But if Henry's plan makes him seem
more devoid of value than even his sister (whose value for money isn't particularly dignified but is, at least, a value), it is also the case that his absence of
interest makes Henry peculiarly well suited to be Fanny's suitor. For if we are
familiar with Austen's critique of the marriage market as, above all, a system
in which individuals are treated as exchangeable or at least acquirable values,
the indifference to money Henry's suit exhibits (since he doesn't stand to
make any) is not obviously susceptible to this same sort of critique. That
Henry seems to be a character almost without a preference, then, produces
his action as the manifestation of a detached interest that is love subtracted of
its otherwise overwhelming risks of possession. Love restored, we might say,
if not to the principled neutrality of classical art, then at least to something
like its indifference.

It is on these grounds that, three-quarters of the way through the novel,
he makes a particularly well-conceived proposal to Fanny. Henry's first good
decision is to put conduct over words—"it is not by telling you that my affections are steady. My conduct shall speak for me"—but his real genius is to
define conduct itself as a form of inaction and desert as out of the question:
"absence, distance, time," he says, "shall speak for me.—They shall prove,
that as far as you can be deserved by any body, I do deserve you" (*M*, 397).
This is not, to be sure, Darcy's late-hour heroism. But what Henry seems, in
his way, to have figured out is that Fanny cannot be earned but can only, and
maybe not even then, be acquired over time. "It is not," Henry goes on to
say, "by equality of merit that you can be won. That is out of the question":

> You are infinitely my superior in merit; all *that* I know. You have qualities
> which I had not before supposed to exist in such a degree in any human
> creature. You have some touches of the angel in you beyond what—not merely
> beyond what one sees, because one never sees anything like it—but beyond

what one fancies might be. . . . It is he who sees and worships your merit the
strongest, who loves you most devotedly, that has the best right to a return.
There I build my confidence. (*M*, 397–398)

The proposal is, we can see, awkward precisely because it is pointed, or
trying to be pointed, in the right direction. Its strange mix of superlatives
and comparatives, of categorical absolutes and relative metrics—"infinitely
my superior," "touches of the angel," "not merely beyond what one sees . . .
but . . ."—strains at putting the manor in marriageable terms, at fitting the
beyond of contract into the form of a marriage license. The terms of the
liberal market seep in—"merit," "merit," even the particularly creepy investment language of "the right to a return"—but one can, even so, appreciate
the shape of the effort. We don't have to like Henry—Fanny continues not
to like him "as a man" (*M*, 193)—but what his real obstacle here isn't his
potentially long list of personal foibles but a problem of literary genre.

The marriage that the novel settles on, of course, is—like the public
impersonality of "a volume of Shakespeare" versus the denatured but still
palpable individualism of *Lovers' Vows*—the even more impersonal one. As
many critics have pointed out, Fanny's marriage to Edmund, her first cousin,
is as endogamous as it's possible for a marriage to be, and if marrying your
first cousin seems unsurprising in aristocratic circles, the novel has suggested,
in its first pages, that the fact of their shared upbringing makes it impossibly
proximate ("You are thinking of your sons," says Mrs. Norris, "—but do
not you know that of all things upon earth that is the least likely to happen;
brought up, as they would be, always together like brothers and sisters? It
is morally impossible. I never knew an instance of it" [*M*, 7]).[96] But what
is more interesting, for my purposes, is not simply the fact that the novel
handles the problem of marriage's connection to merit and the market by
pulling the family strings tighter than even Mrs. Norris can imagine but that
it handles this problem by (on a minimal reading) dodging the responsibility
of narrating the marriage at all and even (on a more maximal one) suggesting
the very impossibility of doing so.

It is important, then, that Fanny and Edmund's marriage takes place
not through the proleptic hindsight of an epilogue (happily ever after) but
through the essentially unqualified prospect of a story yet to come. "I pur-
posely abstain from dates on this occasion," says a narrative voice that has
hardly, as we have seen, been overly precise in its chronometry,

> that every one may be at liberty to fix their own, aware that the cure of uncon-
> querable passions, and the transfer of unchanging attachments, must vary much
> as to time in different people. I only entreat everybody to believe that exactly at

the time when it was quite natural that it should be so, and not a week earlier, Edmund did cease to care about Miss Crawford, and became as anxious to marry Fanny as Fanny herself could desire. (*M*, 544)

What we have here is the return of manorial style, the mode of the "such a one." Its enjoinments of our readerly imaginations as to time—just imagine that it happens at whatever time it would be natural—are both premised on and distract us from the logical impossibility of the thing we are enjoined to imagine: "the cure of unconquerable passions" and "the transfer of unchanging attachments." Imagine, the narrative is instructing, that the incurable was cured and the unchanging was changed at the time when such things are possible. But what time is that? How long does it take to cure the incurable or to weather the transferred into the unchanging? The paradox or contradiction here is not bourgeois or Burkean; it has nothing do with squaring sentiment and structure. The paradox is, rather, manorial; it's about how long a thing needs to be in order to be immemorial, about how long is forever. Austen is, in effect, doing the impossible: narrating the creation of a new manor. Or, more precisely, she's enlisting us in a project—the new creation of timelessness—that happens where the novel intersects with and crosses over into the romance.

This marriage, if that's what it is, is certainly not the reward many critics have taken it to be. But it's probably better just to say that this isn't so much a marriage as the shape of a marriage, a marriage plot (always a form) steered even more strongly toward an abstract formalism. How happy is Edmund's "happiness in knowing himself to have been so long the beloved of such a heart"? It's "great enough to warrant any strength of language in which he could clothe it to her or to himself." But how great is something that "warrants any strength"? Trust me, the narrative says, "It must have been a delightful happiness." And how happy is Fanny's happiness? It was a "happiness . . . no description can reach" (*M*, 545). Thus beggared, like Henry Crawford before it, the narrative voice turns away from persons (and content and sentiment) and toward form: everything is as "thoroughly perfect in her eyes, as everything else within the view and patronage of Mansfield Park had long been." It is an ending virtually Keatsian in its convergence on tautology: a perfection that can only be modified by itself, a completeness whose only modification is its own thoroughness. If there are persons, here, the ending must be without perfection. If there is perfection, the ending must be without persons. If the personal and the perfect can be held together in one scene, it must be because they are held together like a curve and its asymptote, converging always and forever, as well as only ever, in prospect.

3. Castes of Exception
Tradition and the Public Sphere in The Private Memoirs
and Confessions of a Justified Sinner

> The general and perpetuall voice of men is as the sentence of
> God him selfe.
> —Richard Hooker, *Of the Laws of Ecclesiastical Polity* (1593)

> [O]n behalf of his Majesty's rights and titles; he therefore, for
> himself, and as prince and steward of Scotland ... hereby grants
> to the said George Colwan, his heirs and assignees whatsomever,
> heritably and irrevocably, all and haill the lands and others
> underwritten ... heritably and irrevocably in all time coming.
> —James Hogg, *The Private Memoirs and Confessions
> of a Justified Sinner* (1824)

Scholars of James Hogg have provided two primary approaches to his most
famous novel, *The Private Memoirs and Confessions of a Justified Sinner*.[1] One
has been to see it as a lengthy, gothic satire on Calvinist faith, particularly
the belief in predestination. The other has been to see it as protesting the
conditions of authorship in an Edinburgh public sphere increasingly under
the sway of a monolithic English literary nationalism. It bears noting that
these views are at cross purposes. Insofar as Scottish Presbyterian religion
amounts to an indigenous tradition, a critique of Calvinism rests uneasily
alongside the claim that Hogg was attempting to develop or assert some
particularly Scottish form of literature over and against (possibly) a British
and (certainly) an English literature.[2] It is certainly possible that Hogg meant
to elevate certain traditions above others. But, beyond the difficulty of saying
just what that alternative, valorized tradition might be, given that the novel's
story of a haunted Calvinist blends the religious tradition with other, and
older, forms of Scottish folklore, the very category of tradition, understood
as a holistic collection of practices, makes it difficult to honor one aspect of
an inheritance over another. There is, thus, a real question about the viability
of taking the novel as both a critique of Calvinism and an endorsement of
folk belief more generally; it looks as though what is true of Calvinism ought
to be true of tradition more broadly construed.

Hogg's novel gains currency by being understood as an engagement
with the broader issue of tradition rather than the more particular subject

matter of the sinner's seventeenth-century religious enthusiasm. It is true that Scottish Presbyterianism, by balancing a sense of Scottish nativism with the desire for a Protestant succession, had been an important and complex political factor in both the run-up to the Act of Union and the monarchical struggles surrounding and following 1707. But by 1824 the specific topic of Calvinism would not have had the political charge that the Jacobite risings (the last of which, in 1745, features in *Waverley*) still contained some sixty years later, helped along by the nearer impact of the French Revolution. In this light, it can be hard to see just why Hogg would have found the subject of Calvinism particularly worth taking up. Broadening the description of the novel's interest, however, from a particular tradition (Calvinism) within Scottish history to a question about the place of tradition itself within Scottish history immediately extends the novel's purchase by making it a visible participant in the development of a romantic nationalism whose emphasis on local cultural identity sought to revivify the abstraction of statehood from within or, in the case of Scotland, to trouble the imposition of multistatehood from without. If Calvinism indexes tradition, Hogg's novel is not only a gothic novel centered on an antiquated theological subject but a gothic novel centered on the question very much alive in the romantic period about the degree to which indigenous antiquity (often in the form of excavated objects and collected folklore) could purvey a national identity different from the one produced by the forces of large-scale historical change, the formal arrangements of government, or the circulatory operations of both mass print culture and modern capital.

Indeed, it is as a staging of the intersections between native tradition and more modern forms of cultural distribution that the novel has gained critical interest. The novel's peculiar structure—essentially a twice-told tale in which an editor's account precedes and situates the first-person account of the justified sinner himself—has helped the criticism to focus on it as a novel that formalizes a cultural antagonism, one between British modernity and native Scottish culture, between an Enlightenment editor and a superstitious memoir writer, between a modern editor and a traditional author, between an alienated editor and a deeply rooted subject, or between an imperialist collector of historical artifacts and a native artisan. In all such descriptions Hogg's novel plays host to a constellation of oppositions in which romantic nationalism is seen as a countermovement within the larger institution of romanticism and in which the authentic work of culture is both under threat from and resistant to its circulation in an age of cultural reproduction.

In this chapter, I want to take a rather different line in order to argue for a view of Hogg's novel as a diagnosis of—rather than an advocate for—the romantic nationalism it has been seen to valorize. Hogg's novel performs this diagnosis, I argue, by presenting three distinct but importantly interrelated problems of representative individuality: briefly, cultural-national, textual, and religious. The first has to do with a romantic nationalism that, by both locating cultural identity in the past and insisting on its purchase within the present, turns the past into a standard of cultural value: the most appreciable culture is the one that most closely resembles the way things were. Hogg's novel, I will argue, comes out against the viability of this model of cultural identity not by asserting the absolute discontinuity between past and present but by seeing the very notion of continuity as necessarily involving forms of change and evolution that make it impossible to set up a relation of identity between any present practice and any past state. So while cultural-nationalist accounts of the Scottish context have frequently stressed the discontinuity to which textual transmission subjected local, and largely oral, practices, Hogg will describe even continuous local practice as necessarily involving modes of transmission in which the past cannot be thought of as having a unitary identity that might be misappropriated or preserved by turns.

This question of historical relation need not, certainly, center around problems of textual materials, but it is not difficult to see why some conception of text has been important both to contemporary accounts (which regularly turn on an opposition between print abstraction and oral immediacy) and to projects within the romantic period like Scott's antiquarian effort to archive and restore ballads in *The Minstrelsy of the Scottish Border*.[3] The objective form that text provides thus proves to be a strongly ambivalent feature: on the one hand, it facilitates the seemingly abstracting forms of distribution by which a Scottish ballad can be sung in an English drawing room; on the other hand, it facilitates the preservation that allows an old Scottish ballad to appear as an authentic piece of Scottish nationalism anywhere at all.[4] Cultural nationalism's ambivalent relation to textuality points to a central structural difficulty: that cultural nationalism is at once strongly presentist, valuing locality and immediacy (which text destroys), and deeply historicist, seeing in the past (which text preserves) the truth of the whole. Hogg's novel addresses this representational concern by presenting text neither as a falsifying abstraction nor as a means toward isolating the authentic version of the particular work. Instead, the novel presents text as an archive of the alterations to which tradition is subjected just by virtue of being handed on. In such an account, text enables a sense of history—since we can see, for example, how the spelling of a name changed over time—without entailing an exclusive claim about identity—because one spelling is not a false version of another. Text, in this description, neither marks our alienation from authentic scenes of cultural production, but neither does it make it possible for us to identify the most authentic instantiation of a culture in quite the way Scott suggested we might with the ballad form.

Any of this discussion could be had (indeed, has just been had) without mention of Calvinism, but it is in Calvinism that Hogg will find his strongest example of a representative identity that consistently undervalues the present moment in relation to a historically disparate one. Cultural nationalism deals with the primeval past while Calvinism, of course, predestines the future, but both see the transactions of the present moment as being always overwritten—at once entirely colored and made negligible by—a past or future state. In his famous essay *Qu'est-ce qu'une nation?*, Ernest Renan sought to overcome this tension between the present moment and a sense of transcendental identity by way of an essentially contractualist model in which citizens constantly recommit themselves to their "clearly expressed desire to continue a common life."[5] But while Renan could see citizens as repeatedly choosing to be what they were, neither cultural nationalism nor Calvinism can operate via the consent of their members. For just as it is the force of cultural nationalism to describe individuals as so many versions of what Herder calls "the internal prototype" provided by "the manners of their fathers," Calvinism's predestination meant that membership not only didn't require contractual renewal but saw such contractualism as a fundamentally heretical assertion that a mortal individual might be in a position to affirm or adjust God's plan. This anticontractualism works against our tendency to see Calvinism as a distinctly modern formation. The most significant studies of Calvinism have emphasized its status as, in Christopher Harvie's phrase, "a social gospel."[6] Both Max Weber's monumental study and more recent histories have repeatedly underscored Calvinism's importance to modernity more generally: Calvinism devalued family ties and inherited status, focused on merit and individual achievement, created formal equality among the elect that made financial contract possible, produced an active public sphere, and promoted the diligence and frugality we all now recognize as its work ethic. But while these descriptions are undoubtedly correct in aligning the social history of Calvinism with the rise of capitalist individualism, Hogg's novel concentrates on the theological position that ensured that, whatever contracts one had signed in life, "all [would] be," as the sinner says, "blotted out" (*P, 75*).

Predestination turned the present into a kind of virtual event—"diligence in worldly business, and yet deadness to the world," recommends a 1641 pamphlet entitled "The Way of Life"—as one's actions became merely the representative face of a past or future state that was itself beyond alteration.[7]

The importance of Hogg's novel, both in this study and more generally, thus lies not in the representation it provided of a particular tradition (Calvinism), nor in the representation it provided of a national tradition more generally (Calvinism as a stand-in for Scottish antiquity), but in the analysis it offers of the corporatizing dynamics of tradition itself. Both romantic nationalism and Calvinism treat present individuals simultaneously as fallen versions of some original prototype and as stand-ins or mouthpieces for transcendent states. In doing so, tradition puts individuals in a position, like the members of a company or the justified sinner himself, to feel that the fault is not theirs for only living in the here and now.

—+—

One can see, simply by thumbing through the text one holds when one holds *The Private Memoirs and Confessions of a Justified Sinner*, that the novel serves as an umbrella for a collection of documents—a fact highlighted by the novel's full title, *The Private Memoirs and Confessions of a Justified Sinner: Written by Himself: With a Detail of Curious Traditionary Facts and Other Evidence by the Editor*. In the order they arrive, this is what we read: an editor's narrative giving one version of the story, the memoirs of the sinner giving another, and the resumption of the editor's narrative, whose "other evidence" includes an "extract from an authentic letter, published in *Blackwood's Magazine for August, 1823*" (P, 165), that tells of the exhumation (not once, but twice—once by "two young men" [P, 168] and again by "another shepherd" [P, 169]) of the rural grave of a suicide found on "a wild height called Cowanscroft, where the land of three proprietors meet all at one point" (P, 165), and provides the "little traditionary history" of that "unfortunate youth" (P, 166). We are then told, after the end of the letter but still within the editor's resumed narrative, that this letter was signed by one James Hogg of "Altrive Lake" and that although it "bears the stamp of authenticity in every line," the editor is wary from having often "been hoaxed by the ingenious fancies displayed in that Magazine" (P, 169). As a result, the editor decides to conduct an independent survey of the grave, during which he learns that, regarding the account provided in Hogg's letter, "hardly a bit o't [was] correct" (P, 170). Having benefited from some improved directions, the editor reaches the spot and exhumes the grave (now for a third time) to discover, among the other, vaguely eerie details ("The breeches still suited the thigh, the stocking the leg, and the garters were wrapt as neatly and as firm below the knee as if they had been newly tied" [P, 172]), *"a printed pamphlet"* (P, 173), which, after "a thorough drying," unfolds itself to reveal a title page reading "the private memoirs and confessions of a justified sinner: written by himself. fideli certa merces" (P, 174).

It is a difficult case to summarize, but it is not quite without precedent. Insofar as it comprises a number of texts, Hogg's novel has relatives in the history of the novel both earlier—in the compiled letters of the epistolary novel—and later—most proximately in the testimonial novels popularized by Wilkie Collins. And, in its willingness to go "to unusual lengths to reproduce authenticating devices, in the form of documentary evidence," Hogg's novel has relatives within the romantic tradition in texts like MacPherson's *Ossian* and Walpole's *The Castle of Otranto,* which presented themselves as documents that had been brought to light rather than written to the moment.[8] Hogg's novel, however, differs importantly from these affiliates. It does so, first, in that it does not use these documents to produce a single story told, as Collins's preamble in *The Woman in White* puts it, "by more than one pen"; the editor and the sinner and Hogg's letter do not in any obvious way collaborate to document a single chain of events, in the way that Collins's novel, by collecting eyewitnesses to various events, does.[9] The second important difference is that these documents are manifestly less interested in proving the authenticity of a single text (the memoirs) than they are in describing the operations by which "traditionary history" sustains itself not only by repeating certain stories over and over (the usual version of an oral or literary tradition) but by telling stories *about* stories—letters and narratives about the discovery of (in original italics) *"a printed pamphlet."* As practical exemplifications of tradition, rather than of the management or verification to which tradition might be subjected, the complied documents are devoted neither to the unifying efforts of story nor to the empirical ones of history but, instead, to the production of tradition as itself a form of metacommentary.

"What can this work be?" the editor asks about the sinner's printed pamphlet. But it is immediately clear that he does not really care about the answer: "Sure, you will say, it must be an allegory; or (as the writer calls it) a religious parable, showing the dreadful danger of self-righteousness?" (*P,* 165). Maybe this is right, but our editor "cannot tell" (*P,* 165). What *is* important, he says, what we should "attend to," is "the sequel," "a thing so extraordinary . . . that if there were not hundreds of living witnesses to attest the truth of it, I would not bid any rational being believe it" (*P,* 165). The "sequel" we are being enjoined to believe by all these "hundreds of living witnesses" is not, then, the facts within the justified sinner's narrative but something like its "miraculous" resurrection as an item of traditionary history. The editorial project, here, can practically dispense with its obligations to the objective text—maybe it's an allegory, maybe it was the product "of a religious maniac," who knows?—in favor of its interest in the way information about the text circulates—the sequelae that are rumors of its existence, indications of its possible whereabouts, or already available versions of the story it provides.

Some of these forms of circulating discourse—like the editor's narrative or Hogg's letter—have a material existence, and some, like the information about the grave's whereabouts provided by a passing shepherd, do not. But the distinction between material and immaterial, or between written and oral, forms of circulation is here minimized by the larger way in which this second-order information (information, that is, about the primary text of the confessions themselves) takes on a self-sufficiency, if never a primacy, of its own. This thought helps explain why it might be possible for the editor to claim that there are hundreds of living witnesses to an event—the "sequel"—that seems, on a rough headcount of those involved in the text's unearthing, to have no more than a half-dozen. For in laying its emphasis on the nearly endless possibilities for reception rather than on the lonelier act of exhumation or the singular instance of production, the editorial effort to compile traditionary history always involves multitudes of participants. Tradition has, the editor tells us in the first paragraph of the novel, "been handed down to the world in unlimited abundance" (P, 3). And because the inexhaustible abundance of tradition, by definition, already exists as a gathering, an editor's work has already been done: "I am certain," the editor begins his narrative, "that in recording the hideous events which follow, I am only relating to the greater part of the inhabitants of at least four counties of Scotland, matters of which they were before perfectly well informed" (P, 3). It is, then, one of the defining characteristics of tradition that it is always in the position of having been received without ever exactly seeming to have been authored; because tradition exists as a definitionally popular form, the question of authorship has been rendered unimportant (if not properly unanswerable). Thus the particular appropriateness of the editor's opening remark that he is "only relating to the greater parts of the inhabitants of at least four counties of Scotland, matters of which they were before perfectly well informed" (P, 3). Tradition is both always redundant (a repetition of a tale already told) and a body of discourse that never repeats since it exists as nothing but an endless series of additions, editions, and metareflections.

Tradition's priority—its ability always to be there first—and its abundance—its irreducibility to any finite set of texts or experiences—makes an editor's work simultaneously easy and infinite. More dramatically, though, it reconfigures the question of literature (or culture more generally) from one of production and authorship to one that revolves around reception and assembly. It is not that tradition wholly dispenses with the idea of generation—even talk has to start somewhere—but that, by making the question of origin as unanswerable as it is unimportant, the idea of generation is retained only as an idea, as something that exists in principle but not in fact. As I will review more particularly in a moment, it is customary for treatments of Hogg's novel to see the editor's excavating and classificatory efforts as a form of damage to the original body of Wringhim's narrative, an outsider usurping or co-opting a fragment of authentic culture. But the force of tradition as I have been describing it is rather the opposite: to emphasize the processes of transmission and co-option by which things get handed down—and without which nothing does. This displacement of authorship by audience, of production by reception, is nicely and succinctly marked by Hogg's appearance in the supplementary materials gathered up in the conclusion of the editor's narrative. Given the importance of reception, Hogg's appearance as the contributor of a response to the novel he in fact authored is more than a clever exploitation of the affordances of a public sphere in which art and opinions could be offered up anonymously; it also, and more interestingly, begins to look like a moment in which the circulatory operations of the public sphere have made it possible for the author of a text to take himself as part of his own audience—and to be right in doing so. Circulation produces a world in which all information, even information that one has offered personally, comes secondhand.

Many accounts, of course, have described Hogg as an author who, in his writings for *Blackwood's* and as a member of the *Noctes Ambrosianae* (a collective made up of other *Blackwood's* writers, John Gibson Lockhart foremost among them), took enthusiastic advantage of the opportunities the Edinburgh public sphere offered for proliferating authorial identities. What all these pen names and print personae seem meant to disturb, a disturbance that has made them particularly attractive to poststructuralist criticism, is the relation between writer and written. But the usefulness of approaching the novel through the question of reception (rather than through production) is that it provides a way of talking about the novel's metatextual interests in a way that allows it to cease "revolving," as Ian Duncan puts it, "around figures of its own production." Production, this is to say, is no longer at stake. And far from a novel that, as Duncan writes, "predicts its own condition as an outcast text, not to be brought to life in a reader's imagination, circulated in a market, or perpetuated in a tradition," we get a novel that theorizes the paradoxical ontology of any lived, circulated tradition—always repeated and never the same.[10] Duncan argues that the text's outcast position and its obsessive revolutions are, at the end of the day, part of the book's strategy of self-preservation, a way of closing its system of circulation since "textuality unleashes a lethal alienation from common life in its original condition of a traditional community which, as the medium of natural belief, cannot be recovered in the commodity form of fiction."[11] I would argue, by contrast, that the novel never imagines an "original condition" and, further, that, even if it did, the "original condition" could not be the same as Duncan's "traditional community" since tradition in this novel functions as the opposite of preservation.

The oppositions Duncan produces or to which he gestures at the close of his essay—Edenic past versus fallen present, natural condition versus modern alienation, tradition versus modernity, belief versus skepticism—repeat oppositions that have governed the criticism on the novel but that I think it is the novel's real brilliance to treat as continuous. In the cultural-nationalist reading, the goal, as Douglas Mack argues, is to preserve a culture. In this view, all of the bad information about the grave's location in the *Blackwood's* letter ("hardly a bit o't correct") should be understood as an effort to preserve the "sanctity of the grave . . . a shrine of the culture of an old pre-Union Scotland."[12] You can't circulate or commodify the culture you can't reach. But you can't practice it either (or, obviously, hand it down to the next generation). So fear about the "lethal alienation" of text produces a kind of terror of circulation that ends up cutting against the very life it means to preserve. What might be alienated by text gets alienated (anyway) by being hidden in the ground. A tradition whose sanctity has been preserved is a dead culture housed in shrine you cannot enter.[13]

Mack bases his claim for Hogg's role as a preservationist on the bad information his letter provides and on its description of the excavation as "a pity" because of the deterioration resulting from "exposures to the air" and "the impossibility of burying" anything dug up "again as closely as it was before" (*P*, 169). This concern with preservation and resurrection reappears in John Barrell's reflections on the figure of what he calls "the rising" (in which an apparently dead corpse sits upright or is otherwise recovered) in Hogg's work. Both the frequency with which Hogg recurs to the theme and its ambivalence (are these risings welcome recoveries or horrific returns?) lead Barrell to see "the rising" as the "obsessive figure at the heart" of Hogg's narratives, a sign of his abiding unease about "how Scotland should regard its violent history"; can, Barrell finds Hogg asking, "the identity of Scotland be based on the disavowal, the concealment of its past wounds, or must they be acknowledged?"[14] Barrell's account of Hogg's historical ambivalence obviously differs from Mack's account of Hogg's preservationist enthusiasm, but both rely on the same notion of the past as an object that, like any object lying in the ground, can either be left buried or (in Barrell's vivid phrase) "rak[ed] up" and (as Mack says) "revive[d]."[15] But even though the remarks in Hogg's letter about the "impossibility of burying anything up as closely as it was before" are assimilable to both Mack's preservationist reading (it's why one shouldn't violate graves) and Barrell's portrayal of historical anxiety (it's why one should be nervous about rising bodies), the example of decomposition as a consequence of revivification we see in the letter reveals the contradiction between a view of tradition as an object and a view of tradition as nothing but the changes and alterations to which an object is subjected. More succinctly, the decomposition that attends the text's excavation reveals that the preservationist project and the revivification effort are not complementary but antithetical. The cultural tradition that exists, the letter shows us, does so only insofar as it exists in a state of change.

The force of this claim is to recast entirely the question of local culture in the romantic period, an issue we have largely understood as a question about who has a legitimate right to a cultural legacy. Thus, Mack's admiration for what he sees as Hogg's preservationist strategy rests on the presumption that there are certain people who are (and others who are not) the legitimate inheritors of a tradition; the sinner's body and the sinner's text are Hogg's to protect in a way that they are not the editor's to disseminate. Here, for instance, is Katie Trumpener's rendering of that cultural-nationalist position: "Bardic nationalism insists on the rich fullness of national knowledge" preserved by "anchoring discursive traditions in landscape, in a way of life, in custom. The English, in comparison, have only borrowed words."[16] The culture that is really yours, as opposed to the culture you "have only borrowed," is the culture that you live—the one "anchor[ed] in landscape, in a way of life, in custom." But Hogg's novel has already shown us that the culture that is lived is the culture that changes. Anchored in a landscape (for example, buried) is the antithesis of "a way of life," which isn't an anchoring at all. It's thus a mistake to think that the culture that is really yours can ever be stolen or borrowed—a mistake, really, to think it can be owned at all—since culture does not have an objective form; it has only the expansively conceptual form of "a way of life." In pointing to the alteration that any circulation, any cultural life, requires, Hogg's novel identifies a contradiction between bardic nationalism's two thoughts about cultural value: that value could be both stored up in the past (anchored in the landscape like what Scott describes as "the ore of antiquity") and imagined to have a present existence as an ongoing "way of life."[17] Because living, Hogg's novel shows us, means changing, preservation (in what only feels like a paradox) means death.

This abiding tension between a conception of culture as a value preserved (anchored, rooted, grounded) in the past and a conception of culture as made up of ongoing practice should be seen as itself an inheritance of a romantic effort to come to grips with the consequences the notion of popular art (art as a way of life) had for conceptions of the work of art (art as object). The tension receives an illustrative instantiation (if not exactly analysis) in one of the essays Scott used to introduce *Minstrelsy of the Scottish Border*. "Introductory Remarks on Popular Poetry" (1830) oscillates between two versions of culture: as an unchanging essence and as an evolutionary system. The essay, Scott tells us, was meant to be of "a literary nature," in order to complement the "historical" one of the original introduction and to "afford the general reader some information upon the character of Ballad Poetry."[18] It becomes clear almost immediately, however, that the literary and the historical cannot, especially in the case of "Ballad Poetry," be handled separately. For as Scott's account makes evident, the ballad's status as "popular poetry" did more than simply mark the difference between balladeers and practitioners of "higher" forms. It becomes clear, as Scott rediscovers the break with neoclassicism represented in the *Lyrical Ballads'* prefatory ambition to write poetry in common speech, that the ballad subordinated a view of poetry as an art of rule-governed or strictly conventional forms (the ode, the sonnet, the sestina, etc.) to a view of poetry as a kind of native speech, an expression of "the climate and country in which it has its origins[,] the temper and manners of the people."[19] On this model of poetry, the differences between one population's popular poetry and another's are assigned to the differences between local contexts, and a collection of ballads in theory could, like core samples of geological strata, represent the continuities (and so also the differences) between historically disparate moments.

In this way the ballad can be seen not just as an important literary form but as a literary form whose very informality (its capacity for change over time) recasts the task of literary history and the idea of cultural transmission more generally. Because this notion of contemporary, ongoing use was built into the formal definition of a ballad, a single ballad could be said to exist in many different versions without there being any logical contradiction. Thus, Scott will describe the "very fine ballad of 'Chevy Chase'" as having "been produced by the gradual alterations of numerous reciters, during two centuries, in the course of which the ballad has been gradually moulded into a composition bearing only a general resemblance to the original."[20] This invocation of "general resemblance" means that, unlike a sonnet, which one can only reproduce whole or not at all, a ballad might be rather markedly altered without losing its identity. One might, as in the example Scott provides, rewrite the lines "The Percy owt of Northumberland, / And a vowe to God mayd he" as "The stout earl of Northumberland / A vow to God did make" without being taken to be writing something other than "Chevy Chase."[21] Like the title Hogg provides for his novel, then, "Chevy Chase" does not exclusively denominate a particular copytext but, rather, functions as the name for a collection—a variorum—that relies on "general resemblance" for its integrity. The rather loose guidelines of resemblance provide a way to talk about continuity through change. Only a misguided literary historian would, in this light, try to decide which version is the real "Chevy Chase"; the job is to talk about how "Chevy Chase" came to be over time.

As clear as those implications are, though, Scott will not in fact dispense with the question of legitimacy or authenticity and goes on to suggest that careful scholarship can, like Tooke's etymology discussed in Chapter 1, purify the "ore of antiquity" of the mistakes inserted by posterity, the "deteriorat[ion] and adulterat[ion]" that occurs when a poem is, "like a book reprinted in a multitude of editions," "transmitted through a number of reciters."[22] Scott, this is to say, is interested in the development of a text across time *only insofar* as such historicizing is a necessary first step in the antiquarian effort to undo it. We need to collect all available versions in order to recover the "rugged sense and spirit of the antique minstrel," in order to turn an ongoing tradition, which always (that's how you know it's ongoing) arrives "reprinted in a multitude of editions," back into an object.[23]

If Scott's aim is to correct the alterations introduced by transmission across (geographical, historical, social) contexts and by the fact of multiple authors, Hogg's novel reveals the instability that attends the inability to change with the times. Scott, like all good preservationists, wants to dispense with alteration; the justified sinner, like all good Calvinists, believes he already has. *"Amen, for ever!"* the sinner's memoirs conclude: "I will now seal up my little book, and conceal it; and cursed be he who trieth to alter or amend!" (*P*, 165). The unalterable state of the sinner—*"Amen, for ever!"*—and the unalterable state of his book thus fall into alignment: unchanging, sealed, concealed, and dead. If that's where the sinner leaves it, the opening paragraphs of the novel offer us an illustration of the opposite principle: an exemplification of the tradition-as-alteration that has yielded us our many different versions of "Chevy Chase." Where Scott's devotion to the authenticity of antiquity would lead him to see this as so many fallings away from a real identity, Hogg's novel presents this sort of alteration as the most normal thing in the world.

> It appears from tradition, as well as some parish registers still extant, that the lands of Dalcastle (or Dalchastel, as it is often spelled) were possessed by a family of the name of Colwan, about one hundred and fifty years ago, and for at least a century previous to that period. That family was supposed to have been a branch of the ancient family of Colquhoun, and it is certain that from it spring the Cowans that spread toward the Border. (*P*, 2)

Just as "Chevy Chase" functioned as both the name for many individual poems across time and, so too, as a name for their general resemblance, the names of places and families in Hogg's first paragraphs are shown to be in a constant state of evolution. They move over time as one standard practice replaces another (from "Colquhoun" to "Cowan"), or they coexist as alternate but noncompeting practices ("Dalcastle" with an "h" or without). The point, clearly, is not—as the ore-of-antiquity position would have to have it—to depict the Colwans as the usurpers of the Colquhouns or to imply that Dalcastle and Dalchastel are two different places. By presenting the ways in which even the names of people change over time or exist simultaneously in different but equally legitimate forms, the editor opens by marking identity as something held by general resemblance rather than by preservationist rigidity.

But if in this way the novel's opening represents traditional identity as flexible just because historically continuous, the plot of the story told in both narratives is immediately set in motion by the very problem of legitimacy/illegitimacy that the notion of identity by general resemblance seemed meant to defuse. George Colwan, the laird Dalcastle, marries a woman, a Calvinist radical who has not only "imbibed her ideas from the doctrines of one flaming predestinarian divine alone" (P, 4) but brings this divine, Mr. Wringhim, to live with her. In time she bears a son and, soon thereafter, another. The first son "the laird acknowledged as his son and heir." The second son—"though a brother he certainly was," the editor tells us, "in the eye of the law, and it is more than probable that he was his brother in reality"—is denied by the laird, who refuses to "take the baptismal vows on him in the child's name" (P, 14). Accordingly, the second child is forced to "live and remain an alien from the visible church for a year and a day; at which time, Mr. Wringhim, out of pity and kindness, took the lady herself as sponsor for the boy, and baptized him by the name of Robert Wringhim—that being the noted divine's own name" (P, 14). Thus begins a story that will depict an antagonism between the two brothers, an antagonism that, forwarded on by the devil-like figure of Gil-Martin who haunts the young Robert Wringhim, will lead to George's murder at the hands of his brother before his disappearance (in the editor's narrative) and his suicide (in the sinner's own).

In these basics the plot is fundamentally a gothic tale in which, as in so many such, the issues of inheritance shade into representations of psychological instability and supernatural agency. Given the novel's setting just prior to the Act of Union (though it omits direct mention), we might see the novel as a fairly straightforward instance of the nationalist gothic genre that, in Trumpener's characterization, emphasizes "the traumatic consequences of historical transformation and the long-term uneven development, even schizophrenia, it creates in 'national characters.'"[24] But even as it seems plausible that the illegitimacy forced onto Wringhim by his father's neglect might be responsible for a certain psychic vulnerability, the novel makes clear that Wringhim's loss of individuality is attendant not on his having been denied by his probably (?) or possibly (?) biological father but upon his adoption, first by his namesake and, then, into the Calvinist faith. Schizophrenia (or something like it) is caused not by the absence of a patrimony but by what both the law and the Calvinist elect call "adoption" (P, 13)—not, then, from the unavailability or incoherence of national character but from the nonnegotiable singularity of one.

In her reading of the novel, Eve Sedgwick suggests that the easy-going, physically strong, and basically generous (as well as tellingly named) George represents traits that came "ever more overtly to denominate the British racial ideal" and that the jealous, weak-bodied, and anxiously intellectualized Robert is the foil against which that British ideal is developed.[25] But we might work this characterological juxtaposition another way: by seeing them not as antithetical national characters—as if national characters were natural kinds—but as antithetical nurtures.[26] Here's a description from the early pages:

> George was brought up with his father, and educated partly at the parish-school, and partly at home, by a tutor hired for the purpose. He was a generous and kind-hearted youth. Robert was brought up with Mr. Wringhim . . . and there the boy was early inured to all the sternness and severity of his pastor's arbitrary and unyielding creed. He was taught to pray twice every day . . . but he was only to pray for the elect, and, like David of old, doom all that were aliens from God to destruction. (P, 14)

In both instances it seems that character is cultural—as a product of experience or, as Scott put it, of "the climate and country" and "the temper and manners" in which one lives—but the difference between the two cultures could hardly be more stark—a varied and multisourced education and an arbitrary and unyielding ("stern and severe") indoctrination into an "arbitrary and unyielding creed." One open, semipublic, catholic; the other hived off, exclusive, and Calvinist. And, given this unchanging rigidity, it may make sense to think of Calvinism less a culture or an upbringing than—like a text buried in the ground—an outcast state that can never, as Duncan puts it, "be brought to life." The chronological inversion (but the logical twin) of a culture so perfectly preserved that it doesn't exist, Calvinism looks forward to a future so fixed it might as well be a dead end. Unlike legal adoption—which puts the development of a child in the care of an adult—Calvinist adoption is premised on the nondevelopment of its children. "The grace of adoption," as the *Westminster Confession of Faith* (1646) describes it, is the process by which the justified "are taken into the number, and enjoy the liberties and privileges of the children of God, have His name put upon them . . . are enabled to cry, Abba, Father, are pitied, protected, provided for, and chastened by Him as by a Father: yet never cast off, but sealed to the day of redemption; and inherit the promises, as heirs of everlasting salvation." The *Westminster Confession* flirts with the idea that divine adoption entails something like life and experience—there's pitying, and protecting, and chastening—but it is fundamentally a dead state ("sealed to the day of redemption") whose only conclusion comes already foregone. The lessons or guidance the *Westminster Confession* imagines coming from the divine Abba thus become something like time-killing exercises—a way to while away the centuries until the day of redemption: a form of cultivation and action on which it is the defining Calvinist position that nothing could hang.

Belief in predestination produces a world in which, because all conclusions are forgone, all actions take place in ironizing quotation marks. This is not, of course, what the Calvinist historiography of the twentieth century has emphasized. Following Weber's foundational analysis of the ways in which Calvinist regulation "penetrate[d] to all departments of private and public life," other historians have detailed the ways Calvinism, as Michael Walzer writes, "gave rise to a collectivist discipline marked above all by a mutual 'watchfulness.'"[27] It could hardly be more *Surveiller et Punir:* a regime of what Susan Manning calls "the unremitting self-scrutiny which must accompany action."[28] This unremitting scrutiny is, in one sense, a social mechanism designed to compensate for the fallenness of human vision on whose fallibility the doctrine of predestination rests (since we can't reliably perceive good and evil, our salvation can't be left up to us). Accordingly, the accounts of Weber and Walzer describe the ways Calvinists came to substitute society for the God from whom they were estranged: if one couldn't see like God, the social world at least provided a polling place made up of people who had been successful at adhering to a more or less codified set of behaviors and achievements. But it is, at the same time, hard to see how a lot of people seeing imperfectly together might manage to replicate, let alone reduplicate, the God from whom we are, as Walzer says, "permanent[ly], inescapabl[y], estranged."[29] And even if it could—even if, that is, social consensus could provide a reliable indicator of one's future state—it's hard to see, given its unchangeablity, how the conclusion could matter. The fixity of one's final state would make knowing potentially interesting, but in terms of its influence on action in the lived world, of absolutely no importance. It might be better, then, to think of the Calvinist regimes of scrutiny not (as Walzer and others have argued) as a way to control a rising and inherently unpredictable individualism by approximating divine vision but—quite differently—as a necessary counterweight to the thoroughly antinomian entailments of Calvinism's own fundamental tenet: that one's final state can't hang on what you do in this world and that knowing it (being in or out) couldn't change a thing.[30]

The *Memoirs* offer a striking representation of the way the fact of predestination (whichever way the coin flips) formally nullifies action by showing that what follows on adoption is not, as Robert Wringhim Sr. suggests, the ability to do anything one wants ("Who would not envy the liberty wherewith we are made free?" his adopted father asks [P, 11]) but the inability to see oneself as doing anything. "I seemed hardly to be an accountable creature," says young Robert. "Either I had a second self who transacted business in my likeness, or else my body was at times possessed by a spirit over which it had no controul, and of whose actions my own soul was wholly unconscious" (P, 125). This is already late in the novel, from those unhappy days when Wringhim wants nothing more than the nonexistence ("My principal feeling . . . was an insatiable longing for something that I cannot describe properly, unless I say it was for utter oblivion that I longed") of which he is already possessed (P, 126): "Could I have again been for a season in utter oblivion to myself, and transacting business which I neither approved of, nor had any connection with" (P, 128).

In one sense, of course, Wringhim is right: the shapeshifting Gil-Martin *is* performing actions in his likeness. And in this sense the problem does not seem to be the philosophical one of belief—that Wringhim believes in his election and therefore cannot see himself as acting—but the factual, if in this case supernatural, problem of being framed. But we might just as easily say that the novel's supernatural elements do not so much provide a way of getting outside of the problems that Calvinist predestination poses for individual action as they literalize those problems by giving a body to the conception of agency Calvinism provides. For it was not only the case that predestination made earthly action finally irrelevant but that seeing the relevant constituencies—the just and the reprobate—to be already established made it possible to see all of one's actions as nothing more than emanations of one's state. "We have no more to do with the sins of the wicked and unconverted here, than with those of an infidel turk," the elder Robert Wringhim explains, "for all earthly bonds and fellowships are absorbed and swallowed up in the holy community of the Reformed Church. . . . To the

wicked, all things are wicked; but to the just, all things are just and right"
(*P*, 11). Calvinism's view of the world as divided into the wicked and the
just made it seem that the nature of one's action derived from one's status
rather than having—as in any conventional account—the nature of one's
status derive from one's action.

Some moments suggest that the status of election produces an outsized
sense of one's capacity ("I am the sword of the Lord, and Famine and Pes-
tilence are my sisters," says the younger Wringhim in a particularly ecstatic
moment [*P*, 103]), but its broader effect is to evacuate agency of meaning.
The Wringhim who finds himself God's instrument upon election spends
his preelection days sinning without doing much of anything at all. "It was
about this time," he recalls,

> that my reverend father preached a sermon, one sentence of which affected me
> most disagreeably. It was to the purport, that every unrepented sin was produc-
> tive of a new sin with each breath that man drew; and every one of these new
> sins added to the catalogue in the same manner. I was utterly confounded at the
> multitude of my transgressions; for I was sensible that there were great num-
> bers of sins of which I had never been able thoroughly to repent, and these
> momentary ones, by a moderate calculation, had, I saw, long ago, amounted to
> a hundred and fifty thousand in the minute, and I saw no end to the series of
> repentances to which I had subjected myself. A life-time was nothing to enable
> me to accomplish the sum, and then being, for any thing I was certain of, in
> my state of nature, and the grace of repentance withheld from me,—what was
> I to do, or what was to become of me? In the meantime, I went on sinning
> without measure. (*P*, 74)

Although Wringhim here speaks of actions as countable instances—the
problem of sin appears to be one of "number," of "multitude"—the interest
of the passage clearly is to point out the categorical incommensurability of
a case-by-case count of one's actions and, on the other hand, an overarching status like grace or gracelessness. The contradiction in terms (status
versus action) we find in Wringhim's "grace of repentance" runs throughout
the passage, as Wringhim frantically tries to proceed, sin by countable sin,
through what is, thanks to his gracelessness, an infinite set. "I always *tried* to
repent of these sins by the slump," Wringhim goes on, "for individually it
was impossible" (*P*, 78). The problem, though, still is that even a very large
"slump" can never equal Wringhim's "state of nature." He is, as he says,
"a transcendent sinner" (*P*, 78) not because he has committed many sinful
actions but because when sin (or election) is transcendent one can sin (or act
justly) with "each breath."

It is in this triumph of transcendent status over ongoing action that we can see the dividends Gil-Martin's supernaturalism pays, for the fact that he haunts Wringhim, that he is always, eerily present—"When I lay in bed, I deemed there were two of us in it; when I sat up, I always beheld another person, and always in the same position from the place where I sat or stood, which was about three paces off me toward my left side" (*P*, 106)—causes Gil-Martin to become rather more of an afflicting condition (Wringhim calls him a "distemper" [*P*, 106]) than an individual. "The tendency to belief in supernatural agency is natural," Scott wrote in *Demonology and Witchcraft*, "and, indeed, seems connected with, and deduced from, the invaluable conviction of the certainty of a future state."[31] But in being haunted by Gil-Martin, Wringhim looks less like a man who can, as in Scott's description, see the plausibility of ghosts and spirits because he believes that he himself "shall not wholly die" than he does a man forced to drag his own future state along with him. The supernatural here, then, does not externalize subjective states, making what is in the mind appear in the world, but is instead (and quite the contrary) a feature of the memoir's persistent depiction of individual consciousness as constantly shadowed, indeed overshadowed, by transcendent conditions.

I began this chapter by describing the continuities between cultural nationalism, textual antiquarianism as represented by Scott, and Calvinism as represented by Hogg. More particularly, I have been arguing that each of these representational situations sets up a tension between the ongoing nature of existence (the cultures people actually practice, the ballads people transmit, the actions a Calvinist commits) and a fixed, transcendent status (the Scottishness that subsumes practice; the real ballad of Chevy Chase that, whether it actually exists or not, causes all other ballads of Chevy Chase to be only mistaken versions; the final state that is yours no matter what you do). If Calvinism provides the most intense version of the disconnect between the immediate and the transcendent, because it makes psychological what might otherwise remain an academic question about the definition and operations of culture, Wringhim's memoirs themselves show that the strain of having a foot in both worlds is a risk occasioned not only by extraordinary religious enthusiasm but by something as ordinary as coming into property.

For it is one of the surprises of the memoirs that Wringhim's psychological crisis should reach its peak not, as we might expect, in the murder of his brother but in the appearance of a royal decree entitling one Robert Wringhim Colwan to the lands descending down the line of his "more than probable" father. Like a supernatural being who acts on your behalf or a final state that ignores your individual action, the royal grant, which entails the lands to "George Colwan, of Dalcastle and Balgrennan . . . and his heirs and assignees whatsomever, heritably and irrevocably . . . in all time coming" (*P*, 180), represents a model of original, inviolable agency immune to the desires or agencies of its subjects. (As Sandra Macpherson has observed in an argument on forms of entailment in Austen, the whole point of the instrument was to make possible an agency whose effectiveness did not depend on its being seconded or shared by anyone among the living.)[32] Thus, when Wringhim, who seems strongly *not to want* the land, attempts to "deny every thing connected with the business," to "disclaim it in total" by virtue of the fact that he "know[s] no more about it than the child unborn" (*P*, 179), he means to be invoking an obvious figure for innocence—the child unborn—but has, in fact, latched on to the very audience to which an entail is directed. Entails, like nationalist identities, are ways of organizing children unborn and, in this, are the closest man's law can come to Calvin's; entails are the conveyors of future states. And insofar as they convey these states into "all time coming," without the corruptions of transmission or the static generated by there ever having been more than one pen, entails are nearly perfect antiquarian objects, ensuring that the "ore of antiquity" remains unalloyed. But in sealing away the future the entail also opens up the present as nothing more than a waiting room that the generations file through to occupy but never to own, an interim period stretched between an action in the past and a consequence that is always in the future.

4. Nothing Personal

The Decapitations of Character in A Tale of Two Cities

> One could not read the correspondence of an old-regime
> intendant with his superiors and subordinates without noting
> how the similarity of institutions makes the officials of that time
> similar to those of our own. They seem to shake hands across
> the abyss of the Revolution which separates them.
> —Alexis de Tocqueville, *The Old Regime and The Revolution*

As the final pages of *A Tale of Two Cities* lead their hero to the guillotine, Sydney Carton holds the hand of a poor seamstress whom we have never met and whose name we will never know.[1] Headed to the scaffold in place of Charles Darnay, the man to whom Carton has been continually compared and the husband of the woman he loves, Carton has just come into a lead role that has been, until now, something of a shared duty. And here, with the seamstress, he puts the final touches on his centrality, comforting a woman to whom he has no previous connection and in whose fate he has no personal stake. In this moment both Carton's individual importance and personal virtue would seem to be clearly on display. He remains, accordingly, one of Dickens's most loved and best remembered characters. But the singular importance that readers, like the seamstress herself ("You comfort me so much ... I am so ignorant"), have attached to Carton holds no currency within the revolutionary world.[2] At the moment of their execution the differences between the characters "all flash away": "The knitting women count Twenty-Two ... Twenty-three" (*T*, 371). The numbers specify, but they are neither driven by characterization nor open to it. A scene that seems designed to confirm the importance of the personal concludes by asserting its irrelevance.

This scene's replacement of character by number provides a particularly succinct version of the indifference to individual distinction I want to argue is a much more widespread feature of membership in this novel and the French Revolution it imagines. It may seem entirely familiar to think of Dickens as a chronicler of indifference—the Gradgrinds, the Scrooges, the bleak houses, the coke towns—and a critic of the way modern, industrialized, institutionalized life invades and cripples our naturally given inner lives. Only the saintly—the Tiny Tims, the Joe Gargeries—seem to wear the light of their humanity openly; the rest of us, have to, Wemmick-like, hide it under a castle.[3] But what's special about *A Tale of Two Cities* is that, rather than turning on the more familiar competition between inner essence and institutional demands, it adopts and resolutely maintains an understanding of individuals as entities so thoroughly representative that the very question of inner life disappears. What we have in *A Tale of Two Cities*—a novel often mistakenly criticized for its sentimentalism and its disinterest in history—is in fact a rigidly unsentimental novel about a set of political perspectives—the ones animating the French Revolution—that were themselves programmatically indifferent to the personality of persons.

This alignment of form and theme is estranging since it makes it more difficult to continue seeing Dickens as one of history's great humanists. We can, I think, continue to hear a critique of the indifference to persons in the brutal energy with which Dickens renders it; a description of the guillotine, for instance, as a "crashing engine that constantly whirrs up and falls" (*T*, 387) is not, after all, exactly proguillotine. But it's not exactly antiguillotine, either, and one can feel in moments like this—or in the clinical distance of the knitting women's body count or the detached scope that lends the opening antitheses their majestic citability—signs of a certain enthralled ecstasy at the possibilities of this starkly depersonalized perspective. In August 1859, Dickens wrote to his friend and eventual biographer, John Forster, about his plan to write "a story of incident" that would, with echoes of the crashing engine of the novel's final paragraphs, "pound the characters in its own mortar ... beating their interest out of them." The marginal notations in Forster's biography capture one version of that plan ("Not dialogue but incident."), but Dickens's own descriptions of the program put its depersonalizing aims in even starker relief; the goal, Dickens wrote, was to have "characters true to nature, but whom the story itself should express, more than they should express themselves, by dialogue."[4] As programs go, it was not easy: "Nothing but the interest of the subject," Dickens wrote, "and the pleasure of striving with the difficulty of the form of treatment—nothing in the way of mere money, I mean—could repay the time and trouble of the incessant condensation."[5] Those demands for incessant condensation were, most immediately, an effect of the serial format in which the novel originally appeared (launching *All the Year Round*), but this was hardly Dickens's first brush with the exigencies of magazine publication, and it's clear from Dickens's properly theoretical remarks about the priority of incident or story over character that these issues of form were active ambitions rather than passive functions of format.

The problem of plot—or, really, of plottedness—in *A Tale of Two Cities* thus goes well beyond a question of the density of incident—beyond, that is, the need to arrange for what Dickens called a "rising in every chapter."[6] The idea that a novel might pound its characters in the mortar of story involves a thorough recasting of action from something that might plausibly be said to originate in the intentions and volitions of the characters into something that, by definition, transcends the "small creatures" (*T*, 7) who appear on the novel's pages. Some five decades ago the critic G. Robert Stange aptly observed that *A Tale of Two Cities*, "almost uniquely in Dickens, [is] a single plot, that is unraveled with speed and concision, and which always dominates both the characters and their *milieux*."[7] But we might equally take the despairing words of Charles Darnay—one of *A Tale*'s "small creatures"— himself: "It could not be otherwise," Charles says on being sentenced to death, "all things have worked together as they have fallen out . . . a happier end was not in nature to so unhappy a beginning" (*T*, 347). The absence of a counterfactual where we ought to hear one (*it could not have been . . .*) and the odd tautology that follows it—things have worked together as they have fallen out—bespeak a world whose unfolding arrives as a constant and unstoppable conspiracy carried out through, but never exactly by, the persons who inhabit it. If earlier in the novel Charles can still engage in some liberal self-scolding—"His renunciation of social place," he thinks, "had been hurried and incomplete. He knew he ought to have systematically worked it out and supervised it, and that he had meant to do it, and that it had never been done" (*T*, 251)—he has, by novel's end, come to see his life not as a series of (insufficiently) willed actions but as a top-to-bottom byproduct of plot's self-administration. Plot, Charles has learned, resides "in nature," not in "persons."

One conventional term for this state of affairs would be historical determinism. And as moments like this one from the opening pages make clear—"It is likely enough," we are told, "that rooted in the woods of France and Norway, there were growing trees . . . already marked by the woodman, Fate, to come down and be sawn into boards, to make a certain movable framework with a sack and a knife in it, terrible in history" (*T*, 6)—it's not entirely wrong to think of *A Tale of Two Cities* (or *Hard Times* before it) as an early instance of what would come to be known as literary naturalism. As what follows will make clear, though, Dickens's novel engages history in ways that are more precise than simply casting it as a warehouse of suprapersonal forces. For what interests Dickens about the French Revolution is not simply the more obvious paradox—that what might look like a shift toward the individualist ideals of liberty and equality occurs as a mass event in which individuals wash up as mere flotsam—but the deeper and more interesting paradox that the revolution, as codified in the Declaration of the Rights of Man and theorized by Robespierre (who made speech after speech laying out the philosophical entailments of its assorted articles), did not so much abolish the representative forms of personhood found in aristocracies and monarchies (in which a son stands for a family or a king for a country) as apply them to everyone. For if the aristocracy sowed the seeds of its downfall by insisting on the absolute nature of its power in the manner of Louis XIV's "*L'état, c'est moi,*" the claims of the People were no less absolute. "What is the Third Estate?" Abbé Sieyès famously asked. His immediate answer: "*Everything.*"[8] To describe the French Revolution as a conflict between political forms is thus to miss exactly what Dickens finds to lament in the event: that the popular, national membership the First Republic instated simply repeated the categorical force of the aristocracy it overthrew. The novel is, I am suggesting, about what de Tocqueville calls in this chapter's epigraph "the similarity of institutions."[9] The similarity between the aristocracy and the republic that replaced it lies in their identical commitment to a naturalized political order in which rights were ordained by—and only by—birth. This version of entitlement will be described, with shades of the Calvin we saw in the prior chapter, by the novel's most antirevolutionary character, the Marquis d'Evremonde, as "natural destiny" (*T*, 129). The impulse to describe questions of social organization as natural conditions is not, however, limited to aristocrats asserting the divine rights of provincial nobles. Indeed, the feature of the novel I mean to bring out is its rather remarkable refusal to limit a sense of unearned membership to the class of hereditary nobility. *A Tale of Two Cities* treats the French Revolution as if its goal were not to do away with nobility but to extend nobility to everyone.

It's true that certain strains of French revolutionary thought have what can feel like a liberal—that is, individualistic—aim. In a 1791 speech on the right to vote, for example, Robespierre came down extremely hard on an early Republican proposal to make suffrage a function of personal income, railing against "the monstrous distinctions drawn between [men] by the decrees that make a man active or passive, or half active and half passive, according to the varying degrees of fortune that permit him to pay three days' wages in taxes, ten days, or a silver mark."[10] Political agency should not, the argument is, be a function of financial wherewithal; all men, regardless of wage, are equally agents in a political sense. But Robespierre's argument against partitioning the electorate according to wage was not, as a liberal dispensation might receive it, a defense of the individuality of individuals but, instead, a way to insist on the generality of the general will: "Can the law be termed an expression of the general will when the greater number of those for whom it is made can have no hand in its making?"[11] As he put the thought in an earlier speech arguing against restrictions on eligibility for public office, "all citizens, whoever they are, have the right to aspire to all levels of office-holding. Nothing is more in line with your declaration of rights, according to which all privileges, all distinctions, all exceptions must disappear. The Constitution establishes that that sovereignty resides in the people, in all the individuals of the people."[12] Throughout his speeches, this is Robespierre's strategy: to remind his listeners of the new political ontology contained in the Declaration of the Rights of Man, which insisted that distinctions disappear so that sovereignty might be recognized as a property of the people. "The principle of sovereignty resides essentially in the nation," Article III reads, and "no body of men, no individual, can exercise authority that does not emanate expressly from it." Robespierre's arguments against restrictions on political activity thus are something like the opposite of the liberal principle that every individual is entitled to voice an individual pref- erence. Instead, they rest on what Slavoj Žižek calls the "state-centralized" insistence that sovereignty and agency are properties of a demographic entity (the People) rather than the particular entities that are persons.[13] No politics is personal, for Robespierre, because all politics is popular.

What *A Tale of Two Cities* offers us, then, in its competition between aristocrats and republicans, is an account of the French Revolution as an event that, from the perspective of the individual, was essentially without sides. The novel has, as Cates Baldridge notes, been seen as frustratingly indecisive in terms of its political ideology, but the novel's real insight, I'm arguing here, is that there wasn't really a choice to be made.[14] The French Revolution, here, is not the advent of a politics responsive to the individual but a conflict between two versions of naturalized membership in which identity is inherited and individuality a matter of whom you represent. The aristocratic indifference to an individual's actions and preferences is an indif- ference that, in this novel, has become a common property. And the Terror is just what you get when you attach a system of punishment to a political ontology whose founding gesture is to make, as Robespierre says, "all privi- leges, all distinctions, all exceptions . . . disappear." The French Revolution's prioritization of the general over the particular is so thorough that Dickens will formulate death—the erasure of particularity—as a kind of national ideal. As reread by Dickens's novel, the conjunction in the revolutionary motto—"Liberty, Equality, Fraternity, or Death" (*T*, *285*)—does not signal an alternative (as, say, in Patrick Henry's famous phrase) but an equivalence: "The last much the easiest to bestow, O guillotine" (*T*, *285*). Death, that is, is not merely a tactic or a punishment by which the "Republic One and

Indivisible" (*T*, 255) protects itself; it's the most perfect instantiation of the absence of distinction—the One-and-Indivisibility—at which it aims: a way to protect the singularity of the nation from the possibility that someone might take something personally.

On the one hand, it may seem surprising that this assessment of a totalizing social form should take place through the relatively small cast of characters with whom we spend most of the novel. It's true that the novel does not cast a wide net and engages in a typically Dickensian plot of revealed affiliation. (Briefly: a banker, Mr. Lorry, informs Lucie Manette that her long-lost father has been discovered above a Paris wine shop owned by the novel's revolutionaries, Monsieur and Madame Defarge, whose sister, it turns out, was raped and whose brother-in-law was murdered by the father of the young nobleman, Charles Darnay, who ends up married to Lucie and saved by Sydney Carton's sacrifice.) The French Revolution presented, as Lukács's well-known and not entirely unreasonable critique saw it, as an eight-person soap opera.

Lukács takes the interconnection of character as a form of bourgeois introversion, arguing that Dickens had turned the historical event of the French Revolution into nothing more than "a Romantic background."[15] But looked at in light of Robespierre's insistence that every particular must be seen as continuous with (and as a mouthpiece of) the general, we can also see that there's a perfect appropriateness in the idea that the household might be entirely continuous with the historical. The French Revolution's conditionless synecdoche—in which, as in romantic aesthetics, each represents the all and the all represents the each—collapses the distinctions (between background and foreground, major and minor, private and public) on which Lukács's criticism relies. So while Lukács wants characters with a greater capacity to represent the "popular"—"They write about the French Revolution," he says, "and we see neither Danton nor Robespierre, they write about the Napoleonic Wars without Napoleon"—he's missing the force of Robespierre's insistence that every individual is equally representative of the generality.[16] Robespierre's point, in so many words, is that he could be anyone.

Thus unlike the liberal individualist assumption of, say, the prelude to *Middlemarch*—which claims that everyone, even an uncanonized Theresa or a seamstress or a drunk barrister, has a "loving heart-beat" that goes on below the horizon of the "long-recognizable deed"—the interest of Dickens's historical mode lies in its opposite insistence that there is no such thing as an individual story.[17] We should thus see the especially tight interconnection of characters across the plot—an interconnection brought to a limit case in the nonbiological twinning of Sydney Carton and Charles Darnay—not as closed-off introversion but as part of Dickens's experiment in what it would mean to imagine that both character and plot are the properties of structures rather than individuals. In this novel, identity, including the kinds of identity that derive from action (for example, guilt or innocence), is a function of interrelation rather than a property premised on individual volition or idiosyncratic depths. In a small but telling moment midway through the novel, Madame Defarge shows up to speak with Lucie and says not "I'm here to speak with you" but "It is the daughter of your father who is my business here" (*T*, 278). Identity, as Madame's remarkably vexed syntax makes clear, is entirely a function of position rather than content. Familial and domestic, yes—husband, daughter, father—but also as purely graphic and depsychologized as a family tree.

In one sense, this indifference to the deep person reconfirms—and, more importantly, revalues—observations made by an earlier generation of critics who noticed how little interest Dickens's art manifested in psychological interiors. As early as 1927 E. M. Forster rather harshly assessed Dickens's "flat people" and his reliance on "types and caricatures."[18] Even in Forster, though, the claim that the characters *are* flat sets up the observation that they don't *seem* flat. "Nearly every one can be summed up in a sentence," writes Forster in a particularly memorable moment,

> and yet there is a wonderful feeling of human depth. Probably the immense vitality of Dickens causes his characters to vibrate a little, so that they borrow his life and appear to lead one of their own. It is a conjuring trick; at any moment we may look at Mr. Pickwick edgeways and find him no thicker than a gramophone record. But we never get the sideway view. . . . He always has the air of weighing something.[19]

Recasting God's inspiration of Adam as an acoustic experiment, Forster imagines some of Dickens's "immense vitality" causing flat characters to resonate, producing the effect of depth from the fact of flatness. From here we can begin to see the importance of *A Tale* as a novel at home in its characterization, a novel that both openly thematizes and importantly politicizes the aesthetic Forster is content to describe as an attractive sleight of hand. In this novel, the fact that life has been borrowed is so prevalent that even nameless border officials know it. When the young nobleman Charles Darnay returns home to France and is told that "his cursed life is not own," the revolutionary official does not mean that Charles is only pretending to be "thicker than a gramophone record," but he does mean something that Charles had already begun to understand in his failure to renounce his "social place": that he remains far more a function of his historical position than an intentional agent. It's not the case that Charles is entirely without an inner life—as we've seen, he scolds himself for failing to meet "the force of these circumstances" with "continuous and accumulating resistance"—just that no one is interested in whatever intentions, views, or sympathies those depths might harbor. Charles is, in this sense, an individual who has wandered into an allegorical world.

But in another, even broader sense, the fact that the novel turns on this dichotomy—between self-representing individuals and representative selves—puts it outside of the flat-deep dichotomy that organizes both Forster's and Alex Woloch's more recent account of novelistic character. Woloch's well-known study *The One vs. the Many* argues that the depth of main characters is a kind of surplus value accumulated off the backs of the masses—the deep Ones get to be that way only because of the minoritized Many.[20] Woloch's account has proven especially useful to students of the novel (including myself) because it offers a way to see character as a product of narrative form; he can thus dispense with something like Forster's hazily extratextual suggestion that an author's "vitality" somehow spills into the text itself. But even an account so attuned to the ways in which character is not always deeply rendered still can't quite get at the peculiarity of *A Tale of Two Cities*, in which one's individuality is so consistently understood to be a function of "social position," of the many every one represents. *A Tale of Two Cities* replaces the opposition of Woloch's "versus" with something like equality: every individual is the face of a many. So deep is this emphasis on taking singulars for plurals that the novel will describe it as practically its own model of perception. "It was nothing to her," the novel will tell us of its most furious revolutionary, Madame Defarge, "that an innocent man was to die for the sins of his fathers. She saw not him, but them" (*T*, 376).

What we have in a moment like this, then, is the programmatic expansion—the expansion, that is, into a program—of the numerical logics with which we began the chapter. In precisely the way twenty-three (Carton's place in the executioner's count) can be thought of as the representative of numbers one through twenty-two, identity in the revolutionary world is a matter of how many an individual represents. Woloch's account frequently returns to the individual consciousness as a litmus test for the justice of character's "distributional system"; characters are fortunate to the degree they are deep, and they are mistreated to the degree that they are flat. But Madame Defarge's version of character doesn't care to—and, in a strict sense, cannot—make any appeal to an individual's inner life. For her external description is not an outline to be filled in by an internal psychology; it is not the grounds of an identity so much as a means of identification:

"It is necessary to register him. How do they call that man?"

"Barsad."

"Barsad," repeated madame. Good. Christian name?"

"John."

"John Barsad," repeated madame, after murmuring it once to herself.

"Good. His appearance; is it known?"

"Age, about forty years; height, about five feet nine; black hair; complexion dark; generally, rather handsome visage; eyes dark, face thin, long, and sallow; nose aquiline, but not straight, having a peculiar inclination towards the left cheek; expression, therefore, sinister."

"Eh my faith. It is a portrait!" said Madame, laughing. (*T*, 183–184)

With room for characters no bigger than the seamstress with whom we began, Madame Defarge's knitted registry of the condemned points out just how thin an operative characterization might be. The compilation of details might suffice for a police sketch, but it is not likely to count either as a literary character or even as what Forster calls "caricature." The parodic, flowery attention to detail ("aquiline, but not straight") suggests that Madame might do with less and underlines how much she is already doing without. Even the characteristics that ought to suggest character are treated as pragmatic, identifying marks. Barsad's "sinister" expression is not proof of his character (he'll turn out to be a hapless spy) in the way a bloated visage might, for a Hogarth, index a libertine's moral corruption. The "sinister" expression is, at most, the accidental effect of Barsad's slanting nose and perhaps nothing more than a pun on its leftward "inclination." A "portrait," then: not a psychology, not even a minor character, really—just enough representation to recognize one.

Given the prominence of gothic spaces of this novel, however—the graves, keyholes, prison cells, gargoyles—it is not surprising that critics have frequently read it along the plumb lines of an excavation than the sketch lines of a "portrait." In one of the strongest treatments of the novel, Catherine Gallagher argues that Dickens's narrative produces occasions, in the form of occlusions, in order to demonstrate its omniscience. Gallagher connects these novelistic exhibitions to the French Revolution's violation of individual privacy. "The resemblances" of the revolution, she writes, "to Dickens's novels, with their insistence on omniscience and their concomitant need for someone always to be hiding something are obvious. . . . [The novel's] continuation is as dependent on the discovery of plot as is that of the Revolution itself."[21] For Gallagher, then, the novel does not just describe "monstrous violators of the realm of the private"; it is itself one such violator.

Gallagher's account is beautifully methodical, but it hinges on seeing the novel's most absolute claim for the secrecy of secrets as merely the setup for its most significant "duplicity." It is in the novel's famed Night-Shadows passage that Gallagher finds the novel theorizing the opacity it invents in order to ignore:

> My friend is dead, my neighbour is dead, my love, the darling of my soul, is dead; it is the inexorable consolidation and perpetuation of the secret that was always in individuality, and which I shall carry in mine to my life's end. In any of the burial places of this city through which I pass, is there a sleeper more inscrutable than its busy inhabitants are, in their innermost personality, to me, or than I to them? (*T*, 14–15)

Some forty years ago E. D. H. Johnson began his chapter on the "Presentation of Characters" in Dickens by observing the way in which the "true identities" of characters are "masked even from themselves under conventionally prescribed poses."[22] In Johnson's version of the problem, social form veils real character. For Gallagher, who has a very different account of social prescription, social form insists that characters reveal more and more of themselves. It seems to me, however, that neither alternative—the difficulty of exposure (in Johnson) or the demand for it (in Gallagher)—is operative if secrecy is understood in the absolute way this passage understands it. Secrets, the passage is clear, are categorical rather than elective, the consequences of form rather than instances of intentionally concealed content. The speaker does not seek to know each of the "city's busy inhabitants" as well as he knows his "friend." He says, rather, that if knowing innermost personality is what we mean by knowing someone, then even the "darling of [his] soul" is as "inexorab[ly]" dead to him as any nameless sleeper. "Mysteries arise out of close love," Dr. Manette will tell us later in the novel, "as well as out of wide division" (*T*, 140).

The opposite of this categorical secrecy isn't disclosure or intimacy but something equally categorical: the absolute visibility Michel Foucault described as the "Rousseauist dream that motivated many of the revolutionaries." "It was," as Foucault describes it, "the dream of a transparent society, visible and legible in each of its parts, the dream of there no longer existing any zones of darkness . . . the dream that each individual, whatever position he occupied, might be able to see the whole of society, that men's hearts should communicate, and that opinion of all reign over each." In the interview from which this is taken, Foucault goes on to equate the "Rousseauist dream" with the Benthamite regime of an "'all-seeing' power." But Foucault's claim that "Bentham was the complement to Rousseau" misses the way in which the dream of Rousseau makes the regime of Bentham beside the point.[23] A world without zones of darkness does not need better methods of surveillance, and the world that needs them is not the world Foucault's Rousseau dreams for us.

Dickens's contribution to this line of thinking, then, is to suggest the cohabitation of these categorical alternatives: the "perpetuation of the secret" and the secret's abolishment. In the Rousseauist model of absolute visibility individuals may still have depths (they appear at least to have "hearts"), but these depths are no longer experienced as dark spots in need of illumination. Rousseau's dream, we can see, runs Forster's conjuring trick in reverse, taking something deep and making it appear flat. And in the model of the secret's "perpetuation" innermost thoughts are, by definition, permanently out of reach. Both alternatives—the world as a flat plane, the world as a closed book—make disclosure inoperative. In the world of absolute visibility, disclosure is pointless; in the world of absolute secrecy, it's impossible. Seen in this light, the Night-Shadows passage makes much more radical claims about the relation of disclosure and characterization. The deep subjectivity and meaningful disclosure that novels have been seen, as a genre, to provide make sense only if characters really have bottoms, if their depths are finite and therefore finally mappable. If, however, characters are bottomless, they may as well be flat. A politics that really believes in bottomless subjects cannot, at least not practically, be a politics that rests on disclosure. And the politics that seriously imagines that people are finally and forever secrets does not go begging for people; it does without.

The scandal of Dickens's revolution, then, lies less in its violation of personal depths than in its ability to operate as if no one had them. This indifference to individuality helps explain what might otherwise be a surprising feature of a Dickens novel: the narrative's allegiance to its banker (Mr. Lorry: "I have no feelings; I am a mere machine" [T, 25]). As in Bleak House or Great Expectations's Wemmick, here too law and finance capital treat persons as bureaucratic functionaries—but the private realm of authentic experience that might otherwise be the oppositional term is strangely missing. In fact, the narrative has so little trouble sharing itself with a banker that it is occasionally at pains to remind us of the difference between them: "It is Jarvis Lorry who has replied to all the previous questions" (T, 370), the narrative voice will inform us after a series of utterances unmarked by quotation. The moment's self-consciousness, its appearance as an overt narrative glitch, simply formalizes an imbrication of character and narrative voice that in fact begins as early as the second chapter's first sentence, in which the novel turns itself over to the vocabulary of Mr. Lorry: "It was the Dover road that lay, on a Friday night late in November, before the first of the persons with whom this history has business" (T, 8).

The novel is, of course, not a first-person novel, and Mr. Lorry is not even "the first of the persons with whom this history has business," but the business of history's persons will turn out to be both the novel's and Mr. Lorry's chief trade. For, as his conversation with Lucie Manette makes clear, the oddest feature of his banking business is that it has practically nothing to with money and everything to do with the location of missing daughters missing their fathers. "These are," Mr. Lorry will tell Lucie,

> "mere business relations, miss; there is no friendship in them, no particular interest, nothing like sentiment. I have passed from one to another, in the course of my business life, just as I pass from one of our customers to another in the course of my business day; in short, I have no feelings; I am a mere machine. To go on—"
>
> "But this is my father's story, sir . . ."
>
> . . .
>
> "So far, miss (as you have remarked), this is the story of your regretted father. Now comes the difference. If your father had not died when he did— Don't be frightened! How you start!"
>
> . . .
>
> "As I was saying, if Monsieur had not died; if he had suddenly and silently disappeared; if he had been spirited away; . . . if he had an enemy in some compatriot who could exercise a privilege . . . of filling up blank forms for the consignment of any one to the oblivion of a prison for any length of time . . .—then the history of your father would have been the history of this unfortunate gentleman, the Doctor of Beauvais."
>
> . . .
>
> "You know that your parents had no great possession, and that what they had was secured to your mother and to you. There has been no discovery, of money, or of any other property; but—"
>
> "But he has been—been found. He is alive. . . . Still, alive."
>
> A shiver ran through her frame, and from it through his. She said, in a low, distinct, awe-stricken voice, as if she were saying it in a dream,
>
> "I am going to see his Ghost! It will be his Ghost—not him! . . . I have been free and happy, yet his Ghost has never haunted me." (*T*, 25–28)

It is a strange banker who makes trips in dank coaches and across rough water to tell his client that "there has been no discovery, of money, or of any other property," who imagines that he has clients with neither property nor money to speak of. But banking in this novel is an entirely formal occupation—it trades in families and relation rather than property. Or, when property does seem involved, it's because it's been redefined as family history, and banking is just the practice of "carry[ing] over" "accounts" (*T*, 269) from one generation to the next. In the absence of "money, or of any other property," one can always (indeed, one always does) inherit one's parents.

In this arrangement the financial inheritance that defines aristocracy's hold on property looks like a second-order translation of blood into money, biology into property. Neither money nor title, what Lucie inherits from her father is, rather, "a forehead with a singular capacity [of] lifting and knitting itself into an expression." "The young forehead" is capable of "lift[ing] itself into that singular expression," but this "expression" turns out to be "characteristic, besides being singular" (*T*, 23)—singular, that is, but in its singularity shared, characteristic of a group. Although it seems odd to stage an inheritance drama around a body part as mundane as a forehead, forehead may work even better than property in dramatizing identity-by-inheritance. Unlike spendable "money" or some alienable "other property," a forehead seems far less separable from the question of who one is. Once we start thinking of faces as inherited property, we are much closer to seeing identity not as something that we just have, in some *sui generis* way, but as something that we *come into*.

Putting the matter in this way makes *A Tale* seem a little like *Dombey and Son*, perhaps Dickens's most emphatic account of the idea that individuals might inherit who they are. In *Dombey and Son*, though, this way of thinking will be set up as the object of critique and the plot predicated on its eventual abandonment. To treat people as property is, in *Dombey and Son*, a moral mistake. In *A Tale*, by contrast, there no such revelation of error—no return to deep and authentic sentiment. Quite the opposite: the conclusion's famous twist depends on one person's taking over the debt on someone else's account. Carton's final words, famous as they are, arrive with the odd, objective neutrality of a comparative assessment ("a far, far better thing I do, than I have ever done" [*T*, 390]), and the narrative—as if to limit even further what might have been an impassioned final statement—seals those last words off in a counterfactual time ("if he had given any utterance to his [thoughts], . . . they would have been these" [*T*, 389]). The counterfactual positioning means that Carton's last words only *could have* been his (not that they actually were); the comparative phrasing suggests that they could have been anyone's (that anyone could see that this thing is better).[24] Redemption: the telos that in, say, the conversion of Scrooge requires a sentimental revolution is, in *A Tale*, returned to a purely formal, virtually economic transactionalism. And it's to supply such a system's need for a universal equivalent that all our heroes in this novel—Lucie, Lorry, Charles, Carton—are set up to be versions of one another: to be singular—yes—but above all to be "characteristic," not just to *have* an "expression" but to be able to function as one.

Thus the value of Lucie's forehead's—its ability to identify her—results not from the fact that no one else has a forehead like that but from the fact that someone else (her father) does, just as Carton's final value results from his ability to stand in for someone else. Woloch will call this, writing of Austen, "the transformation of characters into characteristics" and describe it as part of the inequality machine that conserves inner representation for the well-to-do.[25] In *A Tale*, though, it's difficult to maintain that kind of critique of inequality since everyone is dealing with what the novel calls "second-hand cares" (*T*, 20)—Mr. Lorry, whose fundamental job is to see that no one's cares are ever entirely their own, is always near at hand. When Ms. Pross, Lucie's caretaker, enters after Lucie has lost consciousness at the news of her father's existence, her question's amusing fussiness—"Look at her, with her pretty face and her cold hands. Do you call *that* being a Banker?"—does not obscure for an "exceedingly disconcerted" (*T*, 30) Lorry the fact that its answer is yes. As Mr. Lorry's exceeding unease admits, banking is a practically necromantic (pretty faces, cold hands) affair, one in which the living and the dead share an account. "How many accounts with Tellson's never to be balanced in this world," the novel muses, and "must be carried over into the next; no man could have said that night any more than Mr. Jarvis Lorry could" (*T*, 269). The novel returns with some frequency to the ghostliness of banking—the carrying of accounts over to another life: "As was natural, the head-quarters and great gathering-place of Monseigneur, in London, was Tellson's Bank. Spirits are supposed to haunt the places where their bodies most resorted, and Monseigneur without a guinea haunted the spot where his guineas used to be. Moreover, it was the spot to which such French intelligence . . . came quickest. . . . Tellson's was at that time, as to French intelligence, a kind of High Exchange" (*T*, 244). Like a repetition of the connection between the insurance industry and the public sphere (born together at Lloyd's London coffee shop), at Tellson's the linked currencies of money, information, and family ties—and of information and family ties even after the guineas are gone—stitch together the living and the dead, the patriot and the expatriate. If others of Dickens's works—*Bleak House, Dombey and Son, A Christmas Carol*—have led us to see the transactional realms of law and finance as soulless affairs, here we are presented with the opposite view. Banking's focus on inheritances and estates, like the idea that one might have to (or be able to) settle accounts in the hereafter, is absolutely dependent on a view of individuals as the faces (what Lloyd's of London knows as "Names") for bundled, essentially institutional accounts. The individualist mindset of modern finance—that most bourgeois of provinces—thus conserves an essentially aristocratic intuition in the idea that one does not only acquire wealth of property but *transmits* it, hands it down.

A Tale renders this paradoxical system—in which every individualist is also thinking like an aristocrat—by constantly presenting the biological family as if it were as institutional as any bank. The result is that children start to look like ghostly versions of their fathers and vice versa: "I am going to see his Ghost! It will be his Ghost—not him," says Lucie. Without the convention of aristocratic succession (in which there is only one lord at a time) to mark the dead from the living, the biologization/bourgeoisification of the family causes everyone to look like a ghost—as if everyone were inheriting from everyone else at once. The novel, once entitled *Buried Alive*, runs enough mutations on the phrase "recalled to life" to suggest that there is no birth that is not a rebirth. The phrase "recalled to life" itself, Lorry tells us, is valuable not because of its untranslatable specificity but because of its generality. It may, he says, "mean anything" and "comprehend[s]" his "credentials, entries, and memoranda" (*T,* 29). A catch-all in the truest sense, the phrase's comprehension of "anything" and everything makes even future additions to its meaning—"entries, and memoranda"—look like recollections. The phrase is simply the semantic version of the fact that Lucie's daughter is named Lucie or that the line of children Carton's death makes possible are named Sydney. Where even future people appear as commemorative editions it's no surprise that the present should be understood as an echo: "[His voice] was like the last feeble echo of a sound made long and long ago. So entirely had it lost the life and resonance of the human voice, that it affected the senses like a once beautiful color faded away into a poor weak stain. So sunken and suppressed it was that it was like a voice underground" (*T,* 42). The attenuated version of some other original person: recovered people are not colors; they're stains.

Even Lucie, as we see more of her, is less a character than a principle of formal connection and, importantly, of equal distribution: "Ever busily winding the golden thread that bound them all together, weaving the service of her happy influence through the tissue of all their lives, and making it predominate nowhere" (*T,* 218). The golden thread may, of course, testify that Lucie is as much the (blonde, of course) angel of the household as, say, *Bleak House*'s Esther. It also, though, lays an important emphasis on what's economic about domestic economy. The problem of the household, here, is not that it finally cannot hold up against the pressure of institutional structures but that it is itself an institutional structure. And the problem with institutional structures is not that they don't care about souls but that they could not exist without them. In a world with no vocabulary for the extension of the individual past the boundaries of their physical existence, people who die are just dead. In a world structured by the extension of the individual past their physical borders, the fact that no one dies is the correlative of no one's ever really living. The death's-head compulsion formerly reserved for the *mortmain* of property is here no longer restricted to Portias with wealthy fathers; it has become the inalienable inheritance of anyone with a dad.

Like the birth that grounds Robespierre's notion of equal citizenship—absolutely equal because entirely unavoidable: they tell the world, Robespierre complained, "that there are men without birth, as if any living man had not been born"—the ineluctability of family is made clear in the novel's linkage of the two characters who ought to be most opposed in their conception of the family's structure.[26] Both the novel's most vehement revolutionary, Madame Defarge, and the novel's most entitled aristocrat, the Monseigneur d'Evremonde, understand themselves as familial representatives rather than discrete individuals. In the coalescence of these two ostensibly opposed positions, we can see how different Dickens's imagination of the French Revolution was from the description Thomas Paine famously gave of it:

> There never did, there never will, and there never can exist a parliament, or any description of men, or any generation of men, in any country, possessed of the right or the power of binding and controlling posterity to the "end of time." . . . Every age and generation must be free to act for itself, in all cases, as the ages and generation which preceded it. The vanity and presumption of governing beyond the grave, is the most ridiculous and insolent of all tyrannies.
>
> Man has no property in man; neither has any generation a property in the generations which are to follow. . . . It is the living, and not the dead, that are to be accommodated. When man ceases to be, his power and his wants cease with him; and having no longer any participation in the concerns of this world, he has no longer any authority in directing who shall be its governors.[27]

Paine's claim in the *Rights of Man* is premised on a very powerful rejection of the rights of the dead. The point, for Paine, of restricting the duration of political arrangements to the term of a natural life is to curtail the kind of ghostly continuities for which the family in Dickens's novel is the most fertile ground. Paine, here, is basically indifferent to property as a material matter, but he is explicitly concerned with it as an *immaterial* one. Where the ghostly monseigneurs derive comfort from their ghostly guineas, Paine sees property's immateriality as the source of its tyrannical persistence. For this reason his rejection of the notion that a generation might have "property in the generations which are to follow" is premised on his reassertion of the material facts of life. Paine wants to insist that death means only and entirely death: "When a man ceases to be . . . he has no longer any authority." Dickens's novel, then, is remarkable for setting one *Rights of Man* against another, for critiquing the French Revolution on the very grounds Paine found for admiring it. Nowhere is this critique more clear than in the novel's refusal to provide an alternative to the "governing beyond the grave" Paine sought to abolish.

Their names' aristocratic preposition of origin is only the first indication that both Defarge's and d'Evremonde's will both represent the opposite of Paine's pastless subject. This is not to say that Madame Defarge doesn't imagine the revolution as a chance for personal vengeance, only that her sense of what is personal to her requires a family as thoroughly institutionalized as any aristocrat's:

> I was brought up among fisherman of the sea shore [Madame tells us], and that peasant family so injured by the two Evremonde brothers . . . is my family. . . . That sister of the mortally wounded boy on the ground was my sister, that husband was my sister's husband, that unborn child was their child, that brother was my brother, that father was my father, those dead are my dead, and that summons to answer for those things descends directly to me! (*T*, 354)

The origins Madame describes are personal insofar as they are no one else's—like Carton's number or Barsad's nose, they identify—but they are also strongly extrapersonal insofar as they depend on a model of appropriation by which "those dead" become "my dead." Madame's status as the novel's most explicit embodiment of the revolution is directly related to her sense of herself as the inheritor of the experiences of others. The French Revolution is not, in this sense, opposed to nobility but, in fact, extends it by ensuring that even families without property have "those things [which] descend." This version of identity is in complete keeping with the description the novel will provide of its Everynoble figure, Monseigneur: "Monseigneur had the other truly noble idea, that the world was made for them. The text of his order (altered from the original by only a pronoun, which is not much) ran: The earth and the fullness thereof are mine, saith Monseigneur" (*T*, 109). What is "truly noble," here, is the alteration "by only a pronoun" that allows what belongs to someone else to be understood as one's own. A sense of entitlement—"that the world was made for them"—no longer requires a title, just a change of pronoun—"which is not much": "that sister . . . was my sister," "that brother . . . was my brother," "those dead are my dead."

It is not surprising that Madame imagines that the harm done to those close to her requires her to seek out those responsible for the harm, but by the time she makes the above speech she already knows that both of the Evremonde brothers responsible for it are dead. By seeing her project as the persecution of a family (rather than the prosecution of a harm), the category of individual action disappears. This is the force of Madame's thinking of Evremonde not just as a name that certain people have but as a "race": "I have this race a long time on my register doomed to destruction and extermination" (*T*, 353). Because she thinks Evremonde is a race, Charles can belong to it without his ever having done anything bad to her family and even after—since he's turned over the family lands to its tenants—his having done a fair amount of good. It also makes clear why Charles's change of last name, from Evremonde to an anglicized version of his mother's maiden name, matters so little: it may mark his personal displeasure, but it will not exempt him (nothing could) from his race. As the system of racial identification lends no weight to Charles's personal history, it also deletes even the action Madame thinks she is avenging. Madame can take herself as not needing to have any feelings in particular about Charles because once the task is the extermination of the family, individual stories disappear, and this is as true for the stories of a family's rapists as it is for the stories of its most benevolent members.

The father's rapacity and the son's charity don't outweigh each other since neither one carries any weight: who the revolution thinks you are is not a matter of what you have or haven't done. On June 22, 1791, Robespierre made a speech in front of the Constituent Assembly arguing against the death penalty. He did so on basically utilitarian grounds similar to the ones Cesare Beccaria popularized in his 1764 *On Crimes and Punishments*, namely, that "the death penalty is unjust" and that "it multiplies crimes more than it prevents them."[28] On December 3, 1792, Robespierre made another speech, this time arguing for the execution of Louis XVI. What looks like a wholesale reversal on capital punishment, though, has to do not with a change of heart on the death penalty but on Robespierre's insistence that the king, unlike some other possible convict, is not and never could be on trial precisely because he is not an individual. "There is no question of a trial," Robespierre says and blasts the Assembly for having been "drawn far from the actual question" by misunderstanding the roles involved: "Louis is not an accused; and you are not judges; you are only, and can only be, statesmen, the representatives of the nation."[29] Judges judge actions; representatives just represent. And what Louis represents, Robespierre argues, is the natural antithesis to what the representatives of the republic represent: "When a nation has been forced to resort to the right of insurrection it returns to the state of nature as regards its tyrant ... the effect of tyranny and insurrection is to break [the social contract] entirely as regards the tyrant ... it is to throw them into mutual war." "Insurrection" isn't a response to injustice in the way a trial is the response to a crime because tyranny isn't an illegal action; it's a failed representative order. It's not always clear, in Robespierre's speech, which side—the tyranny or the insurrection—made the first leap from contract to representation, but like an early version of mutually assured destruction (Robespierre's "mutual war"), once you're there, we're there. Unlike the state of law, which hands out sentences in relation to actions, the state of nature Robespierre describes is suddenly, irreversibly zero-sum:"Peoples do not judge like judiciary courts. They pass no sentences; they hurl the thunderbolt. They do not condemn kings; they thrust them back into oblivion."[30]

I know of no study claiming that Dickens was reading texts of Robespierre's speeches in the run-up to writing *A Tale of Two Cities* (though one imagines versions might have been somewhere in the boxes Carlyle packed up for him), but the echoes of the "oblivion" that lies on the other side of Robespierre's categorical antitheses are unavoidable in Madame Defarge's "doctrine" of "extermination" (*T*, 353). In fact, a discussion between Madame and her husband rather exactly restages the question between Robespierre and the Assembly over the execution of Louis XVI. Madame has her "doctrine" of "extermination," and, like Robespierre's statesmen, her job is not to "pass ... sentences" but to deal in "oblivion." Monsieur Defarge, by contrast, understands "extermination" as something akin to a series of individual verdicts. And because he's thinking of "extermination" as just a lot of individual death sentences, Monsieur Defarge's question is about how to know when one has punished enough:

> "It is true what madame says," observed Jacques Three. "Why stop? There is great force in that. Why stop?"
>
> "Well, well," reasoned Defarge, "but one must stop somewhere. After all, the question is still where?"
>
> "At extermination," said madame.
>
> . . .
>
> "Extermination is good doctrine, my wife," said Defarge, rather troubled; "in general, I say nothing against it. But this Doctor has suffered much; you have seen him to-day; you have observed his face when the paper was read."
>
> . . .
>
> "As to thee," pursued madame, implacably addressing her husband, "if it depended on thee—which, happily, it does not—thou wouldst rescue this man even now."
>
> "No!" protested Defarge. "Not if to lift this glass would do it! But I would leave the matter there. I say, stop there." (*T*, 352–353)

The immediate question at hand is the execution of Charles, but the discussion is not about whether he should be executed; both Madame and Monsieur think he should die. The difference (one cannot, really, even call it a disagreement) between the couple has to do with whether extermination is a personal question, with whether Charles is in fact at issue in his own execution. Monsieur Defarge acts as if each person were to be given an up-or-down vote by the revolutionary tribunal. Madame, whose doctrine of extermination treats people as if they were neither personal nor meaningfully personalizable, doesn't imagine that these are individual rulings. This, of course, is the point of her suggestion that Monsieur is acting as if something depended on him ("if it depended on thee") and her snide quip about it being fortunate that "it does not."

In a certain sense she's right. These demonstrations of Madame's "doctrine" allow her to come out looking like the objective one, like the one with reasons that lie outside of her own feelings. When the question moves from Charles to Charles's wife, Lucie, to their daughter (also Lucie), and then to Lucie Darnay's father, Dr. Manette, the weakness of Monsieur's reliance on personal feeling becomes almost immediately clear. Sympathy for Dr. Manette, for whom Monsieur Defarge worked and served as a caretaker upon his release from prison, or for Lucie looks like an argument for leniency toward Charles: "It is very strange," Defarge will say, "now, at least is it not very strange that, after all our sympathy for Monsieur her father, and herself, her husband's name should be proscribed under your hand at this moment?" (*T*, 192–193). There is, for Monsieur, a kind of natural trickle-down effect to sympathy. But the effect, a few steps down the chain, though, is that one begins to appear inconsistent, almost whimsical. The stopping point in which he is so interested can only have an arbitrary end determined by some sentimental fiat: "I would leave the matter there. I say, stop there." Madame, by contrast, is one side in Robespierre's "mutual war"; unlike her husband, she is not ruling on individuals, and because she's not ruling on individuals she's never going to be inconsistent. So programmatic as to be tautological, extermination stops "at extermination."

The novel goes on to provide a scene that literalizes the emphasis on position (rather than personality) entailed by Madame's zero-sum logic. In advocating the execution of Charles, Madame is firmly within an identitarian logic premised on blood, but the question becomes more vexed when it comes to the execution of Charles's father-in-law, Dr. Manette, long the figure of revolutionary sympathy and tied to Charles, after all, only by the legal bonds of his daughter's marriage. Madame, it appears, has no particular interest in killing Dr. Manette—"This Doctor . . . may wear his head or lose it, for any interest I have in him; it is all one to me" (*T*, 373)—but given that Lucie is to die and Dr. Manette *is* related to her, why not? "I cannot speak of one without the other," says Madame, "and I must not be silent"

(*T*, 374). So that's that: those who share a sentence share a sentence. Virtually grammatical in its operations (recall, for example, "the daughter of your father"), Madame Defarge's doctrine here widens from a genocidal principle to a social one: the prosecution of blood expands to become the prosecutions of association. If Monsieur's model of judgment is sentiment, Madame's is syntax, as if wrong place, wrong time were especially indicting rather than absolving circumstances.

On the other side of the class divide, an identical problem comes to the fore in Charles's discussions with his uncle, the Marquis d'Evremonde. Like Madame, Charles will find himself "unable to speak of one without the other": "Why need I," he asks his uncle, "speak of my father's time, when it is equally yours? Can I separate my father's twin-brother, joint inheritor, and next successor from himself?" (*T*, 129). Charles, of course, no more thinks his father and his uncle are the same person than Madame Defarge imagines that Lucie and her father share a body. But what's being underlined in both these moments is the possibility that being a separate body is no grounds for separation. Charles's objection to the family as a set of social structures ("joint inheritor, and next successor") is only exacerbated by the biological rarities of twin brothers:

> "Sir," said the nephew, "we have done wrong, and are reaping the fruits of wrong."
>
> "*We* have done wrong?" repeated Marquis, with an inquiring smile, delicately pointing first to his nephew then to himself.
>
> "Our family; our honourable family, whose honour is of so much account to both of us, in such different ways. Even in my father's time we did a world of wrong, injuring every human creature who came between us and our pleasures, whatever it was." (*T*, 128–129)

Charles is laying out a pretty standard complaint against the aristocracy: that, backed by the privilege of title, they set about the satisfaction individual whims ("whatever" they are). But as the Marquis's "delicate" mock fingering of himself indicates, the real privilege of nobility is that one's individual whim was never exactly individual. The entitlement of noble action is not the ability to do anything; instead, because guilt doesn't accrue to noble agents any more than it accrues to justified sinners, it is the appearance of never having done anything at all. For this reason, Charles will describe himself as "bound to a system that is frightful to me, responsible for it, but powerless in it; seeking to execute the last request of my dear mother's lips" (*T*, 129). What looks to Charles like powerlessness, that is, looks to the Marquis like immunity.

Though they differ in their feelings about it, Charles and his uncle share a position, and though they would probably be surprised to hear it, Marquis and Madame share one too. If it seems strange to describe nobles as disenfranchised by their title, it is equally strange that the novel's revolutionary should argue for the absence of individualism as a condition with its own "consolation":

> Vengeance and retribution take a long time; it is the rule. . . . How long . . . does it take to make and store the lightning? . . . It does not take a long time . . . for an earthquake to swallow a town. Eh well! Tell me how long it takes to prepare an earthquake? . . . But when it is ready, it takes place, and grinds to pieces everything before it. In the meantime, it is always preparing, though it is not seen or heard. That is your consolation. Keep it. (*T*, 185)

Vengeance that rolls down like water may be "consolation," but it isn't justice. The natural rhythms of birth and death that Paine thought could secure a clean political slate for each new generation are forsaken here in favor of chronological metrics large enough to ensure the insignificance of any individual lifespan. The "consolation" for individual injustice, as Madame lays it out, lies not in the possibility of its redress in one's lifetime but in a faith, religious in all but name, that while the injustice of the moment may be your earthquake, it will not be the last one the world will see. Death by family, earthquake, or lightning feels unjust (no one, as Oliver Wendell Holmes Jr. observed in Chapter 1, *deserves* lightning), but it may be (as in fact Holmes argued) a mistake to think of them as questions of justice in the first place. People, Robespierre said, don't judge like tribunals, they "hurl the thunderbolt," and Madame, likewise, doesn't think she's judging: "Tell the wind and the fire where to stop. But don't tell me." For individuals who think of themselves as nature's agents, death means nothing at all. "Not to the death. . . . It is not necessary to say, to death," the Marquis tells Charles. "I will die, perpetuating the system under which I have lived" (*T*, 129).

What we are seeing in Dickens's novel, then, is an analysis of the surprisingly anti-individual implications of natural rights—rights, that is, that invoke the state of nature as a warrant. Edmund Burke, as Lord Acton would after him, saw the French Revolution as a case study in individualism out of control: a society governed by nothing, Acton wrote, but "bare cupidity and vengeance . . . brutal instinct and hideous passion."[31] But what we have seen emerging in Robespierre's understanding of the event as well as in Madame and d'Evremonde's understanding of their position in it is the way this clash of representative ontologies (the aristocracy and the people) deletes the possibility of individual action. When Acton rehearses some facts of Robespierre's biography—that he would die "leaving less than twenty guineas in depreciated assignats" and that "he lived on a deputy's allowance of eighteen francs a day"—he does so as if this modesty were an ironic counterweight to Robespierre's political self-aggrandizement. But in putting it that way, Acton is missing the more important fact that *both* the modesty and the magnification derive from Robespierre's understanding of himself as, above all, a "deputy." When Acton describes Robespierre's "private life [as] inoffensive and decent" in contrast with the bloodiness of his public one, he misses what was most radical in Robespierre's claims—their wholesale refusal of the private life—for a much more typical (and classically liberal) distinction/contradiction between one's public conduct and one's private virtues.[32]

You behead sworn friends and former schoolmates (at Robespierre's behest George Danton and Camille Desmoulins would be executed on the same day in 1794) for the same reason that you live on eighteen francs a day: you work for the people, not yourself. It is for the same reason, too, that Mr. Lorry, however comedic or benignly stammering he may appear, should nevertheless be understood as being in perfect seriousness when he says that these are "mere business relations." "No matter what individual qualities or defects a man may have," Hannah Arendt writes, "once he has entered the maelstrom of an unending process of expansion, he will, as it were, cease to be what he was and obey the laws of the process, identify himself with anonymous forces that he is supposed to serve . . . he will think of himself as mere function, and eventually consider such functionality . . . his highest possible achievement."[33] Arendt is writing about imperialism (and about Cecil Rhodes in particular), but her description could equally serve for Robespierre or Mr. Lorry—two embodiments of the "laws of process" that, as John Forster noted above, govern both the novel's formal ambitions and the revolution it takes as its subject. What Dickens and Arendt help us see, then, is the French Revolution's key role in the incorporation—the thoroughgoing corporatization—of modernity. Colonial trading companies, multinational banks, and democratic nations all now sit alongside the older corporate persons who are aristocrats and monarchs: as far as their deleterious effects on individualism go, these "laws of process" and "anonymous forces" are the same; what has changed (by exponentially increasing) is their scale.

Like Arendt, who ties the "death factories" of Germany into a longer rise of totalitarianism within Western history, Dickens's novel will locate death as the French Revolution's absolute political—or, better, biopolitical—aspiration.[34] A satirical cartoon of the revolutionary time depicts the guillotining of Sanson, the executioner under the Terror. In a shift from the usual view of these cartoons, which typically feature Sanson holding the head of the guillotine's latest victim out to an incredibly dense crowd of onlookers, this particular cartoon has traded the crowds of spectators for a crowd of guillotines that overlook what appears to be the second-to-last execution in France, as Robespierre prepares to behead the executioner. A second cartoon completes the trajectory as Robespierre, now apparently the last person in France, lies on the machine, his arm still in position to operate the blade in an awkward, but apparently successful, effort to take off his own head. As both these cartoons indicate, there is in these representations an apocalyptic fascination with last things. Like the political version of artistic minimalism, the purest republic is the republic that has done away with representation by doing away with all its representatives. "What we need," Robespierre wrote, "is a single will," but the trick of the single will is that it looks self-identical—single—not when there is just one will but when there are *no* more personal wills for it to include. As long as there are individual wills, the generality of the general will is a fiction. These cartoons and Dickens's novel combine to show us that the event, which looked like the greatest expansion of popular representation the world had seen, in fact bore within it the desire to do away with representation altogether, to have a republic that *was* the people rather than just their reflection—a republic that could, like Coleridge's symbol in Chapter 1, body forth the general will rather than simply stand (as a sign) for it. The result is not a politics of consensus because the general will does not amount to (or allow) compromise or the reconciliation of individual differences; the result is, rather, Madame Defarge's dream of "extermination," Robespierre's dream of "annihilation."

As Sydney Carton's conversation with the Wood-sawyer—the character who is the guillotine's greatest enthusiast within the novel—makes clear, the guillotine is not an instrument of punishment that supports the Republic; it is the Republic:

> "How goes the Republic?"
>
> "You mean the guillotine. Not ill. Sixty-three today. We shall mount to a hundred soon. Samson and his men complain something of being exhausted. Ha, ha, ha! He is so droll. Such a Barber!"
>
> "Do you often go to see him—"
>
> "Shave? Always. . . . Go and see him when he has a good batch. Figure this to yourself, citizen; he shaved the sixty-three today, in less than two pipes!"
>
> (*T*, 324)

In the Wood-sawyer's enthusiasm for scale and speed ("sixty-three today, in less than two pipes") we see an inversion of the innovation in punishment Joseph-Ignace Guillotin had meant to bring about in inventing the machine that now bears his name. Guillotin argued that a death sentence should inflict only death and not, say, torture or the collateral damage of visible suffering or the shaming appearance of sexual arousal that hanging can produce. By minimizing the personal depths involved in execution, Guillotin hoped to clarify the connection between individual crime, sentence, and punishment. But here we see that individualizing goal—to deliver a fate more precisely to an individual—perfectly inverted by a government that used the machine to serialize executions and make death a mechanism of membership. For what's republican about the guillotine is that it ensures no one dies individually, that everyone dies, as Robert Wringhim might put it, by "the slump." The guillotine, that is, does not just publicize the individual moment of death; it pluralizes it. It is hardly beside the point that Sanson (the family name of the executioner, itself an inherited position) might really be joking about being tired. The guillotine replaced the laborious infliction of individual agony with an operation so quick as to be barely observable, and what impresses the Wood-sawyer is the number of sentences it has become possible to carry out in a day's shaving. If Kafka's penal colony develops this trend even further, by imagining a machine capable of individually tailored sentences, the guillotine insists that one size fits all.[35]

The novel picks up on the guillotine's erasure of individuality by making the notion of a singular execution seem beside the point. Far from confining the trope of numbers to Carton's execution, death is throughout imagined to be an aggregate experience. Even the tumbrils that cart the lots of condemned are counted: "One. Two. Three. Three tumbrils" (*T*, 290). It is this serial repetition of death and its associates that Sir James Fitzjames Stephen pointed out in one of the novel's earliest and still most scathing reviews:

> Almost any subject will do, because the pathetic power of the scene lies in
> the fact of the death; and the artifice employed consists simply in enabling the
> notion of death to be reiterated at short intervals by introducing a variety of
> irrelevant trifles which suspend attention, and allow it after an interval to revert
> to death with the additional impulse derived from the momentary contrast.
> The process of doing this to almost any extent is so simple that it becomes,
> with practice, almost mechanical. To describe the light and shade of the room
> in which the body lies, the state of the bedclothes, the conversation of the
> servants, the sound of the undertaker's footsteps, the noise of driving the coffin
> screws, and any number of other minutiae, is in effect a device for working on
> the feelings by repeating at intervals, Death-death-death-death-death.[36]

Stephen's review reads much like a critique of Edgar Allan Poe's "Philosophy of Composition" (a text that begins by naming *Barnaby Rudge*, Dickens's other novel of revolution and beheading). What Stephen is noticing (though clearly not appreciating) is the importance for both Poe and Dickens of terminal results. Poe's famous plan for art does not simply suggest starting with where the story ends and then figuring out how to get there. Instead, the essay develops into the recommendation that we begin with an effect (an affect, really) and then set about repeatedly producing it. As Poe's essay progresses, it becomes less and less about how one gets to the end of *"The Raven"*'s plot—since, as a dialogue that consists almost entirely of conclusions ("nevermore"), it doesn't really have one—and becomes increasingly about how many senses of an ending a single poem might be structured to provide. The "-ore" phoneme—the saddest sound—is tied to the saddest scene—the death of a beautiful woman—and the interest of repeating "Nevermore" is not just to indicate that Lenore is dead but to tell us, as Stephen would say, that she's "Dead-dead-dead-dead-dead." And what Stephen imagines as grounds for a critique—that this kind of mechanically produced sensation is so simple even a raven could do it—is, for Poe as for Dickens, less interesting than the revelation that only a raven could:

> In observing the difficulty which I had at once found in inventing a sufficiently plausible reason for its continuous repetition, I did not fail to perceive that this difficulty arose solely from the pre-assumption that the word was to be so continuously or monotonously spoken by a *human* being—I did not fail to perceive, in short, that the difficulty lay in the reconciliation of this monotony with the exercise of reason on the part of the creature repeating the word. Here, then, immediately arose the idea of a non-reasoning creature capable of speech.[37]

Poe settles on the raven for the same reason we see Mr. Lorry describe himself as a "mere machine"—"a non-reasoning creature capable of speech." In both Poe's aesthetic theory and Dickens's French Revolution the realm of human experience—of life, and personality, and feeling—has been replaced by institutional structures so thoroughly that the human appears, if at all, as merely sentimental static that needs to be muted in order for the impersonal personality of a structure to give itself voice. These texts thus suggest not only that personality might be accorded to unconscious objects—Corporations, Republics, Ravens, Mr. Lorrys, Tumbrils, Guillotines—but that we have arrived at a timeless, interiority-less world in which what we used to think of as a personality has no place at all. "Above all, one hideous figure grew as familiar as if it had been before the general gaze from the foundations of the world—the figure of the sharp female called La guillotine" (*T*, 264). A snapshot of the world after persons, Dickens's sublime image captures the "general gaze" staring at its eloquent, nonreasoning mother forever.

As many historical sources point out, when Guillotin presented his device (it had not yet been given his name) he was not so much presenting a new invention as making an argument for the popularization of beheading.[38] Death by beheading was nothing new, and similar machines had been used around Europe for several centuries, but it had been typically reserved for nobles and aristocrats, with the lower classes left the grosser ordeals of hanging. Dickens does not miss the democratic impulse behind Guillotin's arguments for decapitation: "Two score and twelve were told off. From the farmer general of seventy, whose riches could not save him to the seamstress of twenty, whose poverty and obscurity could not save her . . . The frightful moral disorder . . . smote equally and without distinction" (*T*, 360). In decapitation—in its mechanical method and its depersonalizing effects—Dickens finds the clearest instantiation of the life without distinction the French Revolution sought to establish. The guillotine is not just a (not-so) new way of administering death but looks like an improvement on the leveling work that has more or less always been claimed for it:

> Death is Nature's remedy for all things, and why not Legislation's? Accordingly, the forger was put to Death; the utterer of a bad note was put to Death; the unlawful opener of a letter was put to Death; the purloiner of forty shillings and sixpence was put to Death; the holder of a horse at Tellson's door who made off with it was put to death . . . the sounders of three-fourths of the notes in the whole gamut of Crime were put to death. Not that it did the least good in the way of prevention—it might have almost been worth remarking that the fact was exactly the reverse—but it cleared off (as to this world) the trouble of each particular case, and left nothing else connected with it to be looked after. (*T*, 56)

Death looks natural not because it is an organic process—hanging and decapitation, obviously, aren't—but because, like all organic processes (Robespierre's "thunderbolt," say, or Madame's "lightning"), it is indifferent to both person and personality. The novel describes death, in an inversion of Robespierre's comment on the inevitability of birth, as our "natural and not to be alienated inheritance," according to which "the messenger on horseback had exactly the same possession as the King" (*T*, 15). It's not a new move: it runs back at least to Odysseus's visits to the underworld, in which distinctions are no longer operative, or to Lucian's description of the afterlife as a place where the dead all look like the same person. But if all death performs this equalizing work—erasing the distinctions of wealth, station, and talent—it remains a state to which people are thought to arrive in their own good time or, even in the case of capital punishment, on some conception of their merits. "La guillotine" washes away these last shreds of individuality in a way that only an artificial and arbitrary machine could: promising that one might now mass produce death's defining indistinction. Death by art, unlike death by nature or death by punishment, need no longer stoop to correcting the illusions of individuality individually. If what made natural death natural was its indifference to "each particular case"—that is, death is natural because it's beyond our choosing—the massified, artificial death in the Terror is even more natural for clearing away "the trouble" of imagining that there ever was such a thing as a personal case in the first place. "Legislation's" end turns out to be the remedy for "Nature's remedy." The guillotine, by delivering people in batches to an identical death in the name of the republic, made it impossible for individuals to think even of their deaths as their own.

The guillotine is thus not simply an instrument of political maintenance but a significant emblem of political achievement. The fact that the Terror led to the death of many innocents is not, for this novel, just a regrettable fact of history; it is also the signal fact of its political arrangement and the logical outcome of the depersonalized ontologies it imagined. The irrelevance of innocence (or guilt) in the time of Terror is a statement about the irrelevance of the individual, and it is this irrelevance that makes the Terror a terror and not just a particularly draconian set of laws. By making a law out of suspicion, the French Revolution did more than to encourage individuals to act on their most worst impulses by inventing information about innocent neighbors in retaliation for petty aggravations. More broadly, the Law of the Suspected provided a method for the instant translation of the personal into the public; calling everyone an Enemy of the People ensured that there was no such thing as a personal suspicion or a private dispute. And the guillotine, for the same reasons, is not really a punishment; it neither punishes action nor encourages individuals to police their own. It is, rather, the machine that teaches the people it is meant to serve its indifference toward them and their indifference from one another.

If the guillotine is a machine personified by family name, the novel does, I've argued, provide it with plenty of company. Madame's insistence that her target is not a person but a "race," Monseigneur's insistence that his birth is his "natural destiny," Charles's discovery that the allotments of social station are unadjustable by personal action, Mr. Lorry's sense of his profession as a "great trust not his own," Lucie's status as a "golden thread": these are, I've argued, all versions of the same story in which an individual ability to stand for a group obviates the claims of anything internal to them. And it's under these depersonalizing because personifying lights that we need to return to

Sydney Carton and the logic of redemption we touched on earlier. His death at the end of the novel looks redemptive, and it is a much-loved scene. But it's hard to imagine that substituting one person for another is going to wash clean a plot made bloody by treating individuals as exchangeable units. His death may change the tone of the plot—from vengeance to sacrifice—but it alters neither its impersonal logic nor its mortifying force.[39] It's true that Carton's hypothetical last words imagine the guillotine converted from a machine of depersonalized vengeance into one of individualized "retribut[ion]": "I see Barsad, and Cly, Defarge, The Vengeance, the Juryman, the Judge, long ranks of the new oppressors who have risen on the destruction of the old, perishing by this retributive instrument, before it shall cease out of its present use" (*T*, 389). But the inclusion of revolutionary abstractions (The Vengeance, the Juryman, the Judge) alongside actual persons and the seemingly endless ranks of the condemned ("the long ranks of the new oppressors") point to an open-ended and thoroughly biopolitical (rather than retributive) future: one that conducts itself in terms of populations rather than persons and is, therefore, a permanent stranger to justice. "Ever busy and ever worse than useless" was how the first pages described a Hangman trying to prosecute a social problem, and there's no reason to think the lesson has ceased to hold. Indeed, when, in a move Bram Stoker will borrow in the final "Note" of *Dracula*, Carton (whose name, as an empty form, has started to take on some weight) projects a series of Sydney Cartons—

> I see that child who lay upon [Lucie's] bosom and who bore my name, a man winning his way up in that path of life which once was mine. I see him winning it so well, that my name is made illustrious there by the light of his. I see the blots I threw upon it, faded away. I see him, fore-most of just judges and honoured men, bringing a boy of my name, with a forehead that I know and golden hair, to this place—then fair to look upon, with not a trace of this day's disfigurement—and I hear him tell the child my story, with a tender and a faltering voice. (*T*, 390)

—we can see that he has begun to think even of himself as both a population and what *The Private Memoirs and Confessions* would call a "traditional history," an endlessly recycled feature of popular memory. Both fully popular and endlessly recycled without ever losing his identity ("my name," "was mine," "my name," "my name," "my story"): the deepest fantasy Carton's never-spoken last words hold forth—one so attractive it hurts to see through it—is that the personal and the popular might, by a romantic symbol or a romantic hero, be held together in a single view, that the "beautiful city" and "brilliant people" our projected Carton projects and the lives he imagines for them ("rising from this abyss," "struggl[ing] to be truly free, in their triumphs and defeats, through long years to come" [*T*, 389]) could somehow be conceivable as the direct effects of the "far, far better" death he has just died. The fantasy of sacrifice is that you might be the first cause of history, and the fantasy of martyrdom is that someone will remember you—tell *your* story "with a tender and faltering voice"—as if you could still be thought of as a person rather than, as Victor Frankenstein will discover, an arbitrary link in the "laws of process" and "anonymous forces." In the fantasized last words the novel dreams for us, everyone still bears a name. But in the actual last words of the novel—"Twenty-three"—no one does.

5. Not World Enough

Easement, Externality, and the Edges of Justice (Caleb Williams)

> And the land was not able to bear them, that they might dwell
> together: for their substance was great, so that they could not
> dwell together. . . .
> And Abram said unto Lot, Let there be no strife, I pray
> thee, between me and thee, and between my herdmen and thy
> herdmen; for we be brethren.
> Is not the whole land before thee? separate thyself, I pray
> thee, from me: if thou wilt take the left hand, then I will go to
> the right; or if thou depart to the right hand, then I will go to
> the left.
>
> —Genesis 13:6, 7–9

> Does the common water make the floods,
> That's common everywhere?
>
> —John Clare, "Distant Hills"

In his 1781 *Essay on the Right to Property in Land*, the Scottish land reformer William Ogilvie proposed some "general outlines" for what he calls "a progressive Agrarian law."[1] At the heart of his plan was the desire to "encrease the number of independent cultivators" under the thought that "of two nations equal in extent of territory and in number of citizens, that may be accounted happiest in which the greatest number of independent cultivators is the greatest."[2] This increase in independent cultivators, Ogilvie thought, could be brought about by redistributing England's territory such that "every citizen aged twenty-one years or upwards [could], if not already in possession of land, be entitled to claim from the public a certain portion not exceeding forty acres."[3] Ogilvie's basic pitch—known to American schoolrooms as Jeffersonianism—takes an interesting angle into a late eighteenth-century land regime increasingly defined by the politics of parliamentary enclosure. The plan is, on the one hand, a form of resistance to enclosure, a way to decrease what Ogilvie calls the "artful strictness" of the "monopoly of land." But the proposal also, we can see, doubles as a plan of enclosure in its own right; the idea is to hive up the national territory into many more and much smaller, but still decidedly private, parcels.[4]

Put up against our conventional ways of understanding the problem of property in the romantic period, Ogilvie's proposal looks like—and is—an outlier, one not easily squared with our deeply entrenched assumption that hostility to private property is the *sine qua non* of radical politics in the period. As useful and familiar as it is, though, that divide (between the pro property and the con) obscures another problem very much alive around 1800, which I want to take up here—a problem not about ownership, exactly, but about sharing or, as we now call it, social cost: how should we handle the inevitable fact that certain resources (like light, air, and water) must be shared and that uses will, sooner or later, interfere? These questions, I will be arguing, are conspicuously neglected by both Ogilvie's propertied utopia and the alternative, antiproperty utopias we see in projects like Coleridge and Southey's pantisocracy and Thomas Spence's radical communalism. Ogilvie's hyperprivatized vision can't account for the fact that some things (say, rivers) have to remain common, and the radical commonality of a pantisocracy can't account for the fact that some things (those same rivers) can only be used in a finite number of ways by a finite number of users.[5] What both of these opposed utopias need, I will argue, is a theory of easement—the section of law that handles use rights—and, as if written to make exactly that point, the dystopia that is *Caleb Williams* shows us what the world looks like without one.

Coleridge and Southey's plan for a propertyless society on the banks of the Susquehanna will likely be known even to casual students of the romantic period, but theirs was only one of many voices in the period arguing for the fundamental unnaturalness and illegitimacy of private property. In a series of lectures, pamphlets, utopian schemes, and a short-lived (but amazingly titled) 1793 periodical called *Pig's Meat; or, Lessons for the Swinish Multitude*, for instance, Thomas Spence argued that the very idea of the ownership of land ran contrary to natural right. In one pamphlet entitled "The Restorer of Society to Its Natural State," for instance, Spence contended that the ownership of land is wrong in exactly the same way that slavery or selling your children is wrong: it involves treating something that is, by natural right, fundamentally above or beyond ownership as if it were a material good like any other.[6] The argument for thinking of access to the land as a natural right was simple. As Article 3 of the constitution for his utopia Spensonia put it, "All human beings, have a continual and inalienable property in the Earth, and its natural productions."[7] "For upon what must [the people] live," Spence asked in a 1775 lecture titled "The Real Rights of Men," "if not upon the productions of the country in which they reside? Surely to deny them that right is in effect denying them a right to live . . . [and] the right to deprive anything of the means of living, supposes a right to deprive it of life."[8] Spence's objection to property in land was, we can see, properly biopolitical. Even if one's exclusive ownership of a certain parcel of land does not *seem* to be immediately or obviously murderous, the very claim to ownership means arrogating to oneself the power to withhold or sustain life, the right to extend life to these ones here at the cost of those over there—a power that, for Spence anyway, no human has (or ought to have) over any other.

It is from arguments like these that our familiar identification of romantic radical antipropertyism emerges. When supplemented by further examples— like Rousseau's thoughts about the first evil genius who, "having enclosed a piece of ground, bethought himself of saying *This is mine*" or even Sir William Blackstone's assertion "that (accurately and strictly speaking) there is no foundation in nature or in natural law" for giving "man an exclusive right to retain in a permanent manner that specific land, which before be- longed generally to every body, particularly to nobody"—a broad chorus of consensus radicalism gets organized around what Jonathan Bate calls the "Rousseauesque" commitment to "a state of nature prior to the fall into property [and] into inequality."[9] To be for property is, in this view, to be against the common, and to be against the common is to be unromantic.

One of the very useful things about Ogilvie's *Essay on the Right to Property in Land*—which is both proequality *and* proproperty—is the pressure it puts on the assumptions underlying this conventional graph of romantic politics. Contrary to our Rousseauesque assumptions, it seems not to have occurred to Ogilvie to see commonality and equality as mutually entailed ends. In- deed, quite the opposite: because equality for Ogilvie *just is* the equality of property in land, achieving equality did not forbid but actually required writing property directly onto the face of the earth. Because equality can be established and maintained only through the comparison of one thing with another, there is no equality without division. Indeed, once presented with Ogilvie's approach to the problem, it becomes possible to see that what Coleridge and Southey were trying to achieve wasn't the end of inequality so much as the establishment of unity or oneness. But unity, for obvious reasons, not only doesn't ensure equality; it actually makes the question of equality—which requires comparing at least two entities—irrelevant. For this reason, Ogilvie's plan to implement equality relied on the separateness of individual persons. There are, he wrote, "two maxim[s] of natural law": on the one hand, there's the fact that we all have a "right to an equal share of the soil"; on the other, there's the fact that "every one, by whose labour . . . the soil has been rendered more fertile, has a right to the additional produce of that fertility."[10] These two rights—equality and individualism—are, he says, bound up and evenly distributed through nature's ground:"The whole extent of soil is affected by both rights at once, and not different parts by each," and "the limits by which their influence and extent may be discriminated from each other, do not readily present themselves to the mind."[11] Property and equality, the suggestion is, arrive originally and permanently entangled, and while it's all too clear that you can be for property without being for equality, it turns out that if you believe in persons you can't really be for equality without also being for property. It's thus that Ogilvie can see the universalization of private ownership as an acknowledgment of our common entitlement to nature's materials rather than, as in Rousseau's fable, civilization's original sin against it.

But while one can see the force of Ogilvie's proposal in theory, it's not necessarily easy to imagine putting it into practice: it's hard to avoid immediately projecting the natural discrepancies that will make equality's establishment either impossible or, at best, merely nominal. Since all land is not arable, and since all arable land is not created equal, and since certain agricultural necessities—particularly the access to water—don't seem to be redistributable even by act of Parliament, there is no way to ensure the equality of any two acreages. The inequality that thinkers like Rousseau and Coleridge see *originating* with the fiat of ownership in fact preexists it; the drawing of lines in the dirt discovers discrepancies even before it enshrines and extends them. If Ogilvie's proposal is going to mitigate these differences, his plan for equality is going to need to include a version of what English property law recognizes under the heading of easements and servitudes—ways of managing the naturally occurring differentials between one parcel and another and of ensuring rights of access to common goods (like a river or a coastline) in spite of the private ownership of adjoining land. But if we add easement to the equation, the "compact form[s]" of Ogilvie's scheme—whose whole point was to insist on equality without having to insist on commonality—start to leak. Once citizens have to cross one another's land or negotiate rights to water, people can't really see themselves as farming exclusively "for their own account." The world's natural inequality—the fact that some parts of it are more upstream than others, say—means that accounts will always have to be, at least in some degree, shared. The commons thus creeps back in, and what makes Ogilvie's scheme for equalizing (rather than abolishing) property finally impossible is the material self-*in*sufficiency of any particular parcel: not the injustice of private property, then; just the impossibility of property's privacy.

One might take this flaw in Ogilvie's scheme as a sign that the Asphereterists (as Coleridge called the antiproperty position) had it right all along—that all property is a lie told against nature. But it's not necessarily the case that simply doing away with property does away with the questions of distribution that Ogilvie was trying to answer. One might, with Coleridge and Southey, generalize individual property as a legal matter, but because this propertyless world is presumably still going to have discrete persons in it (persons who do not understand themselves to be absolutely fungible), and because those discrete persons will be needing things from this world (water, food) and, at least occasionally, bumping into one another in their pursuit of those goods, deleting property does not do away with the problem of how to distribute the commons.

Take, for example, Spence's *Crusonia*. This dialogue between a visitor and one of the members of the egalitarian society set up after Robinson's departure from the island lays out the basic tenets of Spence's utopian vision. In Crusonia there is, first and foremost, no personal ownership of land; instead, every citizen rents from a number of incorporated parishes who are themselves the proprietors. Our Crusonian tour guide testifies at length to the harmony and civilized progress that have resulted from abolishing the private ownership of land. The island, he says, "has more the air of a garden, or rather a paradise, than a general country scene," for it boasts an "infinite number of real gardens," and even the meadows and pastures "are strewed very thick with fruit-trees"; the corn is "cultivated in rows, . . . as carefully as garden-herbs"; the houses are "surprisingly neat," "delightful dwellings" and "are scattered, very rank over the whole country."[12] This vaunted density (infinite gardens! thick trees! rankly scattered dwellings!) is meant, of course, as a proof of prosperity and a preemptive shot at a budding Malthusianism. But for as tightly as he wants to pack his island, Spence does not take up the crucial question of distribution that density raises—of how to share resource X among Y users. Don't worry, Spence's tourguide seems to say, there's enough to go around. But enoughness is hard to know in advance since there are many kinds of scarcity that our rankly scattered lives can produce. What happens when your neighbor sets up a pig farm that damages the river that's irrigating the orchard you've started? Or when he builds a silo so big (for all that corn) that it swamps your garden in shadow? The Crusonian constitution does not say, but it's hard to imagine that the fact that everyone is, Fanny Price–like, a renter rather than an owner is going to keep such issues from rearing their thorny heads. Simply doing away with property does not, this is to say, explain how to live together, and even in a situation based entirely on usufruct uses may well interfere, and certain common resources will need, after all, to be divided.

Sharing, as Ogilvie intuited, thus *requires* some notion of property, some question about the particular distribution of a good to a specific person given a specific place or time. It's true that the kind of property that sharing requires need not look much like property in fee simple: it wouldn't have to be permanent, or exclusive, or alienable. But to the degree that the happy renters of Crusonia are, in fact, happy, it's at least in part because they will have found a way to manage their access to truly common resources like light, air, and water. And managing that access requires being able to say something that is *not exactly* the thing Rousseau's impostor says ("this is mine") but also isn't exactly *unlike* it either. Sharing requires being able to say, *"This (for now) is mine"* or *"I—and not you—am using some of this at the moment."* In a densely settled world ("we encrease continually, laying parish to parish as occasion requires," says Spence's Crusonian tour guide), there is nothing that, in Blackstone's words, belongs "particularly to nobody." Once we live "parish to parish," everything is someone's, at least for now and by fact if not by law, and it's only the presumed plenteousness of certain resources that keeps us able to think of them as the opposite of property: light, water, air—and, if you're Spence, land. For when, as one might expect, the prosperity of Crusonia increases such that "no parish had an uninhabited spot left," the decision is "resolved in parliament, to take a considerable piece of the continent, on the side next us, into possession, and constitute a few new parishes on the shore." "Into possession," then, *et in Arcadia.* And out of Arcadia—which is to say in the age of Malthus or the California Water Board—one can instantly see some of the many ways a theoretically plenteous nature comes to function, in practice, as a very contentious field.

Although it makes no explicit appearance in the governance structure of Crusonia, the question about how to negotiate both the commonness of property and the kinds of property we have in the commons does in fact have a long history in England in the law of easements and servitudes. Under this heading fall both the specific "ancient rights" of common—such as the rights of turbary (to cut peat or turf for fuel) or estover (to take wood from the lord's waste for building or fuel)—and the history of conventions developed for negotiating things like access to resources like water, light, and air. Easements are typically termed either positive (things someone is permitted to do) or negative (things an owner is prevented from doing). My right to walk across your land in order to access a public coastline is positive; the right of a windmill owner to prevent his neighbor, as one well-known case from 1862 has it, from "erect[ing] a house so high that the wind was stopped from the windmills in Finsbury fields" is negative.[13] But in all their forms easements deal with rights we have in land we don't own (like the lord's waste) and to things (like the wind) that seem beyond owning. Easements are, in short, how property law understands sharing.

So while we are certainly right, in one sense, to think of the romantic period as one in which private property was ascendant (as emblematized by enclosure), our recourse to an easy opposition between the private and the common oversimplifies the way property in land had long comprised (and still does comprise) a dense and always partially case-specific set of rights and obligations.[14] The version of the question I am urging, then, is not the Blackstonian or Rousseauvian one: how did a world in which land "belonged generally to every body" get replaced by a world in which all land seemed to belong to somebody? The question is, rather, a more vexed one about how even land that belongs in some sense to somebody always also belongs, at least a little, to someone—and maybe to everyone—else. The question, then, is not how the regime of property replaced the regime of the commons; it's about how certain versions of commonness remain central even once we're within a regime of property in which, as Hardy says, even "the inches of land had value," and about how it is we negotiate the terms of that commonness.[15]

Easements thus occupy a crucial and necessarily difficult position in the institution of liberal property, since they both presume it (you can't have easements if you don't first have a concept of ownership) and push against it by limiting the absoluteness of any dominion. This duplicity has caused easements and servitudes to seem oddly uncategorizable. In a very early attempt, for instance, Henry de Bracton's eleventh-century *De legibus et consuetudinibus Angliæ* entitled divides the world of things into those that can be owned and those that cannot: some things are "within our patrimony" and others, like those "things [that are] sacred or are dedicated to religion, or are common," are "beyond our patrimony." But immediately a third, more confusing group appears: a set of "certain things [that] are neither within nor beyond our patrimony." This uncertainly located set includes things "such as rights and servitudes, uses and fruits [usufruct]," as well as "bridleways, roads, and aqueducts, and such like." These things "are not reckoned amongst goods, for they cannot be alienated of themselves and without the ground," but at the same time they "are not said to be outside [the class of] goods, since those who possess them have a right of exception, and those who don't possess them, have [or may have] a right of action."[16] So servitudes—our rights of use, access, crossing, etc.—are things that seem both possessed and beyond possession. That easements and use rights are not detachable from the ground—lawyers often speak of covenants "running with the land," meaning that whoever owns the land also thereby enters into whatever rights or obligations run with it—makes them seem both rather like a form of property and (because these rights can't be "alienated of themselves") like a kind of nonproperty.

This ambiguity pushes Bracton to develop a new division of things that seems potentially more overarching than the within-/without-patrimony with which he begins: there is, he goes on, "another and second division of things, because some are corporeal and others incorporeal."[17] Corporeal things are easy: they are "those things, which by their nature, may be touched" ("such as a man, a ground, a robe, gold, silver," and even "a thing which has fallen into the depth of the sea" or "the stars fixed in the firmament").[18] But incorporeal things are more mysterious: they "can neither be seen nor touched"—like "the right of going, or of driving or of leading water"—and therefore "cannot [in fact] be possessed, but [only] can be as it were [the Latin original is *quasi*] possessed."[19] In Blackstone's much later redescription of the same issue, he continues to see incorporeal hereditaments as entities defined by their secondary nature. They are understood to be rights "issuing out of a thing corporate" and as such appear merely as "a sort of accidents, which inhere in and are supported by that substance" but which in and of themselves have no existence but "in idea and abstracted contemplation."[20]

But while there's a sort of poetry to this abstraction (one that only increases when Bracton adds "good and evil spirits" and "the soul of the world and the souls of men" to his list of incorporeal things), the mysterious quasiness of the servitude belies its necessarily lived particularity.[21] Easements may be abstract things in the sense that George Crabb articulated in his 1846 *Law of Real Property*—they are "not," he wrote, "the objects of sense but exist in the mind only."[22] But because all easements and servitudes are inherently site-specific arrangements, in which one specific set of people can do some particular thing (drive cattle, carry water, take turf, etc.) on or across this section of some other specific person's property, there is no such thing as an easement in the abstract or in general. Easements are, as Blackstone says, "supported by . . . substance," and in this sense they are inherently nonuniversal and, therefore, nonuniversalizable.[23] We may, as both Spence and Ogilvie argue, all have a right to sustenance from the land, and making good on that right may require that there be such a thing as easements, but those easements are themselves necessarily particular and incapable of being universalized. Thus in his analysis of the various rights of common, Blackstone speaks not only of "common appendant" (the right to put "commonable beasts upon the lord's waste" for food and purposes of manuring) but also of a kind of metacommons, "common because of vicinage, or neighbourhood." Commons because of neighborhood, Blackstone observes, comprise the many cases in which "the inhabitants of two townships, which lie contiguous to each other, have usually intercommoned with one another" such that "the beasts of the one" are constantly "straying mutually into the other's fields, without any molestation from either." This mutual tolerance for mutual straying is what Blackstone calls a "permissive right": a practice "intended to excuse *what in strictness is a trespass in both*, and to prevent a multiplicity of suits." Either township would, that is, be fully within their rights to "enclose and bar out the other" since although "they have intercommoned time out of mind" neither one has any actual "right to put his beasts originally into the other's common." "But if they escape," Blackstone says, they escape, and when they "stray thither of themselves, the law winks at the trespass."[24] The law of easement is a quasi-formal—and necessarily quasi—recognition of the way commonness happens but does so in necessarily site-specific ways. There is no implication, for example, that townships A and B ought to let all the cows in England share their intercommon. So easement always moves in two directions at once. Like the broader parameters of "action on the case" examined in Chapter 1, easement is the longstanding wink the formal law gives to the messier strayings of social practice as well as the way the law formalizes that straying as something that is, after all, a practice.

Still, to think of easement as the wink the law gives to trespass is to imply that the default position is property defined as exclusive and permanent domain. The law's formal rigidity is simply compelled to flex in acknowledgment of the quotidian fact that the world is inevitably shared with others (and cows)—but only within certain cases and limits. As the terms easement and servitude suggest, the law describes such flexing as a courtesy or convenience one property pays to another. Bracton, for example, describes easement as "the institution by which one house is subjected to another."[25] This way of talking indicates the law's desire to treat property's formal conception—in which parcel X is fundamentally discrete from parcel Y—as if it were the true state of the matter and to treat easement as an always-only nonce performance. "Really," the law seems to say, "we are separate, but since it seems we are in this together ..." (wink). But, as our troubles with Ogilvie have shown, we are never *not* in this together, and because truly to hive a parcel off from those things we share—light, air, water, and ways—would be to create a quite literally dark and airless vacuum, the viability of any property always depends on its rights to unownable things.

Thus Charles Gale, in the first full-length treatment of easements in English law, published in 1839, argued that "the origin of some easements is as ancient as that of property."[26] This was so not only because easements are nothing but a modification made to private property but because they are a *necessary* modification. No easements, no property: as Gale's translation of Jean Marie Pardessus's 1806 *Traité des servitudes* puts it: "the extension of cultivation brought men nearer together," and it therefore became necessary "to restrict in certain cases rights legitimate in themselves" since "the absolute exercise" of individual rights "could not take place, *without rendering some properties almost valueless.*"[27] There's still a hint here of something like Blackstone's wink—the rights ("to enclose and bar out the other," as Blackstone says) are "legitimate in themselves"—but Gale and Pardessus stress the sustained necessity much more heavily than does Blackstone's glancing courtesy. Easement is needed if properties are to be valuable at all. The "absolute exercise" of property rights might make sense if the world were the kind of abstract, frictionless space of high school physics. But in the real world, where any action is liable to bump against another, easement is indispensable. So while we tend to think of land as the realest and most substantial form of property, what Gale and Pardessus before him are recognizing is the way land's very materiality makes it one of the most inevitably and fragilely social of all possessions (second only, perhaps, as Godwin will show, to reputation). And in this light the law of easement, which defines and regulates the social life of property, isn't a grudging exception paid to property but the sine qua non of property itself.

It is not an accident, then, that Gale's important study (it remains in print today; its nineteenth edition appeared in 2012) should appear in the already industrialized and thoroughly enclosed England of the 1830s. If it was "the extension of cultivation" and the bringing of "men nearer together" that first necessitated easement way back when, easement grew only more essential and (correlatively) more contentious as modernity densified and privatized. Although very few people still avail themselves of the "ancient rights" (cutting turf for fuel, repairing their homes with wood from the lord's waste), we remain at least as adept at treating land less as a single property than as a bundle of natural resources, rights to which may be distributed differentially over many parties. In the United States today, for instance, a parcel of land might be simultaneously (1) privately owned; (2) protected from further development, even by the owner, under a conservation easement; and (3) subject to an easement allowing for the exploration and extraction of natural gas or other resources from beneath the surface. It's possible for a single parcel to be private, preserved for the greater good, and aggressively exploited by an outside party all at the same time.[28] Much as the law sees persons as miscellaneous bundles of rights and obligations, our geographies are now extensively crisscrossed by complicated arrangements of permission and limitation.

If easements haven't attracted literary scholars and cultural theorists as readily as other subspecialties of property law (inheritance, coverture, contract), it is perhaps because they are a kind of equal-opportunity embarrassment to any theory of property as categorically private or constitutively public. Easements function to build openness into privacy and closure and, on the other side, to build privacy and closure (or what we might think of as limitedness or specificity) into conditions of open or unfettered access. Caveating what would otherwise be absolute privacy or absolute commonality, easements have not only seemed decidedly unuseful for developing utopian programs but have frustrated roughly two centuries of attempts, from Blackstone to Bentham and on into the twentieth century, to develop a hermetically systematic account of property law.[29] Like the externality that concerns rational choice theory and the tort law that has to treat accidents as if they had agents, easement can seem doubly dissatisfying for trading the categorical clarity of either absolute commonality or absolute privacy for a view of property as a perennially dissonant and inevitably local settlement between the two. The blunt dichotomy of common versus private can't capture this, and it's been hard to find a place for easement in a romantic period divided between utopian commonality and heartless privacy.

Easement's duplicity, then, as modernity's: separate but living together, private but never alone. Works of romantic literature that capture this odd ambivalence are, it seems safe to say, much more rare than those seeking to extol a lost community. Still, there are some moments in which this difficult bind seems to rise to the surface. Is Wordsworth's "Michael," for instance—a poem whose first line reads, "If from the public way you turn your steps"—a lament for a lost commons or a lost privacy? When we visit the ruined wall of the lost sheepfold, are we paying a visit to something exemplarily private (the family farm, the nonpublic way) or something exemplarily communal (a pastoral community)? The poem is founded on this ambiguity: it describes the sacrifice of the communion between father (Michael) and son (Luke) to the effort to save the farm they hold between them, thus setting up a tragically self-defeating structure where leaving becomes the only condition for staying and where independence (Luke is sent on a transatlantic profit-seeking venture) is the only way to save community. And because the poem's central crisis results from the fact that the father has much earlier offered the farm "in surety for his brother's son," the division of one communion (between father and son) is brought about by the claims of another communion (between uncle and nephew, or brother and brother), from which the first cannot, and presumably would not want to, establish its independence.[30]

The good and bad news of property, then, is that its inevitable sociability turns it, perhaps in spite of itself, toward the common, but does so in ways that disable property from warding off what "Michael" calls "the unlooked for claim" (the claim, in this case, on the farm as collateral). What makes a poem like "Michael" seem ideologically unsortable is that it arrives as a lament for an independence, a privacy (the family farm) that the plot shows to have been already put into public play as collateral. A happier settlement, perhaps, would be something like the best of both worlds—a communion that would have all the self-identity and protection of property—but without some structure to mediate this relation between the private and the common (and maybe even with it) one runs the risk of the opposite: a world of unlooked-for claims in which the liabilities of commonness produce the debt that is commonality's own ruin.

And nowhere does that ruin seem more ruinous than in *Caleb Williams*, a novel whose serial disasters swing guardrail to guardrail between the impossibility of ever finding a true outside to property—of establishing something that could be held in common—and the inability to find a true inside to property—of establishing something that could be exclusively someone's. It is not only in its general pessimism, then, that the novel stands in stark contrast to Godwin's just-prior *Enquiry Concerning Political Justice*, a work that had argued for the inevitability of reason's progress, but in the specific doubts the novel raises about the smooth fit the *Enquiry* had imagined between the public and the private—a smoothness that had been central to the earlier work's political optimism more generally. It was, in the *Enquiry*, reason's simultaneous universality (*every*one has it) and individuality (every*one* has it) that had allowed Godwin to align a strong notion of privacy with the fact of commonality. Because each person possesses reason, they ought to be allowed, Godwin argued, to use it unmolested by others. Much like J. S. Mill's later *On Liberty*, Godwin's political vision thus requires that individuals be left uncoerced by their neighbors, governmental forces, social institutions, and even—famously—the promises that they may have made yesterday.[31] "Every man has a certain sphere of discretion," Godwin declared, "which he has a right to expect shall not be infringed by his neighbours," and therefore "no man must encroach upon my province, nor I upon his."[32] It is declarations like these—in favor of the rights of individual reason and against the corrupting (or at least distorting) effects of positive institutions—that get Godwin regularly cited as a founder of philosophical anarchism.[33] But while it's true that Godwin imagined individuals as the proper possessors of reason, the whole value of reason to his political vision more generally was its *im*personality. Reason is thus personal only in the kind of technical sense that it is humans who put it into operation. But reason's actual mandates, Godwin frequently reiterates, are unchanging and universal. It thus ought to be possible, in a world of perfected reason, to trust that any individual would act as every other individual would. "There is," Godwin wrote, "no sphere in which a human being can be supposed to act, where one mode of proceeding will not, in every given instance, be more reasonable than any other mode [and that] mode the being is bound by every principle of justice to pursue."[34] The more reasonable course and the less reasonable one are not, Godwin thinks, matters of perspective. To the degree that they seem so, it's because we remain in reason's adolescence; our uncertainty or disagreements about which "mode of proceeding" is most reasonable are local failings and do nothing to gainsay the fundamentally universal structure of reason that exists below the irregularity of our actually existing behavior. "What has society a right to require of me? The question is already answered: everything that it is my duty to do." Will it sometimes ask me to go beyond my duty to reason? Yes, of course it will. Should it? "Certainly not." Why not? Because society cannot "change eternal truth."[35] Where the determinations of reason are understood to be eternal and unchanging, it doesn't—or shouldn't—matter who is doing the reasoning. And for Godwin it doesn't make sense to speak about feeling entitled to one's personal opinion or to the gratification of one's individual proclivity. "Few things," Godwin writes, "have contributed more to undermine the energy and virtue of the human species, that the supposition that we have a right, as it has been phrased, to do what we will with our own."[36] Because all of us are beholden to the universal standard of reason, we and everything we have are under public obligation. Nothing can "be more incontrovertible" than the assertion "that princes and magistrates have no rights" since "there is no situation of their lives that has not its correspondent duties." But it is, Godwin argues, equally incontrovertible that "the same restrictions [are] applicable to subjects and citizens." Princes, every last each of us, "we have in reality nothing that is strictly speaking our own."[37]

Thus it is that reason, in the *Enquiry*, underwrites the alignment of two principles that would otherwise be decidedly opposed: the liberal commitment to nonencroachment on anyone's "sphere of discretion" and the belief that nothing is "strictly speaking our own." A world ruled by reason would be a world that didn't need a law of easements because it would be a world that had solved the problem of sharing: reason would ensure that everyone's individual province should seamlessly function "to the benefit of the whole."[38] As in Coleridge's theory of the symbol discussed in Chapter 1, reason's great trick is thus to delete the friction between what's mine (the part) and what's ours (the whole). In light of this hopeful solution it is particularly striking that Godwin, having completed the first version of the

Enquiry in 1793, turned almost immediately to a novel whose title promises to address *Things As They Are* rather than as they ought to, or might someday be, and in which a series of tragedies is generated by nothing so much as the stark absence of any notion of easement, any universal reason that could negotiate the commonality of property and the kinds of rights each of us have to that which is common.[39]

As readers will recall, the main plot of the novel revolves around two case studies in long-brewed antipathy—first, between the cultured noble Ferdinando Falkland and the rougher-hewn squire Barnabas Tyrrel, and second, between Falkland and his servant, Caleb Williams.[40] Given the seemingly obsessive nature of these resentments, we might take the novel as a lesson in the depth of irrational ill will that one individual might bear another. Godwin himself came close to describing the plot in psychological terms as one of sadistic pleasure, in which the "ingenuity and resources" of a "pursuer" keep a "fugitive" in a state of "fearful alarm" for pages on end.[41] But to read the novel as a study in the pleasures of malice would be to miss the way the novel's deep interest in how inadvertent (and therefore nonmalicious) actions and even clearly locally beneficial actions can produce scarcity and discord somewhere else in the system.[42] Positioned in this way the issue that the novel raises about action is not so much psychological—what Godwin called the "entrails of mind and motive"—as it is both formal (it's about relation) and empirical: a question about how to read the value of an action once it takes its place in Godwin's "diversified scene of human life."[43]

So where the political vision of the *Enquiry* rested on the assumption that the inalterable "eternal truth" of reason was something that might be apparent to any temporal actor, *Caleb Williams* presents a world in which, if there is a general good, it seems to exist only as a noumenal realm—a theoretical ideal beyond the math of any imminent actor.[44] It's not, then, that the characters in *Caleb Williams* are unreasonable but that they are confined to an insistently local economy in which aid or virtue extended in one direction produces harm or hatred in another. The earlier, overarching faith that we are always guaranteed a "sphere" in which "one mode of proceeding" will "in every given instance, be more reasonable than any other" is here traded for an equally insistent perspectivalism. Because the consequences of action continually expand, one's calculations about the value of an act are never complete, are only ever some particular one's.

In the end, it is this ineluctable perspectivalism and not malice that is the crucial engine of the novel's tragedies. Indeed, because the problem is perspectivalism and the challenges it poses to adducing an objective valuation of action, the engine cannot be malice since bad intentions as much as good ones are likely to be gainsaid by circumstance. Malice, to the degree it matters at all, is nothing more than the byproduct of a much larger structural crisis about how the fact that we share a world interrupts our attempt to get a reliable or final account of the value of any action. Some one hundred and fifty years, then, before the theories of social cost, spillovers, and externality that would revolutionize economics in the twentieth century (see Chapter 1 for more on this), Godwin's novel understood that the crucial problem of property was not (as it was for Spence, Coleridge, and the mainline critique of romanticism) how to get rid of it once and for all but—quite the contrary—how to have it in the first place.

Like so many gothic novels *Caleb Williams* is based around a failure of boundaries—the lines that mark off the past from the present (*Otranto*), the human from the monster (*Dracula*), the sacred from the profane (*The Monk*), etc. But the novel is perhaps unique in its insistence that little more than the sheer fact of sharing a space with someone else is sufficient to make us plagues and monsters to each other. The novel can thus dispense with the psychological claims of the doppelganger—of uncanny likeness and secret similitude—in order to concentrate on the ways the world constantly throws up new problems of sharing, new crises for the commonness of property, just by virtue of having other people in it.

It's true, though, that certain parts of the novel do seem caught in a gothic rut of anxiety about teleology and origin. In his notes on the composition of the novel, written to accompany the 1832 Standard Novels edition, for instance, Godwin describes (in the remark that excited Poe as a precedent for "The Philosophy of Composition") his decision to work backward "from the ultimate conclusion to the first commencement of the train of adventures upon which I purposed to employ my pen."[45] That comment—along with Caleb's own oft-repeated hypotheses on the fated nature of history ("from the moment of . . . taking a step like this, . . . his misfortunes took their commencement" [14]; "The very next incident in the story was in some degree decisive of the catastrophe" [36]; "all are but links in one chain" [132])—puts its emphasis on what Godwin in his introduction for the 1832 Standard Novels edition called "the entire unity of plot."[46] But Caleb's strangely serial recognitions of that unity—this was where it all started, and then here is also where it all started, and also over here was the decisive thing—suggests that what's really being observed is not the actual teleological linearity of events but the way their entanglement makes the origin of any present circumstance constantly revisable and any particular step seem like the decisive one.

Indeed, Caleb's obsession with origins seems out of place in a plot that tends to be driven not by the iron hand of a singular intention (say, *Lear*) but the happenstance, occasional shape of the run-in. From the opening vignette detailing Falkland's near brush with violence in Italy (he's been

giving reading lessons to the fiancée of a jealous and not-reassuringly named
Count Malvesi) to the pointedly mundane origins of his enmity with Tyrrel
(over the attentions of a woman at a dance, over airtime at the local assembly); to the problems triggered when a famous poet, one Mr. Clare, happens
to retire "in this very neighbourhood"; to the accidental intersections that
keep making Falkland look like a hero (he rescues a burning village that
he happens to be riding by; he interrupts an abduction while out on an
unrelated nocturnal mission to catch "a man who lurked about this wood for
robbery or some other bad design" [75]); to the random meetings that keep
bringing Caleb back into Falkland's orbit ("instead of pursuing the proper
direction, I had taken one that led to [Falkland's brother-in-law] rather than
to my own habitation"—oops [143]), the novel is a story about treating the
ineluctable, because always accidental, fact of copresence as if it were in and
of itself a malicious action. More like *Oedipus* than *Lear*, *Caleb Williams* is
a situation tragedy. And when the very fact of running into someone else
makes us thieves of the regard, confidence, respect, or affection that "belongs" to someone else, there is no need for buried origins or the monstrous
revelations of history. In fact, one doesn't even need fate: the quotidian fact
of simultaneousness, our being in this together, is understood to be its own
and distinctly plentiful form of disaster.

"The arrival of Mr. Falkland," we learn, "gave a dreadful shock to the
authority of Mr. Tyrrel" (18), who has, until now, been thuggishly enjoying
his local preeminence in the small pond of what the novel insistently refers
to as "the neighbourhood" (for example, 22, 23, 30, 35).[47] The men, the
narrative tells us, "were like two stars fated never to appear at once above the
horizon," but that's actually a confusing way to put it since unlike Orion and
Sagittarius, who manage to take their seasonal turns, Falkland's and Tyrrel's
ellipticals are peculiarly interfering. Even when Mr. Tyrrel sits himself "at
the extremity of [the] circle" that has Falkland at its center, in order "to
withdraw himself," he is as if "by enchantment retained . . . in his place" and
forced to "consent to drink the dregs of the bitter portion which envy had
prepared for him" (24). Extraterritoriality, as Caleb will later have extensively
illustrated for him, is the one thing that is not on offer. "It is my business,"
says Falkland's agent to Caleb just before the novel's conclusion,

> to see that you do not break out of bounds. . . . Beware the salt seas! They are
> out of my orders. You are a prisoner at present, and I believe all your life will
> remain so. . . . As long as you think proper, you are a prisoner within the rules,
> [but] you are not to go out of these climates. . . . I would advise you for the
> future to keep at a proper distance from the sea, for fear of the worst. (228)

Both early and late, then, the novel shows itself to be a distinctly *island* gothic—a story whose unnerving horror comes not primarily from the physical threats to which one man is subjected by another (Falkland will tell Caleb he has, in fact, been *protecting* him) as by the finitude and finality of geography itself. "I cannot stir abroad," Tyrrel says, "without meeting some mortification in which you are directly or remotely concerned, I am determined [a word we can now hear as indicating confinement rather than intention] to hate you. Now, sir, if you will only go out of the county or the kingdom ... I will promise never to quarrel with you as long as I live" (29). But, of course, no one leaves. In later episodes Caleb, like Tyrrel before him, continually finds himself circling accidentally into Falkland's orbit: he runs into Mr. Forester even after taking a road that "led in a direction wholly wide of the habitation of our late visitor" (142); he runs into Falkland's agent even after having "decided upon making a circuit, the direction of which should seem at first extremely wide of my intended route, and then suddenly striking into a different path" (153); he runs into Mr. Falkland's carriage even after "the only rule that I laid down to myself in traversing the forest was to take a direction as opposite as possible to that which led to the scene of my late imprisonment" (227); he disguises himself as an Irishman only to be arrested (bad luck: the police were looking for an Irishman who resembles not Caleb but Caleb's disguise) and "dragged to the very centre of the kingdom" (236); and so on. No one, not Tyrrel and not Caleb (and not Caleb-as-Irishman or Caleb-as-Jew), is ever very far from the "centre of the kingdom." What we have, then, is all the rank density of Spence's Crusonia minus the mercifully uninhabited (was it?) continent "on the side next us." The fact of what Blackstone called vicinage is absolute; there is nowhere that isn't "neighbourhood," and everyone is always straying.

What one needs in neighborhoods, what one needs when there are no more continents to settle, is the wink of easement. But the novel raises the prospect of easement—the idea that you could share without losing or take without stealing—only in order to present it as immediately self-canceling. Here's the easement Falkland proposes early on as a solution to the growing animosity between himself and Tyrrel. "We are," Falkland warns, "upon the brink of whirlpool," and "if we be enemies, who shall tell where our enmity will stop? Every new event will feed it; it will swell beyond imagination or limit; ever seeming enlarged to its utmost size, it will still become more monstrous" (26). As the terms to which Falkland resorts (whirlpools, limits, brinks, etc.) indicate, the problem is one of unmanageable overlap—and the solution is to stop overlapping. "We neither of us wish to change roads," says Falkland in a reworking of Abraham's proposal to Lot in Genesis, "let us each suffer the other to pursue his own track unmolested. Be this our compact; and by mutual forbearance let us preserve mutual peace" (28). "We are formed," Falkland says, "in different habits; why should we interfere? The world is wide enough for both" (28). Separate spheres thus provide the ground for accord, as Godwin's *Enquiry* promised they would: "Every man . . . has a sphere of discretion, but that sphere, is limited by the co-ordinate sphere of his neighbour."[48]

But in this novel there is no such thing as coordination—only incessant coincidence—and in one of the story's most darkly brilliant turns this peaceable offer of easement is immediately converted into a second-order scarcity, in which the very suggestion that two could share the world is treated as if it were a form of theft.[49] "This," says Tyrrel about the *offer* to share, "is only a new debt added to the score, which he shall one day richly pay" (30). To be sure, there's nothing in this moment to prevent us from reading it as proof of Tyrrel's peculiar perversity, his special hatefulness. But as the novel works variations on this theme, the slightly strange conservation of matter Tyrrel's response implies—in which generosity here is debt somewhere else—expands from a personal idiosyncrasy into a larger claim about the impossibility of forwarding an abstraction like the public good. Here there are only ever public, or potentially public, *goods*—plural, countable, and all of them, no matter how immaterial, like respect or honor, potentially scarce.[50] In this system, taking a benefit from one place and putting it somewhere else relocates or redistributes that particular good but can't be said to *forward* or improve anything. There is no better, only different: this distribution or that other one. We can divide things—rivers, light, respect—one way or another, but we can't make more of them, and if this is true then there's no way, as Tyrrel sees, that more for me isn't going to mean less for you.

It's a bit as though Godwin was playing his own Malthus, since the core bar to happiness, here, is economic before and above its being moral. And it is to hit this home that two early episodes, which seem on their surface designed to dramatize the temperamental differences between Falkland and Tyrrel, in fact make the same formal point about the impossibility of justly negotiating property's distribution. In an early instance of heroism, Falkland, out for a night ride, discovers that a nearby village is burning. "There were," the novel says, "eight or ten houses already on fire, and the whole seemed to be threatened with destruction" (53). Falkland's immediate resolution is to "pull down a house, next to one that was wholly on fire, but which itself was yet untouched" (53–54). The befuddled residents, whose response has thus far been limited to the self-interested conveyance of "their movables and furniture into the adjoining fields" (53), are "astonished at a direction which implied a voluntary destruction of private property" (54). Falkland, far-sighted noble that he is, ascends the nonburning house in an instant and loosens the support of a stack of chimneys in order to force them "headlong into the midst of the fire." "By his presence of mind," Caleb's narration extols, and "by his indefatigable humanity and incessant exertions, he saved three fourths of the village from destruction" (54). As a moment it seems a fairly successful application of the kind of utilitarian calculus Godwin had suggested in his *Enquiry*, most famously in the hypothetical problem about who to save, the Archbishop Fénelon or the valet, from a burning room. There Godwin argued that one would be morally obligated to save Fénelon and that this was so even "suppos[ing] the valet had been my brother, my father, or my benefactor," on the grounds that "the life of Fénelon" mattered more to the general good, that his life, as Godwin puts it, "was really preferable to that of the valet."[51] Falkland's burning village problem seems even easier: no humans, only houses, and none of them particular to him. But even in these less strenuous circumstances the novel is careful to show the gaps in the apparently airtight logic of the moral-philosophical story problem. Here, Falkland's heroism happens to save Tyrrel's niece, Emily (in a strange, outlying village, apparently, since there are no outliers), who falls in love with him, so that when he saves her again a little later (through another nighttime happenstance), it only increases her affections for Falkland and dramatically decreases her affections for Tyrrel, which makes Tyrrel unhappy and jealous enough to imprison Emily, who ends up dying in house arrest thanks to some lethal combination of grief and lack of care. A case that begins as a perfect exemplification of reasonable action—no one would think it would be better to let a village burn than to destroy a single, albeit nonburning house—turns out not to be immune to the spillover effects that emerge a few days, or weeks, or months later as hostile witnesses. The novel thus admits what the *Enquiry* does not: that it is never really a choice between an archbishop and a valet; it's a choice between one unpredictable future and another. Mitigating one flood of catastrophe only diverts it into a new channel. In the words of the novel: "these waters of bitterness, extending beyond him, poured their deadly venom upon others" (15).

This spread of bitter waters makes Falkland's obviously philanthropic actions practically indistinguishable from Tyrrel's obviously malicious ones. When Tyrrel finds one of his renters, a Mr. Hawkins, guilty of ingratitude (Hawkins has declined to put his son into Tyrrel's service), Tyrrel takes advantage of what the novel describes as "the particular situation of Hawkins's house, barns, stacks, and outhouses" (43). Observing that the "land of one part of Hawkins's farm . . . was lower than the rest and consequently exposed to occasional inundation from a river by which it was bounded," Tyrrel has "a dam belonging to this river privately cut to [lay] the whole under water" (42). The corn he cannot "privately" flood he decimates by "pull[ing] away the fences of the higher ground ... and turn[ing] in his cattle" (42), and then, as the coup de grâce, Tyrrel closes access to "the road to the market town" by fencing off what the novel calls, with the important uncertainty characteristic of easement, "a path, or private road" that "had been a broad path time out of mind" and "led directly from Hawkins's house to the road" (43). The geographic explicitness of the passage and odd oscillations between what's private and what isn't suggest that Tyrrel's actions are not or are not only blindly malevolent but are designed to illustrate the ineluctable imbrications of material properties in a material world. We are, one imagines, meant to sympathize with Hawkins's efforts to establish his family's independence—"I do not see any good," Hawkins tells Tyrrel, "that comes of servants" (40)—but Tyrrel's response points up their structural futility. Tyrrel is, to be sure, no good, but in its twin belief that no property is ever solitary and no communion is ever equal, the novel makes it clear that the special forms of despotism it takes as its subject—"the modes of domestic and unrecorded despotism, by which man becomes the destroyer of man"—turn out not really to require despots.[52]

The impersonality of the reading I am suggesting here is meant to push away from—though not to disagree with—the long history of understanding the novel (beginning with Godwin himself) as a parable about the social power one class has over another (see, for instance, Marilyn Butler's reading of the novel as "hav[ing] to do with the power exercised over individuals by the community in general, and by rich or great men in particular; a power which advanced societies have institutionalized as law").[53] At stake in my reading, then, is less whether the rich have power over the poor (obviously they do) than the fact that, as underlined by Falkland's sense that Caleb's existence is as much a torment to him as vice versa, the novel's model of enmity does not, in fact, require class difference. Though clearly both wealth and temperament can exacerbate it, enmity is, I am arguing, a formal product of sheer togetherness, not a byproduct of class difference or psychological proclivity.

It's as if to secure fully the impersonality of this despotism that the novel turns, immediately following Falkland's failed plea for reason, temperance, and easement, to a new case of "distemper" (31) that—because it actually is a fever—has nothing to do with temperament.[54] "It was not long after," the fifth chapter begins, "that a malignant contagious distemper broke out in the neighbourhood, which proved fatal to many of the inhabitants, and was of unexampled rapidity in its effects." The person that the disease strikes first is the poet Mr. Clare, a gentlemen who, the novel is careful to tell us, "in this scene of rural retreat at least ... had not an enemy" (30) except for, now, this "universal foe" and "general affliction" (31). His efforts to explain the disease—perhaps his "intellectual efforts" had been too strenuous (30)? Or, "I should have acquitted myself better" (31)?—all seem decidedly beside the point since what a contagious disease makes clear is the stark unimportance of one's behavior (let alone one's preferences or intentions). "The strange seeds of distemper," Clare says, "seem to float in the air, and to fasten upon the frame without its being possible for us to tell what was the method of their approach" (31). The novel will gild the lily of its key idea over the next pages by making Falkland's kind attendance on Clare in his illness yet another source of diminishment for Tyrrel, who can't seem to go unwronged, but the indispensable interest of the episode, otherwise entirely extraneous to any of the mainline plots of the novel, is in the turn toward the epidemiological itself.[55] For it is in a virus—at once a preeminent disrespecter of borders *and* the kind of thing that you seem to need other people to contract—that the novel finds its starkest image of a togetherness—a "general affliction"—that is in and of itself, and later if not sooner, a disaster.

What recourse, then, is available? There is, as Caleb and Tyrrel have learned, no outside to the neighborhood, which is also to say that there is no inside to anywhere either: no place to which one could, like Clare, retire from society, no private place from which one could plead, as Caleb once does of Falkland, "Suffer me at least to call life and the pursuits of my life my own!" (200). No place to call one's own, then, and no place that can be safely shared; these are the unhappy options. And, thus barred from both virtue rewarded and social peace, it's not hard to see why a novel that had rather courageously written itself into this easementless corner would struggle to find a way to conclude. Godwin, as is well known, composed two different endings for his novel. Both of them follow on a final hearing between Caleb and Falkland, an event this time held—unlike the novel's previous depositions, which have taken place in Falkland's home and in explicitly public venues like town halls and courtrooms—in a site carefully situated so as to offer "a medium between the suspicious air of a private examination and the indelicacy as it was styled of an examination exposed to the remark of every accidental spectator" (295–296). That studious placement in a kind of public privacy or a private publicity is the first sign that Godwin's conclusion is searching for a third way between the two more obvious options: the one in which Caleb's story is vindicated and Falkland tried for the murder he's been hiding all these years, or the other, in which Falkland's narrative (my life, he says in the manuscript ending, "had been irreproachable" and lived publicly "in the face of [my] country" [306]) is upheld and Caleb jailed for his actual slanders and alleged thefts.

That Godwin turns away from both of these verdict-granting options is telling. If the goal of the novel has been to expose the unjust torment of an innocent man by a more powerful, jealous one, either of the more obvious, unpursued options would seem to work: either Falkland is found guilty of murder and his mistreatment of Caleb, in which case our conventional sense of justice is satisfied, or Caleb is found guilty of a theft he didn't commit, and the novel becomes a more despondent indictment of a system of justice that allows the rich and well regarded to sail clear. But what we see in both of the endings Godwin actually wrote—though this is more clear in the second, published one—is something like neither/nor: not justice and not injustice but, first, the discovery (a little vaguely in the manuscript ending) of the dissatisfactions of justice's strict allocation of guilt to a single account and then, much more clearly in the rewritten, published ending, the elaboration of a philosophy that seeks to move beyond the terms of strict justice and its promise of absolute summation in favor of one side or the other.

On a quick read, it is easy enough to see the second, published ending not as an extension but the contradiction of the manuscript version.[56] In the manuscript ending, Caleb ends up in a sort of private prison tended by the henchman, Jones, who has, at the behest of Falkland, pursued Caleb throughout the second half of the novel, and the final passages of the manuscript detail Caleb's stunned sense of injustice ("I am still in the highest degree perplexed ... to account for the entire and ignominious miscarriage of my last accusation" [309]) and remarks on rumors of Falkland's continued life and health ("I understand that Mr. Falkland ... still lives, nay, that he is considerably better in his health" [309]) before finally plunging Caleb into a dash-riddled and apparently unstable monologue that includes an odd parable about a traveler trying to assist a crocodile and strange claims ("I am like a log" [311]) that are hard to assemble into clear meaning. The published ending, by contrast, ends with what looks much more clearly like victory for our hero: "Williams," says Falkland, "you have conquered!" (301). The ending of injustice, then, replaced by justice.

But it's very important that the novel doesn't leave things here but in both versions extends its meditations beyond the verdict that would seem to conclude the main action of the plot. In the first ending, Caleb suffers his own disintegration, his pleas unheard. But in the second, in which Caleb *is* heard and *is* believed, the prospects of what would have looked only moments earlier like success have turned into their own form of punishment even before he's begun to speak. Seeing the guilt-wracked Falkland hobbling into the courtroom, Caleb asks whether he can bring himself to "trample upon a man thus dreadfully reduced." "Shall I point my animosity," he wonders, "against one whom the system of nature has brought down to the grave?" The remark picks up on and reworks, now as an almost positive philosophy, the abandonment of justice the last paragraphs of the manuscript ending hint at in their broken resignation: "Well," Caleb says, "it is all one at last—I believe there was nothing in life worth making such a bustle about—no, nor in secrets—nor in murders neither, for the matter of that—when people are dead, you know, one cannot bring them to life again! . . . Well then,—It is wisest to be quiet it seems . . . True happiness lies in being like a stone" (311). Hiding in that final despondence (I am "a stone—a grave-stone!—an obelisk to tell you, here lies what was once a man!") is the thought that the true sources of difficulty are not the secret keepers or the murderers but those who cannot let bygones be bygones. Put in those terms, the recommendation is for passivity, a way of suffering a world too broken to bother trying to fix. But reformulated in the published ending, the pains of a will toward justice are made more explicit and the peculiar kind of activity that is forbearance more clearly understood. His voice "suffocated with agony" (298), Caleb expresses his willingness to abandon the hearing altogether and ends up mounting something that is neither an accusation nor a defense but a lament about his and Falkland's mutual inability to be either truly together or truly apart: "You began in confidence," he says to Falkland, "why did you not continue in confidence" or, alternatively, "Why did you not suffer me to depart"? The old problem, then: not together, but not separate. But, here, for the first time in the novel, Caleb formulates an alternative to the either/or: "I am sure that, if I had opened my heart to Falkland, if I had told to him privately the tale that I have now been telling, he could not have resisted my reasonable demand. After all his precautions, he must ultimately have depended on my forbearance." It's a solution hatched over by the quasi-ness of easement, but what Caleb is suggesting is something like Blackstone's intercommoning. When "the inhabitants of two townships have intercommoned time out of mind," the thought went, they "excuse what in strictness is a trespass in both." As there, Caleb's emphasis on the ideal of forbearance suggests a lost world in which both men not only might have suffered each other but, in a complex way, depended on the forbearance of the other not to prosecute what "in strictness" would be "a trespass in both." That complexity already lends some moral heft to what Blackstone lightens by describing as a wink, but *Caleb Williams* will go even further still in describing the forbearance of easement as a kind of blessing. "I came hither to curse," says Caleb, "but I remain to bless" (300). "You have inflicted on me the most fatal of all mischiefs," says Falkland to Caleb, "but I bless the hand that wounds me" (302). As with all final acts of forgiveness granted in ruin, there's no way to salvage from this ending a strict sense of justice. Even more strongly, the lesson, if there is one, is about the way a strict theory of justice itself partakes too much of the fiction of a perfectly private property. Both land and morals as the law imagines them are divisible into discrete parcels and assignable by exclusive titles. But here even guilt is shared and therefore comes to be something that is not quite, not *properly*, guilt. Quasi guilty or quasi innocent is how things are left, is things as they are.

As Celeste Langan has noted, at the beginning of the nineteenth-century easement's outlook was not clear. In Langan's account easement is one of the casualties of the ever more absolute forms of ownership that cancelled an earlier freedom—what Langan (and Wordsworth) call "vagrancy" and what Benjamin Constant defined as the right "to come and go without permission."[57] But easement, since it always involves case-specific forms of subordination, was never really the same as vagrancy or crossing without permission. Easement belongs to the sphere of rights and obligations, not the sphere of freedom. In an interesting turn toward the end of the nineteenth century a number of the large landowners who hold the titles to large open, periurban spaces (like Hampstead Heath) will make this point. Because easements and "ancient rights" were, they argued, held by particular commoners in relation to particular commons, there was no such thing as an "easement in gross," no right of way that literally anyone might claim.[58] They lost. So if the quasi-ness of easement lost to the absoluteness of property in the time of enclosure, it would also lose to the absoluteness of publicity (to the pure anonymity of anyone) at the end of the century. Still, if it seems in general that we have de-quasi-ed our notions of property—so that all land is either perfectly private or perfectly public—it's not hard to find cases that illustrate the currency of easement. For the question that *Caleb Williams* leaves us with is less about the future of easements and servitudes as Blackstone or Bracton would have understood them—as ancient rights of common—than it is about the (very bright, very busy) future of the problems of togetherness and sharing that easements were meant to manage. Here, for instance, is recent information from a website run by TransCanada explaining to landowners their options regarding the proposed building of the Keystone XL pipeline designed to bring oil from Canadian tar sands down to Texas refineries:

> TransCanada has been working with landowners throughout Montana, South Dakota and Nebraska on easement agreements. We are incredibly pleased with

the progress we've made thus far. In Montana and South Dakota, we've reached voluntary agreements with 100 per cent of landowners. And in Nebraska, we've reached agreements with 78 per cent of all landowners along the approved route. . . . Our commitment is to treat landowners with honesty, fairness and respect, to work with them and come up with the best possible solution. . . . *In the event we cannot reach an agreement, the value of the compensation paid to a landowner for an easement is determined by a state-approved eminent domain process.*[59]

Clearly, the problems easement was meant to solve have not disappeared with the dwindling of the other rights of common. The problems of togetherness are formal—built into the structure of things—rather than historical. And if it's the case that at this moment in history landowners in Nebraska have only two choices—to sell an easement to TransCanada or to sell one to the state of Nebraska under the "state-approved eminent domain process"—one can only imagine the kind of blessing they are preparing for the next wounding hand.

Epilogue: Everything Counts
(*Frankenstein*)

> Your disaster is irreparable. What do you intend to do?
>
> —*Frankenstein*

The goal of this study has been to shift our understanding of the problem that the individual person presents in the British nineteenth century—indeed, to argue that the individual was *a problem* rather than a unit that went without saying—by examining the budding incoherence, registered in both the law and the novel, of commonsense understandings of action, responsibility, and justice.[1]

What we have seen is the materialization of a now long-running conflict between the first-person, accountable action on which both liberalism and justice depend and the emergent forms of collective personhood and distributed action that are characteristic of modern life. This history differs markedly from the more familiar narrative in which individualism slowly rises over and against older collective forms. It differs, for instance, from the kind of narrative Nancy Armstrong has recently offered, in which "what we now call 'the novel' won its title in a field of argumentation as it figured out how to adjust, incorporate, and abject competing [that is, collective] ways of thinking about the individual." Armstrong is, I think, right to stress the difficulties that faced the individuality of what she calls "the individual subject," but what we have seen written across of the face of these novels are the signs of a *permanent* strain. There is, this is to say, no title to win, no winning. It has thus been one of the points of this study to show some of the reasons why it is too narrowing, too teleological to say that novels become novels only when they fend off collective personhood as if their liberalism were being constantly buffeted by exclusively external winds. For while it's true that the novel did recognize that forms of collective personhood are disruptive to "the development of individualism," it also recognized, in a way that the shape of Armstrong's claim does not, that collective personhood is absolutely built into the history of both modernity and liberalism.[2] So it is not just that the collective continued to haunt what would have otherwise been a happy novelistic liberalism, for what structures the drama of these novels—and what bears on everything about them, from their formal decisions (for example, the muting of free indirect discourse in *Mansfield Park* or the assembled texts of *Justified Sinner*) to their rethinking of plot (Dickens), or setting (Godwin), or what they think a character is (Austen, Dickens)—is the impossibility of drawing a bright line between individuals and collectivities.

So, as disruptive as it may have been to "the novel" as it would have preferred to be (if genres, like corporations, can have wishes), the collective personhood that kept putting the brakes on modernity's smooth ascent was coming from those very developments—freedom of contract, scientific investigation, industrial development, democratic reform, and, yes, the novel itself—central to the "progress" of modern individualism. Thus we have seen how empiricism both rested its case on the composite nature of thought, language, and the body even as—which is to say *at the same time as and for just that reason*—it found itself unable to reckon with the complexity its own methods revealed. The result, as we saw with Hartley in chapter 1, was the reemergence of the very approximation and figurative representation it had been the whole point of empiricism to avoid. Similarly, we saw how the effort in romantic aesthetics to dignify neglected fragments by understanding them as the natural representatives of some greater whole (as in Coleridge's symbol or the cultural nationalism I've argued Hogg's *Justified Sinner* addresses) effectively replaced persons with personifications—a move that works just fine until you want to think of your personification or your symbol *doing* something (besides, that is, merely personifying or symbolizing). In Dickens's treatment of the French Revolution we saw how both the birth of modern democracy and the aesthetic program of the novel might be turned to decidedly anti-individualist ends, thanks to a nationalist reconceptualization of agency and a particularly aggressive experiment in the subservience of character to plot. And so on.

As Dickens's famous opening projects, the period that stretches between "the Squib Case" and the rise of the limited liability corporation was a contradictory time: the age of contract but also (as well as *therefore*) the corporate person; the presumptive heyday of laissez-faire industrialism but also (as well as *therefore*) a period that was forced to reckon with the attendant complications of social costs, conflicting uses, and the widening scale of industrial accidents. I have not argued that we have no warrant for seeing liberal individualism as the dominant ideology of the nineteenth century;

we do. But I have tried to bring out the remarkable degree of uncertainty that hovered around that notion even in the arenas most committed to it. The idea that "everybody [ought] to count for one, nobody for more than one," as Mill summarized the Benthamite principle in his 1861 *Utilitarianism*, seems simple enough.[3] Putting it into practice, however, required the active maintenance of the conceptual scaffolding necessary to bracket the many forms of collectivity that shadow the idea of singularly countable action. The twentieth-century critiques of the liberal subject have been eloquent about its theoretical inadequacies and its ethical blindsides, but many of the charges would have seemed familiar even to people like Mill and Godwin, champions of individualism who were nevertheless deeply aware of how easy it is to lose the individual behind webs of relational circumstance and merely representative action. The story of that awareness is part of what I have traced here.

Whatever its difficulties, the correlation of individual persons with particular actions is not a project easily abandoned. Simply recognizing the fictionality of liberal individuality, its artifactual or ideological character, does not in and of itself get one (or us, rather) out of it. We might well decide, as Robert Owen did, that the fictional nature of liberal individuality means that all punishment, all accountability, is unjust. Because, as Mill paraphrased the Owenite position, "the criminal did not make his own character" but was the product of "education, and the circumstances which surround him," it was "unjust to punish at all." And we might even extend Owen's argument (since if circumstances make criminals, presumably they make noncriminals, too) and disband not only our criminal but also our civil institutions of accountability: contracts, promises, debts, etc.[4] But even if we did away with accountability as a social matter, we would probably still find vestiges of justice hanging around just as a matter of ordinary thinking and saying. Since we can't (or have yet to find a way to) describe the world without attributing actions to some someone or some something, we also can't help but make it seem as though the infinity of contributing agents were so much circumstantial noise. Until we have a way of talking without subjects and verbs, we are bound to suggest misleadingly that there are some individuals that are to be held accountable (and some that we can ignore) and that action reliably arrives in neatly packaged cases.

All of the time, then, we face a version of the problem the law knows as the distinction between action and action on the case. And like the nineteenth-century judge who, as we saw in Chapter 1, saw the threat that an expanded notion of circumstance posed to the law, we find ourselves forced to insist on more or less strict forms of pleading in cases that we know might always have been more expansively construed. As materialists like Joseph Priestley saw, the multiplicity, complexity, and agential force of circumstances is guaranteed to go continually understated. And if this limitation is really inborn, then we are without any justified ground from which to critique institutions of accountability (like liberalism or the law) for the oversimplifications and reifications that make its judgments possible. Description and reification go hand in hand. And because they do, the question can't really be *whether* we should reify or not. The question is, rather, one of scale—a question about which units, which scales, which entities, which *reifications* we prefer to which others—and why.

As it was for the nineteenth-century courts that gradually widened the scale of action they were willing to recognize, the question for us is not whether we should be positivists. It's about how we want to go about being them. It's a question that resonates in our contemporary moment, a period as extensively populated by personifications and as manifestly rippling with superpersonal agencies as any Wordsworth or Coleridge could have wished. We push back, maybe, against the personhood of corporations. We try to understand the place of human agency within the large-scale eventfulness of oil spills and chemical disasters. We try to calculate responsibility for climate change. We try to manage access to common goods like water and breathable air. These are not projects we can accomplish simply by thinking "beyond" our human scale or by seeing through the artificiality of any organizing unit. They are, rather, projects that require us to think about the relation between one scale and another and, even more pointedly, about which scales—the human? the nonhuman? the state? the federal? the corporate? the environmental?—we want to put at the head of the table, and why, and when.

Clearly, the entity we put there need not always or ever be the human individual. Indeed, there are plenty of arguments on both the right ("corporations are people, too, my friend," said the Republican presidential candidate Mitt Romney) and the left (in, for example, the many varieties of theoretical posthumanism) that human personhood should not have pride of place. Thus freed of our retrograde humanism, we may decide to concern ourselves with the life (the agency, the experience, and perhaps even the political representation) of other units—nimbus clouds, or caribou herds, or multinational banks, or concepts, or languages. Or perhaps, as in the "flat ontology" recommended by Levi Bryant, we will simply choose to stand back under a principle of noninterference (one that feels a little liberal, actually, but whatever) and just let all these different forms of being, like the usurers of old, go about their being-business.[5] We may want to think at the level of the planet (rather than the state or the nation or the globe) or in terms of the multitude (rather than the individual), or to toggle between these different scales or talk about their interactions.[6] But we will only be able to avoid reducing this "promiscuous harmony" to a limited set of "singular" or "individual" agents by delaying forever the moment in which we describe them in action or want to characterize some particular relation between them. When we ask what IBM is doing for the environment, or how the Dow is responding to the Ukraine, we are thinking about scale-scale relations. But even to ask the question we have had to winnow the multitude, to start talking as though we think it really is reducible to a few especially important agents and a few conspicuous actions and effects. If we can't stand to winnow, we can't stand to ask, and we will never be able to answer.

Without winnowing—without buying into the fiction of personhood at some level of corporateness—our questions will be endlessly hypothetical, merely speculative rather than theoretical. They will be models for the kinds of questions we *could* ask ("let us consider," we will enjoin, "the multiple effects different scales have on one another"), but we will not really be able to ask any particular question (what X means for Y, or what A did to B), and we will therefore spare ourselves (more's the pity) having to offer a defense of why we thought it right or useful to frame the case in that particular way. The recent interest in thinking about "agency" (rather than action) preserves this less demanding, because only speculative, freedom while still offering us the feeling that we are being dutifully empirical about things that are actually transpiring. But as soon as we want to ask an actually specific question—which fields of force are in play and what are they doing to the others—we're back to our (both bad and necessary) reductions. No matter how intensively we remind ourselves, as Bryant argues we should, "that humans occupy no privileged place within being" and "that objects of all sorts and at all scales are on equal ontological footing," there's no way to avoid stepping on the spirit of that recognition as soon as we start to describe, as Bryant also thinks we should, the actual "collectives and entanglements" that exist "between a variety of different types of actors, at a variety of different temporal and spatial scales."[7] Ontology may be flat; descriptions, however various, never are.

Or, in the terms I've suggested here: persons may be collective, but justice never is. It was the late eighteenth and early nineteenth century, I have been arguing, that clearly recognized both the brute fact of our ontological entanglement *and* the need to think of action as if the brute facts were otherwise. And it is this intellectual history, I'm (still) arguing, that can usefully illuminate a tension that remains largely latent in our current theoretical moment's propensity to extoll the heterogeneity and multiplicity of being, as if reduction were something that the right lens might finally eliminate. What we have seen across the nineteenth century's philosophy, law, science, and, above all, narrative fiction is the generation of a characteristically modern (as true then as it is today) double vision: a perspective that both admits our commitment to the special agency of the objects that are human persons and, *at the same time*, acknowledges the merely heuristic, only *quasi* nature of all objects. Materialism, romanticism, economics, law, the novel—all recognized the ways even our most personal- and substantial-seeming bodies had come to seem a little incorporeal, collective, attenuated. But they did not, at the same time, just dispense with personhood altogether. This is the interesting puzzle. "A man must be very criminal indeed," writes Joseph Priestley, "who can maintain what he, at the same time, believes to be ill founded."[8] Criminal—maybe. But on the other hand, how else?

In the two hundred and fifty years since Priestley discovered oxygen and started really to worry about the doctrine of the Christian Resurrection—to worry about whether he was going to have to maintain something ill founded—our particles have gotten more nano, but the fundamental problem has retained its shape. "There is," John Searle has recently proclaimed, "exactly one overriding problem in contemporary philosophy": how to square the "basic facts" (that "the universe consists entirely of particles" organized into "fields of force" or "systems") with the widespread intuition that we humans are "conscious, intentionalistic, rational, social, institutional, political, speech-act performing, ethical and free will possessing agents."[9] It may be that today relatively few of our physicists are worried about what Priestley called "the great doctrine of future retribution."[10] But a quick glance at any new report on climate change will show that our ostensibly secular world is hardly free of the specter of future retribution and that our ostensibly liberal one remains confused about how to understand any single person's individual agency in relation to the structural crisis of the globe's climate.[11]

Our instruments are better and our data bigger. But the increasingly reliable, plentiful information rearticulates rather than solves the problem. The detail with which we can map our interconnection means that there are many more entities than there used to be, many more conceivable stakeholders (to use the go-to word of public policy). But the problem—for Priestley, as for Searle—was never about whether there were two or twenty scales of being. The problem is about how to understand the relevance (or irrelevance) one scale has to another. As Bruno Latour suggests in a new article on agency in the Anthropocene, the problem is that we are "not equipped with the mental and emotional repertoire to deal with such a vast scale of events."

And as we wobble between scales the vertigo is evident: we feel passively sucked along for the ride, as if we are simply "submitting to such a rapid acceleration" of our contemporary crises, all the while knowing that our air-conditioned and animal-proteined lives are responsible for some part of that acceleration and that we haven't voted for governments that might have stopped it (or even talked about it). So in a version of the paradox Ian McEwan's novels mine so successfully and so often, we cringe with guilt (and rightly so), all the while being reminded, as we blow by the tipping point of one feedback loop after another, that there is nothing any of us, individually, certainly, but maybe even together, can do to stop the system. We are, Latour argues, so entirely responsible and "so utterly impotent."[12] Nothing counts, and everything does; it's a strange combination: on the one hand, a triumph of positivism—everything so measurable—yet the question of action, the question of causality, keeps slipping out of our conceptual grasp. "Our disaster," as Henry Clerval, our good friend from 1818, puts it, "is irreparable" (75). But, as he asks his friend Victor, what will we do? Or—more to the point—what is "doing" in conditions of irreparability? In the weird twist of this moment *anthropogenic* has started to sound as much like the end of responsibility—"It's not *me*, it's anthropogenic!"—as a confession.

This perplexity of agency may feel new. But what I want to do in this epilogue is to turn to one last major text of the nineteenth century—Mary Shelley's *Frankenstein*—in order to forward it as a prescient diagnosis of the curious contradictions that appear in a situation where a tragedy seems to have been authored by many hands. On the one hand, as we will see, culprits are everywhere. We are all to blame. But, on the other hand, because when culprits are everywhere no one is especially culpable, "guilty" no longer seems like a useful verdict, and, indeed, the very idea of a verdict itself seems based in misunderstanding.

———+———

Everyone—from its first readers to people who have never read it at all—knows that *Frankenstein* is a modern morality tale about the dangers of over-reaching knowledge. The playbill for Richard Peake's *Presumption*, an 1823 stage adaptation of Shelley's novel, captured this thought early on: "The striking moral exhibited in this story," it read, "is the fatal consequence of that presumption which attempts to penetrate, beyond prescribed depths, into the mysteries of nature."[13] Nearly two hundred years later, when the popular media regularly refers to the novel as if it were a self-evident warning about the perils of scientific development (say, genetically modified "Frankenfoods"), we remain pretty much where Peake left us. Here, for instance, is the first sentence of Maurice Hindle's introduction to my 2003 Penguin edition: "As a cautionary tale warning of the dangers that can be cast into society by a presuming experimental science, *Frankenstein* is without equal." So that would seem to be that: knowledge needs to know its place. A well-managed experimental science might be ok, but a *"presuming"* one? Watch out.

To be fair, this ultracommon reading is not exactly coming from nowhere. Victor himself presents his story as a cautionary lesson in the ills of scientific hubris: "how much happier [is] that man," Victor says, "who believes his native town to be the world, than he who aspires to become greater than his nature will allow" (54). But for all its ubiquity, what I want to suggest here is that this reading of the novel as a warning about the moral pitfalls of "playing God" with an overreaching science is missing the story's more important, and more basic, observation about the way in which scientific knowledge causes our moral frameworks to fail by greatly expanding the number of causes we can see contributing to any single state of affairs. In a certain sense, then, the universal reading is right—science is dangerous—but it's not dangerous for the reasons that the common line assumes. The moral danger is not that we "become greater than [our] nature will allow"; it's in the greatness (the size) and the systematicity (the connectedness) of nature itself. The danger lies not in what we do with science but in the fundamental assumption of natural philosophy: that causality is never merely a one-to-one relationship (where one X is the cause of one Y) but a complex structure of relations in which the explanation for any event can be traced back to a potentially unlimited number of contributory causes and in which the "event" in question is itself simply one link in a proliferate chain that stretches off into an endless future. The problem, that is, is not that Victor is an irresponsible scientist (although he's not the best person ever) but that science, even as it foregrounds itself as nothing but the investigation of causes, makes responsibility a meaningless term.

Under this description we can see that the problem Shelley identifies in her novel is the same one that bogged down the materialist empiricisms on which she's drawing. In the first chapter of this book, we saw how Hartley, Priestley, and James Mill all came to recognize that the enormous amount of data their anatomizations of mind and body produced had begun to interfere with what had been the aim of the anatomizations in the first place: the ability to say exactly what elements had gone into which things. Just imagine the amazing complexity of vibrations "in the air a little above the streets of such a city as London," Priestley said, and you can see what you're up against: the street sweeper, the apple vendor, the clopping horse—but who knows what slighter tremors one is missing? And if one understands vibrations, as these natural philosophers did, not only as elements of one's experience but as causes—as material events that impact the material structure of the world (and the minds that are in it)—then it's easy to see why all our descriptions of causality are going to suffer from the same philosophical flimsiness that dogs the legal doctrine of "proximate cause." As John Stuart Mill has already pointed out for us, our descriptions of cause reach for what's ready to hand—the icy step, the carelessly hoisted anvil—and in doing so they let hosts of other causes—the friend who sent us on that errand, the mothers who fed us—walk scot-free.

When we offer our moralizing reading of the novel—the one in which we wish that Victor hadn't waded beyond the "prescribed depths"—we are treating proximate causes as though they were absolute, as though our conventions of ascribing agency to nearby things and persons were not merely an adequate or sufficient convention but not a convention at all. It is to read the novel, in other words, as a world in which causation runs back only a page or two, as if the dispersed factors that have affected Victor's course to this inflection point could be pared down to only the most local suspects. To think that the world is divided up into "prescribed depths" and proscribed ones requires imagining that there is such a thing as a truly cautious experimental science—one that can not only anticipate but actually know what its effects will be—and entails believing that we can draw a bright line between the good work of discovering facts about the world and the dangerous work of tampering with "essences." Our critique of overreaching knowledge thus requires us to imagine a fully taxonomized world, one in which the entities and relations are sufficiently settled and known for us to be able to keep our investigations in bounds. And because our moralized reading depends on this perfect taxonomy we're left with the odd fact that the reading that sees *Frankenstein* as a critique of Enlightenment rationality has way more confidence in the Enlightenment than the Enlightenment ever did.

"More confidence" because actually practicing empiricists don't think they have a full list of the relevant stuff (a better list is precisely what they are after). There's the stuff we know and the stuff—whether it's DNA, or stem cells, or quarks, or dark matter—we haven't fully grasped, either because of some methodological limitation or because some arbitrary piety has convinced us not to ask. It's the arbitrariness of these limits that Victor indicates when he says that "life and death" had come to seem merely "ideal bounds" (55). What makes them seem "ideal" rather than real boundaries is that he's come to understand everything in terms of cause: he's seen, he says, "how the fine form of man was degraded and wasted," he's "beheld the corruption of death succeed to the blooming cheek of life," and he's examined "all the minutiae of causation, as exemplified in the change from life to death, and death to life" (53). The result, as the now-reversible terms "life to death"/ "death to life" indicate, is that what used to seem like categorical opposites are now just names for different places on a continuum of causality. Like his great predecessor Matilda in Matthew Lewis's *The Monk*—who sees that her guardian's "deep researches into causes and effects" has allowed him to "reverse the order of nature"—the problem isn't that Victor has looked "too far" (for example, beyond his "native town") but that the idea of "far" doesn't make any sense once one has reconceived the world as an infinite web of "all the minutiae of causation."[14] Limits, in this sea of infinite relation, are a thing of the past, and metrics and categories just nonce boxes. "The consequences are too terrible," says *The Monk*'s whinging Ambrosio, who, after raping the woman he loves and murdering her mother, seems finally to have reached his limit. "Ridiculous prejudices," says Matilda.[15]

And fair enough—for both of them. For while we can all get the Victor/ Matilda point—that it's all just stuff, all just cause and effect, and so why stop at the arbitrary line of some "ideal bound" (chemotherapy good, stem cells bad)—we can also probably all imagine cases in which we would want to favor certain causal elements over others (at least until the vitalists foreswear antibiotics). One might, with Victor or Matilda, adopt the stoically antievaluative position Percy Shelley recommended for Necessarians. "A Necessarian," he wrote,

> is inconsequent to his own principles, if he indulges in hatred or contempt. . . . He looks with an elevated and dreadless composure upon the links of the universal chain as they pass before his eyes; while cowardice, curiosity, and inconsistency only assail him in proportion to the feebleness and indistinctness with which he has perceived and rejected the delusions of free-will.[16]

But one also might, on the other hand, seek to reinstall the possibility of morality even at the cost of engaging a prejudicial or "delusi[ve]" humanism.

The darkest lesson of *Frankenstein* is its insistence that (a) these are the options and (b) that there is no peace to be established between them. In this it is unlike *The Monk*, whose conclusion resorts to the intervention of divine punishment to reinstall the possibility of morality. (God's limits might be arbitrary but are not—just ask Job—any less effective for it.) *Frankenstein*, by contrast, bars the transcendence and leaves us in a resolutely material world where there is no way to be but torn between, on the one hand, our recognition that we are simply "links of the universal chain" and, on the other, the hatred, and guilt, and monstrosity that we feel in spite of or, as Percy puts it with precise resonance, "inconsequent to" our enchained condition. This is why thinking of *Frankenstein* as a morality tale doesn't account for the complexity of the problems of justice it raises. Our moral reading treats justice as if the terms on which it depends (actions, persons, intentions) were stable and available notions when the whole force of the novel is to point out the way our different and equally plausible ways of construing these ideas cut against one another in entirely irresolvable ways. Not a morality tale but something like the opposite: a testament both to the manifest pointlessness of trying to apply moral limits to a materialist world and, at the same time, to the stickiness of our commitment to our human evaluations and categories. Like *Pride and Prejudice*, a novel fueled by the incoherence between two ways of valuing persons (family versus merit), *Frankenstein* is fueled by the incoherence between two ways of construing action: as merely one part of an endless series or as something that might be meaningfully, especially, specifiably *yours*.

   To focus this question about action the novel takes what seems like it should be the big event (and it *is* the big event in the movies)—the creation of the creature—and moves it to the beginning. (It's described in the fifth chapter but, as an element of *fabula*, precedes word one). The important drama, this is to say, inheres not, as in other gothics, in the hemming and hawing of desire and suspense that precedes a signal action (the lust consummated, the curtain drawn back, the revenge enacted) but in the post-hoc hemming and hawing of how to understand what (if anything) has been done and what (if anything) one is responsible for. It is in its capturing of this new moral problem—not whether to act out one's desires but about how to read an action—that the modernity of "The Modern Prometheus" lies. And it's for this reason that the crucial moment of the creature's education comes not in the discovery of fire (the overreach of the premodern Prometheus) but in the discovery that the value of fire has everything to do with one's proximity to it. "One day," the creature says, "when I was oppressed by cold, I found a fire which had been left by some wandering beggars, and was overcome with delight at the warmth I experienced from it. In my joy I thrust my hand into the live embers, but quickly drew it out again with a cry of pain. How strange, I thought, that the same cause should produce such opposite effects!" (107). Or, more exactly, how strange that the oppositeness of effects is so entirely a function of where one is standing: too proximate is burning, and just right is warm, but a county or two over someone else's apple trees are starting to wheeze. What we have in the novel, then, is not a lesson about the unpredictability of effects or the ease with which philanthropy goes awry (and in this *Frankenstein* pushes past its parent text,

Caleb Williams) but a lesson in the absolutely crucial bearing nearness has on the value of an action. If all Victor has done is create a creature, it's hard to fault him very much; lots of people bring new creatures into the world. If, however, Victor has killed his brother, hanged the babysitter, strangled his best friend, and murdered his sister-wife on her wedding night, the case is obviously very different—which is to say that the very boundaries of "case" have been redrawn.

And has he done these things? Sort of yes and sort of no. The novel's model for picturing this ambivalence—in which one is both totally and not really to blame—is parentage, since what's odd about parentage is that it seems to imply both unlimited liability (for what cannot be chalked up either to nature or nurture?) and, at the same time, the very minimized responsibility of being a bit player. As we all know, everything is Victor's fault since if Victor had been a better father/mother to his creation the creature wouldn't have ended up cold and alone and rejected by the cottagers he's tried to help and therefore would not have been quite so full of hurt and anger and then would never have killed Victor's brother and so on.... But as we also all know: really? And what about the other abuses that seem so remote from Victor's failures—for example, the father that chases the creature away after he's saved a young boy from drowning? Do we charge the ungrateful father as well—and with what? In the alternate version in which the creature is warmly welcomed into the Frankenstein household, it's probably true that he wouldn't have been at that particular river at that particular time, but who knows? Leave work a few minutes earlier and make it home safe. Maybe things would have gone better if Victor had been a better father—more love could have hardly hurt—but even if Victor had been perfectly loving we wouldn't expect it to guarantee anything. The world, we know, takes vicious swerves. So while we might prefer that Victor welcome his creature, we do so knowing there is no level of care that would ensure the creature's goodness, let alone the justice of anyone else's fate. It would be nice for all involved if Victor were kinder. But it would not, necessarily, be the cause of anything particular, and it therefore feels misguided, like a different kind of overreach, to lay all the disasters at Victor's feet, unable as we are to say what course could have made things go otherwise.

It's worth noting that, at least in nineteenth-century England (although our practices on this seem to be changing), we would not be apt to blame Victor if the creature were a human child since we do not tend to prosecute parents for the actions of their children.[17] And so our uncertainty about Victor's liability is importantly linked to the novel's other great moral question: the question of the creature's humanity. What are creatures of "gigantic stature" made up of the "collect[ed] and arrang[ed] materials" that were once human parts—are they humans? Victor says no: "there can be no community between you and me," he tells the creature (103). But we've been hard on Victor for that, and many have argued that he should grant the creature recognition as a member of the human species. But if this is a problem between humans, it seems strange to dehumanize the creature by treating him as if he were simply a stone Victor has carelessly let careen down a mountain instead of a person who has committed a crime. If the creature is human, Victor may be deeply unsympathetic—but he's not a criminal. And if the creature is a thing (like a rock or a vicious dog), Victor isn't guilty of a failure of sympathy, although he might be considered negligent if the creature was foreseeably murderous (but was he?). Are our children things, or are they people? Are they our effects, or are they their own most proximate causes? Exactly.

So while it makes sense that the feminist and psychoanalytic scholarship that did much of the important work of returning the novel to critical importance in the 1980s and early 1990s would have seen something particularly gendered in all the novel's talk of birth giving and "hideous progeny," what I'm suggesting here is that we can also see the novel using the issue of parentage to capture a much more general problem about the nature of responsibility within a complex chain of antecedent causes and more or less distal effects.[18] We may be the parents of our actions, but some of our children, we also want to say, are seriously on their own. And indeed as Victor is careful to observe—

> If instead of this remark, my father had taken pains to explain to me that the principles of Agrippa had been entirely exploded, and that a modern system of science had been produced, which possessed much greater powers than the ancients, because the powers of the latter were chimerical, while those of the former were real and practical; under such circumstances I should have certainly thrown Agrippa aside and have contented my imagination, warmed as it was, by returning with greater ardour to my former studies. It is even possible that the train of my ideas would never have received the fatal impulse that led to my ruin ... (40)

—there is no father that isn't also someone else's son.

So this is how the case lies: Victor's father is to blame, but also Victor, but also the assorted cottagers and panicked fathers, but also, while we're at it, the creature himself. The novel's real brilliance lies in its ability to make all the answers seem equally right and absolutely contradictory. The problem is not ours alone. Here, for instance, is Victor returning to his hometown after William's murder: "I could hardly sustain," he says, the multitude of feelings that crowded into my mind. I passed through scenes familiar to my youth, but which I had not seen for nearly six years. How altered everything might be during that time! One sudden and desolating change had taken place; but a thousand little circumstances might have by degrees worked other alterations, which, although, they were done more tranquilly, might not be the less decisive. Fear overcame me; I dared not advance, dreading a thousand nameless evils that made me tremble, although I was unable to define them.

As in the creature's discovery in his pocket of the papers detailing his creation, which not only "minutely described . . . every step" Victor "took in the progress of [his] work" but "mingled" this history "with accounts of domestic occurrences" (132), what's remarkable about Victor's sentiments on his return is not that he's full of dread (who wouldn't be?) but that he isn't exactly sure which form of change he should dread more: the "sudden and desolating" one of his brother's murder or the mundane but no "less decisive" ones wrought by "a thousand little circumstances" working "other alterations." Indeed, to the degree that this question is answered by the last sentence of the passage—"a thousand nameless evils that made me tremble"—the untraceable multiplicity of culprits seems more dreadworthy than the idea that you are your younger brother's killer. This isn't to say that Victor won't also think he's a murderer—"I called," he says later, "myself the murderer of William, of Justine, and of Clerval" (181)—just that he won't *always* think this. All this, and "I the cause," he says at one point; "but," he adds, "I was absent when it was committed" (83), so . . . And thus it revolves: "I felt as if I had committed some great crime, the consciousness of which haunted me. I was guiltless, but I had indeed drawn down a horrible curse upon my head, as mortal as that of crime" (167).

Victor's story, which turns the connective tissue of materialism against its own oft-repeated doctrine that "nothing may act where it is not," does not belong to him alone. "Oh, God!" exclaims Elizabeth on learning of William's death, "I have murdered my darling child" (74)—a statement whose confusion of both maternity (she's not the mother) and murder (she's not the killer) speaks not only to the specifically gendered problem of motherhood but to the more generally structural one of causality itself. Indeed, even the creature's murder of William and the framing of Justine are presented as the (incoherent) result of forcing a commitment to justice down a causal chain. For while the journal pages the creature discovers allow him to locate Victor as the proper object of his reparative suit—"But on you only had I any claim for pity and redress, and from you I determined to seek that justice which I

vainly attempted to gain from any other being that wore the human form"
(141)—that singularity does not last long. "Frankenstein!" says the creature
to Victor's brother, "you belong then to my enemy—to him towards whom
I have sworn eternal revenge; you shall be my first victim" (138). One can,
of course, already see the serial logic emerging ("first victim"), but as the
creature continues the ordering of referents and the identification of culprits
become even harder to track. Discovering around the newly dead William's
neck a miniature of William and Victor's mother, the creature decides to
plant it in the pocket of the sleeping Justine:

> Not I, but she, shall suffer; the murder I have committed because I am forever
> robbed of all that she could give me, she shall atone. The crime had its source
> in her: be hers the punishment! Thanks to the lessons of Felix and the sangui-
> nary laws of man, I had learned how to work mischief. (139)

More important than the creature's murderous "mischief" is the unhinged
grammar that it follows. The "she" who shall suffer is, presumably, Justine—there's no doubt that it's Justine who's the "sleeper" who stirs at the
beginning of the paragraph—though the referent is made ambiguous by
the presence of another woman, Frankenstein's mother, who is pictured
on the locket and is much more easily understood as the source (since she's
the source of Victor) of "the crime"—the absence of love—the creature
imagines he's punishing. It's not clear how the creature's unlovedness could
have its source in Justine (she's just about the only one who *hasn't* seen him).
Maybe she's been diverting Victor's love, which might otherwise flow to
the creature? But then this doesn't seem like a "source," exactly. The creature
suffers what Clerval has called an "irreparable" condition—"forever robbed"
of love—and understands its irreparability as proof that everyone, even those
who have never even had the chance to shudder at his presence, is in on its
production.

And, in a way, he's right, since when no one loves you, it is kind of everyone's fault. But everyone's fault isn't really fault at all (as the men in Carlyle's
description of the Manchester uprising showed us in this book's Introduction). Or it is fault, but there's nothing to do about it. What's frightening
about this novel isn't so much the murderous creature as the asymmetry
the creature lights up between a punishment that can only be meted out to
one individual or another for a crime that has its source in everyone. "Not
only you and your family," the creature threatens, "but thousands of others
shall be swallowed up in the whirlwinds of [my] rage" (103). In this sense,
the creature simultaneously instantiates both the materialist and the moral

options for thinking about action. And in his final speech to Walton in the Arctic he gets, finally, to the heart of both matters. On the one hand: "Am I to be thought the only criminal? Why do you not hate Felix, who drove his friend from the door ...?" And on the other: "But it is true that I am a wretch" (224). Two different views, then: both of them true and (therefore) neither of them just.

Acknowledgments

Although the usual caveat about the errors being mine alone is totally in effect here, there is no better (and, for me, no happier) proof of my basic contention in this project than the many aiders, abettors, saving graces, and roadside rescuers without whom this book would not have been possible. I started working on this project nearly a decade ago and have carried it through several institutions and at least as many cities. Along the way, I've benefitted in ways I cannot number from a host of people I'm very happy to be able to acknowledge here.

Adrienne Chapman, Maria Caswell, Tom Murdock, Charlie Shaw, and Jeffery Welch made words and stories important. Oliver Arnold, Karen Beckman, Diana Fuss, Mark Hansen, Tom Keenan, Yousef Komunyakaa, Jeff Nunokawa, James Richardson, Tom Roche, and Laurie Sheck made it clear that words about words and stories can be their own kind of art. Amanda Anderson, Isobel Armstrong, Sharon Cameron, Simon During, Alan Grossman, Richard Halpern, Susie Herman, Simon Jarvis, Jonathan Goldberg, and Michael Moon did me the enormous favor of teaching me to ask better questions. Special thanks to Bradley Grant for just about the best place I've ever lived; to Neil Hertz, the man about Baltimore (and Chicago, and Ithaca, and . . .), for making the stones talk like people; to Matt Benedetto, Tara Bynum, Rachel Cole, Bryan Conn, Meredith Evans, Naomi Fry, David and Stephanie Hershinow, James Kuzner, Claire Jarvis, Benj Myers, Mark Noble, Ben Parris, John Rockefeller, Jordan Stein, Michael Snediker, Matt Taylor, and Tony Wexler for making graduate school sharp and well intentioned; to Todd Burner, Dan Kemp, Jay Liddell, Stephen Moeller, Nick Rankin, Cameron Snaith, Desi Van Til, and Laura Vaughn for seeing the whole picture and not holding it against me; to Ian Lockey, Tim Poovey, the Werehouse (especially Mandy, Mitchell, JB, and Jay), and the Brown-Rodgers-Dixon water tower (my nonvegetable love) for giving Winston-Salem anchorage and light; to Amy and Jamie Montgomery for letting me paint their house and hang out with their pit bulls; to Paul Saint-Amour for his continually generous spirit and radically open intelligence; to Rod Bantjes, Marie Gillis, Richard Nemesvari, Maureen Moynagh, and Cory Rushton for making St. Francis Xavier University and Antigonish, NS a good place to live, teach, write, and, sometimes, to surf; to Tom Brady, April Harriell, Brad and Meg Hayden, Mary Miller, Jordan Smith, and Lucky Tucker for making Oxford feel like home; to Magalí Armillas-Tiseyra, Lindy Brady, Erin Drew, Derrick Harriell, Melissa Ginsburg, Dan Novak, Chris Offutt, Peter Reed, Ian Whittington, and Caroline Wigginton for making work feel like home, too. Michael D'Arcy, Hilary Emmett, Jason Gladstone, Ed Goode, Jason Hoppe, Maica Murphy, Emilio Sauri, Jannette Vusich, and Daniel Worden have always been there (even when I didn't deserve it and often with oysters). Mathias Nilges drives a white dog in a purple pickup, but that's just because he lives near where thanks breaks down on its way into words.

As a critic and a teacher, I've received encouragement from the example of Mark Canuel, Anne-Lise François, Douglass Sullivan-Gonzales, Irene Tucker, and Michael Warner—who make it look easy when they aren't making it look hard in the best way possible. To my great benefit, portions (and often way more than portions) of this project were read with energetic attention and enormous good will by Ian Balfour, Andy Franta, Lisa Siraganian, and the Extraordinarily Long Eighteenth-Century Reading Group at the University of Mississippi (thanks to Marc Lerner, Peter Reed, and Jason Solinger, troopers all).

I'd like to think the Andrew W. Mellon Foundation for the grant that helped get graduate school started and the Department of English and the Dean of Arts at the University of Mississippi for the time and support needed to finish this project off. At Mississippi, I'm especially grateful for our terrific (ask anyone!) department chair, Ivo Kamps, and for my many colleagues in the English Department who prove over and over again that warm and smart aren't opposites. It's hard to imagine having had a more supportive, good-humored group in favor of my finishing this.

An earlier version of Chapter 3, "Castes of Exception: Tradition and the Public Sphere in *The Private Memoirs and Confessions of a Justified Sinner*," appeared in *ELH* 77, no. 2 [2010]: 536–560. An earlier version of Chapter 4, "Nothing Personal: The Decapitations of Character in *A Tale of Two Cities*," appeared in *Novel: A Forum on Fiction* 41, no. 1 [2007]: 29–52. I am grateful to both journals for their permission to use that material here—and for putting it out there in the first place.

I am grateful to Brian McGrath and Sara Guyer for their early interest in this project and their patience in seeing it to print. Helen Tartar allowed me to feel like I was on to something, and Tom Lay made sure I didn't fall off. The challenging, intelligent responses provided by the two readers for Fordham made this book into a far better thing than I could have done on my own. One of those readers remains anonymous, though the set of incredibly useful provocations, wisdom, and insight he or she sent my way makes me grateful every day; the other reader—I've now discovered—was Billy Galperin, who, in 2005, helped me get on the program at my first real-live academic conference, which makes for a full decade of extraordinarily generous input, engagement, and assistance. The talented Nathan Likert helped copy edit and index this book with extraordinary speed and precision. Eric Newman at Fordham University Press was a great help in bringing this from text to book.

Jason Potts is one of the most astute readers/editors of a critical argument—in probably, like, this hemisphere. He's been making my work better for a long time now, and, more important, he helped keep me in the game when it wasn't even clear to me where the game was. It wouldn't have been harder without him; it would have been impossible.

Among Frances Ferguson's many graces is her ability to hear in what you're saying a project that is not only better than the one you think you're talking about but so much better than the one you're thinking/talking about that it may well take you years (+ luck and a tailwind) to catch up to it. All I can say is that I'm really happy to have arrived, after ten years of work, somewhere around the year 2008 and that I will be forever grateful for the futures her example has created—for me as for so many others.

And, finally, my beloved and beyond-thanking conditions of possibility: my parents, John and Lora; my sister, Molly; my brother, Ben; the Ellis family—Peter, Cynthia, Dai, Liz, Tari, Tom; and my family: Cristie, Northrop, Tina. You put up with me when I was trying to write this, and when I was trying not to. This book is for you. Any good lawyer would recommend holding out for better, but I hope you can be persuaded to take this for now.

Notes

Introduction: Personification and Its Discontents

1. Chapter epigraph sources: William Hazlitt, "On Personal Identity," in *Sketches and Essays; and Winterslow (Essays Written There)* (London: Bell & Daldy, 1872), 322; Novalis, *Logological Fragments I,* § 55, in *Philosophical Writings,* trans. and ed. Margaret Mahony Stoljar (Albany: State University of New York Press, 1997), 58.

2. Charles Taylor, *A Secular Age* (Cambridge, Mass.: Harvard University Press, 2007), 146.

3. Karl Marx and Friedrich Engels's remark is from *The Communist Manifesto, a Modern Edition,* introduction by Eric Hobsbawm (London: Verso, 2012), 37; "getting and spending" is from William Wordsworth's sonnet "The world is too much with us," in *The Poetical Works of William Wordsworth,* ed. E. de Selincourt and Helen Darbishire, 2nd ed. (Oxford: Clarendon, 1954), 3:18.

4. Henry Sumner Maine, *The Ancient Law,* 4th ed. (London: John Murray, 1870), 168.

5. E. P. Thompson, *The Making of the English Working Class* (New York: Vintage, 1966), 832; Eric Hobsbawm, *The Age of Revolution, 1789–1848* (New York: Vintage, 1996), 3.

6. John Plotz, *The Crowd: British Literature and Public Politics* (Berkeley: University of California Press, 2000), 2. See also Adela Pinch, *Strange Fits of Passion: Epistemologies of Emotion, Hume to Austen* (Stanford, Calif.: Stanford University Press, 1996); Linda Colley, *Britons: Forging the Nation, 1707–1837* (New Haven, Conn.: Yale University Press, 1992); Mary Poovey, *Making a Social Body: British Cultural Formation, 1830–1864* (Chicago: University of Chicago Press, 1995); Audrey Jaffe, *The Affective Life of the Average Man: The Victorian Novel and the Stock Market Graph* (Columbus: Ohio State University Press, 2010); Audrey Jaffe, *Scenes of Sympathy: Identity and Representation in Victorian Fiction* (Ithaca, N.Y.: Cornell University Press, 2000); and Mary Fairclough, *The Romantic Crowd: Sympathy, Controversy, and Print Culture* (Cambridge: Cambridge University Press, 2013).

7. The question of how "we feel, think, or believe together" is the subject of a large body of work. Virtually all of it is indebted to Benedict Anderson's *Imagined Communities* (London: Verso, 1983), though over the past thirty years scholars have moved away from the rational, print-based publics described by Anderson and in Jürgen Habermas's seminal *The Structural Transformation of the Public Sphere* (Cambridge, Mass.: The MIT Press, 1989). For an important description of publics that exist below the presumed transparence of the Habermasian one, see Michael Warner, *Publics and Counterpublics* (New York: Zone, 2005). For an account of lyric poetry as nocturnal counterpublic, see Daniel Tiffany, *Infidel Poetics: Riddles, Nightlife, Substance* (Chicago: University of

Chicago Press, 2009). For an account of publics constituted less through rational discourse than collective attachment and public feeling, see Lauren Berlant, *Cruel Optimism* (Durham, N.C.: Duke University Press, 2011); and Anne Cvetcovich, *Depression: A Public Feeling* (Durham, N.C.: Duke University Press, 2012). For an account of interrelation that blurs lines between the actors (or "actants") and the "spheres" in which they move, see Bruno Latour, *We Have Never Been Modern*, trans. Catherine Porter (Cambridge, Mass.: Harvard University Press, 1993). For a view of the social that minimizes the place of human-human interaction, see Niklas Luhmann, *The Reality of the Mass Media* (Stanford, Calif.: Stanford University Press, 2000). For an account of worldly sensation as a public constitutively beyond the human, see Mark N. B. Hansen, "The Primacy of Sensation: Psychophysics, Phenomenology, Whitehead," in *Theory Aside*, ed. Jason Potts and Daniel Stout (Durham, N.C.: Duke University Press, 2014); and Mark N. B. Hansen, *Feed Forward: On the Future of Twenty-First-Century Media* (Chicago: University of Chicago Press, 2014).

8. Quoted in Thompson, *Working Class*, 105–106.

9. This is not to say, though, that thoughts about prose genres were entirely missing from the period: see James Beattie's 1783 "On Fable and Romance"; Clara Reeve's 1785 *The Progress of Romance*; William Godwin's 1797 "On History and Romance"; Anna Laetitia Barbauld's 1810 "On the Origin and Progress of Novel Writing." For a helpful account of Barbauld's importance in helping define the novel of the romantic period as a genre, see Claudia L. Johnson, "'Let Me Make the Novels of a Country': Barbauld's *The British Novelists* (1810/1820)," *Novel* 34, no. 2 (2001): 163–179. Although the standard thought (as Reeve's title suggests) is that romance was gradually ceding its cultural ground to the novel, modern criticism has often suggested the longevity of the romance tradition. Michael McKeon's important work *The Origins of the English Novel, 1600–1740* (Baltimore, Md.: Johns Hopkins University Press, 1987), for example, makes "the persistence of romance and the aristocracy" (4) central to his history of the novel as a dialectical (rather than strictly linear) progression. For an account of the importance of romance in relation to the romantic novel in particular, see Ian Duncan, *Modern Romance and Transformations of the Novel: The Gothic, Scott, Dickens* (Cambridge: Cambridge University Press, 2005). For an account of romance's relation to political economy and nation building, see Miranda Burgess, *British Fiction and the Production of Social Order, 1740–1830* (Cambridge: Cambridge University Press, 2005).

10. Samuel Taylor Coleridge, *Biographia Literaria* (London: Rest Fenner, 1817), 1:60.

11. See Mark Philip, "The Fragmented Ideology of Reform," in *The French Revolution and British Popular Politics*, ed. Mark Philip (Cambridge: Cambridge University Press, 1991), 50–77. Kevin Gilmartin's interesting *Print Politics: The Press and Radical Opposition in Early Nineteenth-Century England* (Cambridge: Cambridge University Press, 2005) tracks the way the "revisionist idea of multiple and overlapping spheres"—"a plebian counterpublic sphere"—emerged within the period even as it threatened to fragment a radical movement committed to unanimity and universal representation (6). Thus the ambivalence, Gilmartin argues, congealed in "key formulas like 'radical reform' and 'independent opposition,'" which indicate "a divided motivational structure" according to which the reform movement "attempted to constitute itself in terms that were both fundamental (radical, independent) and negative or relative (reform, opposition)" (5–6).

12. See James Chandler, *England in 1819: The Politics of Literary Culture and the Case of Romantic Historicism* (Chicago: University of Chicago Press, 1998), esp. chap. 2, "The Art of the State."

13. For an account of the centrality of language to these debates about social form—the degree to which both radicals and loyalists understood their struggle to be about the definition of things like constitution, equality, treason, and imagination—see John Barrell's magisterial *Imagining the King's Death: Figurative Treason, Fantasies of Regicide, 1793–1796* (Oxford: Oxford University Press, 2000).

14. "Exceptionally turbulent" is Franco Moretti's assessment of 1790–1810 in *Graphs, Maps, Trees* (London: Verso, 2005), 18. "Exceptionally turbulent," then, in relation to an already turbulent time: "Forty-four genres," Moretti writes, "over 160 years" (from 1740–1900). Moretti's quantification of this generic tumult gives graphic shape to a complexity already familiar to many critics working on prose fiction around 1800. Robert Kiely's seminal study *The Romantic Novel in England* (Cambridge, Mass.: Harvard University Press, 1972) offered an early and important chronicle of the contradictions the romantic novel seemed to involve. His observations have been seconded by people like Katie Trumpener, who in *Bardic Nationalism* (Princeton, N.J.: Princeton University Press, 1997) describes "the history of the British novel" over "the course of the romantic period" as "a history of dislocations, bifurcations, and disengagements" as much as a story of "continuity or accretion" (xv). Trumpener's engagement with "the problem of culture" offers a new source for the generic instability Julian Moynahan had earlier observed in the period's novel: "Romanticism had temporarily unhinged—derailed—the novel by overwhelming it with new expressive possibilities, a new politics of crisis and change, and a new expectation that any substantial story about private persons would reflect the experience of a whole society" (quoted in ibid., xiv). For an important bibliographic survey of the novel in this period, see Peter Garside, *The English Novel, 1770–1829*, 2 vols. (Oxford: Oxford University Press, 2000). For an attempt to turn the "generic promiscuity of the romantic-era novel into an opportunity for "exploring and mapping the contours and conditions" (147) of the period, see Amanda Gilroy and Wil Verhoeven's introduction to and the essays collected in their special issue on the romantic-era novel (*Novel: A Forum on Fiction* 34, no. 2 [2001]: 147–162). For a groundbreaking history of reading in the period, see William St. Clair, *The Reading Nation in the Romantic Period* (Cambridge: Cambridge University Press, 2004).

15. For accounts of the gothic as a genre, see Eve Kosofsky Sedgwick, *The Coherence of Gothic Conventions* (New York: Arno, 1980); Elizabeth R. Napier, *The Failure of Gothic: Problems of Disjunction in an Eighteenth-Century Literary Form* (Oxford: Oxford University Press, 1987); James Watt, *Contesting the Gothic: Fiction, Genre, and Cultural Conflict, 1764–1832* (Cambridge: Cambridge University Press, 1999); Michael Gamer, *Romanticism and the Gothic: Genre, Reception, and Canon Formation* (Cambridge: Cambridge University Press, 2000); and Marshall Brown, *The Gothic Text* (Stanford, Calif.: Stanford University Press, 2005). The mandatory touchstone in discussions of the historical novel as a genre remains Georg Lukács's *The Historical Novel*, which I discuss later, although Avrom Fleischman's *The English Historical Novel: Walter Scott to Virginia Woolf* (Baltimore, Md.: Johns Hopkins University Press, 1971) offers a more standard (and thorough) account of the genre's history. James Chandler's monumental *England in 1819* reshaped contemporary thinking about romantic historicism. For an account

arguing that both Lukács and Chandler position the rise of the historical novel (and, possibly, historical consciousness) too late, see Ruth Mack, *Literary Historicity: Literature and Historical Experience in Eighteenth-Century Britain* (Stanford, Calif.: Stanford University Press, 2009).

16. For a recent view of generic diversity in the romantic period as well as an account of how the very idea of genre came to be inflected within the period, see *Romanticism, History, and the Possibilities of Genre: Re-forming Literature 1789–1837*, ed. Tilottama Rajan and Julia M. Wright (Cambridge: Cambridge University Press, 2006); see also *Recognizing the Romantic Novel: New Histories of British Fiction, 1780–1830*, ed. Jillian Heydt-Stevenson and Charlotte Sussman (Liverpool: Liverpool University Press, 2008). For a collection examining the place of the urban within a presumptively rural romanticism, see *Romantic Metropolis: The Urban Scene of British Culture, 1780–1840*, ed. James Chandler and Kevin Gilmartin (Cambridge: Cambridge University Press, 2011). For issues of the global, see Evan Gottlieb, *Romantic Globalism: British Literature and Modern World Order, 1750–1830* (Columbus: Ohio State University Press, 2014); and *Global Romanticism: Origins, Orientations, and Engagements, 1760–1820*, ed. Evan Gottlieb (Lewisburg, Penn.: Bucknell University Press, 2015). For an account of war's centrality to the romantic imagination, see Mary A. Favret, *War at a Distance: Romanticism and the Making of Modern War Time* (Princeton, N.J.: Princeton University Press, 2010), esp. chap. 4, "Everyday War," which reads Austen's *Persuasion* as a study in the relation between the domestic spaces of the novel and the militarized space abroad. For a discussion of colonial gothic, see Janina Nordius, "Racism and Radicalism in Jamaican Gothic: Cynric R. Williams's *Hamel the Obeah Man*," *ELH* 73, no. 3 (2006): 673–693; for a more "local" version of colonial gothic, see Ian Duncan, "Walter Scott, James Hogg, and Scottish Gothic," in *A New Companion to the Gothic*, ed. David Punter (Chichester: Wiley-Blackwell, 2012), 123–134.

17. For a map of these other genres, see Moretti, *Graphs*, esp. "Figure 9: British novelistic genres, 1740–1900." For a sustained reflection on Chartism and midcentury prose fiction, see Chris R. Vanden Bossche, *Reform Acts: Chartism, Social Agency, and the Victorian Novel, 1832–1867* (Baltimore, Md.: Johns Hopkins University Press, 2014); see also M. O. Grenby, *The Anti-Jacobin Novel: British Conservatism and the French Revolution* (Cambridge: Cambridge University Press, 2001).

18. Kiely, *The Romantic Novel in England*, 1, 12.

19. Walter Scott, *Waverley*, ed. Claire Lamont (Oxford: Oxford University Press, 2015), 7.

20. Edmund Burke, *Reflections on the Revolution in France*, in *Select Works of Edmund Burke: A New Imprint of the Payne Edition*, ed. Francis Canavan (Indianapolis: Liberty Fund, 1999), 2:169, 2:171.

21. Marx and Engels, *The Communist Manifesto*, 37–38.

22. See Elaine Hadley, *Living Liberalism: Practical Citizenship in Mid-Victorian Britain* (Chicago: University of Chicago Press, 2010); Lauren Goodlad, *Victorian Literature and the Victorian State: Character and Governance in a Liberal Society* (Baltimore, Md.: Johns Hopkins University Press, 2004); David Wayne Thomas, *Cultivating Victorians: Liberal Culture and the Aesthetic* (Philadelphia: University of Pennsylvania Press, 2004); and Amanda Anderson, *The Powers of Distance: Cosmopolitanism and the Cultivation of Detach-*

ment (Princeton, N.J.: Princeton University Press, 2001). For three position papers—by Rohan McWilliam, Jordanna Bailkin, and Elaine Hadley—addressing the liberal turn in Victorian scholarship, see the "Forum on Liberalism" published in *Victorian Studies* 48, no. 1 (2005).

23. Eugenio Biagini, *Liberty, Retrenchment, and Reform: Popular Liberalism in the Age of Gladstone, 1860–1880* (Cambridge: Cambridge University Press, 1992), 6.

24. Jonathan Parry, *The Rise and Fall of Liberal Government in Victorian Britain* (New Haven, Conn.: Yale University Press, 1993), 3.

25. It is not possible to give a complete list of work that has positioned itself as a critique of liberalism, in part because this critique was closely tied to other critical projects—the critique of humanism, logocentrism, positivism, interpolation, etc. So broadly construed, the critique of liberalism would include much of the major work of later twentieth-century critical theory: most of Foucault (though perhaps not the later turn to "technologies of the self"); all of Deleuze and Guattari; all of Judith Butler, Jameson, and Derrida; and a vast amount of work by scholars writing from a variety of critical perspectives: e.g., feminist (see, for instance, Mari Matsuda's critique of Rawls in "Liberal Jurisprudence and Abstracted Visions of Human Nature," *New Mexico Law Review* 16 [1986]: 613–30; or Elaine Hadley's critique of Rawls's "inattentiveness to bodily form" [*Living Liberalism*, 21]); psychoanalytic (see Lee Edelman, *No Future: Queer Theory and the Death Drive* [Durham, N.C.: Duke University Press, 2004]); communitarian (e.g., Charles Taylor, *Sources of the Self* [Cambridge: Cambridge University Press, 1989]; or Michael Walzer, "The Communitarian Critique of Liberalism," *Political Theory* 18 [1990]: 6–23); and postcolonial (e.g., Uday Singh Mehta, *Liberalism and Empire: A Study in Nineteenth-Century British Liberal Thought* [Chicago: University of Chicago Press, 1999]; Gayatri Chakravorty Spivak's landmark essay "Can the Subaltern Speak?" in *Marxism and the Interpretation of Culture*, ed. Cary Nelson and Lawrence Grossberg [London: Macmillan, 1998], 271–313; and, more recently, her arguments for "planetarity" in *Death of a Discipline* [New York: Columbia University Press, 2003], esp. chap. 3).

Many of these critiques contest liberalism's universalism: because not everyone or not everywhere (or not everywhen) thinks about the subject as liberalism does, liberalism's ostensible universality is actually culturally specific and can't help but force (in obvious contradiction to its own ideals of tolerance and equality) its demands (for self-monitoring subjects [Foucault], self-authored subjects [Derrida], "rational" and culturally neutral subjects [feminism, postcolonialism, communitarianism], future-oriented and heteronormative politics [Edelman]) onto this landscape of diverse alternatives. In this sense, the focus of this enormous wave of critiques was on the *ideology* of liberalism.

Another diverse set of critiques is now emerging from what we might think of as a more *formal* direction. These critiques tend not to go so much after liberalism's political values (though they may not agree with those either) as they do its ontological assumptions: namely, that it sees the world as if human individuals were the important units, the important actors. This resistance to the monopoly of the human individual funds a variety of recent projects. Some seek to show the fictionality of the divisions that separate the human from the nonhuman (see, for instance, Roberto Esposito, *Bios:*

Biopolitics and Philosophy, trans. Timothy Campbell [Minneapolis: University of Minnesota Press, 2008]; or Cary Wolfe, *Animal Rites: American Culture, the Discourse of Species, and Posthumanist Theory* [Chicago: University of Chicago Press, 2003]) and/or to point out the complex interconnections that give the lie to humanity's presumptive claims to agency (see, for instance, Karen Barad, *Meeting the Universe Halfway: Quantum Physics and the Entanglement of Matter and Meaning* [Durham, N.C.: Duke University Press, 2007]; Marjorie Levinson, "Of Being Numerous: Counting and Matching in Wordsworth's Poetry," *Studies in Romanticism* 49, no. 4 (2011): 633–657; Timothy Morton, *The Ecological Thought* [Cambridge, Mass.: Harvard University Press, 2010]; and Jane Bennett, *Vibrant Matter: Toward a Political Economy of Things* [Durham, N.C.: Duke University Press, 2010]). Still others want to move us past the exclusive claims the human seems to have on our ethical categories (see, for instance, Claire Colebrook's two volumes of essays *Death of the Posthuman: Essays on Extinction* [Ann Arbor, Mich.: Open Humanities Press, 2014]) and to alert us to the limitations of a humancentric ethics and phenomenology (see Graham Harman, *Towards Speculative Realism: Essays and Lectures* [Hants: Zero, 2010]; Timothy Morton, "Here Comes Everything: The Promise of Object-Oriented Ontology," *Qui Parle* 19, no. 2 (2011):163–190; and Ian Bogost, *Alien Phenomenology; or, What It's Like to Be a Thing* [Minneapolis: University of Minnesota Press, 2012]). This list is not exhaustive. I consider the bearing of some of the more formalist/materialist perspectives in relation to Shelley's *Frankenstein* in the epilogue.

26. Edmund Fawcett, *Liberalism: The Life of an Idea* (Princeton, N.J.: Princeton University Press, 2014), 4.

27. Friedrich Engels, *The Condition of the Working Class in England*, trans. Florence Kelley Wischnewetzky (London: Swan Sonnenschein & Co., 1892), 23.

28. In speaking of a character's ending as "a plausible outcome of her actions" I have expressed the idea as simply as I could, but this is not to underrate (indeed, it is almost impossible to overstate) the significance and sophistication of accounts describing the novel as juridical, consequence-dispensing form. From Watt's now-classic comparison of readers to a "jury in a court of law" (*The Rise of the Novel: Studies in Defoe, Richardson, and Fielding* [Berkeley: University of California Press, 2001], 31); to the Foucauldian or surveillance-prone novel of D.A. Miller (*The Novel and the Police* [Berkeley: University of California Press, 1989]), Nancy Armstrong (in *Desire and Domestic Fiction* [Oxford: Oxford University Press, 1987] and her more recent *How Novels Think* [New York: Columbia University Press, 2005]), and John Bender (in *Imagining the Penitentiary: Fiction and the Architecture of Mind in Eighteenth-Century England* [Chicago: University of Chicago Press, 1987], and, more recently, his *Ends of Enlightenment* [Stanford, Calif.: Stanford University Press, 2012]); to the sociologies of individualism in work by Alex Woloch (*The One Versus the Many* [Princeton, N.J.: Princeton University Press, 2005]) and Deidre Shauna Lynch (*The Economy of Character: Novels, Market Culture, and the Business of Inner Meaning* [Chicago: University of Chicago Press, 1998]); all the way up to accounts that engage with evolutionary science like William Flesch's *Comeuppance* (Cambridge, Mass.: Harvard University Press, 2009) or Blakey Vermeule's *Why Do We Care About Literary Characters* (Baltimore, Md.: Johns Hopkins University Press, 2009), the novel has been read as a genre that supports (and reproduces) the systems that ensure we get what we have coming. What has made this general argument

convincing is its ability to yoke the novel's formal features to its social function. The capacity of novelistic narrative to move fluidly between interior psychologies and the external world of social values (particularly after the invention of free indirect style) affirms the reliability of public judgment in the face of modernity's "disembedding." As Michael McKeon has put it, the novel "originat[es] to resolve . . . a cultural crisis in attitudes" about how "external social order is related to the internal, moral state of its members" (*The Origins of the English Novel*, 20). And as free indirect style manages the relation of inner and outer, the novel's diachronic plot makes coherent the relation of earlier and later, the correspondence of good behavior to good ending (or bad to bad) that, Flesch argues, we all expect from novels. The novel's affiliation with social or legal evaluation more generally hasn't been universally approved. Many accounts (including the Foucauldian ones listed here) register the conscripting power of evaluation. Others, like William Galperin (*The Historical Jane Austen* [Philadelphia: University of Pennsylvania Press, 2003]) and Amanda Anderson (*The Powers of Distance: Cosmopolitanism and the Cultivation of Detachment* [Princeton, N.J.: Princeton University Press, 2001]), portray the realist novel as far less conscriptive than the Foucauldian account suggests. In Galperin's account, Austen's novels set themselves against the impetus toward closure that seems to lie in the narrativity of any narrative. In Anderson's account, novels highlight modes of reflection and detachment that allow individuals to deliberate meaningfully about their social relations. Both Galperin and Anderson suggest that novels can contain an extraterritorial space—one not immediately conscripted by the machinery of evaluation—but their accounts thus also necessarily testify to the general pressure of an evaluative world from which those alternative spaces have to be carved.

29. Franco Moretti, *The Bourgeois: Between History and Literature* (London: Verso, 2013), 48.

30. Nancy Armstrong, "The Fiction of Bourgeois Morality" in *The Novel*, ed. Franco Moretti (Princeton, N.J.: Princeton University Press, 2006), 2:349. Armstrong's argument in this essay offers a kind of condensed version of her argument in *How Novels Think*, which writes the history of the English novel as a competition between "individual demands" and "those of the larger community" (7). "The novel," she writes, is "a ubiquitous cultural narrative that not only measures personal growth in terms of an individual's ability to locate him- or herself productively within an aggregate but also and simultaneously measures the aggregate in terms of its ability to accommodate the increasing heterogeneity of individuals" (51). Armstrong's focus on accommodation—individual to group and vice versa—picks up a line on the novel established earlier in Elizabeth Deeds Ermarth's interesting and (it seems to me) underdiscussed work in *Realism and Consensus in the English Novel: Time, Space, and Narrative* (Edinburgh: Edinburgh University Press, 1998).

31. Clarissa as a victim of "relentless brutality" is from Wendy Anne Lee's reading of *Clarissa* in light of Locke's theory of "indifferency" ("A Case for Hard Heartedness: *Clarissa*, Indifferency, and Impersonality," *Eighteenth-Century Fiction* 26, no. 1 [2013]: 35). For Lee, Clarissa's importance as a character lies in her indifference to the mechanisms of reward and punishment and the depth-model psychologies (self-management, consent, etc.) they involve. For a reading of Sade's *Justine* as a novel that refuses to bridge the gap between individual and social conceptions of value, see Frances Ferguson, *Por-*

nography, the Theory: What Utilitarianism Did to Action (Chicago: University of Chicago Press, 2004), esp. chap. 2, "Justine, or the Law of the Road." Ferguson's reading of the novel form in the light of utilitarianism depsychologizes the utilitarianism we have associated, since D. A. Miller and Nancy Armstrong's seminal Foucauldian readings, with the gaze of modern surveillance by stressing how external assessments (scoreboards, spelling bees, Lancastrian classrooms) measure only what we did, not what we meant to do. Thus Sade's *Justine* "enlists [its heroine] in a cartoonlike" parody of her "commitment to the primacy of her intentions. It does not matter in her view that her body has been through the proverbial wars. She can, she thinks, preserve a mental chastity" (63). Intending is, for Ferguson, just another feeling. All the intention in the world isn't going to make "mental chastity" the same as chastity. For Neil Hertz's advice about what to do if George Eliot puts "poor" before your first name ("duck"), see *George Eliot's Pulse* (Stanford, Calif.: Stanford University Press, 2003), esp. chap. 6, "Poor Hetty." The phrases quoted here are from page 96.

32. I have cited it above, but William Flesch's *Comeuppance* should be noted again in relation to this point. The strength of Flesch's book is its ability not just to give a deep account of how our psychological architecture manages these feats of consistent scorekeeping and claim adjusting but to connect them to the diachronic operations of narrative form. For an extension of Flesch's thoughts on reading and bargaining, see his essay "Hyperbolic Discounting and Intertemporal Bargaining" in *Theory Aside*. For an account of the physiology—the anatomy mental and otherwise—of novel reading, see Nicholas Dames, *The Physiology of the Novel: Reading, Neuroscience, and the Form of Victorian Fiction (Oxford: Oxford University Press, 2007)*. Both Flesch and Dames treat reading as a necessarily diachronic activity. For an account of our need—therefore—for a theory of the middle, see Catherine Gallagher's essay "Formalism and Time" *MLQ* 61, no. 1 (2000): 229–251; and the introduction to and essays in *Narrative Middles: Navigating the Nineteenth-Century British Novel*, ed. Caroline Levine and Mario Ortiz-Robles (Columbus: Ohio State University Press, 2011). Both Gallagher and Levine/Ortiz-Robles oppose "middles" to "beginnings/ends." But what Flesch shows is how it is our ability to project many different possible endings, and to bargain between them, that shapes our experience of any narrative middle. For Flesch, it's our orientation to various ends that makes the in-process the process it is.

33. See V. A. C. Gattrell, *The Hanging Tree: Execution and the English People, 1770–1868* (Oxford: Oxford University Press, 1994), esp. chap. 10, "Executing 'Social Others.'"

34. In focusing on the parallels between questions that appeared in nineteenth-century law and the nineteenth-century novel, I am clearly operating in the broad field of law and literature. That field contains a few characteristic modes of proceeding. One mode is theoretical or linguistic, applying questions developed within critical theory, linguistics, or philosophy to legal issues. See, e.g., the debate in *Critical Inquiry* 9, no. 1 (1982), between Richard Dworkin ("Law as Interpretation," 179–200) and Stanley Fish ("Working on the Chain Gang: Interpretation in Law and Literature," 201–216). For a slightly broader view of the connections between law and literature, see Richard A. Posner, *Law and Literature: A Misunderstood Relation* (Cambridge, Mass.: Harvard University Press, 1988); and for a broader view of the range with which critical and poststructuralist theories might be brought to bear on legal and literary concepts, see

Wai Chee Dimock's important *Residues of Justice: Literature, Law, Philosophy* (Berkeley: University of California Press, 1996). A second mode is more sociological/ethical— treating both law and literature as parallel exercises in cultural (rather than linguistic) meaning making. See Richard Weisberg, *Poethics: And Other Strategies of Law and Literature* (New York: Columbia University Press, 1992); Peter Brooks, *Troubling Confessions: Speaking Guilt in Law and Literature* (Chicago: University of Chicago Press, 2000). For a brilliant, catholic, and basically *sui generis* reflection on various issues of legal thinking and social meaning, see Stephen Sedley, *Ashes and Sparks: Essays on Law and Justice* (Cambridge: Cambridge University Press, 2011). My project belongs to the third mode—the historical—which often looks at narrower, period-specific questions (e.g., the place of circumstantial evidence, the rise of negligence law, etc.). Important forerunners of my work here include Alexander Welsh, *Strong Representations: Narrative and Circumstantial Evidence in England* (Baltimore, Md.: Johns Hopkins University Press, 1992); Jonathan Grossman, *The Art of Alibi: English Law Courts and the Novel* (Baltimore, Md.: Johns Hopkins University Press, 2002); Lisa Rodensky, *The Crime in Mind: Criminal Responsibility and the Victorian Novel* (Oxford: Oxford University Press, 2003); Sandra Macpherson, *Harm's Way: Tragic Responsibility and the Novel Form* (Baltimore, Md.: Johns Hopkins University Press, 2010).

35. Hannah Arendt, *The Human Condition* (Chicago: University of Chicago Press, 1998), 240.

36. Mark Canuel has, for instance, made the novel's interest in action central to his account, which argues for "its unflagging effort to make punishments thoroughly answerable to a character's utility" and its commitment to show how "Fanny is perpetually reforming herself by perpetually enduring sanctions" (*The Shadow of Death: Literature, Romanticism, and the Subject of Punishment* [Princeton, N.J.: Princeton University Press, 2007]). My reading of *Mansfield Park* differs from Canuel's, but I am grateful for his book for highlighting an important history of conflict and contradiction in romantic thinking about punishment.

37. This "translucence" is the basic feature of Coleridge's definition of the symbol (*The Statesman's Manual; or, The Bible the Best Guide to Political Skill and Foresight* in *Lay Sermons*, ed. R. J. White, in *The Collected Works of Samuel Taylor Coleridge* [London: Routledge and Kegan Paul, 1972], 6:30). Coleridge's discussion of Wordsworth's figures as channels for a "living and acting power" can be found in *Biographia Literaria* (London: Rest Fenner, 1817), 2:113; Percy Bysshe Shelley, "On Life," in *Percy Bysshe Shelley: Selected Poetry and Prose* (New York: Holt, Rinehart and Winston, 1951), 221. For a book-length meditation on romantic things and the way an everyday object can "become a vessel for pouring, outpouring, hieratic consecration," see Mary Jacobus, *Romantic Things: A Tree, a Rock, a Cloud* (Chicago: University of Chicago Press, 2012), 2.

38. Hazlitt saw this quite quickly: "His Muse," he wrote about Wordsworth, "is a levelling one" ("Mr Wordsworth," in *The Spirit of the Age* [London: George Bell and Sons, 1886], 152).

39. For a literary version of this problem, see M. H. Abrams's essay on "diction and figures" that opens his classic collection *The Correspondent Breeze* (New York: Norton, 1984). There Abrams singles out personification, as practiced by Wordsworth's poetry and theorized by Coleridge, as the central poetic innovation of the period. Whereas

personification is conventionally understood as, in the words of *The Princeton Ency-clopedia of Poetics* (ed. Alex Preminger and T.V. F. Brogan [Princeton, N.J.: Princeton University Press, 1993]), the endowing of "nonhuman objects, abstractions, or creatures with life and human, characteristics" (902), Wordsworth returned it to its etymological roots in "sounding through"—*per/sonarae*. The idea, as Abrams helps show, was not to make things seem like persons but to show how even marginal figures—the leech gatherer, the discharged soldier, etc.—are, in effect, already sounded through by Coleridge's "living and acting power." It is true, I am arguing, that the idea that everyone is sounded through by a universal voice makes prejudice, selfishness, and arbitrary distinction seem like glaringly false impositions, but that war on distinction makes it impossible for romantic personification to reserve a particular place for human persons.

40. Friedrich Schelling's discussion of "allness" comes from *The Philosophy of Art*, as a way of emphasizing the necessary partialness of any representation; divine "allness" is by definition beyond representation. "Phenomenal nature as such," Schelling writes, "is not a complete revelation of God." "God is not equal to the particular result of his affirmation but rather only to the *allness* of these results" (*The Philosophy of Art*, ed. and trans. Douglas W. Stott [Minneapolis: University of Minnesota Press], 27).

41. Habermas, *Structural Transformation of the Public Sphere*, 13, 7.

42. Charles Dickens, *A Tale of Two Cities*, ed. Gillen D'Arcy Wood (New York: Barnes and Noble, 2004), 359.

43. Dickens was not alone in thinking about this incommensurability. George Eliot's *Felix Holt* (1866), for instance, turns on the question of an individual's liability for a collective action (Felix's attempts to lead a drunken mob *away* from destructive action get him charged with manslaughter). In 1856, Walter Bagehot worried about the way "complicated networks of ramified relations" made it impossible to know what effect "any force or any change may produce" (quoted in Richard Menke, *Telegraphic Realism: Victorian Fiction and Other Information Systems* [Stanford, Calif.: Stanford University Press, 2008], 15). In 1862, Margaret Oliphant published her essay "Sensation Novels" in *Blackwood's* (vol. XCI, January–June 1826), an important theorization of both the genre and Wilkie Collins's *The Woman in White* as signs of a new situation in which "we who once did, and made, and declared ourselves masters of all things have relapsed into the natural size of humanity before the great events which have given a new character to the age" (564). Against this backdrop, Dickens's 1859 invocation of the French Revolution and his decision to write "a story of incident pounding the characters in its own mortar, and beating their interest out of them" seems decidedly of its age (John Forster, *The Life of Charles Dickens* [Philadelphia: J. B. Lippincott & Co., 1874], 3:358).

44. For an account of this distinction between species and individual instance as the founding conceptual innovation of political economy, see Irene Tucker's *The Moment of Racial Sight: A History* (Chicago: University of Chicago Press, 2012), esp. chap. 4, "Observing Selection: Charles Darwin and the Emergence of the Racial Sign." "What distinguishes Malthus from those Scottish Enlightenment thinkers immediately preceding him"—and, Tucker will also argue, from Kant's critical method—"is his willingness to imagine the health of the social body as something other than the sum of health of the various individual bodies" (156). For a literary exploration of this same distinction,

see Emily Steinlight's article on *Bleak House*'s "supernumeraries," which argues that political economy yields "the paradox of a total in excess of the total" ("Supernumeraries and the Biopolitical Imagination of Victorian Fiction," *Novel* 43, no. 2 [2010]: 229).

45. See Georg Lukács, *The Historical Novel*, trans. Hannah Mitchell and Stanley Mitchell (Lincoln: University of Nebraska Press, 1983), 23ff. Lukács argues that changes in military organization made history a mass experience for the first time. War, he says, played a role in the "extraordinary broadening of horizons" (24) by which "the national idea becomes the property of the broadest masses . . . that a feeling of nationhood became the experience and property of the peasantry, the lower strata of the petty bourgeoisie and so on" (25). Dickens, I'm arguing, reverses this view, showing the way a nationalized nation belongs to no one individually and, even more, that to act as though one could align the population with particular persons is as apt to yield the Terror as it to create a "broadening of horizons."

46. Ian Duncan's ambitious rethinking of Scott's historical novel (*Scott's Shadow: The Novel in Romantic Edinburgh* [Princeton, N.J.: Princeton University Press, 2012]) positions *Waverley* not simply as a story that fuses the development of individual and national character but, at the same time, a case study in the alienating aestheticism required to make such a union possible (98).

47. Caroline Levine's *Forms: Whole, Rhythm, Hierarchy, Network* (Princeton, N.J.: Princeton University Press, 2015) reads *Bleak House* as staging a similar question about the relation between the individual and the social body: where "most conventional novels that seek to capture a whole society use characters to stand for entire social groups—the dissipated aristocrat, the honest laborer . . . [*Bleak House* casts] narrative persons less as powerful or symbolic agents in their own right than as moments in which complex and invisible social forces cross" (126). Thought of in these terms, *A Tale of Two Cities* stages not a move *from* the synecdochal to the network but the simultaneous functioning of both modes: a networked world characterized by its dynamism and institutionally scaled agency *and* a justice system compelled to resort to synecdoche (making characters stand for social groups) in order to give institutional agency human (and therefore *punishable*) form. This bloody both/and is, for instance, at the heart of *A Tale*'s famous first chapter, which concludes with a virtuoso overview of social conditions ("all these things," the novel says, "and a thousand like them") that continually highlights the difference between those conditions and the "myriads of small creatures" who live through them. Everyone, the novel says, is "environed by" a set of ongoing circumstances that includes currency instability, inflation, and national debt ("making money and spending it"); agricultural crisis and the rural poverty of "rustic mire"; the social disintegration evinced by "daring burglaries by armed men, and highway robberies"; and, worst of all, a justice system entirely inept and meaninglessly cruel in the face of properly social unrest: a "hangman, ever busy and ever worse than useless . . . now stringing up long rows of miscellaneous criminals; . . . now, burning people in the hand at Newgate by the dozen." The problem that interests Dickens, then, right from the beginning of the novel is the discrepancy between structural, population-level dynamics and the mechanism of individual accountability that tries to bring it to order. The mechanisms of justice, here, continue to bang away, administering justice by "the long

row" or "the dozen." But their ceaseless labor—"ever busy"—is a sign of their complete lack of traction—"worse than useless." The gavels keep banging, but the effort now seems perverse—the punishments now a conceptual error and, as such, their own form of injustice.

48. For a claim that runs exactly parallel to this one, see Achille Mbembe's much-cited essay *Necropolitics* (trans. Libby Meintjes), *Public Culture* 15, no. 1 (2003): 11–40. "In France," Mbembe writes, "the advent of the guillotine marks a new phase in the 'democratization' of the means of disposing of the enemies of the state. Indeed, this form of execution that had once been the prerogative of the nobility is extended to all citizens. In a context in which decapitation is viewed as less demeaning than hanging, innovations in the technologies of murder aim not only at 'civilizing' the ways of killing. They also aim at disposing of a large number of victims in a relatively short span of time" (19).

49. The scaling up of modern life and the political-economic or biopolitical perspectives required to think it have been an object of increasing interest to scholars of the Victorian period in the past decade. Both Mary Poovey (in *Genres of the Credit Economy: Mediating Value in Eighteenth- and Nineteenth-Century Britain* [Chicago: University of Chicago Press, 2008]) and Catherine Gallagher (in *The Body Economic: Life, Death, and Sensation in Political Economy and the Victorian Novel* [Princeton, N.J.: Princeton University Press, 2009]), for instance, have suggested the need to rethink our well-worn habit of opposing literature to the Gradgrindism of political economy and offered important accounts of how the novel internalized social science's governing interest in distribution and systemic operation. Even more recently, Lauren Goodlad has argued (in *The Victorian Geopolitical Aesthetic* [Oxford: Oxford University Press, 2015]) that liberalism may, after all, be inadequate for understanding the political dynamics of a Victorian England that was less a nation than it was a massively extended network of economic relations and decidedly unliberal forms of governance. Her book joins ongoing work by Emily Steinlight (see "Supernumeraries"; "Hardy's Unnecessary Lives: The Novel as Surplus," *Novel: A Forum on Fiction* 47, no. 2 [2014]: 224–241; and "Why Novels Are Redundant: Sensation Fiction and the Overpopulation of Literature," *ELH* 79, no. 2 [2012]: 501–535), John Plotz ("Speculative Naturalism and the Problem of Scale: Richard Jefferies's *After London*, After Darwin," *Modern Language Quarterly* 76, no. 1 [2015]: 31–56), and others tracing how Victorian literature engaged the problem of social dynamics whose connection to the individual life seems difficult—or, strictly, impossible—to map.

50. Horace Walpole, "Preface to the First Edition," in *The Castle of Otranto*, ed. W. S. Lewis and E. J. Clery (Oxford: Oxford University Press, 2008), 7.

51. William Godwin, *Enquiry Concerning Political Justice, and its influence on morals and happiness* (London: G. G. and J. Robinson, 1798), 167.

52. In its focus on the incapacity of judicial forms to make sense of the world, my reading of *Frankenstein* follows Jonathan Grossman's argument in *The Art of Alibi*. The question in *Frankenstein*, Grossman argues, is whether "personal relations" can be extracted from the "legal contexts" that give them shape (69). Grossman shows how Percy Shelley, following a Godwinian line, had argued that personal relations not only *could* be extracted from law but that they *needed* to be freed from its "artificial shackles" (71). Mary Shelley's novel, then, appears as a dystopic follow through on the Perceyan posi-

tion: a story about how horrible things might be between two people who operate in the absence of any legal framework at all. The novel is "a monstrous myth of social relations conducted outside of society," its characters "floundering without a framework—even an unjust one—of legal adjudication for their relationship" (82). Like Grossman, I am interested in the unavailability of legal forms. My interest centers not on the personal versus the formal but on the way the very logic of causality on which the law relies also incapacitates it by yielding a world in which anything might be seen to be the effect of everything else.

53. See Hannah Pitkin, *The Concept of Representation* (Berkeley: University of California Press, 1967).

54. See Sandra Macpherson, *Harm's Way*; Jonathan Kramnick, *Actions and Objects from Hobbes to Richardson* (Stanford, Calif.: Stanford University Press, 2010).

55. See David Kurnick, *Empty Houses: Theatrical Failure and the Novel* (Princeton, N.J.: Princeton University Press, 2011).

56. For a recent account of the collective as a mode of resistance to an individualist system of wage labor, see Anne Janowitz, *Lyric and Labour in the Romantic Tradition* (Cambridge: Cambridge University Press, 2005). Janowitz's interests are in what she calls "a lyric of sociality, of transpersonality rather than transcendence, of achieved connections, and one which embod[ies] in poetic structure the argument between individualism and communitarianism" (10). In a similarly utopian vein, Anahid Nersessian's "Radical Love and the Political Romance: Shelley After the Jacobin Novel," *ELH* 79, no. 1 (2012): 111–134, reads "free love as a limit case of Romantic liberalism and, with it, of political modernity" and Shelley's *Revolt of Islam* as a text that "turns against liberal postures of self-possession to improvise an egalitarian community organized not by right of ownership or marriage, but by an erotics of mutual dependence that makes ecstasy political and—more to the point—the political ecstatic" (112). Nersessian's book, *Utopia, Limited: Romanticism and Adjustment* (Cambridge, Mass.: Harvard University Press, 2015), though, is less ecstatic, arguing for the importance of formal concepts (limitation, boundedness, etc.) to romanticism's particular version of utopianism understood as a plan for a "minimally harmful relationship between human beings and a world whose resources are decidedly finite" (16). Its recent publication date means I have not been able to engage very fully with Nersessian's project, but it seems to me that her focus on allocation—of how to manage resources, make adjustments, put this here and that there—is congenial to my interest in justice and the way romantic authors registered (against their more transcendent reputations) the need to lay some specifically bounded responsibility to some "decidedly finite" account.

57. Thompson, *The Making of the English Working Class*, 832.

58. M. H. Abrams, "Structure and Style in the Greater Romantic Lyric" (1965), in *The Correspondent Breeze* (New York: Norton, 1984), 76–108.

59. Thomas Carlyle, *Past and Present* (London: Chapman and Hall, 1872), 13.

1. The Pursuit of Guilty Things: Corporate Actors, Collective Actions, and Romantic Abstraction

1. Chapter epigraph sources: John Milton, *Paradise Lost*, Norton Critical ed., ed. Gordon Teskey (New York: Norton, 2005), book 2, lines 666–670. Samuel Taylor

Coleridge, "John Donne," in *Marginalia II,* in *The Collected Works of Samuel Taylor Coleridge* (Princeton, N.J.: Princeton University Press, 1985), 12:264.

2. Samuel Taylor Coleridge, *Coleridge's Lectures on Shakespeare and Other Dramatists* (London: J. M. Dent & Sons, 1907), 427.

3. Thomas Kyd, *A Treatise on the Law of Corporations* (London: J. Butterworth, 1793), 18. The philosophical puzzle of identity given the exchange of "members" is, of course, not new in 1793. Discussions of the problem—often known as the ship of Theseus after Plutarch's example—or versions thereof turn up across the history of philosophy.

4. William Wordsworth, *The Thirteen Book Prelude of 1805,* in *The Prelude: The Four Texts (1798, 1799, 1805, 1850),* ed. Jonathan Wordsworth (London: Penguin, 1995), book 6, line 558; P. B. Shelley, "Mont Blanc: Lines Written in the Vale of Chamouni (Version A)," in *The Major Works,* ed. Zachary Leader and Michael O'Neill (Oxford: Oxford University Press, 2003), line 64.

5. Wordsworth, *1805 Prelude,* book 6, line 557.

6. See Gilles Deleuze, *The Logic of Sense,* trans. Mark Lester with Charles Stivale, ed. Constantin V. Boundas (New York: Columbia University Press, 1990), 1.

7. Section epigram source: William Hazlitt, "On Corporate Bodies," in *Table Talk* (London: Grant Richards), 362.

8. For a history of attempts at some kind of limited liability prior to its official recognition in law (in England this was in the Limited Liability Act of 1855), see Robert W. Hillman, "Limited Liability in Historical Perspective," *Washington and Lee Law Review* 54, no. 2 (1997): 613–627.

9. For a view minimizing the effects of the Bubble Act on business activity, see Ron Harris, "The Bubble Act: Its Passage and Its Effects on Business Organization," *Journal of Economic History* 54, no. 3 (1994): 610–627. For a description of the inchoate state of the joint stock market in the wake of the Bubble Act, see Philip Mirowski, "The Rise (and Retreat) of a Market: English Joint Stock Shares in the Eighteenth Century," *Journal of Economic History* 41, no. 3 (1981): 559–577.

10. Bishop Carleton Hunt, *The Development of the Business Corporation in England, 1800–1867* (Cambridge, Mass.: Harvard University Press, 1936), 21. Hunt's view is seconded by Harris's more recent characterization of the legal instability following the Bubble Act's repeal. Harris summarizes the unsettled legal situation this way: "An interjudicial conflict that was viewed by outsiders as a massive zigzag existed between 1825 and 1843: prohibitive judgments in King's Bench, Common Pleas, and Chancery in 1825–30, a permissive judgment in Chancery in 1833, a prohibitive one in 1837, and two permissive ones in Common Pleas in 1843. The legal rule was not settled and the outcome of discrete disputes was not predetermined." Ron Harris, *Industrializing English Law: Entrepreneurship and Business Organization, 1720–1844* (Cambridge: Cambridge University Press, 2000), 248.

11. Harris, *Industrializing English Law,* 286.

12. First Report of the Commissioners Appointed to Inquire . . . Whether Any and What Alterations and Amendments Should Be Made in the Law of Partnership (London: George Edward Eyre and William Spottiwood, for Her Majesty's Stationery Office, 1854), 4. Entwhistle's remarks are quoted in R. A. Bryer, "The Mercantile Laws

Commission of 1854 and the Political Economy of Limited Liability," *Economic History Review*, n.s. 50, no. 1 (1997): 37.

13. For an account depicting neoliberalism as an extension of an earlier liberalism, see David Harvey, *A Brief History of Neoliberalism* (Oxford: Oxford University Press, 2005), esp. chap. 2, "The Construction of Consent."

14. The editorial is quoted in Hunt, *The Development of the Business Corporation in England*, 40.

15. J. S. Mill, "Appendix to the Report from the Select Committee on the Law of Partnership," *Parliamentary Papers 18* (1851): 182. Signed; not republished. Original heading: "1.—Reply to Queries by J. Stuart Mill, Esq."

16. Adam Smith, *Wealth of Nations* (New York: Modern Library, 2000), 149. For a smart and recent critique of a common tendency to read Smith's commitment to contract as also a commitment to globalized corporations, see Sankar Muthu, "Adam Smith's Critique of International Trading Companies: Theorizing 'Globalization' in the Age of Enlightenment," *Political Theory* 36, no. 2 (2008): 185–212.

17. Harris, *Industrializing English Law*, 258.

18. Marx's remarks are quoted in James Taylor, *Creating Capitalism: Joint-Stock Politics in British Politics and Culture, 1800–1870* (Suffolk: Boydell and Brewer, 2006), 27. For a further treatment of Marx on limited liability, see Bryer, "The Mercantile Laws Commission of 1854."

19. *The Times* editorial is quoted in Hunt, *The Development of the Business Corporation in England*, 69.

20. See the translator's introduction Maitland writes for Otto von Gierke's *Political Theories of the Middle Age* (Cambridge: Cambridge University Press, 1900). For a cynical account of Innocent's incentives to create the *persona ficta*, see John Dewey, "The Historical Background of Corporate Personality," *Yale Law Journal* 35, no. 6 (1926).

21. It's thanks to this derivation that, Adam Smith points out, "the university of smiths, the university of taylors, &c. are expressions which we commonly meet with in the old charters of ancient towns" (*Wealth of Nations*, 138).

22. William Blackstone, *Commentaries on the Laws of England*, book 1, chap. 18: "Of Corporations." All quotations from Blackstone are from this chapter and in this online edition. http://avalon.law.yale.edu/18th_century/blackstone_bk1ch18.asp.

23. Frederick Pollock, *Principles of Contract at Law and in Equity*, 3rd American ed. (New York: Baker, Voorhis and Co., 1906), 124. Blackstone places a lot of emphasis on the corporation's use of a common seal—"It is," he stresses, "the fixing of the seal, and that only, which unites the several assents of the individuals, who compose the community, and makes one joint assent of the whole." The seal, here, is an administrative talisman, the protocol that, like a magic ring or the pronouncement of marriage, converts discrete numerousness into unity—without it, we are just so many actors.

24. The idea of public benefit flickers around discussions of the corporate form throughout the nineteenth century. Grant's 1850 treatise cited above, for instance, doesn't insist that the public good must be the end of a corporation, but his examples don't do much to suggest otherwise. "By this means [of the corporation] municipalities were furnished with a form of government that never wore out; charitable trusts were secured to the objects of them; . . . the protection, improvement and encouragement

of trades and arts were permanently provided for; and learning and religion kept alive and cherished in times through which probably no other means can be mentioned that would appear equally well qualified to preserve them" (4). See also Brian M. McCall, "The Corporation as an Imperfect Society," *Delaware Journal of Corporate Law* 36 (2011): 511–575; and Reuven Avi-Yonah, "Cyclical Transformations of the Corporate Form: A Historical Perspective on Corporate Social Responsibility," *Delaware Journal of Corporate Law* 30 (2005): 768–818. McCall points out that it was not until the 1830s that Massachusetts and Connecticut removed the requirement that a corporation be engaged in some form of public work to obtain limited liability.

25. Harris, *Industrializing English Law*, 127.

26. Sir Edward Coke, *The Reports of Sir Edward Coke, Knt. In Thirteen Parts* (London: Joseph Butterworth and Son, 1826), 5:303.

27. Sir Frederick Pollock and William Maitland, *The History of the English Law Before the Time of Edward I*, 2nd ed. (Cambridge: Cambridge University Press, 1899), 1:490.

28. In the 1866 case *Vaughan v. Taff Vale Railway* (Mr. Vaughan's woods had been repeatedly set on fire by, he claimed, sparks from passing locomotives), an earlier ruling for the plaintiff was reversed on the grounds that the railway had been given statutory authorization to use steam engines and could not be shown to have been using them negligently. For a description of the case and its importance, see Thomas Beven, *Negligence in Law* (London: Stevens and Haynes, 1895), 1:341.

29. Beven, *Negligence in Law*, 1:381. *Priestley v. Fowler* (1836) is the *first* documented case of an employee seeking compensation for an accident via a tort action. In 1926 John Dewey authored a famous critique of the corporation's ability to have it both ways: "With respect to its property, the fictitious entity has a clear title as an entity; with respect to its liabilities *outside of property and contract, its position is not so clear*; its fictitious character may be cited to relieve it of some obligations usually regarded as moral" ("The Historical Background of Corporate Legal Personality," 668; my emphasis). The notion of corporate tort continues to make trouble. "The history of [limited liability's] application to corporate torts," writes Daniel R. Kahan, "remains somewhat of a mystery and, to date no comprehensive treatment of the subject exists" ("Shareholder Liability for Corporate Torts: A Historical Perspective," *Georgetown Law Journal* 97 [2008–2009]: 1087–1088). For a critique of how limited liability in the twentieth and twenty-first centuries has been "carried unthinkingly beyond the original object of insulating the ultimate investor from the debts of the enterprise," see Phillip I. Blumberg, "Limited Liability and Corporate Groups," *Journal of Corporate Law* 11 (1986–1986): 575. For an even more stringent critique of the current regime, see Henry Hansmann and Reinier Kraakman, "Toward Unlimited Shareholder Liability for Corporate Torts," *Yale Law Journal* 100 (1990–1991): 1879–1934. Hansmann and Kraakman argue that "limited liability in tort cannot be rationalized" (1880).

30. F. W. Maitland, "Moral Personality and Legal Personality," *Journal of Society of Comparative Legislation*, n.s. 6 (1905): 198.

31. Ibid., 200. For additional commentary on Maitland's lecture, see David Runciman, *Pluralism and the Personality of the State* (Cambridge: Cambridge University Press, 1997), chap. 5.

32. Maitland, "Moral Personality and Legal Personality," 200.

33. Hazlitt, "On Corporate Bodies," 369.

34. Section epigram source: Rene Girard, *Desire and the Novel: Self and Other in Literary Structure*, trans. Yvonne Freccero (Baltimore, Md.: Johns Hopkins University Press, 1965), 86.

35. John William Graham, *The Destruction of Daylight: A Study in the Smoke Problem* (London: George Allan, 1907), 1.

36. Joel Franklin Brenner, "Nuisance Law and the Industrial Revolution," *Journal of Legal Studies* 43, no. 3 (1974): 414.

37. William Farr, "Commentary on Coroner's Returns of Violent Deaths, 1852–6," in *Vital Statistics: A Memorial Volume of Selections from the Reports and Writings of William Farr, M.D.*, ed. Noel A. Humphreys (London: Offices of the Sanitary Institute, 1885), 3.

38. Brenner, "Nuisance Law and the Industrial Revolution," 414.

39. Nuisance deals with actions that are typically intentional in origin but diffuse and/or unpredictable in their effects. It goes back at least to 1608, when one William Aldred won a suit against a neighbor who had built a pig sty near Aldred's house, but it extends much earlier if one includes the longer-running penchant for treating "free possession" and "undisturbed possession" as synonymous phrases.

Negligence holds individuals responsible even for those effects they did not intend. It has a hazier legal history. Oliver Wendell Holmes Jr. found no "satisfactory evidence that a man was generally held liable [in Roman or early English law] for [his] accidental consequences," but S. F. C. Milsom's history of the common law suggests that this apparent absence of negligence is, at least in part, an illusion created by the law's adherence to rote forms of trespass (i.e., intentional harm) even in cases where we might now use a different word. Thus, rather than "complaining that the smith did his work so badly that the horse died," Milsom suggests, "his writ would run something like this: why with force and arms the defendant killed the plaintiff's horse, to his damage and against the king's peace." Under this reading (ingeniously suggested by Milsom's noticing how many accused horse-killers "are named or described as smiths") "duty of care" would be a much earlier invention. See S. F. C. Milsom, *Historical Foundations of the Common Law* (Oxford: Butterworth-Heinemann, 1969), 249.

Proximate cause is typically traced to a comment in Francis Bacon's 1630 *Maxims*. Because, Bacon wrote, "it were infinite for the law to judge the cause of causes, and their impulsions from one of another, [the law] contenteth itselfe with the immediate cause, and judgeth of acts by that, without looking to any further degree" (cited in Patrick J. Kelley, "Proximate Cause in Negligence Law: History, Theory, and the Present Darkness," *Washington University Law Quarterly* 69 [1991]: 54). Despite the precedent offered by Bacon's comment, though, Kelley argues that "modern proximate cause doctrine in tort law seemed to spring up, without identifiable tort law antecedents, in the middle of the nineteenth century" (56).

40. Oliver Wendell Holmes Jr., *The Common Law* (Boston: Little, Brown, and Company, 1881), 4.

41. Ibid., 96.

42. *Scott v. Shepherd* (1773) 96 Eng. Rep. 525.

43. William Selwyn, *An Abridgement of the Law of Nisi Prius*, 3 vols., 4th ed. (Lon-

don: W. Clark and Sons, 1817). For the description of the chain of events in the Squib Case, see 417; for the distinction between action and case, see 416.

44. Ibid., 418.

45. Ibid.

46. Holmes, *The Common Law*, 92.

47. Ibid.

48. For thoughts on the practices of coroner's juries, see Harry Smith, "From Deodand to Dependency," *American Journal of Legal History* 11 (1967): 389–403.

49. *Hansard* (May 7, 1846).

50. For a similar reading of the deodand's formality, see Sandra Macpherson, *Harm's Way: Tragic Responsibility and the Novel Form* (Baltimore, Md.: Johns Hopkins University Press, 2010).

51. For a conceptually related discussion of the law in light of the anti- or a-intentionalism in contemporary neuroscience, see Joshua Greene and Jonathan Cohen, "For the Law, Neuroscience Changes Nothing and Everything," *Philosophical Transactions of the Royal Society of London* 359 (2004): 1775–1785.

52. It ought to be no surprise, given this thought, that the deodand is making something of a comeback in our own moment. See, for instance, Tim Maughan, "Could Ancient Laws Help Us Sue the Internet?," an article published in *New Scientist* describing a proposal by Kate Crawford, a principal researcher at Microsoft Research and visiting fellow at the MIT Center for Civic Media, to revive the deodand to handle, among other things, the accountability of algorithms. https://www.newscientist.com/article/mg22630200-600-could-ancient-laws-help-us-sue-the-internet/.

53. The report of the Royal Commission on Noxious Vapours is published in *The Sanitary Record* (November 29, 1878): 345–347.

54. In *Gerard v. Muspratt,* the plaintiff won on grounds that "the law did not tolerate that any person should erect works and carry them on to the injury of the health and property of another." Sir Cresswell Cresswell's ruling in *Gerard v. Muspratt* is cited in A. W. Brian Simpson, *Leading Cases in the Common Law* (Oxford: Clarendon, 1995), 187. Two decades later in *Tipping* the court repeated Cresswell's thought: "if a man by an act . . . sends over his neighbour's land that which is noxious or hurtful to an extent which sensibly diminished the comfort and value of the property . . . that is an actionable injury." Tipping's case against St. Helen's Smelting Company is reported in *Reports of Cases Argued and Determined in the English Courts of Common Law* (Philadelphia: T. & J. W. Johnson & Co., 1871), 116:1093, and it is discussed in Simpson, *Leading Cases in the Common Law*, chap. 7.

55. Sir John Byles, quoted in Simpson, *Leading Cases in the Common Law*, 172. A concurring opinion held that the right of a proprietor to uncontaminated air is "subject to this qualification, that necessities may arise for an interference with that right pro bono public" (Simpson, *Leading Cases in the Common Law*, 173–174).

56. Simpson, *Leading Cases in the Common Law*, 190. The concerns Pollock raised in his dissenting opinion in *Bamford v. Turley* are reported in John Goddard, *A Treatise on the Law of Easements*, 2nd ed. (London: Stevens and Sons, 1877), 291.

57. Coase makes a version of this point forcefully, arguing that our commonsense answer about "who caused the smoke nuisance" (the man who made the smoke) is a fundamental misunderstanding: "The smoke nuisance was caused both by the man who

built the wall and by the man who lit the fires. Given the fires, there would have been no smoke nuisance without the wall; given the wall, there would have been no smoke nuisance without the fires. Eliminate the wall or the fires and the smoke nuisance would disappear." See R. H. Coase, "The Problem of Social Cost," *Journal of Law and Economics* 3 (1960): 12.

58. Coase, "The Problem of Social Cost," 44.

59. J. S. Mill, *A System of Logic: Ratiocinative and Inductive, Being a Connected View of the Principles of Evidence and the Methods of Scientific Investigation*, 8th ed. (New York: Harper & Brothers, 1882), 403.

60. Ibid., 406 ("logical fictions," "assemblage of conditions"); 404 ("dignif[y]," "capricious manner").

61. Section epigram source:"Corporations and Corporation Law," *The Law Magazine; or, Quarterly Review of Jurisprudence* 25, no. 13 (1850): 146.

62. Samuel Taylor Coleridge, *The Statesman's Manual; or The Bible the Best Guide to Political Skill and Foresight*, in *Lay Sermons*, ed. R. J. White, in *The Collected Works of Samuel Taylor Coleridge*, vol. 6 (London: Routledge and Kegan Paul, 1972), 77.

63. David Hartley, *Observations on Man, His Frame, His Duty, and His Expectations*, in 2 parts, 6th corr. and rev. ed. (London: Thomas Tegg and Son, 1834), 47.

64. Wordsworth, *1805 Prelude*, book 6, lines 346–348.

65. Hartley, *Observations*, 48. Coleridge, "The Eolian Harp: Composed at Clevedon, Somersetshire," in *Poetical Works: Part 1. Poems (Reading Text)*, ed. J. C. C. Mays, in *The Collected Works of Samuel Taylor Coleridge*, vol. 16 (Princeton, N.J.: Princeton University Press), line 18.

66. John Horne Tooke, *Epea Pteroenta, or the Diversions of Purley* (London: Thomas Tegg, 1840), 13.

67. Joseph Priestley, *A Course of Lectures on the Theory of Language and Universal Grammar* (Warrington: W. Eyres, 1762), 35.

68. Tooke, *Epea Pteroenta*, 24.

69. John Horne Tooke, "A Letter to Dunning, Esq. by Mr. Horne" (London: J. Johnson, 1778), 11.

70. Ibid., 7.

71. Tooke, *Epea Pteroenta*, 312–313.

72. Susan Manly, *Language, Custom, and Nation in the 1790s: Locke, Tooke, Wordsworth, Edgeworth* (Aldershot: Ashgate, 2007), 12; Tooke, *Epea Pteroenta*, 2:314.

73. Tooke, *Epea Pteroenta*, 313.

74. Hazlitt, quoted in Hans Aarsleff, *The Study of Language in England 1780–1860* (Princeton, N.J.: Princeton University Press, 1967), 71.

75. William Wordsworth, "Preface to *Lyrical Ballads*" (1802), in *William Wordsworth and Samuel Taylor Coleridge, Lyrical Ballads and Related Writings*, ed. William Richey and Daniel Robinson (Boston: Houghton Mifflin, 2002), 393.

76. Hartley, *Observations*, 77–78.

77. Hartley, *Observations*, 22.

78. James Mill, *Analysis of the Human Mind with Notes Illustrative and Critical by Alexander Bain, Andrew Findlater, and George Grote*, ed. John Stuart Mill (London: Longmans, Green, Reader and Dyer, 1878), 136.

79. Joseph Priestley, "Introductory Essays" to *Hartley's Theory of the Human Mind on*

the Principle of the Association of Ideas with Essays Relating to the Subject of It (London: J. Johnson, 1775), xiii.

80. Coleridge, *Statesman's Manual*, 30.

81. Ibid., 19.

82. Ibid., 20.

83. Ibid., 17.

84. Ibid., 18.

85. Ibid., 28.

86. Ibid., 30.

87. Nicholas Halmi, *Genealogy of the Romantic Symbol* (Oxford: Oxford University Press, 2008), 13.

88. Joseph Priestley, in *A Free Discussion of the Doctrines of Materialism and Philosophical Necessity in a Correspondence Between Dr. Price and Dr. Priestley* (London: J. Johnson, 1778), ix. The quote from the *Book of John* is John 5:28–29.

89. Joseph Priestley, *Disquisitions Relating to Matter and Spirit* (London: J. Johnson, 1782), xxiii.

90. Ibid., 195.

91. *Letters on Materialism and Hartley's Theory of the Human Mind Addressed to Joseph Priestley* (London: G. Robinson, 1777), 88.

92. Richard Price, in *A Free Discussion*, 64.

93. Ibid., 74.

94. *Letters on Materialism*, 87.

95. Priestley, *Disquisitions*, 195–197.

96. Ibid., 200.

2. The One and the Manor: On Being, Doing, and Deserving in *Mansfield Park*

1. Chapter epigraph source: Lionel Trilling, *The Opposing Self: Nine Essays in Criticism* (New York: Viking, 1955), 230.

2. Philip Larkin, "Talking in Bed," in *Collected Poems*, ed. Anthony Thwaite (London: Marvell, 1988), 129.

3. See Kingsley Amis, "What Became of Jane Austen?" *The Spectator* (October 4, 1957): 339–340.

4. See Janet Todd, *The Cambridge Introduction to Jane Austen (Cambridge: Cambridge University Press, 2011):* "It is not absolutely clear," writes Todd, "when she began the work, in 1811 or 1812, but it was concluded in the summer of 1813" (75). "Too light, bright and sparkling" is Austen's famous assessment of *Pride and Prejudice* in a letter to her sister Cassandra dated February 4, 1813. *Jane Austen's Letters*, ed. Deirdre Le Faye, 4th ed. (Oxford: Oxford University Press, 2011), 212. For a longer discussion of Amis's question, see Claudia Johnson, "What Became of Jane Austen? *Mansfield Park*," *Persuasions* 17 (1995): 59–70.

5. The good phrase "gradations of liking" is Nina Auerbach's in *Romantic Imprisonment: Women and Other Glorified Outcasts* (New York: Columbia University Press, 1985), 22.

6. For thoughts on the unreviewedness of *Mansfield Park*, see William Galperin, *The Historical Austen* (Philadelphia: University of Pennsylvania Press, 2003), 154.

7. Jane Austen, "Opinions on *Mansfield Park*," in *Minor Works*, in *The Works of Jane Austen*, ed. R.W. Chapman (Oxford: Oxford University Press, 1954), 6:431–435.

8. To be a "stylist" is, as readers will likely know, high praise for Miller (*Jane Austen, or The Secret of Style* [Princeton, N.J.: Princeton University Press, 2003], 42). Sometimes Miller reads Mary as an example of failed style—a stylist whose excesses or laboriousness keep her from the level of "stylothete" (42)—and other times he holds her up, if briefly, as an example of style's claim for autonomous exteriority, its "freedom from contingency" (39).

9. I haven't been able to track down the first use of the now-common phrase "character of the neighborhood," but the idea that zoning laws are necessarily site-specific clearly runs back to the nineteenth-century cases we reviewed in Chapter 1. The legal scholar J. E. Penner traces "the neighbourhood character standard" back to *Sturges v. Bridgeman* (1879) and, in particular, to Thesiger LJ's opinion that "what would be a nuisance in Belgrave Square would not necessarily be so in Bermondsley" ("Nuisance and the Character of the Neighborhood," *Journal of Environmental Law* 5, no. 1 [1993]: 10).

10. Jane Austen, *Pride and Prejudice*, ed. Pat Rogers (Cambridge: Cambridge University Press, 2006), 3. Jane Austen, *Mansfield Park*, ed. John Wiltshire (Cambridge: Cambridge University Press, 2005), 3. Hereafter abbreviated *M* and cited parenthetically by page number.

11. Claudia Johnson, *Jane Austen: Women, Politics, and the Novel* (Chicago: University of Chicago Press, 1988), 73.

12. Jane Austen, *Emma*, ed. Fiona Stafford (London: Penguin, 1996), 9.

13. Ibid., 7; *Pride and Prejudice*, 5.

14. Jane Austen, letter to Cassandra Austen, January 29, 1813 (*Jane Austen's Letters*, 210). The remark has been a sustained topic of critical reflection. See, for instance, Charles Edge, "Mansfield Park and Ordination," *Nineteenth-Century Fiction* 16, no. 3 (1961): 269–274; Joseph W. Donohue Jr., "Ordination and the Divided House at Mansfield Park," *ELH* 32, no. 2 (1965): 169–178; and Michael Karounos, "Ordination and Revolution in Mansfield Park," *SEL* 44, no. 4 (2004): 715–736. Trilling's remarks on the statement can be found in *The Opposing Self*, 214. John Halperin's biography of Jane Austen, *The Life of Jane Austen* (Baltimore, Md.: Johns Hopkins University Press, 1996), 244ff.

15. Galperin, *Historical Austen*, 159, 11.

16. Ibid., 158.

17. Clara Tuite, *Romantic Austen: Sexual Politics and the Literary Canon* (Cambridge: Cambridge University Press, 2002), 101.

18. Alistair Duckworth, *The Improvement of the Estate: A Study of Jane Austen's Novels* (Baltimore, Md.: Johns Hopkins University Press, 1971), 46–47. For another reading showing how "neoclassic esthetic ideals . . . furnish both the novel's structural framework and an analogue of its moral system" (3–4), see Ann Banfield, "The Moral Landscape of *Mansfield Park*," *Nineteenth-Century Fiction* 26, no. 1 (1971): 1–24.

19. For a much broader application of this paradox, see Kevin Gilmartin's *Writing*

Against Revolution: Literary Conservatism in Britain, 1790–1832 (Cambridge: Cambridge University Press, 2007). Gilmartin is working in relation to a field of romantic studies that has often equated "literary expression and the life of the imagination . . . with some primary sympathy for the French Revolution" (1) by surveying the ways in which the "counterrevolutionary culture . . . was itself obsessed" with the relation between "literary expression" and "radical social change" (2). That counterrevolutionary writing needed to avail itself of the expressive power of writing in general opens the door for rethinking the politics that attach to expressivism as well as for exploring the interesting "ambiguities" of Gilmartin, in a phrase whose interest is in the fact that it feels contradictory, "an enterprising and resourceful conservatism" (7).

20. This wouldn't be the first time that Austen had engaged this dichotomy—see Sandra Macpherson, "Rent to Own; or, What's Entailed in *Pride and Prejudice*," *Representations* 82, no. 1 (2003): 1–23—though, again, *Mansfield Park* seems to move in the opposite direction (toward renting) from the one Macpherson lays out.

21. Section epigram source: Jane West, *A Tale of The Times* (London: T. N. Longman and O. Rees, 1799), 1:4.

22. Jane Austen, *Catherine, or the Bower,* in *Catherine and Other Writings*, ed. Margaret Anne Doody and Douglas Murray (Oxford: Oxford University Press, 1993), 148.

23. Gilmartin, *Writing Against Revolution*, 5.

24. Austen, *Catherine*, 146.

25. Ibid., 148.

26. Johnson, *Jane Austen*, 6.

27. For an account of conduct literature's relation to the rise of the novel and, in particular, the shifting gender dynamics of this transformation, see Nancy Armstrong, *Desire and Domestic Fiction: A Political history of the Novel* (Oxford: Oxford University Press, 1987), esp. chap. 2, "The Rise of the Domestic Woman." For an account of this rise of conservative fiction in relation to Austen, see Johnson, *Jane Austen*, esp. chap. 1, "The Novel of Crisis."

28. Joseph Litvak, "The Infection of Acting: Theatricals and Theatricality in Mansfield Park," *ELH* 53, no. 2 (1986): 331.

29. Marilyn Butler, *Jane Austen and the War of Ideas* (1975; Oxford: Oxford University Press, 1987), 296.

30. The third volume of Michel Foucault's *The History of Sexuality*, entitled *The Care of the Self,* trans. Robert Hurley (New York: Pantheon, 1986), for instance points out that "individualism" is "frequently invoked, in different epochs, to explain very diverse phenomena," a looseness that allows "entirely different realities" to be "lumped together." Sometimes "individualism entails an intensification of the values of private life," but "these connections are neither constant nor necessary" (42). There are, for instance, "societies or social groups" where "the individual is invited to assert his self-worth by means of actions that set him apart . . . without his having to attribute any great importance to his private life" (42–43), and there are others where "the relation to self is intensified and developed without this resulting, as if by necessity, in a strengthening of the values of individualism or of private life"—e.g., in Christian asceticism (43). For another take on similar questions, see Foucault, "The Care of the Self," in *Technologies of the Self: A Seminar with Michel Foucault*, ed. Luther H. Martin,

Huck Guttman, and Patrick H. Hutton (Amherst: University of Massachusetts Press, 1988), 16–49. For William Flesch's account of how we weigh the values of differently timed risks and rewards, see his "Hyperbolic Discounting and Intertemporal Bargaining," in *Theory Aside*, ed. Jason Potts and Daniel Stout (Durham, N.C.: Duke University Press, 2014).

31. Butler, *War of Ideas*, 276, 284.

32. Elaine Hadley's *Living Liberalism: Practical Citizenship in Mid-Victorian Britain* (Chicago: University of Chicago Press, 2010), for instance, speaks of "liberal cognition" as a "wide range of strikingly formalized mental attitudes, what the Victorians might call 'frames of mind,' such as disinterestedness, objectivity, reticence, conviction, impersonality, and sincerity, all of which carried with them a moral valence" (9).

33. Butler, *War of Ideas*, 296.

34. For Butler's comments on Scott's willingness to entertain the thought that duty kills, see ibid., 293; the quoted passage comparing Austen to Burke is from page 299.

35. Edmund Burke, *Reflections on the Revolution in France*, in *Select Works of Edmund Burke: A New Imprint of the Payne Edition* (Indianapolis, Ind.: Liberty Fund, 1999), 2:169.

36. Anne-Lise François, *Open Secrets: The Literature of Uncounted Experience* (Stanford, Calif.: Stanford University Press, 2008), 222.

37. See David Marshall, *The Frame of Art: Fictions of Aesthetic Experience, 1750–1815* (Baltimore, Md.: Johns Hopkins University Press, 2005), 72.

38. Section epigram source: Sir Frederick Pollock and William Maitland, *The History of the English Law Before the Time of Edward I*, 2nd ed. (Cambridge: Cambridge University Press, 1899), 1:408.

39. For an account of decades (1790–1825) central to Austen's *oeuvre* as particularly important for confirming (or rediscovering in microcosmic form) the larger historical transition from manor to capitalism, see Ann Bermingham, *Landscape and Ideology: The English Rustic Tradition, 1740–1860* (Berkeley: University of California Press, 1986), esp. 73–74.

40. The Liberty of Havering, for instance, a uniquely prosperous manor, benefited enormously from its location eleven miles from London. For a detailed history of Havering, see Marjorie Keniston McIntosh's two studies, *Autonomy and Community: The Royal Manor of Havering, 1200–1500* (Cambridge: Cambridge University Press, 1986), and *A Community Transformed: The Manor and Liberty of Havering, 1500–1620* (Cambridge: Cambridge University Press, 1991).

41. Sir Edward Coke (?), *The Compleat Copy-Holder*, in *Three Law Tracts* (London: J. Worrall, 1764); quotation is from the prefatory note entitled "To the Reader," n.p.

42. Pollock and Maitland, *The History of the English Law*, 276–277.

43. That liberty runs against the "distinction between land and moveables" established by what Maitland and Pollock, summarizing Glanvill, call "the broad rule . . . that no one can give rights in his land by his will" (*The History of the English Law*, 288).

44. For an important collection of essays covering many aspects of manor life, see *Medieval Society and the Manor Court*, ed. Zvi Razi and Richard Smith (Oxford: Clarendon, 1996). For a similarly detailed look, see the introductory essay to *Select Cases in Manorial Courts, 1250–1550*, ed. L. R. Poos and Lloyd Bonfield (London: Selden Society, 1998).

45. Pollock and Maitland, *The History of the English Law*, 332. The depopulation caused by the Black Plague produced many cases in which lords were without (or without very many) tenants. For an account of the depopulation caused by the Black Death and its effects on manorial organization, see Richard Lachmann, *From Manor to Market: Structural Change in England, 1536–1640* (Madison: University of Wisconsin Press, 1987), esp. chap. 3. Christopher Brooks similarly sees the Black Death diminishing lordly power: "Court rolls from the Tudor and Stuart periods never record cases reflecting the control of the lords over the family lives of base tenants, presumably because the power of enforcing such obligations had been lost during the relative glut of land that followed the fourteenth-century Black Death and the withering away of serfdom." Christopher Brooks, *Law, Politics, and Society in Early Modern England* (Cambridge: Cambridge University Press, 2008), 255.

46. This indifference is part of what made the manor so useful for centralizing and standardizing control in postconquest England since it creates a kind of delegated, modular absolutism. So long as Sir Robert pays the 18*s* he owes for his lands at Greatham, the king doesn't care if it takes one or many villeins to produce it. As S. F. C. Milsom explains, when the monarch looked down from his court he saw a nation of manors and lords, not a nation of manors and lords and the various subordinate statuses below them: "Royal courts would not help the unfree, and rationalized the matter by saying that in their law unfree land belonged to the lord, at whose will the unfree tenants held. Seen from above, therefore, there were no rights in the land, no courts, and no judges: there was a gathering at which the lord's will was declared and recorded" (*The Historical Foundations of the Common Law* [London: Butterworths, 1969], 12).

47. Pollock and Maitland, *The History of the English Law*, 211.

48. For an important account of deep character, see Deidre Shauna Lynch, *The Economy of Character: Novels, Market Culture, and the Business of Inner Meaning* (Chicago: University of Chicago Press, 1998). Lynch gives Austen pride of place in her history of how novelists came to generate characters who "succeed in prompting their readers to conceive of them as beings who take on lives of their own and who thereby escape their social as well as their textual contexts" (8), but—perhaps tellingly—*Mansfield Park* doesn't appear in her book.

49. Nina Auerbach, *Romantic Imprisonment: Women and Other Glorified Outcasts* (New York: Columbia University Press, 1985), 10. For an account of both Fanny Price and Anne Eliot as exemplars of constancy, see Alisdair MacIntyre, *After Virtue: A Study in Moral Theory*, 3rd ed. (Notre Dame, Ind.: University of Notre Dame Press, 2007), esp. chap. 16 and pp. 238–243. MacIntyre's reading of Austen as an advocate of constancy as a virtue is the jumping-off point for Joyce Kerr Tarpley's *Constancy and the Ethics of Jane Austen's Mansfield Park* (Washington, D.C.: Catholic University of America Press, 2010).

50. Jane Austen, *Persuasion*, ed. Patricia Meyer Spacks, 2nd ed. (New York: Norton, 2013), 22.

51. Trilling, *Opposing Self*, 212.

52. François, *Open Secrets*, 235.

53. Trilling, *Opposing Self*, 212.

54. For a history of the centrality (and surprising longevity) of the manorial court,

see Brodie Waddell, "Governing England Through the Manor Courts, 1550–1850," *The Historical Journal* 55, no. 2 (2012): 279–315. The impersonality I am describing as a feature of the manorial system has not always been emphasized. E. P. Thompson, for example, sees the manor not as an impersonal structure but as the basis for what he calls "a customary consciousness in which rights were asserted as 'ours' rather than mine or thine" (*Customs in Common: Studies in Traditional Popular Culture* [London: Penguin, 1993], 179). For Thompson, whose interest in consciousness runs throughout his work, the manor is not psychologically neutral or indifferent to the personal; it grounds a communal psychology that animates each of its members. For another account of individuals "inherit[ing] a certain kind of social or communal psychology of ownership," see E. P. Thompson, "The Grid of Inheritance: A Comment," in *Family and Inheritance: Rural Society in Western Europe, 1200–1800*, ed. Jack Goody et al. (Cambridge: Cambridge University Press, 1978), 337. As I hope is clear, this is not the route that, in my view, Austen takes. Had she done so we would have in *Mansfield Park* something like the English gentry equivalent of *Waverley*, which, published in the same year, deals with the developing "customary consciousness" of its main character. Austen does not, like Thompson and Scott, think that the personality of the collective unit can be so easily transferred into the terms of individual consciousness. Thompson argues that a person could have a manor for a mind, but Austen is interested in the gap that exists between the personality of a place and the personality of a person.

55. Pollock and Maitland, *History of English Law*, 363. Vinogradoff takes a similar line: "One of the most potent factors productive of communalism is the joint liability of members of a village in regard to duties primarily imposed on every single one of them. . . . This communal liability may indeed be at the root of the usual description of all organised local subdivisions as commons or communities" (*Growth of the Manor* [London: Swann Sonnenschein, 1905], 318–319).

56. On the absence of corporate funds and fines in severalty, see Pollock and Maitland, *History of English Law*, 365–366.

57. Frederick Pollock, "The English Manor," in *Oxford Lectures and Other Discourses* (London: Macmillan & Co., 1890), 119.

58. For an efficient overview of these changes, see Lachmann, *Manor to Market*.

59. Ibid., 16.

60. The treatise is often attributed to Sir Edward Coke, though doubts about his authorship are growing, see Brooks, *Law, Politics, and Society in Early Modern England,* 336, n. 132; and David Chan Smith, *Sir Edward Coke and the Reformation of the Laws: Religion, Politics, and Jurisprudence, 1578–1616* (Cambridge: Cambridge University Press, 2014), 29n62.

61. *Compleat Copy-Holder,* 4, 5.

62. Ibid., 45.

63. Wolfram Schmidgen, *Eighteenth-Century Fiction and the Law of Property* (Cambridge: Cambridge University Press, 2006), 15. As Christopher Brooks points out in *Law, Politics, and Society in Early Modern England,* the politics behind this idealization were variable and complicated. Both radical reformers and royalists pointed to the manor's timelessness as warrant for their political visions: reformers saw manors as proof that "local jurisdictions stretched back to the days before the Conquest" and that "true En-

glish justice was to be found in traditional local courts where laymen sat as both judges and juries" (249); royalists saw in the manor "a petty kingdom, where the lord was the king, the tenants the subject, and the courts equivalent to the equitable and common-law jurisdictions at Westminster" (247).

64. *Compleat Copy-Holder*, 46.

65. William Blackstone, *Commentaries on the Laws of England* (San Francisco: Bancroft-Whitney, 1915), 1211.

66. John Scriven, *A Treatise on the Law of Copyholds: And of the Other Tenures (Customary & Freehold) of Lands Within Manors . . .*, 7th ed., rev. Archibald Brown (London: Butterworths, 1896), 5.

67. See, for instance, *Encyclopaedia of the Laws of England with Forms and Precedents by the Most Eminent Legal Authorities*, 2nd ed. (London: Sweet and Maxwell, Ltd., 1907), 8:556.

68. Pollock, *English Manor*, 112.

69. Schmidgen, *Eighteenth-Century Fiction and the Law of Property*, 14.

70. *Compleat Copy-Holder*, 142.

71. Section epigram source: Elizabeth Inchbald, *Lovers' Vows, a Play in Five Acts, from the German of Kotzebue* (Philadelphia: Neal and Mackenzie, 1829), 12; my italics.

72. Austen, *Pride and Prejudice*, 272.

73. Trilling, *Opposing Self*, 212.

74. Ibid.

75. Claudia Johnson reads the novel as an anatomization of "conservative mythology" designed to "expose not only the hollowness but the unwholesomeness of its moral pretensions" (*Jane Austen*, 96). Fanny, in this reading as in Trilling's, remains a site of discomfort—not because Fanny shouldn't be rewarded and is, but because her rewarded-ness merely confirms the grip of a bad system, making her "a heroine ideologically and emotionally identified with the benighted figures who coerce and mislead her" (*Jane Austen*, 96). Duckworth, *Improvement*, 8.

76. Marshall makes this idea of nothingness central to his impressive reading of the novel (to which I return). Marshall (*The Frame of Art*, 85) quotes the part of the novel in which this line ("What a piece of work here is about nothing") is given to Mrs. Norris, who uses it in scolding Fanny for her refusal to play the Cottager's Wife. Marshall does not concentrate on the phrase's origin in the play itself, perhaps because his reading centers on the nothingness of linguistic meaning rather than, as I am emphasizing and as the original scene suggests, the irrelevance of action and reward. Marshall is interested in what it would mean for a work to be "about nothing." I'm interested in the question of doing something for nothing. My interest thus turns away from the individualist terms of sincerity/insincerity, meaning/not-meaning, or intending/not-intending that have been at the forefront of our readings of the theater in *Mansfield Park*. My reading isn't directly opposed to any of these arguments, but they are subsidiary to my argument for the broader irrelevance of merit and action to the world of the novel. To care about whether one acts sincerely or insincerely requires imagining a world in which action matters—a world, I'm arguing, *Mansfield Park* presents only in negative. For more, though, on the question of theatricality, see Kathleen E. Urda, "Why the Show Must Not Go On: 'Real Character' and the Absence of Theatrical

Performances in *Mansfield Park*," *Eighteenth-Century Fiction* 26, no. 2 (2013–2014): 281–302; Anna Lott, "Staging a Lesson: The Theatricals and Proper Conduct in *Mansfield Park*," *Studies in the Novel* 38, no. 3 (2006): 275–287; William Galperin, "The Theatre at Mansfield Park: From Classic to Romantic Once More," *Eighteenth-Century Life* 16, no. 3 (1992): 247–271; Syndy McMillen Conger, "Reading *Lovers' Vows*: Jane Austen's Reflections on English Sense and German Sensibility," *Studies in Philology* 85, no. 1 (1988): 92–113; Elaine Jordan, "Pulpit, Stage, and Novel: *Mansfield Park* and Mrs. Inchbald's *Lovers' Vows*," *Novel: A Forum on Fiction* 20, no. 2 (Winter 1987): 138–148; Joseph Litvak, *Caught in the Act: Theatricality in the Nineteenth-Century English Novel* (Berkeley: University of California Press, 1992); Dvora Zelicovici, "The Inefficacy of Lovers' Vows," *ELH* 50, no. 3 (1983): 531–540; and William Reitzel, "*Mansfield Park* and *Lovers' Vows*," *Review of English Studies* 9, no. 36 (1933): 451–456.

77. Johnson, *Jane Austen*, 73.

78. My argument here closely parallels Anne B. McGrail's in "Fanny Price's 'Customary' Subjectivity: Rereading the Individual in *Mansfield Park*," in *A Companion to Jane Austen Studies*, ed. Laura Cooner Lambdin and Robert Thomas Lambdin (Westport, Conn.: Greenwood, 2000), 57–70. McGrail's aim, like my own, is to suggest the limited purchase possessive individualism has in the novel. She argues that domestic space "retained many of the features of precapitalist society: nonabsolute property relations, a system of obligations to owners and the rules of custom developed through consensus over time" (58) and argues that Fanny's relation to her rooms is closer to "the common cottager who uses wasteland that the lord of the manor does not want" (64).

79. In this section of his reading Marshall (*The Frame of Art*, 88) cites Leo Bersani's descriptions of Fanny as "a negative presence" and as a being who "almost is not."

80. See ibid.

81. Ibid., 89.

82. That there may be costs to adopting the nonpersonality of authorship/art seems implied by Aristotle's original praise: presumably, part of the reason that Homer deserves applause for keeping himself in reserve is because it would be understandable if he were to do otherwise. Marshall's similar sense that self-reservation entails some amount of psychic pain can be seen in his suggestion that Fanny's reticence is an effect of the ideology of male dominance: "We must wonder if the style of silence . . . is for Austen the true womanly style—or whether, rather, the style or persona of silence must mask the true woman style" (ibid., 89). It's not clear to me how this political-ideological reading of this inability to come forward is meant to line up with his more thoroughly poststructuralist claim at the end of the chapter that true self-presentation is a kind of categorical impossibility (because "even the language of real feeling and the integrity of the true self must be spoken in persona, personated in the mask of true acting" [90]). In any case, Marshall's sense that the position of the author is one whose psychic costs may be legitimated but never really erased or compensated by the affordances of impersonal style is repeated, as I will lay out in a moment, in the opening gambit of Miller's *Jane Austen*, where the exacting provinces of style are aligned with particularly minoritized subject positions in the real world.

83. Miller, *Jane Austen*, 51.

84. Ibid., 56.

85. Ibid., 29.

86. M. H. Abrams, "Wordsworth and Coleridge on Diction and Figures," in *The Correspondent Breeze (New York: Norton, 1984)*, 23.

87. The slightly covert reference here is to the discussion in chap. 6, "In Search of the Natural Sublime: The Face on the Forest Floor," of Frances Ferguson's *Solitude and the Sublime: Romanticism and the Aesthetics of Individuation* (New York: Routledge, 1992); particularly germane, here, is her account of William Gilpin's distinction between maps, which don't have faces, and portraits, which do (139). For Ferguson's much more recent discussion of taking impersonal forms (ideological hailing, literary genres, search-engine algorithms) personally—on the ways we respond to these generic structures as if they had not just our number but our name—see her treatment of Miller's reading of Austen in "Now It's Personal: D. A. Miller and Too-Close Reading," *Critical Inquiry* 41, no. 3 (2015): 521–540. That article articulates what's involved in the kind of personalization Miller deploys in his account of style in Austen and close reading. My interest here is, essentially, in the other direction—in the depersonification of persons rather than personification of nonpersons—so I'm limiting my engagement with this more recent text, but I trust that my debts here are as clear to others as they are to me.

88. Johnson, "What Became of Jane Austen?" 65.

89. "demesne, n." *OED Online*, my emphasis. Maitland's explanation here is quoting from his own work with Pollock; see *History of the English Law*, 211.

90. Miller, *Jane Austen*, 68.

91. Leo Bersani, *A Future for Astyanax: Character and Desire in Literature* (New York: Columbia University Press, 1984), 76.

92. Austen, *Pride and Prejudice*, 19.

93. For an account of "the frigid complacencies of wealth and the mechanical mediations that serve them" (1) in Merchant Ivory and Henry James, see Garrett Stewart, "Citizen Adam: The Latest James Ivory and the Last Henry James," *The Henry James Review* 23, no. 1 (2002): 1–24.

94. Austen, *Pride and Prejudice*, 25.

95. Marshall's chapter has an excellent reading of the way in which the characters play roles, paradoxically, as themselves—see *The Frame of Art*, 77.

96. For readings of the endogamous marriage, see Glenda A. Hudson, *Sibling Love and Incest in Jane Austen's Fiction* (London: Macmillan, 1992); Eileen Cleere, "Reinvesting Nieces:'Mansfield Park' and the Economics of Endogamy," *NOVEL: A Forum on Fiction* 28, no. 2 (1995): 113–130; Ellen Pollock, *Incest and the English Novel, 1684–1814* (Baltimore. Md.: Johns Hopkins University Press, 2003); Mary Jean Corbett, "'Cousins in Love, &c.' in Jane Austen," *Tulsa Studies in Women's Literature* 23, no. 2 (2004): 237–259. The politics of the question are complicated—and Corbett offers a particularly nuanced account of the question—but as will soon be clear, I'm less interested in the question of cousin/sibling relation than I am in the problem of manorial narration that the closing paragraphs model. For a broader account of marriage and close kinship in eighteenth- and early nineteenth-century novels (including *Mansfield Park*), see Ruth Perry, "'All in the Family': Consanguinity, Marriage, and Property," in *The Oxford History of the Novel in English*, vol. 2: *English and British Fiction, 1750–1820*, ed. Peter Garside and Karen O'Brien (Oxford: Oxford University Press, 2015), 407–423.

3. Castes of Exception: Tradition and the Public Sphere in *The Private Memoirs and Confessions of a Justified Sinner*

1. James Hogg, *The Private Memoirs and Confessions of a Justified Sinner,* ed. P. D. Garside (Edinburgh: Edinburgh University Press, 2002). Hereafter abbreviated *P* and cited parenthetically by page number.

2. I am marking the difference between a Scottish literature as a part of British literature and Scottish literature as a part of English literature to reflect a discrimination made by Hogg himself. The criticism that has taken up the issue of nationalism most explicitly has tended to see both Britishness and Englishness as, if not themselves synonymous, equally non-Scottish. Scottishness is neither British- nor Englishness. This view is different than the one Hogg himself expresses in a prefatory remark to his (very nationalistic) poem "The Harp of Ossian": "I have always felt it painfully that the name of Scotland, the superior nation in every thing but wealth, should be lost, not in Britain, for that is proper, but in England. In all dispatches we are denominated the English, forsooth! We know ourselves, however, that we are not English, nor ever intend to be." James Hogg, *Songs by the Ettrick Shepherd* (1831; Oxford: Woodstock, 1989).

3. See Sir Walter Scott, *Minstrelsy of the Scottish Border,* ed. T. F. Henderson (Edinburgh: William Blackwood, 1902).

4. For an account of the exportation of ballads in particular, see Leith Davis, "At 'Sang About': Scottish Song and the Challenge to British Culture," in *Scotland and the Borders of Romanticism,* ed. Leith Davis et al. (Cambridge: Cambridge University Press, 2004), 188–203. Davis's argument rests on an opposition between local transmission and international transmission, the difference, that is, which I am arguing Hogg's novel importantly disregards.

5. Ernest Renan, "What Is a Nation?" in *The Nationalism Reader,* ed. Omar Dahbour and Micheline R. Ishay (New York: Humanity Books, 1995), 43.

6. Christopher Harvie, *Scotland and Nationalism,* 3rd ed. (London: Routledge, 1998), 12.

7. Quoted in Susan Manning, *The Puritan-Provincial Vision: Scottish and American Literature in the Nineteenth Century* (Cambridge: Cambridge University Press, 1990), 21.

8. Ian Duncan, "Authenticity Effects: The Work of Fiction in Romantic Scotland," *South Atlantic Quarterly* 102, no. 1 (2003): 95.

9. Wilkie Collins, *The Woman in White* (New York: Harper and Brothers, 1861), 5.

10. Duncan, "Authenticity Effects," 112.

11. Ibid., 112–113.

12. Douglas Mack, *Scottish Fiction and the British Empire* (Edinburgh: Edinburgh University Press, 2005), 77.

13. In his book *Making the English Canon: Print-Capitalism and the Cultural Past, 1700–1770* (Cambridge: Cambridge University Press, 1999), Jonathan Kramnick has offered a broader analysis of this contradiction. See also his article "The Making of the English Canon," *PMLA* 112, no. 5 (1997): 1087–1101, for a discussion of the way "a retrospective investment in the past" was "elaborated in positions often taken in opposition to one another. Seen from one perspective, the past was an object of irrecoverable loss. . . . Seen from another, this Gothic nimbus only obscured the past's essential continuity with the present" (1087).

14. John Barrell, "Putting Down the Rising," in *Scotland and the Borders of Romanticism*, ed. Leith Davis et al. (Cambridge: Cambridge University Press, 2004), 135.

15. Ibid., 136; Mack, *Scottish Fiction and the British Empire*, 77.

16. Katie Trumpener, *Bardic Nationalism: The Romantic Novel and the British Empire* (Princeton, N.J.: Princeton University Press, 1997), 34.

17. Scott, "Introductory Remarks On Popular Poetry," in *Minstrelsy of the Scottish Border*, 12.

18. Ibid., 1.

19. Ibid., 5.

20. Ibid., 12.

21. Ibid., 13.

22. Ibid., 11–12.

23. Ibid., 12, 13.

24. Trumpener, *Bardic Nationalism*, xiii.

25. Eve Sedgwick, *Between Men: English Literature and Male Homosocial Desire* (New York: Columbia University Press, 1985), 98.

26. Here I'm following through on Sedgwick's passing observation that the difference between the two brothers represents the "almost complete triumph of nurture over nature" (ibid., 99).

27. Max Weber, *The Protestant Ethic and the Spirit of Capitalism*, trans. Talcott Parsons (New York: Charles Scribner's Sons, 1958), 36. Michael Walzer, *The Revolution of the Saints: A Study in the Origins of Radical Politics* (Cambridge: Harvard University Press, 1965), 301.

28. Manning, *The Puritan-Provincial Vision*, 3. For an explicitly Foucauldian account of Calvinism, see John Stachniewski, *The Persecutory Imagination* (Oxford: Clarendon, 1991).

29. Walzer, *The Revolution of the Saints*, 27.

30. For Calvinism as way to control rising individualism after Locke, see ibid., 303.

31. Sir Walter Scott, *Demonology and Witchcraft . . . in a series of letters addressed to J. G. Lockhart* (London: William Tegg, n.d.), 75.

32. See Sandra Macpherson, "Rent to Own; or, What's Entailed in *Pride and Prejudice*," *Representations* 82, no. 1 (2003): 1–23.

4. Nothing Personal: The Decapitations of Character in *A Tale of Two Cities*

1. Chapter epigraph source: Alexis de Tocqueville, *The Old Regime and the Revolution*, ed. François Furet and Françoise Mélonio, trans. Alan S. Kahan (Chicago: University of Chicago Press, 1998), 138.

2. Charles Dickens, *A Tale of Two Cities*, ed. Richard Maxwell (London: Penguin, 2003), 389. Hereafter abbreviated *T* and cited parenthetically by page number.

3. For a reading of Dickens's domesticity as a way to staunch modern alienation and the instability of the commodity form, see Jeff Nunokawa, *The Afterlife of Property: Domestic Security and the Victorian Novel* (Princeton, N.J.: Princeton University Press, 2003), in particular chap. 3, "For Your Eyes Only: Private Property and the Oriental Body in *Dombey and Son*." For a reading of Dickens's characterization in light of melodramatic

stage tradition (and a defense against a criticism and culture that privileges interiority and mindedness), see Juliet John, *Dickens Villains: Melodrama, Character, Popular Culture* (Oxford: Oxford University Press, 2003).

4. John Forster, *Life of Charles Dickens* (London: Chapman and Hall, 1904), 2:352.

5. Ibid., 2:350.

6. Ibid., 3:352.

7. G. Robert Stange, "*A Tale of Two Cities* Reconsidered," *English Journal* 47, no. 7 (1957): 382. Forster, *Life of Charles Dickens,* 3:356.

8. Abbé Sieyès, *What Is the Third Estate,* in *The Nationalism Reader,* ed. Omar Dahbour and Micheline R. Ishay (Amherst, N.Y.: Humanity Books, 1999), 37.

9. For an account of the continuity between the French Revolution and the aristocracy, see François Furet, *Interpreting the French Revolution* (Cambridge: Cambridge University Press, 1981).

10. Maximilien Robespierre, "Speech on the Right to Vote," in *Robespierre,* ed. George Rudé (Englewood Cliffs, N.J.: Prentice-Hall, 1967), 15.

11. Ibid., 13.

12. Maximilien Robespierre, "Speech Denouncing the New Conditions of Eligibility," in *The French Revolution and Human Rights: A Brief Documentary History,* trans. and ed. Lynn Hunt (New York: St. Martin's, 1996), 83.

13. Slavoj Žižek, "Robespierre; or, The 'Divine Violence' of Terror," in *Virtue and Terror,* by Maximilien Robespierre, ed. Jean Ducange, trans. John Howe (London: Verso, 2007).

14. See Cates Baldridge, "Alternatives to Bourgeois Individualism in *A Tale of Two Cities,*" *Studies in English Literature, 1500–1900* (1990): 633–654.

15. Georg Lukács, *The Historical Novel* (Lincoln: University of Nebraska Press, 1983), 243.

16. Ibid., 209.

17. George Eliot, *Middlemarch* (London: Penguin, 1994), 4.

18. E. M. Forster, *Aspects of the Novel* (New York: Harcourt, Brace & World, 1954), 108, 109.

19. Ibid., 109.

20. Woloch describes this as unequal allocation as "narrative asymmetry." Alex Woloch, *The One Versus the Many* (Princeton, N.J.: Princeton University Press, 2005), 43.

21. Catherine Gallagher, "The Duplicity of Doubling in *A Tale of Two Cities,*" *Dickens Studies Annual* 12 (1983): 125.

22. E. D. H. Johnson, *Charles Dickens: An Introduction to His Novels* (New York: Random House, 1969), 115.

23. Michel Foucault, "The Eye of Power," in *Power/Knowledge: Selected Interviews and Other Writings, 1972–1977,* ed. Colon Gordon (New York: Pantheon, 1980), 152.

24. For an extended reading of the novel and its last scene along these lines, see Frances Ferguson, "On Terrorism and Morals: Dickens's *A Tale of Two Cities,*" *Partial Answers* 3, no. 2 (2005): 49–74.

25. Woloch, *The One Versus the Many,* 141.

26. Robespierre, "Right to Vote," 19.

27. Thomas Paine, *The Rights of Man*, in *Reflections on the Revolution in France* and *The Rights of Man* (New York: Doubleday Anchor, 1973), 277–278.

28. Maximilien Robespierre, "On the Abolition of the Death Penalty," in *Robespierre*, ed. George Rudé (Englewood Cliffs, N.J.: Prentice-Hall, 1967), 24.

29. Maximilien Robespierre, "On the Action to be Taken against Louis XVI," in *Robespierre*, ed. George Rudé (Englewood Cliffs, N.J.: Prentice-Hall, 1967), 27.

30. Ibid., 28.

31. Lord John Acton, *Lectures on the French Revolution* (London: Macmillan, 1910), 226.

32. Ibid., 226.

33. Hannah Arendt, *The Origins of Totalitarianism* (New York: Harcourt, Brace & World, 1966), 215.

34. Ibid., 459.

35. See Franz Kafka, "In the Penal Colony," in *The Complete Stories* (New York: Schocken, 1971).

36. James Fitzjames Stephen, "Review of *A Tale of Two Cities*," *Saturday Review* (December 17, 1859).

37. Edgar Allan Poe, "The Philosophy of Composition," in *The Unabridged Edgar Allan Poe* (Philadelphia: Running Press, 1983), 1084.

38. See Daniel Arasse, *The Guillotine and the Terror*, trans. Christopher Miller (London: Penguin, 1989).

39. See Garrett Stewart, *Death Sentences: Styles of Dying in British Fiction* (Cambridge, Mass.: Harvard University Press, 1984), for a very different reading of the novel's conclusion. Stewart sees the ending of the novel as exemplary for its ability to show us the difference between dying in fact and dying in art.

5. Not World Enough: Easement, Externality, and the Edges of Justice (*Caleb Williams*)

1. William Ogilvie, *An Essay on the Right of Property in Land* (London: J. Walter, 1782), 155.

2. Ibid., 30, 31.

3. Ibid., 74.

4. Ibid., 194 ("artful strictness"), 201 ("monopoly"), 225 ("small farms").

5. Southey's letter is reproduced in many places, but see *Robert Southey: The Story of His Life Written in His Letters*, ed. John Dennis (Boston: D. Lothrop, 1887), 92.

6. See "The Restorer of Society to Its Natural State" (1801), http://www.ditext .com/spence/restorer.html. The Thomas Spence society has done a good job at making some of his important work available online and gathering up links such as this one above. Print versions of Spence's writings are hard to come by, but see, for instance, *The Political Works of Thomas Spence*, ed. H.T. Dickinson (Newcastle Upon Tyne: Avero [Eighteenth-Century] Publications, 1982).

7. Thomas Spence, *The Constitution of Spensonia* (1803), http://www.ditext.com/ spence/constitution.html.

8. Thomas Spence, "The Real Rights of Man, Plainly Shewn in a Lecture read at

the Philosophical Society in Newcastle, on the 8th of November, 1775, for Printing of which, the Society did the Author the honour to expel him," in *Pig's Meat; or, Lessons for the People, Alias (According to Burke) The Swinish Multitude,* vol. 3 (London: No. 8, Little Turnstile, High Holborn, 1795), 221. http://thomas-spence-society.co.uk/7.html.

9. Jonathan Bate, *Song of the Earth* (Cambridge, Mass.: Harvard University Press, 2000), 266. Bate describes this as a "myth of the pre-political, the pre-historic," but also seems to credit (?) ecopoetics with believing in it: "ecopoetics," he writes, "may properly be regarded as pre-political" (266). For more on Bate's commitment to seeing romantic literature as central to modern ecological thought, see his *Romantic Ecology: Wordsworth and the Environmental Tradition* (1991; London: Routledge, 2013), especially the closing pages of the introduction, in which he seeks to help Wordsworth "to become once more what he imagined himself to be" (9)—to restore Wordsworth, that is, after the denaturing skeptical turns of deconstruction, new historicism, and "buzzwords" like "'history'" and "'politics'" (7), by "mak[ing] claims for the historical [in a nonbuzzword way, presumably] continuity of a tradition of environmental consciousness" (9). Blackstone, *Commentaries on the Laws of England,* book 2, chap. 1: "Of Property in General," http://avalon.law.yale.edu/18th_century/blackstone_bk2ch1.asp.

10. Ogilvie, *An Essay on the Right of Property in Land,* 17–18. It's worth recalling that Spence's proposals were also clear about protecting the rights of individuals to the unequal produce of their property. People could be industrious and keep the fruits of that industry; they just couldn't turn around and use it to buy more property. In the dialogue by which the constitution of Crusonia is elicited, the visiting captain asks whether "would it not tend to make People more industrious if they could lay out their Riches" by owning land, to which his Crusonian host, Mann, responds: "I am surprised to hear you ask that Question. Look either to us or to the Jews, and see if there be any Want of Industry in acquiring Wealth as far as Law allows, though we can buy no Land; but on the contrary you will find a general Industry, not one idle." The real mystery, Mann says, is that anyone bothers to work in England: "But in your Country, what great Incitement, pray, can it be to Industry, to be obliged to give the Cream of one's Endeavours, unthanked, to the Landlord?"

11. Ibid., 17.

12. Thomas Spence, *A Supplement to the History of Robinson Crusoe, Being the Constitution of Crusonia* (1782). http://thomas-spence-society.co.uk/6.html. All quotations from *Crusonia* above are from this electronic edition.

13. The quoted phrase is attributed to a justice Winch in an *Anonymous case* (reported in *Viner's Abridgment of Law and Equity,* 1741–1753) and discussed in the London legal newspaper *The Jurist* (August 9, 1862) as a contravening precedent to a very similar 1862 case, *Webb v. Bird,* in which the plaintiff was suing his neighbor for having built a building that blocked "the current of air which would have come" to his windmill. In 1862 the plaintiff's suit was denied, but in the earlier *Anonymous case* the judge ordered the obstructing building to be torn down. The relevant issue of *The Jurist* can be found collected in *The Jurist,* vol. 8, part 2, new series (London: V. & R. Stevens, Sons, & Haynes, 1863), 371.

14. The key text on enclosure in romanticism remains John Barrell's *The Idea of Landscape and the Sense of Place, 1730–1840: An Approach to the Poetry of John Clare* (Cam-

bridge: Cambridge University Press, 1972). See also his *The Dark Side of the Landscape: The Rural Poor in English Painting, 1730–1840* (Cambridge: Cambridge University Press, 1983).

15. Thomas Hardy, *Tess of the d'Urbervilles: A Pure Woman*, 2nd ed., ed. Sarah E. Maier (Peterborough, Ont.: Broadview Editions, 2007), 57.

16. Henrici de Bracton, *De legibus et consuetudinibus Angliæ. Libri quinque in varios tractatus distincti. Ad diversorum et vetustissimorum codicum collationem typis vulgate*, ed. Sir Travers Twiss (London: Longman & Co. 1878–1883), 1:55–57, http://bracton.law.harvard.edu/Unframed/English/v2/39.htm.

17. Ibid., 57.

18. Ibid., 83.

19. Ibid., 57.

20. Blackstone, *Commentaries on the Laws of England*, 2:20.

21. Bracton, *De legibus*, 83.

22. George Crabb, *The Law of Real Property* (London: A. Maxwell & Son, 1846), 3.

23. Blackstone, *Commentaries on the Laws of England*, 2:20.

24. Ibid., 2:33–34.

25. Bracton, *De legibus*, from the translation of Samuel E. Thorne, http://bracton.law.harvard.edu/Unframed/English/v3/163.htm.

26. Charles James Gale, *A Treatise on the Law of Easements*, 3rd ed. (London: H. Sweet, 1862), 2.

27. Ibid., 3; my emphasis.

28. For some recent analysis of this conflict see, for example, Nicholas House, "Conflicting Property Rights Between Conservation Easements and Oil and Gas Leases in Ohio: Why Current Law Could Benefit Conservation Efforts," *William and Mary Law Review* 55, no. 4 (2014): 1586–1616; Paige Anderson, "Reasonable Accommodation: Split Estates, Conservation Easements, and Drilling in the Marcellus Shale," *Virginia Environmental Law Journal* 31, no. 1 (2013): 136–167; Rachel Heron, Justin S. DuClos, and Shaun A. Goho, "The Interpretation of Surface Easements in Severance Deeds as a Limit on Hydraulic Fracturing Practices," *Buffalo Environmental Law Journal* 19, no. 1 (2011–2012): 73–106.

29. For a treatment of Bentham on easements, see Mary Sokol, "Bentham and Blackstone on Incorporeal Hereditaments," *Journal of Legal History* 15, no. 3 (1994): 287–305.

30. William Wordsworth, "Michael. A Pastoral Poem," in *The Poetical Works of William Wordsworth*, 2nd ed., ed. E. de Selincourt and Helen Darbishire (Oxford: Clarendon, 1954), line 211.

31. For Godwin on promises, see Ian Balfour, "Promises, Promises: Social and Other Contracts in the English Jacobins (Godwin/Inchbald)," in *New Romanticisms: Theory and Critical Practice*, ed. David L. Clark and Donald C. Goellnicht (Toronto: University of Toronto Press, 1994), 225–250.

32. William Godwin, *Enquiry Concerning Political Justice, and its influence on morals and happiness* (London: G. G. and J. Robinson, 1798), 167.

33. For a reading of Godwin's reliance on reason as a "a uniquely violent conceptual experiment, an attempt to hurl humanity into a space beyond any historical de-

termination," see David Collings, "The Romance of the Impossible: William Godwin in the Empty Place of Reason," *ELH* 70, no. 3 (2003): 848. For Godwin's relationship to the history of anarchism, see John P. Clark, *The Philosophical Anarchism of William Godwin* (Princeton, N.J.: Princeton University Press, 1977), or, more recently, Chris Pierson, "The Reluctant Pirate: Godwin, Justice, and Property," *Journal of the History of Ideas* 71, no. 4 (2010): 569–591.

34. Godwin, *Enquiry*, 158.

35. Ibid., 136.

36. Ibid., 161.

37. Ibid., 164 ("nothing that is strictly . . . our own"), 162.

38. Ibid., 224.

39. How to understand the link between Godwin's political writing and his work as a novelist is a source of perennial debate. Gary Handwerk, for instance, argues that "the tendency of *Caleb Williams*, and indeed of all Godwin's fiction, runs fundamentally contrary to the political assumptions and expectations of *Political Justice*" ("Of Caleb's Guilt and Godwin's Truth: Ideology and Ethics in *Caleb Williams*," *ELH* 60, no. 4 [1993]: 940). Not all critics have taken such a diametric line: Scarlet Bowen's recent study, *The Politics of Custom in Eighteenth-Century British Fiction* (New York: Palgrave Macmillan, 2010), for example, has argued that certain political ideals, particularly the commitment to custom and gradualism, carry over from one project to the other. But most critics (including Bowen) see the transition to involve some major change. Sometimes that change is, as Handwerk suggests, caused by a shift in ideology or Godwin's understandably growing pessimism in light of the 1794 Treason Trials. In other accounts, though, critics have argued what seems to me like a strong line: that the novel form forces issues that might have lain dormant in the political theory. See, for instance, Evan Radcliffe, "Godwin from 'Metaphysician' to Novelist: *Political Justice*, *Caleb Williams*, and the Tension Between Philosophical Argument and Narrative," *Modern Philology* 97, no. 4 (2000): 528–533; or Penny Fielding's argument in "'No Such Thing as Action': William Godwin, the Decision, and the Secret," *Novel* 42, no. 3 (2009): 380–886, that "the novel form's very insistence on instantiation, on the consequences of the action of the moment, or the narrative of decision, allow Godwin to explore some of the tensions already present in *Political Justice*" (382). Both David Collings's essay "The Romance of the Impossible" and John Bender's essay "The Penetrating Gaze and Narration in *Caleb Williams*," in *Ends of Enlightenment* (Stanford, Calif.: Stanford University Press, 2012), see *Caleb Williams* exposing problems with violence (Collings) and authority (Bender) that run against the aims established in the *Enquiry*. In her essay on Godwin's notions of justice, Tilottama Rajan sees the teleological pressure of the novel form as a threat to the sustained self-criticism Godwin imagines judgment to entail ("Judging Justice: Godwin's Critique of Judgment in *Caleb Williams* and Other Novels," *The Eighteenth Century* 51, no. 3 [2010]: 341–362). Rajan, there, is working out a version of the question about narrative form raised in Jonathan Grossman's argument (*The Art of Alibi: English Law Courts and the Novel* [Baltimore, Md.: Johns Hopkins University Press, 2002], 61) about *Caleb Williams* as a key text for marking a larger shift in British fiction from stories that climax with scenes of punishment to stories that climax with trial scenes and "self-justifying storytellers" they involve.

40. Timothy Campbell, "'The Business of War': William Godwin, Enmity, and Historical Representation," *ELH* 76, no. 2 (2009): 343–369, situates the "tortuous enmity" (356) of this novel as just one moment in a larger pattern in Godwin's thought: "an uneasy attraction to enmity" (356) that stood, in one sense, in dramatic contrast to his otherwise "pacific philosophy" (355) but also in opposition to the larger draining of affect (see 350) characteristic of a nation in which even war could be increasingly commercialized.

41. William Godwin, "Godwin's Preface to the Standard Novels Edition," reprinted in *Caleb Williams*, ed. Pamela Clemit (Oxford: Oxford University Press, 2009), 348. Pages from the text of the actual novel will be cited parenthetically in the text.

42. Both Nicole Jordan ("The Promise and Frustration of Plebeian Public Opinion in *Caleb Williams*," *Eighteenth-Century Fiction 19, no. 3* [2007]: 243–266) and David O'Shaughnessy ("Caleb Williams and the Philomaths: Recalibrating Political Justice for the Nineteenth Century," *Nineteenth-Century Literature* 66, no. 4 [2012]: 423–448) have offered accounts that read the novel in relation to changing conceptions of the public sphere in light of plebian and populist movements in the 1790s. My account here is less focused on the problem of public rationality or public decision making than on the ways in which simply belonging to a group whose parameters remain necessarily undefined makes the value of any action incalculable.

43. Godwin, "Preface to the Standard Novels Edition," 351.

44. The line I am taking here is quite close to the one laid out in Fielding's "'No Such Thing as Action.'" Godwin's *Enquiry* had, Fielding argues, set up an uneasy mixture according to which ethical decision making was defined precisely by its freedom from prescription yet also had to be understood as "a consequence of antecedents [which were] ultimately part of Godwin's impersonal, rational universe of 'the boundless progress of things' that traverses and motivates individual subjects." Decision making thus had both to be wholly unconditioned and "take into account specific or singular circumstances." "Squaring this circle," Fielding argues, "seems possible in *Political Justice* (where these circumstances do not have to demonstrate specific social calculations)"; "*Caleb Williams*, a novel in which characters come under the pressure of actual decisions, shows how difficult it in fact is" (383). From this reading—either in Fielding's formulations or mine of the absolutely determinative and, at the same time, absolutely incalculable circumstances that bear on any decision, it becomes possible, as I'll argue more fully in the epilogue, to see how much *Frankenstein* shares with what is in many ways its parent text.

45. Godwin, "Preface to the Standard Novels Edition," 349.

46. Ibid.

47. We might understand "neighbourhood," in this light, as Godwin's more colloquial word for what Clifford Siskin calls "system." *Caleb Williams*, he argues, is a novel obsessed with the ways things "'intrude' into each other" once they enter and are "ordered by system." As a result, Siskin argues, "Caleb comes to feel part of the very things that oppress him." Clifford Siskin, "Novels and Systems," *Novel: A Forum on Fiction* 34, no. 2 (2001): 202–215. Rajan's "Judging Justice" highlights a similar issue of intervolvement in the novel's narrative structure: "The stories of Caleb and Falkland each claim to tell the whole truth and nothing but the truth. But because it contains so

many different stories, the narrative, though told by Caleb, becomes a magnetic field of interactions between characters, and characters and readers, that is in excess of Caleb's actual story" (346).

48. Godwin, *Enquiry*, 218.

49. Andrew Franta offers a view of this absence of coordination in his reading of the "series of failed handshakes" that punctuate the plot of *Caleb Williams* ("Godwin's Handshake," *PMLA* 122, no. 3 [2007]: 697). By historicizing the gesture or action that is a handshake (it was, Franta argues, an enactment of equality before it was a gesture that presumed it), Franta is able to trace Godwin's pessimistic conclusion that "there is no 'due medium between individual and concert'" as well as to reassess the novel as one that calls into question both "the conservative attack on the revolution and the radical defense of it" (697).

50. For a reading of Godwin's engagement with debates about the nature of honor in the 1790s and, more particularly, his effort to generate an abstracted and desentimentalized form of honor that would be public rather than private and, at least in theory, immune to the forms of volatility and scarcity we're seeing here, see Jamison Kantor, "Burke, Godwin, and the Politics of Honor," *SEL* 54, no. 3 (2014): 675–696.

51. Godwin, *Enquiry*, 128.

52. Godwin, "Preface to the 1794 Edition," in *Caleb Williams*, 312.

53. Marilyn Butler, *Jane Austen and the War of Ideas* (Oxford: Oxford University Press, 1987), 61.

54. The point, here, is that an account of psychology or mind (of temperament, intention, obsession) can only take us so far as an explanation for how things go wrong in this novel. For accounts that focus on the psychologism of the novel (often as opposed to the abstraction of the *Enquiry*), see Kenneth W. Graham, "Narrative and Ideology in Godwin's *Caleb Williams*," *Eighteenth-Century Fiction* 2, no. 3 (1990): 215–228; and Eric Daffron, "'Magnetical Sympathy': Strategies of Power and Resistance in Godwin's *Caleb Williams*," *Criticism* 37 (1995): 213–232.

55. For an account that considers *Caleb Williams* in light of epidemiology and "nervous bodies," see Peter Melville Logan, "Narrating Hysteria, 'Caleb Williams,' and the Cultural History of Nerves," *Novel: A Forum on Fiction* 29, no. 2 (1996): 206–222.

56. My argument that Godwin is rethinking—or trying to think his way around—the idea of verdicts runs close to Tilottama Rajan's in "Judging Justice," but the question of how to read the endings has been much discussed in the criticism. Since D. G. Dumas unearthed the original, cancelled ending in the holograph held by the Victoria and Albert Museum ("Things as They Were: The Original Ending of *Caleb Williams*," *SEL* 6, no. 3 [1966]: 575–597), critics have debated possible explanations for and significance of the revision. Dumas argues that the rewritten ending eliminates much of the political tension that defines the novel and had been given greater scope in the unpublished first ending (see also 584): "From one version of the ending to the other we pass from a Caleb victim of the institutions of society to a Caleb victim as much to his own egoism as Falkland's persecution" (591). Gary Kelly argues that the revised ending was designed "to communicate to his readers some of his own sense of elevation and passion in the pursuit of truth," a pursuit much needed "as Government repression increased late in 1793 and early in 1794" (*The Jacobin Novel: 1780–1805* [Oxford: Clar-

endon, 1976], 186). For Marilyn Butler it is the second, published ending's eschewal of structural oppression that makes it "different and [more] profound": "The first version is the more tragic at the level of external action, but it hands over responsibility for the dénouement to an external agent—the law—and so suffers from the rational but excessively flat determinism of so many novels of the period. The new ending is a brilliant idea, a shift on to the inner plane" that "locates the action in Caleb's consciousness, which is as it should be" (*Jane Austen and the War of Ideas*, 68). Kenneth W. Graham's article "Narrative and Ideology in Godwin's *Caleb Williams*," *Eighteenth-Century Fiction* 2, no. 3 (1990): 215–228, offers a useful overview of these and other interpretations as well as a convincing argument that explaining the change of endings simply by recourse to political ideology (without, that is, factoring in other aesthetic considerations such as unity or the novelistic demand for closure) is likely to come up wanting. Rajan's discussion of the two endings in "Judging Justice" seems to me to make good on Graham's call for an account that could merge reflection on aesthetics and politics—Rajan argues that Godwin is "putting on trial the very genre of the Novel as judgment" (344), offering a critique of the imperative toward verdicts in both novels and courtrooms. On this point at least, Rajan's argument runs close to John Bender's argument—which is animated more by Foucault than Derrida but directed, nevertheless, against the objectifying force of novelistic conclusions—that Godwin "is a utopian anarchist whose attack on personified authority in *Caleb Williams* is also staged within a field of narration that profoundly contradicts his enterprise" ("The Penetrating Gaze and Narration in *Caleb Williams*," in his *Ends of Enlightenment*, 163). The claim, that is, is that "Godwin fundamentally undermined his project from the beginning because narration as he undertook it reproduced the constructions of character he was assailing" (167).

57. See Celeste Langan, *Romantic Vagrancy: Wordsworth and the Simulation of Freedom* (Cambridge: Cambridge University Press, 1995), esp. 76–81; Langan quotes Constant on 15.

58. See, for instance, Sir Robert Hunter, *The Preservation of Open Spaces, and of Footpaths and Other Rights of Way* (1896), 2nd ed. (London: Eyre and Spottiswoode, 1902).

59. http://keystone-xl.com/keystone-xl-oil-pipeline-landowner-information-montana-nebraska-easements-compensation-packages-transcanada/. My emphasis.

Epilogue: Everything Counts (*Frankenstein*)

1. Chapter epigraph source: Mary Shelley, *Frankenstein* (London: Penguin, 2003), 75. Hereafter cited parenthetically by page number.

2. Nancy Armstrong, *How Novels Think* (New York: Columbia University Press, 2005), 10.

3. John Stuart Mill, *Utilitarianism* (London: Parker, Son, and Bourn, 1863), 91. The principle Mill attributes to Bentham does not seem to have an identified source in Bentham's writing. See Jeremy Waldron, *God, Locke, and Equality* (Cambridge: Cambridge University Press, 2002), 14n32.

4. Robert Owen's position is being paraphrased by Mill, *Utilitarianism*, 90.

5. Levi H. Bryant, *The Democracy of Objects* (Ann Arbor, Mich.: Open Humanities Press, 2011), 31.

6. Indeed, despite many differences in approach and interest, work in a variety of particularly energetic critical fields—e.g., ecocriticism, posthumanism, the new materialism, speculative realism, object-oriented ontology, and "the new metaphysics"—are joined by a resistance to the humancentrism of our traditional approaches to politics and philosophy. Like a vastly widened version of one of postcolonialism's basic moves, the guiding sense in these newer fields is that human perception and human concerns have harmfully narrowed, reduced, or impinged on other forms of (nonhuman) life, experience, agency. Writing on the Anthropocene is thus almost always antianthropocentric.

7. Bryant, *The Democracy of Objects*, 32.

8. Priestley, in Joseph Priestley and Richard Price, *A Free Discussion of the Doctrines of Materialism and Philosophical Necessity in a Correspondence between Dr. Price and Dr. Priestley* (London: J. Johnson, 1778), xxxi.

9. John Searle, *Freedom and Neurobiology* (New York: Columbia University Press, 2007), 4–5.

10. Priestley, in Priestley and Price, *Free Discussion*, ix.

11. See, for instance, the *Third National Climate Assessment* (2014), http://nca2014.globalchange.gov/report.

12. Bruno Latour, "Agency at the Time of the Anthropocene," *New Literary History* 45, no. 1 (2014): 1.

13. The text of the playbill is quoted in Steven Earl Forry, "An Early Conflict Involving the Production of R. B. Peake's *Presumption; or, The Fate of Frankenstein*," *Theatre Notebook* 39 (1985): 99–103. The full text of the article is available through the extraordinarily useful Pennsylvania Electronic Edition of the novel, edited by Stuart Curran. The homepage for the electronic edition is knarf.english.upenn.edu, and Forry's article can be found at knarf.english.upenn.edu/Articles/forry.html.

14. Matthew Lewis, *The Monk* (London: Penguin, 1998), 229.

15. Ibid., 230.

16. Percy Bysshe Shelley, "Notes on *Queen Mab*," in *The Works of Percy Bysshe Shelley Edited by Mrs. Shelley* (London: Edward Moxon, 1847), 25.

17. The legal history of parental liability for the torts of their children is complicated and currently changing, with courts, beginning around the middle of the twentieth century, becoming more willing to hold parents accountable for the acts of their children. For one overview of the question, see Paula Giliker, *Vicarious Liability in Tort: A Comparative Perspective* (Cambridge: Cambridge University Press, 2010), esp. chap. 7, "Parental Liability for the Torts of Their Children: A New Form of Vicarious Liability?"

18. There are a number of key texts from feminist perspectives that helped revive Shelley's novel as an object of serious critical attention. These include Ellen Moers, "Female Gothic," in *The Endurance of Frankenstein: Essays on Mary Shelley's Novel*, ed. George Levine and U. C. Knoeflmacher (Berkeley: University of California Press, 1979), 77–87; Sandra M. Gilbert and Susan Gubar, *The Madwoman in the Attic* (New Haven, Conn.: Yale University Press, 1979); Mary Poovey, "My Hideous Progeny: Mary Shelley and the Feminization of Romanticism," *PMLA* 95, no. 3 (1980): 332–347; Barbara Johnson, "My Monster/My Self," *Diacritics* 12, no. 2 (1982): 2–10; Mary Jacobus, "Is There a Woman in This Text?" *New Literary History* 14, no. 1 (1982): 117–141;

Gayatri Chakravorty Spivak, "Three Women's Texts and a Critique of Imperialism," *Critical Inquiry* 12, no. 1 (1985): 235–261; Anne K. Mellor, *Mary Shelley: Her Life, Her Fiction, Her Monsters* (London: Methuen, 1988), esp. chaps. 2 ("Making a Monster") and 3 ("My Hideous Progeny"). Many of these feminist approaches focused on comparing the 1818 and 1831 version of the novel, often as an explicit attempt to decouple a sense of Mary Shelley's authorship from the editorship and influence of her husband. I'm not embarking on a comparison of these editions since the central questions of responsibility (authorship, parentage, progeny hideous or otherwise, etc.) cut across both editions.

Works Cited

Aarsleff, Hans. *The Study of Language in England, 1780–1860.* Princeton, N.J.: Princeton University Press, 1967.

Abrams, M. H. *The Correspondent Breeze.* New York: Norton, 1984.

Acton, John. *Lectures on the French Revolution.* London: Macmillan, 1910.

Alborn, Timothy L. *Conceiving Companies: Joint Stock Politics in Victorian England.* London: Routledge, 1998.

Amis, Kingsley. "What Became of Jane Austen?" *The Spectator* (October 4, 1957): 339–340.

Anderson, Amanda. *The Powers of Distance: Cosmopolitanism and the Cultivation of Detachment.* Princeton, N.J.: Princeton University Press, 2001.

Anderson, Benedict. *Imagined Communities.* London: Verso, 1983.

Anderson, Paige. "Reasonable Accommodation: Split Estates, Conservation Easements, and Drilling in the Marcellus Shale." *Virginia Environmental Law Journal* 31, no. 1 (2013): 136–167.

Arasse, Daniel. *The Guillotine and the Terror.* Translated by Christopher Miller. London: Penguin, 1989.

Arendt, Hannah. *The Human Condition.* Chicago: University of Chicago Press, 1998.

———. *The Origins of Totalitarianism.* New York: Harcourt, Brace & World, 1966.

Armstrong, Nancy. *Desire and Domestic Fiction.* Oxford: Oxford University Press, 1987.

———. "The Fiction of Bourgeois Morality." In *The Novel*, 2 vols., edited by Franco Moretti. Princeton, N.J.: Princeton University Press, 2006.

———. *How Novels Think.* New York: Columbia University Press, 2005.

Auerbach, Nina. *Romantic Imprisonment: Women and Other Glorified Outcasts.* New York: Columbia University Press, 1985.

Austen, Jane. *Catherine, or the Bower.* In *Catherine and Other Writings*, edited by Margaret Anne Doody and Douglas Murray. Oxford: Oxford University Press, 1993.

———. *Emma.* Edited by Fiona Stafford. London: Penguin, 1996.

———. *Jane Austen's Letters.* 4th ed. Edited by Deirdre Le Faye. Oxford: Oxford University Press, 2011.

———. *Mansfield Park.* Edited by John Wiltshire. Cambridge: Cambridge University Press, 2005.

———. "Opinions on *Mansfield Park*." In *The Works of Jane Austen*, vol. 6, *Minor Works*, edited by R. W. Chapman. Oxford: Oxford University Press, 1954.

———. *Persuasion.* 2nd ed. Edited by Patricia Meyer Spacks. New York: Norton, 2013.

———. *Pride and Prejudice.* Edited by Pat Rogers. Cambridge: Cambridge University Press, 2006.

Avi-Yonah, Reuven. "Cyclical Transformations of the Corporate Form: A Historical

Perspective on Corporate Social Responsibility." *Delaware Journal of Corporate Law* 30 (2005): 768–818.

Babbage, Charles. *On the Economy of Machinery and Manufactures.* London: Charles Knight, 1835.

Baldridge, Cates. "Alternatives to Bourgeois Individualism in *A Tale of Two Cities.*" *Studies in English Literature, 1500–1900* (1990): 633–54.

Balfour, Ian. "Promises, Promises: Social and Other Contracts in the English Jacobins Godwin/Inchbald." In *New Romanticisms: Theory and Critical Practice,* edited by David L. Clark and Donald C. Goellnicht Toronto: University of Toronto Press, 1994.

Banfield, Ann. "The Moral Landscape of *Mansfield Park.*" *Nineteenth-Century Fiction* 26, no. 1 (1971): 1–24.

Barad, Karen. *Meeting the Universe Halfway: Quantum Physics and the Entanglement of Matter and Meaning.* Durham, N.C.: Duke University Press, 2007.

Barrell, John. "Putting Down the Rising." In *Scotland and the Borders of Romanticism,* edited by Leith Davis, Ian Duncan, and Janet Sorensen. Cambridge: Cambridge University Press, 2004.

Barrell, John. *Imagining the King's Death: Figurative Treason, Fantasies of Regicide, 1793–1796.* Oxford: Oxford University Press, 2000.

Bate, Jonathan. *Romantic Ecology: Wordsworth and the Environmental Tradition.* London: Routledge, 1991.

———. *Song of the Earth.* Cambridge, Mass.: Harvard University Press, 2000.

Bender, John. *Ends of Enlightenment.* Stanford, Calif.: Stanford University Press, 2012.

———. *Imagining the Penitentiary: Fiction and the Architecture of Mind in Eighteenth-Century England.* Chicago: University of Chicago Press, 1987.

Bennett, Jane. *Vibrant Matter: Toward a Political Economy of Things.* Durham, N.C.: Duke University Press, 2010.

Berlant, Lauren. *Cruel Optimism.* Durham, N.C.: Duke University Press, 2011.

Bermingham, Ann. *Landscape and Ideology: The English Rustic Tradition, 1740–1860.* Berkeley: University of California Press, 1986.

Bersani, Leo. *A Future for Astyanax: Character and Desire in Literature.* New York: Columbia University Press, 1984.

Beven, Thomas. *Negligence in Law.* 2 vols. London: Stevens and Haynes, 1895.

Biagini, Eugenio. *Liberty, Retrenchment, and Reform: Popular Liberalism in the Age of Gladstone, 1860–1880.* Cambridge: Cambridge University Press, 1992.

Blackstone, William. *Commentaries on the Laws of England.* Online ed. Avalon Project at Yale University. http://avalon.law.yale.edu/18th_century/blackstone_bk1ch18.asp.

Blumberg, Philip. "Limited Liability and Corporate Groups." *Journal of Corporate Law* 573, no. 11 (1985–1986): 573–632.

Bogost, Ian. *Alien Phenomenology; or, What It's Like to Be a Thing.* Minneapolis: University of Minnesota Press, 2012.

Bowen, Scarlet. *The Politics of Custom in Eighteenth-Century British Fiction.* New York: Palgrave Macmillan, 2010.

Brantlinger, Patrick. "Did Dickens Have a Philosophy of History? The Case of *Barnaby Rudge.*" *Dickens Studies Annual* 30 (2001): 95–112.

Brenner, Joel Franklin. "Nuisance Law and the Industrial Revolution," *Journal of Legal Studies* 43, no. 3 (1974): 403–433.

Brooks, Christopher. *Law, Politics, and Society in Early Modern England.* Cambridge: Cambridge University Press, 2008.

Brooks, Peter. *Troubling Confessions: Speaking Guilt in Law and Literature.* Chicago: University of Chicago Press, 2000.

Brown, Marshall. *The Gothic Text.* Stanford, Calif.: Stanford University Press, 2005.

Bryant, Levi H. *The Democracy of Objects,* Ann Arbor, Mich.: Open Humanities Press, 2011.

Bryer, R.A. "The Mercantile Laws Commission of 1854 and the Political Economy of Limited Liability." *Economic History Review* n.s. 50, no. 1 (1997): 37–56.

Burgess, Miranda. *British Fiction and the Production of Social Order, 1740–1830.* Cambridge: Cambridge University Press, 2005.

Burke, Edmund. *Reflections on the Revolution in France.* In *Select Works of Edmund Burke: A New Imprint of the Payne Edition.* Foreword and biographical note by Francis Canavan. Indianapolis, Ind.: Liberty Fund, 1999.

Butler, Marilyn. *Jane Austen and the War of Ideas.* Oxford: Oxford University Press, 1987.

Campbell, Timothy. "'The Business of War': William Godwin, Enmity, and Historical Representation." *ELH* 76, no. 2 (2009): 343–369.

Canuel, Mark. *The Shadow of Death: Literature, Romanticism, and the Subject of Punishment.* Princeton, N.J.: Princeton University Press, 2007.

Carlyle, Thomas. *History of the French Revolution.* New York: Modern Library/Random House, 2002.

———. *Past and Present.* London: Chapman and Hall, 1872.

Chandler, James. *England in 1819: The Politics of Literary Culture and the Case of Romantic Historicism.* Chicago: University of Chicago Press, 1998.

Chandler, James, and Kevin Gilmartin, eds. *Romantic Metropolis: The Urban Scene of British Culture, 1780–1840.* Cambridge: Cambridge University Press, 2011.

Clark, John P. *The Philosophical Anarchism of William Godwin.* Princeton, N.J.: Princeton University Press, 1977.

Cleere, Eileen. "Reinvesting Nieces: 'Mansfield Park' and the Economics of Endogamy." *NOVEL: A Forum on Fiction* 28, no. 2 (1995): 113–130.

Coase, Ronald H. "The Problem of Social Cost." *Journal of Law and Economics* 3 (1960): 414–440.

Coke, Edward. *The Reports of Sir Edward Coke, Knt. In Thirteen Parts.* 6 vols. London: Joseph Butterworth and Son, 1826.

[Coke, Sir Edward?]. *The Compleat Copy-Holder.* In *Three Law Tracts.* London: J. Worrall, 1764.

Colebrook, Claire. *Death of the Posthuman: Essays on Extinction.* 2 vols. Ann Arbor, Mich.: Open Humanities Press, 2014.

Coleridge, Samuel Taylor. *Biographia Literaria.* 2 vols. London: Rest Fenner, 1817.

———. *Coleridge's Lectures on Shakespeare and Other Dramatists.* London: J.M. Dent & Sons, 1907.

———. "The Eolian Harp: Composed at Clevedon, Somersetshire." In *Poetical Works: Part 1. Poems (Reading Text),* edited by J.C.C. Mays, in *The Collected Works of Samuel Taylor Coleridge,* 16 vols. Princeton, N.J.: Princeton University Press, 2001.

———. "John Donne." In *The Collected Works of Samuel Taylor Coleridge*, vol. 12: *Marginalia II*. Princeton, N.J.: Princeton University Press, 1985.

———. *On the Constitution of Church and State*. London: William Pickering, 1839.

———. *The Statesman's Manual; or The Bible the Best Guide to Political Skill and Foresight*. In *The Collected Works of Samuel Taylor Coleridge*, vol. 6: *Lay Sermons*, edited by R.J. White. London: Routledge and Kegan Paul, 1972.

Colley, Linda. *Britons: Forging the Nation, 1707–1837*. New Haven, Conn.: Yale University Press, 1992.

Collings, David. "The Romance of the Impossible: William Godwin in the Empty Place of Reason." *ELH* 70, no. 3 (2003): 847–874.

Collins, Wilkie. *The Woman in White*. New York: Harper and Brothers, 1861.

Conger, Syndy McMillen. "Reading *Lovers' Vows*: Jane Austen's Reflections on English Sense and German Sensibility." *Studies in Philology* 85, no. 1 (1988): 92–113.

Corbett, Mary Jean. "'Cousins in Love, &c.' in Jane Austen." *Tulsa Studies in Women's Literature* 23, no. 2 (2004): 237–259.

"Corporations and Corporation Law." *The Law Magazine; or, Quarterly Review of Jurisprudence* 25, no. 13 (1850): 145–157.

Crabb, George. *The Law of Real Property*. London: A. Maxwell & Son, 1846.

Cvetcovich, Anne. *Depression: A Public Feeling*. Durham, N.C.: Duke University Press, 2012.

Daffron, Eric. "'Magnetical Sympathy': Strategies of Power and Resistance in Godwin's *Caleb Williams*." *Criticism* 37 (1995): 213–232.

Dames, Nicholas, *The Physiology of the Novel: Reading, Neuroscience, and the Form of Victorian Fiction*. Oxford: Oxford University Press, 2007.

Davis, Leith. "At 'Sang About': Scottish Song and the Challenge to British Culture." In *Scotland and the Borders of Romanticism*, edited by Leith Davis, Ian Duncan, and Janet Sorensen. Cambridge: Cambridge University Press, 2004.

de Bracton, Henrici. *De legibus et consuetudinibus Angliæ. Libri quinque in varios tractatus distincti. Ad diversorum et vetustissimorum codicum collationem typis vulgate*. 6 vols. Edited by Sir Travers Twiss. London: Longman & Co. 1878–1883.

de Tocqueville, Alexis. *The Old Regime and the Revolution*. Edited by François Furet and Françoise Mélonio. Translated by Alan S. Kahan. Chicago: University of Chicago Press, 1998.

Deleuze, Gilles. *The Logic of Sense*. Translated by Mark Lester with Charles Stivale. Edited by Constantin V. Boundas. New York: Columbia University Press, 1990.

Dewey, John. "The Historical Background of Corporate Personality." *Yale Law Journal* 35, no. 6 (1926): 655–673.

Dickens, Charles. *A Tale of Two Cities*. Edited by Gillen D'Arcy Wood. New York: Barnes and Noble, 2004.

———. *A Tale of Two Cities*. Edited by Richard Maxwell. London: Penguin, 2003.

———. *Great Expectations*. Edited by Charlotte Mitchell. Introduction by David Trotter. London: Penguin, 2002.

Dimock, Wai Chee. *Residues of Justice: Literature, Law, Philosophy*. Berkeley: University of California Press, 1996.

Donohue Jr., Joseph W. "Ordination and the Divided House at Mansfield Park." *ELH* 32, no. 2 (1965): 169–178.

DuBois, Armand Budington. *The English Business Company After the Bubble Act, 1720–1800*. New York: The Commonwealth Fund, 1938.

Duckworth, Alistair. *The Improvement of the Estate: A Study of Jane Austen's Novels*. Baltimore, Md.: Johns Hopkins University Press, 1971.

Dumas, D. G. "Things as They Were: The Original Ending of *Caleb Williams*." *SEL* 6, no. 3 (1966): 575–597.

Duncan, Ian. "Authenticity Effects: The Work of Fiction in Romantic Scotland." *South Atlantic Quarterly* 102, no. 1 (2003).

———. *Modern Romance and Transformations of the Novel: The Gothic, Scott, Dickens*. Cambridge: Cambridge University Press, 2005.

———. *Scott's Shadow: The Novel in Romantic Edinburgh*. Princeton, N.J.: Princeton University Press, 2012.

———"Walter Scott, James Hogg, and Scottish Gothic." In *A New Companion to the Gothic*, edited by David Punter. Chichester: Wiley-Blackwell, 2012.

Duncan, William. *Elements of Logic* New York: L. Nichols & Co., 1802.

Dworkin, Richard. "Law as Interpretation." *Critical Inquiry* 9, no. 1 (1982): 179–200.

Edelman, Lee. *No Future: Queer Theory and the Death Drive*. Durham, N.C.: Duke University Press, 2004.

Edge, Charles. "Mansfield Park and Ordination." *Nineteenth-Century Fiction* 16, no. 3 (1961): 269–274.

Engels, Friedrich. *The Condition of the Working Class in England*. Translated by Florence Kelley Wischnewetzky. London: Swan Sonnenschein & Co., 1892.

Ermarth, Elizabeth Deeds. *Realism and Consensus in the English Novel: Time, Space, and Narrative*. Edinburgh: Edinburgh University Press, 1998.

Esposito, Roberto. *Bios: Biopolitics and Philosophy*. Translated by Timothy Campbell. Minneapolis: University of Minnesota Press, 2008.

Evans, Frank. *British Corporation Finance, 1775–1850: A Study of Preference Shares*. Baltimore, Md.: Johns Hopkins University Press, 1936.

———. "The Evolution of the English Joint Stock Limited Trading Company." *Columbia Law Review* 8, no. 5 (1908): 339–361.

Fairclough, Mary. *The Romantic Crowd: Sympathy, Controversy, and Print Culture*. Cambridge: Cambridge University Press, 2013.

Farr, William. "Commentary on Coroner's Returns of Violent Deaths, 1852–6." In *Vital Statistics: A Memorial Volume of Selections from the Reports and Writings of William Farr, M.D.*, edited by Noel A. Humphreys. London: Offices of the Sanitary Institute, 1885.

Favret, Mary A. *War at a Distance: Romanticism and the Making of Modern War Time*. Princeton, N.J.: Princeton University Press, 2010.

Fawcett, Edmund. *Liberalism: The Life of an Idea*. Princeton, N.J.: Princeton University Press, 2014.

Ferguson, Frances. "Now It's Personal: D. A. Miller and Too-Close Reading." *Critical Inquiry* 41, no. 3 (2015): 521–540.

———. *Pornography, the Theory: What Utilitarianism Did to Action*. Chicago: University of Chicago Press, 2004.

———. *Solitude and the Sublime: Romanticism and the Aesthetics of Individuation*. New York: Routledge, 1992.

Fielding, Penny. "'No Such Thing as Action': William Godwin, the Decision, and the Secret." *Novel* 42, no. 3 (2009): 380–386.

First Report of the Commissioners Appointed to Inquire . . . Whether Any and What Alterations and Amendments Should Be Made in the Law of Partnership. London: George Edward Eyre and William Spottiwood, for Her Majesty's Stationery Office, 1854.

Fish, Stanley. "Working on the Chain Gang: Interpretation in Law and Literature." *Critical Inquiry* 9, no. 1 (1982): 201–216.

Fleischman, Avrom. *The English Historical Novel: Walter Scott to Virginia Woolf.* Baltimore, Md.: Johns Hopkins University Press, 1971.

Flesch, William. *Comeuppance.* Cambridge, Mass.: Harvard University Press, 2009.

———. "Hyperbolic Discounting and Intertemporal Bargaining." In *Theory Aside*, edited by Jason Potts and Daniel Stout. Durham, N.C.: Duke University Press 2014.

Forry, Steven Earl. "An Early Conflict Involving the Production of R. B. Peake's *Presumption; or, The Fate of Frankenstein.*" *Theatre Notebook* 39 (1985): 99–103.

Forster, E. M. *Aspects of the Novel.* New York: Harcourt, Brace & World, 1954.

Forster, John. *The Life of Charles Dickens.* 3 vols. Philadelphia: J. B. Lippincott, 1874.

Foucault, Michel. "The Care of the Self." In *Technologies of the Self: A Seminar with Michel Foucault*, edited by Luther H. Martin, Huck Guttman, and Patrick H. Hutton. Amherst: University of Massachusetts Press, 1988.

———. "The Eye of Power." In *Power/Knowledge: Selected Interviews and Other Writings, 1972–1977*, edited by Colon Gordon. New York: Pantheon, 1980.

———. *The History of Sexuality*, vol. 3: *The Care of the Self.* Translated by Robert Hurley. New York: Pantheon, 1986.

François, Anne-Lise. *Open Secrets: The Literature of Uncounted Experience.* Stanford, Calif.: Stanford University Press, 2008.

Franta, Andrew. "Godwin's Handshake." *PMLA* 122, no. 3 (2007): 696–710.

Furet, François. *Interpreting the French Revolution.* Cambridge: Cambridge University Press, 1981.

Gale, Charles James. *A Treatise on The Law of Easements.* 3rd ed. London: H. Sweet, 1862.

Gallagher, Catherine. *The Body Economic: Life, Death, and Sensation in Political Economy and the Victorian Novel.* Princeton, N.J.: Princeton University Press, 2009.

———. "The Duplicity of Doubling in *A Tale of Two Cities.*" *Dickens Studies Annual* 12 (1983): 125–145.

———. "Formalism and Time." *MLQ* 61, no. 1 (2000): 229–251.

Galperin, William. *The Historical Jane Austen.* Philadelphia: University of Pennsylvania Press, 2003.

———. "The Theatre at Mansfield Park: From Classic to Romantic Once More." *Eighteenth-Century Life* 16, no. 3 (1992): 247–271.

Gamer, Michael. *Romanticism and the Gothic: Genre, Reception, and Canon Formation.* Cambridge: Cambridge University Press, 2000.

Garside, Peter. *The English Novel, 1770–1829.* 2 vols. Oxford: Oxford University Press, 2000.

Gattrell, V. A. C. *The Hanging Tree: Execution and the English People, 1770–1868.* Oxford: Oxford University Press, 1994.

Gilbert, Sandra M., and Susan Gubar. *The Madwoman in the Attic.* New Haven, Conn.: Yale University Press, 1979.

Giliker, Paula. *Vicarious Liability in Tort: A Comparative Perspective.* Cambridge: Cambridge University Press, 2010.

Gilmartin, Kevin. *Print Politics: The Press and Radical Opposition in Early Nineteenth-Century England.* Cambridge: Cambridge University Press, 2005.

———. *Writing Against Revolution, Literary Conservatism in Britain, 1790–1832.* Cambridge: Cambridge University Press, 2007.

Gilroy, Amanda, and Wil Verhoeven. "Introduction." *Novel: A Forum on Fiction* 34, no. 2 (2001): 147–162.

Girard, Rene. *Desire and the Novel: Self and Other in Literary Structure.* Translated by Yvonne Freccero. Baltimore, Md.: Johns Hopkins University Press, 1965.

Goddard, John. *A Treatise on the Law of Easements.* 2nd ed. London: Stevens and Sons, 1877.

Godwin, William. *Caleb Williams.* Edited by Pamela Clemit. Oxford: Oxford University Press, 2009.

———. *Enquiry Concerning Political Justice, and its influence on morals and happiness.* London: G. G. and J. Robinson, 1798.

———. "Preface to the Standard Novels Edition." Reprinted in *Caleb Williams*, edited by Pamela Clemit. Oxford: Oxford University Press, 2009.

Goodlad, Lauren. *The Victorian Geopolitical Aesthetic.* Oxford: Oxford University Press, 2015.

———. *Victorian Literature and the Victorian State: Character and Governance in a Liberal Society.* Baltimore, Md.: Johns Hopkins University Press, 2004.

Gottlieb, Evan. *Romantic Globalism: British Literature and Modern World Order, 1750–1830.* Columbus: Ohio State University Press, 2014.

Gottlieb, Evan, ed. *Global Romanticism: Origins, Orientations, and Engagements, 1760–1820.* Lewisburg, Penn.: Bucknell University Press, 2015.

Graham, John William. *The Destruction of Daylight: A Study in the Smoke Problem.* London: George Allan, 1907.

Graham, Kenneth W. "Narrative and Ideology in Godwin's *Caleb Williams.*" *Eighteenth-Century Fiction* 2, no. 3 (1990): 215–228.

Grant, James. *A Practical Treatise on the Law of Corporations.* London: Butterworths, 1850.

Greene, Joshua, and J. D. Cohen. "For the Law, Neuroscience Changes Nothing and Everything." *Philosophical Transactions of the Royal Society of London B* 359 (2004): 1775–1785.

Grenby, M. O. *The Anti-Jacobin Novel: British Conservatism and the French Revolution.* Cambridge: Cambridge University Press, 2001.

Grossman, Jonathan. *The Art of Alibi: English Law Courts and the Novel.* Baltimore, Md.: Johns Hopkins University Press, 2002.

Habermas, Jürgen. *The Structural Transformation of the Public Sphere.* Cambridge, Mass.: MIT Press, 1989.

Hadley, Elaine. *Living Liberalism: Practical Citizenship in Mid-Victorian Britain.* Chicago: University of Chicago Press, 2010.

Halmi, Nicholas. *Genealogy of the Romantic Symbol.* Oxford: Oxford University Press, 2008.

Halperin, John. *The Life of Jane Austen.* Baltimore, Md.: Johns Hopkins University Press, 1996.

Handwerk, Gary. "Of Caleb's Guilt and Godwin's Truth: Ideology and Ethics in *Caleb Williams.*" *ELH* 60, no. 4 (1993): 939–960.

Hansen, Mark N. B. *Feed Forward: On the Future of Twenty-First-Century Media.* Chicago: University of Chicago Press, 2014.

———. "The Primacy of Sensation: Psychophysics, Phenomenology, Whitehead." In *Theory Aside*, edited by Jason Potts and Daniel Stout. Durham, N.C.: Duke University Press, 2014.

Hansmann, Henry, and Reinier Kraakman. "Toward Unlimited Shareholder Liability for Corporate Torts." *Yale Law Journal* 100 (1990–1991): 1879–1934.

Hardy, Thomas. *Tess of the d'Urbervilles: A Pure Woman.* 2nd ed. Edited by Sarah E. Maier. Peterborough, Ont.: Broadview, 2007.

Harman, Graham. *Towards Speculative Realism: Essays and Lectures.* Hants: Zero Books, 2010.

Harris, Ron. "The Bubble Act: Its Passage and Its Effects on Business Organization." *Journal of Economic History* 54, no. 3 (1994): 610–627.

———. *Industrializing English Law: Entrepreneurship and Business Organization, 1720–1844.* Cambridge: Cambridge University Press, 2000.

Hartley, David. *Observations on Man, His Frame, His Duty, and His Expectations. 2 vols.* 6th ed., corrected and rev. London: Thomas Tegg and Son, 1834.

Harvey, David. *A Brief History of Neoliberalism.* Oxford: Oxford University Press, 2005.

Harvie, Christopher. *Scotland and Nationalism.* 3rd ed. London: Routledge, 1998.

Hazlitt, William. "On Corporate Bodies." In *Table Talk.* London: Grant Richards, 1903.

———. "On Personal Identity." In *Sketches and Essays; and Winterslow Essays Written There.* London: Bell & Daldy, 1872.

———. *The Spirit of the Age.* London: George Bell and Sons, 1886.

Heron, Rachel, Justin S. DuClos, and Shaun A. Goho. "The Interpretation of Surface Easements in Severance Deeds as a Limit on Hydraulic Fracturing Practices." *Buffalo Environmental Law Journal* 19, no. 1 (2011–2012): 73–106.

Hertz, Neil. *George Eliot's Pulse.* Stanford, Calif.: Stanford University Press, 2003.

Heydt-Stevenson, Jillian, and Charlotte Sussman, eds. *Recognizing the Romantic Novel: New Histories of British Fiction, 1780–1830.* Liverpool: Liverpool University Press, 2008.

Hillman, Robert W. "Limited Liability in Historical Perspective." *Washington and Lee Law Review* 54, no. 2 (1997): 613–627.

Hobsbawm, Eric. *The Age of Revolution, 1789–1848.* New York: Vintage, 1996.

Hogg, James. *The Private Memoirs and Confessions of a Justified Sinner: Written by Himself: With a Detail of Curious Traditionary Facts and Other Evidence by the Editor.* Edited by P. D. Garside. Edinburgh: Edinburgh University Press, 2002.

———. *Songs by the Ettrick Shepherd.* Oxford: Woodstock, 1989.

Holmes Jr., Oliver Wendell. *The Common Law.* Boston: Little, Brown, and Co., 1881.

House, Nicholas. "Conflicting Property Rights Between Conservation Easements and Oil and Gas Leases in Ohio: Why Current Law Could Benefit Conservation Efforts." *William and Mary Law Review* 55, no. 4 (2014): 1586–1616.

Hudson, Glenda A. *Sibling Love and Incest in Jane Austen's Fiction.* London: Macmillan, 1992.

Hunt, Bishop Carleton. *The Development of the Business Corporation in England, 1800–1867.* Cambridge, Mass.: Harvard University Press, 1936.

Hunter, Robert. *The Preservation of Open Spaces, and of Footpaths and Other Rights of Way.* 2nd ed. London: Eyre and Spottiswoode, 1902.

Inchbald, Elizabeth. *Lovers' Vows, A Play in Five Acts, from the German of Kotzebue.* Philadelphia: Neal and Mackenzie, 1829.

Jacobus, Mary. "Is There a Woman in this Text?" *New Literary History* 14, no. 1 (1982): 117–141.

Jacobus, Mary. *Romantic Things: A Tree, a Rock, a Cloud.* Chicago: University of Chicago Press, 2012.

Jaffe, Audrey. *The Affective Life of the Average Man: The Victorian Novel and the Stock Market Graph.* Columbus: Ohio State University Press, 2010.

———. *Scenes of Sympathy: Identity and Representation in Victorian Fiction.* Ithaca, N.Y.: Cornell University Press, 2000.

Kantor, Jamison. "Burke, Godwin, and the Politics of Honor." *Studies in English Literature* 54, no. 3 (2014): 675–696.

Janowitz, Anne. *Lyric and Labour in the Romantic Tradition.* Cambridge: Cambridge University Press, 2005.

John, Juliet. *Dickens Villains: Melodrama, Character, Popular Culture.* Oxford: Oxford University Press, 2003.

Johnson, Barbara. "My Monster/My Self." *Diacritics* 12, no. 2 (1982): 2–10.

Johnson, Claudia L. *Jane Austen: Women, Politics, and the Novel.* Chicago: University of Chicago Press, 1988.

———. "'Let Me Make the Novels of a Country': Barbauld's *The British Novelists 1810/ 1820*." *Novel* 34, no. 2 (2001): 163–179.

———. "What Became of Jane Austen? *Mansfield Park.*" *Persuasions* 17 (1995): 59–70.

Johnson, E. D. H. *Charles Dickens: An Introduction to His Novels.* New York: Random House, 1969.

Jordan, Elaine. "Pulpit, Stage, and Novel: *Mansfield Park* and Mrs. Inchbald's *Lovers' Vows.*" *Novel: A Forum on Fiction* 20, no. 2 (1987): 138–148.

Jordan, Nicole. "The Promise and Frustration of Plebeian Public Opinion in *Caleb Williams.*" *Eighteenth-Century Fiction* 19, no. 3 (2007): 243–266.

The Jurist 8, part 2, n.s. (1862). London: V. & R. Stevens, Sons, & Haynes, 1863.

Kafka, Franz. "In the Penal Colony." In *The Complete Stories.* New York: Schocken, 1971.

Kahan, Daniel R. "Shareholder Liability for Corporate Torts: A Historical Perspective." *Georgetown Law Journal* 97 (2008–2009).

Karounos, Michael. "Ordination and Revolution in Mansfield Park." *SEL* 44, no. 4 (2004): 715–736.

Kelly, Gary. *The Jacobin Novel: 1780–1805.* Oxford: Clarendon, 1976.

Kiely, Robert. *The Romantic Novel in England.* Cambridge, Mass.: Harvard University Press, 1972.

Kramnick, Jonathan. *Actions and Objects from Hobbes to Richardson.* Stanford, Calif.: Stanford University Press, 2010.

———. "The Making of the English Canon." *PMLA* 112, no. 5 (1997): 1087–1101.

———. *Making the English Canon: Print-Capitalism and the Cultural Past 1700–1770.* Cambridge: Cambridge University Press, 1999.

Kurnick, David. *Empty Houses: Theatrical Failure and the Novel.* Princeton, N.J.: Princeton University Press, 2011.

Kyd, Thomas. *A Treatise on the Law of Corporations*. London: J. Butterworth, 1793.

Lachmann, Richard. *From Manor to Market: Structural Change in England, 1536–1640*. Madison: University of Wisconsin Press, 1987.

Langan, Celeste. *Romantic Vagrancy: Wordsworth and the Simulation of Freedom*. Cambridge: Cambridge University Press, 1995.

Larkin, Philip. "Talking in Bed." In *Collected Poems*, edited by Anthony Thwaite. London: Marvell, 1988.

Latour, Bruno. "Agency at the Time of the Anthropocene," *New Literary History* 45, no. 1 (2014).

———. *We Have Never Been Modern*. Translated by Catherine Porter. Cambridge, Mass.: Harvard University Press, 1993.

Lee, Wendy Anne. "A Case for Hard Heartedness: *Clarissa*, Indifferency, and Impersonality." *Eighteenth-Century Fiction* 26, no. 1 (2013): 33–65.

Letters on Materialism and Hartley's Theory of the Human Mind addressed to Joseph Priestley. London: G. Robinson, 1777.

Levi, Leon. "The Progress of Joint Stock Companies with Limited and Unlimited Liability in the United Kingdom During the Fifteen Years 1869–84, in Continuation of a Paper Read Before the Society in January, 1870." *Journal of the Statistical Society of London* 49, no. 2 (1886): 241–272.

Levine, Caroline. *Forms: Whole, Rhythm, Hierarchy, Network*. Princeton, N.J.: Princeton University Press, 2015.

Levine, Caroline, and Mario Ortiz-Robles. "Introduction." In *Narrative Middles: Navigating the Nineteenth-Century British Novel*. Columbus: Ohio State University Press, 2011.

Levinson, Marjorie. "Of Being Numerous: Counting and Matching in Wordsworth's Poetry." *Studies in Romanticism* 49, no. 4 (2011): 633–657.

Lewis, Matthew. *The Monk*. London: Penguin, 1998.

Litvak, Joseph. *Caught in the Act: Theatricality in the Nineteenth-Century English Novel*. Berkeley: University of California Press, 1992.

———. "The Infection of Acting: Theatricals and Theatricality in Mansfield Park." *ELH* 53, no. 2 (1986): 331–355.

Logan, Peter Melville. "Narrating Hysteria, 'Caleb Williams' and the Cultural History of Nerves." *Novel: A Forum on Fiction* 29, no. 2 (1996): 206–222.

Lott, Anna. "Staging a Lesson: The Theatricals and Proper Conduct in *Mansfield Park*." *Studies in the Novel* 38, no. 3 (2006): 275–287.

Luhmann, Niklas. *The Reality of the Mass Media*. Stanford, Calif.: Stanford University Press, 2000.

Lukács, Georg. *The Historical Novel*. Translated by Hannah Mitchell and Stanley Mitchell. Lincoln: University of Nebraska Press, 1983.

Lynch, Deidre Shauna. *The Economy of Character: Novels, Market Culture, and the Business of Inner Meaning*. Chicago: University of Chicago Press, 1998.

MacIntyre, Alisdair. *After Virtue: A Study in Moral Theory*. 3rd ed. Notre Dame, Ind.: University of Notre Dame Press, 2007.

Mack, Douglas. *Scottish Fiction and the British Empire*. Edinburgh: Edinburgh University Press, 2005.

Mack, Ruth. *Literary Historicity: Literature and Historical Experience in Eighteenth-Century Britain*. Stanford, Calif.: Stanford University Press, 2009.

Macpherson, Sandra. *Harm's Way: Tragic Responsibility and the Novel Form*. Baltimore, Md.: Johns Hopkins University Press, 2010.

———. "Rent to Own; or, What's Entailed in *Pride and Prejudice*." *Representations* 82, no. 1 (2003): 1–23.

Maine, Henry Sumner. *The Ancient Law*. 4th ed. London: John Murray, 1870.

Maitland, F. W. "Moral Personality and Legal Personality." *Journal of Society of Comparative Legislation* n.s. 6 (1905): 192–200.

———. "Translator's Introduction." In *Political Theories of the Middle Age*, by Otto von Gierke. Cambridge: Cambridge University Press, 1900.

Manly, Susan. *Language, Custom, and Nation in the 1790s: Locke, Tooke, Wordsworth, Edgeworth*. Aldershot: Ashgate, 2007.

Manning, Susan. *The Puritan-Provincial Vision: Scottish and American Literature in the Nineteenth Century*. Cambridge: Cambridge University Press, 1990.

Marshall, David. *The Frame of Art: Fictions of Aesthetic Experience, 1750–1815*. Baltimore, Md.: Johns Hopkins University Press, 2005.

Marx, Karl, and Friedrich Engels. *The Communist Manifesto, a Modern Edition*. Edited by Eric Hobsbawm. London: Verso, 2012.

Matsuda, Mari. "Liberal Jurisprudence and Abstracted Visions of Human Nature." *New Mexico Law Review* 16 (1986): 613–630.

Maughan, Tim. "Could Ancient Laws Help Us Sue the Internet?" *New Scientist* (May 6, 2005). https://www.newscientist.com/article/mg22630200-600-could-ancient-laws-help-us-sue-the-internet/.

Mbembe, Achille. "Necropolitics." Translated by Libby Meintjes. *Public Culture* 15, no. 1 (2003): 11–40.

McCall, Brian M. "The Corporation as an Imperfect Society." *Delaware Journal of Corporate Law* 36 (2011): 511–575.

McGrail, Anne B. "Fanny Price's 'Customary' Subjectivity: Rereading the Individual in *Mansfield Park*." In *A Companion to Jane Austen Studies*, edited by Laura Cooner Lambdin and Robert Thomas Lambdin. Westport, Conn.: Greenwood Press, 2000.

McIntosh, Marjorie Keniston. *Autonomy and Community: The Royal Manor of Havering, 1200–1500*. Cambridge: Cambridge University Press, 1986.

———. *A Community Transformed: The Manor and Liberty of Havering, 1500–1620*. Cambridge: Cambridge University Press, 1991.

McKeon, Michael. *The Origins of the English Novel, 1600–1740*. Baltimore, Md.: Johns Hopkins University Press, 1987.

McQueen, Rob. *A Social History of Company Law: Great Britain and the Australian Colonies, 1854–1920*. Farnham: Ashgate, 2009.

Mehta, Uday Singh. *Liberalism and Empire: A Study in Nineteenth-Century British Liberal Thought*. Chicago: University of Chicago Press, 1999.

Mellor, Anne K. *Mary Shelley: Her Life, Her Fiction, Her Monsters*. London: Methuen, 1988.

Menke, Richard. *Telegraphic Realism: Victorian Fiction and Other Information Systems*. Stanford, Calif.: Stanford University Press, 2008.

Mill, James. *Analysis of the Human Mind with Notes Illustrative and Critical by Alexander Bain, Andrew Findlater, and George Grote*. Edited by John Stuart Mill. 2 vols. London: Longmans, Green, Reader and Dyer, 1878.

Mill, John Stuart. "Appendix to the Report from the Select Committee on the Law of Partnership." *Parliamentary Papers* 18 (1851): 182. Signed; not republished. Original heading: "1.—Reply to Queries by J. Stuart Mill, Esq."

———. "Introduction to the Present Edition." In *Analysis of Human Mind*. 2nd ed. London: Longman, 1878.

———. *A System of Logic: Ratiocinative and Inductive, Being a Connected View of the Principles of Evidence and the Methods of Scientific Investigation*. 8th ed. New York: Harper & Brothers, 1882.

———. *Utilitarianism*. London: Parker, Son, and Bourn, 1863.

Miller, D. A. *Jane Austen; or, The Secret of Style*. Princeton, N.J.: Princeton University Press, 2003.

———. *The Novel and the Police*. Berkeley: University of California Press, 1989.

Milsom, S. F. C. *Historical Foundations of the Common Law*. Oxford: Butterworth-Heinemann, 1969.

Milton, John. *Paradise Lost*. Norton Critical ed. Edited by Gordon Teskey. New York: Norton, 2005.

Mirowski, Philip. "The Rise and Retreat of a Market: English Joint Stock Shares in the Eighteenth Century." *Journal of Economic History* 41, no. 3 (1981): 559–577.

Moers, Ellen. "Female Gothic." In *The Endurance of Frankenstein: Essays on Mary Shelley's Novel*, edited by George Levine and U. C. Knoeflmacher. Berkeley: University of California Press, 1979.

Moretti, Franco. *The Bourgeois: Between History and Literature*. London: Verso, 2013.

———. *Graphs, Maps, Trees*. London: Verso, 2005.

Morton, Tim. *The Ecological Thought*. Cambridge, Mass.: Harvard University Press, 2010.

———. "Here Comes Everything: The Promise of Object-Oriented Ontology." *Qui Parle* 19, no. 2 (2011): 163–190.

Muthu, Sankar. "Adam Smith's Critique of International Trading Companies: Theorizing 'Globalization' in the Age of Enlightenment." *Political Theory* 36, no. 2 (2008): 185–212.

Napier, Elizabeth R. *The Failure of Gothic: Problems of Disjunction in an Eighteenth-Century Literary Form*. Oxford: Oxford University Press, 1987.

Nersessian, Anahid. "Radical Love and the Political Romance: Shelley After the Jacobin Novel." *ELH* 79, no. 1 (2012): 111–134.

———. *Utopia, Limited: Romanticism and Adjustment*. Cambridge, Mass.: Harvard University Press, 2015.

Nordius, Janina. "Racism and Radicalism in Jamaican Gothic: Cynric R. Williams's *Hamel the Obeah Man*." *ELH* 73, no. 3 (2006): 673–693.

Novalis. *Logological Fragments I*. In *Philosophical Writings*. Translated and edited by Margaret Mahony. Albany: State University of New York Press, 1997.

Nunokawa, Jeff. *The Afterlife of Property: Domestic Security and the Victorian Novel*. Princeton, N.J.: Princeton University Press, 2003.

Oliphant, Margaret. "Sensation Novels." *Blackwood's* 91 (January–June 1826).

O'Shaughnessy, David. "Caleb Williams and the Philomaths: Recalibrating Political Justice for the Nineteenth Century." *Nineteenth-Century Literature* 66, no. 4 (2012): 423–448.

Paine, Thomas. *The Rights of Man*. In *Reflections on the Revolution in France and The Rights of Man*. New York: Doubleday Anchor, 1973.

Parfit, Derek. *On What Matters*. Oxford: Oxford University Press, 2011.

———. *Reasons and Persons*. Oxford: Oxford University Press, 1984.

Parry, Jonathan. *The Rise and Fall of Liberal Government in Victorian Britain*. New Haven, Conn.: Yale University Press, 1993.

Penner, J. E. "Nuisance and the Character of the Neighborhood." *Journal of Environmental Law* 5, no. 1 (1993): 1–29.

Perry, Ruth. "All in the Family: Consanguinity, Marriage, and Property." In *The Oxford History of the Novel in English, vol. 2: English and British Fiction, 1750–1820*. Edited by Peter Garside and Karen O'Brien. Oxford: Oxford University Press, 2015.

Philip, Mark. "The Fragmented Ideology of Reform." In *The French Revolution and British Popular Politics*, edited by Mark Philip. Cambridge: Cambridge University Press, 1991.

Pierson, Chris. "The Reluctant Pirate: Godwin, Justice, and Property." *Journal of the History of Ideas* 71, no. 4 (2010): 569–591.

Pinch, Adela. *Strange Fits of Passion: Epistemologies of Emotion, Hume to Austen*. Stanford, Calif.: Stanford University Press, 1996.

Pitkin, Hannah. *The Concept of Representation*. Berkeley: University of California Press, 1967.

Plotz, John. *The Crowd: British Literature and Public Politics*. Berkeley: University of California Press, 2000.

———. "Speculative Naturalism and the Problem of Scale: Richard Jefferies's *After London, After Darwin*." *Modern Language Quarterly* 76, no. 1 (2015): 31–56.

Poe, Edgar Allan. "The Philosophy of Composition." In *The Unabridged Edgar Allan Poe*. Philadelphia: Running Press, 1983.

Pollock, Ellen. *Incest and the English Novel, 1684–1814*. Baltimore, Md.: Johns Hopkins Univ. Press, 2003.

Pollock, Frederick. "The English Manor." In *Oxford Lectures and Other Discourses*. London: Macmillan & Co., 1890.

———. *Principles of Contract at Law and in Equity*. 3rd American ed. New York: Baker, Voorhis and Co., 1906.

Pollock, Frederick, and William Maitland. *The History of the English Law Before the Time of Edward I*. 2nd ed. 2 vols. Cambridge: Cambridge University Press, 1899.

Poos, L. R., and Lloyd Bonfield. *Select Cases in Manorial Courts, 1250–1550*. London: Selden Society, 1998.

Poovey, Mary. *Genres of the Credit Economy: Mediating Value in the Eighteenth- and Nineteenth-Century Britain*. Chicago: University of Chicago Press, 2008.

———. *Making a Social Body: British Cultural Formation, 1830–1864*. Chicago: University of Chicago Press, 1995.

———. "My Hideous Progeny: Mary Shelley and the Feminization of Romanticism." *PMLA* 95, no. 3 (1980): 332–347.

Posner, Richard A. *Law and Literature: A Misunderstood Relation*. Cambridge, Mass.: Harvard University Press, 1988.

Preminger, Alex, and T.V. F. Brogan, eds. *The Princeton Encyclopedia of Poetics*. Princeton, N.J.: Princeton University Press, 1993.

Priestley, Joseph. *A Course of Lectures on the Theory of Language and Universal Grammar*. Warrington: W. Eyres, 1762.

———. *Disquisitions Relating to Matter and Spirit*. London: J. Johnson, 1782.

———. "Introductory Essays." In *Hartley's Theory of the Human Mind on the Principle of the Association of Ideas with Essays Relating to the Subject of It*. London: J. Johnson, 1775.

Priestley, Joseph, and Richard Price. *A Free Discussion of the Doctrines of Materialism and Philosophical Necessity in a Correspondence Between Dr. Price and Dr. Priestley*. London: J. Johnson, 1778.

Radcliffe, Evan. "Godwin from 'Metaphysician' to Novelist: *Political Justice, Caleb Williams*, and the Tension Between Philosophical Argument and Narrative." *Modern Philology* 97, no. 4 (2000): 528–533.

Radin, Max. "The Endless Problem of Corporate Personality." *Columbia Law Review* (1932): 643–667.

Rajan, Tilottama. "Judging Justice: Godwin's Critique of Judgment in *Caleb Williams* and Other Novels." *The Eighteenth Century* 51, no. 3 (2010): 341–362.

Rajan, Tilottama, and Julia M. Wright. *Romanticism, History, and the Possibilities of Genre: Re-forming Literature, 1789–1837*. Cambridge: Cambridge University Press, 2006.

Razi, Zvi, and Richard Smith, eds. *Medieval Society and the Manor Court*. Oxford: Clarendon, 1996.

Reitzel, William. "*Mansfield Park* and *Lovers' Vows*." *Review of English Studies* 9, no. 36 (1933): 451–456.

Renan, Ernest. "What Is a Nation?" In *The Nationalism Reader*, edited by Omar Dahbour and Micheline R. Ishay. New York: Humanity Books, 1995.

Renton, Alexander Wood, and Maxwell Alexander Robertson. *Encyclopaedia of the Laws of England with Forms and Precedents by the Most Eminent Legal Authorities*. 2nd ed. 15 vols. London: Sweet and Maxwell, Ltd., 1907.

Reports of Cases Argued and Determined in the English Courts of Common Law. Vol. 116. Philadelphia: T. & J. W. Johnson & Co., 1871.

Ringall, J. M. "Dickens and the Catastrophic Continuum of History in *A Tale of Two Cities*." In *Critical Essays on Charles Dickens's A Tale of Two Cities*, edited by Michael A. Cotsell. New York: G. K. Hall, 1998.

Robespierre, Maximilien. "On the Abolition of the Death Penalty." In *Robespierre*, edited by George Rudé. Englewood-Cliffs, N.J.: Prentice-Hall, 1967.

———. "On the Action to be Taken against Louis XVI." In *Robespierre*, edited by George Rudé. Englewood-Cliffs, N.J.: Prentice-Hall, 1967.

———. "Speech Denouncing the New Conditions of Eligibility." In *The French Revolution and Human Rights: A Brief Documentary History*, translated and edited by Lynn Hunt. Boston: Bedford St. Martin's, 1996.

———. "Speech on the Right to Vote." In *Robespierre*, edited by George Rudé. Englewood-Cliffs, N.J.: Prentice-Hall, 1967.

Rodensky, Lisa. *The Crime in Mind: Criminal Responsibility and the Victorian Novel.* Oxford: Oxford University Press, 2003.

Rovane, Carol. *The Bounds of Agency: An Essay in Revisionary Metaphysics.* Princeton, N.J.: Princeton University Press, 1998.

Runnican, David. *Pluralism and the Personality of the State.* Cambridge: Cambridge University Press, 1997.

Saville, John. "Sleeping Partnership and Limited Liability, 1850–1856." *Economic History Review* n.s. 8, no. 3 (1956): 418–433.

Schelling, Friedrich. *The Philosophy of Art.* Edited and translated by Douglas W. Stott. Minneapolis: University of Minnesota Press.

Schmidgen, Wolfram. *Eighteenth-Century Fiction and the Law of Property.* Cambridge: Cambridge University Press, 2006.

Scott, Walter. *Minstrelsy of the Scottish Border.* Edited by T. F. Henderson. Edinburgh: William Blackwood, 1902.

———. *Waverley.* Introduction by Kathryn Sutherland. Text and notes by Claire Lamont. Oxford: Oxford University Press, 2015.

Scriven, John. *A Treatise on the Law of Copyholds: And of the Other Tenures (Customary & Freehold) of Lands Within Manors: With the Law of Manors and Manorial Customs Generally, and the Rules of Evidence Applicable Thereto: Including the Law of Commons or Waste Lands: And Also the Jurisdiction of the Various Manorial Courts.* Revised by Archibald Brown. 7th ed. London: Butterworths, 1896.

Searle, John. *Neurobiology and Freedom: Reflections on Free Will, Language, and Political Power.* New York: Columbia University Press, 2007.

Sedgwick, Eve Kosofsky. *Between Men: English Literature and Male Homosocial Desire.* New York: Columbia University Press, 1985.

———. *The Coherence of Gothic Conventions.* New York: Arno, 1980.

Sedley, Stephen. *Ashes and Sparks: Essays on Law and Justice.* Cambridge: Cambridge University Press, 2011.

Selwyn, William. *An Abridgement of the Law of Nisi Prius.* 4th ed. 3 vols. London: W. Clark and Sons, 1817.

Shelley, Mary. *Frankenstein.* Introduction by Maurice Hindle. London: Penguin, 2003.

Shelley, Percy Bysshe. *Defence of Poetry.* In *Romantic Poetry and Prose,* edited by Harold Bloom and Lionel Trilling. Oxford: Oxford University Press, 1973.

———. "Mont Blanc: Lines Written in the Vale of Chamouni (Version A)." In *The Major Works,* edited by Zachary Leader and Michael O'Neill. Oxford: Oxford University Press, 2003.

———. "On Life." In *Percy Bysshe Shelley: Selected Poetry and Prose.* New York: Holt, Rinehart and Winston, 1951.

———. "Notes on *Queen Mab.*" In *The Works of Percy Bysshe Shelley Edited by Mrs. Shelley.* London: Edward Moxon, 1847.

Sieyès, Emmanuel Joseph. *What Is the Third Estate?* In *The Nationalism Reader,* edited by Omar Dahbour and Micheline R. Ishay. Amherst, N.Y.: Humanity Books, 1999.

Simpson, A. W. Brian. *Leading Cases in the Common Law.* Oxford: Clarendon, 1995.

Siskin, Clifford. "Novels and Systems." *Novel: A Forum on Fiction* 34, no. 2 2001: 202–215.

Smith, Adam. *Wealth of Nations*. New York: Modern Library, 2000.

Smith, Harry. "From Deodand to Dependency." *American Journal of Legal History* 11 (1967): 389–403.

Sokol, Mary. "Bentham and Blackstone on Incorporeal Hereditaments," *Journal of Legal History* 15, no. 3 1994: 287–305.

Southey, Robert. *Robert Southey: The Story of His Life Written in His Letters*. Edited by John Dennis. Boston: D. Lothrop Co., 1887.

Spence, Thomas. *The Constitution of Spensonia* (1803). http://www.ditext.com/spence/constitution.html.

———. "The Real Rights of Man, Plainly Shewn In A Lecture read at the Philosophical Society in Newcastle, on the 8th of November, 1775, for Printing of which, the Society did the Author the honour to expel him." In *Pig's meat; or, Lessons For the People, Alias According to Burke. The Swinish Multitude*, vol. 3. London: No. 8, Little Turnstile, High Holborn, 1795. http://thomas-spence-society.co.uk/7.html.

———. "The Restorer of Society to Its Natural State" (1801). In *The Political Works of Thomas Spence*, edited by H.T. Dickinson. Newcastle: Avero Eighteenth-Century Publications, 1982.

———. *A Supplement to the History of Robinson Crusoe, Being the Constitution of Crusonia* (1782). http://thomas-spence-society.co.uk/6.html.

Spivak, Gayatri Chakravorty. "Can the Subaltern Speak?" In *Marxism and the Interpretation of Culture*, edited by Cary Nelson and Lawrence Grossberg. London: Macmillan, 1998.

———. *Death of a Discipline*. New York: Columbia University Press, 2003.

———. "Three Women's Texts and a Critique of Imperialism." *Critical Inquiry* 12, no. 1 (1985): 235–261.

St. Clair, William. *The Reading Nation in the Romantic Period*. Cambridge: Cambridge University Press, 2004.

Stachniewski, John. *The Persecutory Imagination*. Oxford: Clarendon, 1991.

Stange, G. Robert. "*A Tale of Two Cities* Reconsidered." *English Journal* 47, no. 7 (1957): 381–390.

Steinlight, Emily. "Hardy's Unnecessary Lives: The Novel as Surplus." *Novel: A Forum on Fiction* 47, no. 2 (2014): 224–241.

———. "Supernumeraries and the Biopolitical Imagination of Victorian Fiction." *Novel: A Forum on Fiction* 43, no. 2 (2010): 227–250.

———. "Why Novels Are Redundant: Sensation Fiction and the Overpopulation of Literature." *ELH* 79, no. 2 (2012): 501–535.

Stephen, James Fitzjames. "Review of *A Tale of Two Cities*." *Saturday Review* (December 17, 1859).

Stewart, Garrett. "Citizen Adam: The Latest James Ivory and the Last Henry James." *Henry James Review* 23, no. 1 (2002): 1–24.

———. *Death Sentences: Styles of Dying in British Fiction*. Cambridge, Mass.: Harvard University Press, 1984.

Tarpley, Joyce Kerr. *Constancy and the Ethics of Jane Austen's* Mansfield Park. Washington, D.C.: Catholic University of America Press, 2010.

Taylor, Charles. *A Secular Age*. Cambridge, Mass.: Harvard University Press, 2007.

——. *Sources of the Self*. Cambridge: Cambridge University Press, 1989.

Taylor, James. *Creating Capitalism: Joint-Stock Politics in British Politics and Culture, 1800–1870*. Suffolk: Boydell and Brewer, 2006.

Thomas, David Wayne. *Cultivating Victorians: Liberal Culture and the Aesthetic*. Philadelphia: University of Pennsylvania Press, 2004.

Thompson, E. P. *Customs in Common: Studies in Traditional Popular Culture*. London: Penguin, 1993.

——. "The Grid of Inheritance: A Comment." In *Family and Inheritance: Rural Society in Western Europe, 1200–1800*, edited by Jack Goody, Joan Thirsk, and E. P. Thompson. Cambridge: Cambridge University Press, 1978.

——. *The Making of the English Working Class*. New York: Vintage, 1966.

Tiffany, Daniel. *Infidel Poetics: Riddles, Nightlife, Substance*. Chicago: University of Chicago Press, 2009.

Todd, Janet. *The Cambridge Introduction to Jane Austen*. 2nd ed. Cambridge: Cambridge University Press, 2011.

Todorov, Tzvetan. *Theories of the Symbol*. Translated by Catherine Porter. Ithaca, N.Y.: Cornell University Press, 1984.

Tooke, John Horne. *Epea Pteroenta, or the Diversions of Purley*. London: Thomas Tegg, 1840.

——. "A Letter to Dunning, Esq. by Mr. Horne." London: J. Johnson, 1778.

Trilling, Lionel. *The Opposing Self: Nine Essays in Criticism*. New York: Viking, 1955.

Trumpener, Katie. *Bardic Nationalism*. Princeton, N.J.: Princeton University Press, 1997.

Tucker, Irene. *The Moment of Racial Sight: A History*. Chicago: University of Chicago Press, 2012.

Tuite, Clara. *Romantic Austen: Sexual Politics and the Literary Canon*. Cambridge: Cambridge University Press, 2002.

Urda, Kathleen E. "Why the Show Must Not Go On: 'Real Character' and the Absence of Theatrical Performances in *Mansfield Park*." *Eighteenth-Century Fiction* 26, no. 2 (2013–2014): 281–302.

Vanden Bossche, Chris R. *Reform Acts: Chartism, Social Agency, and the Victorian Novel, 1832–1867*. Baltimore, Md.: Johns Hopkins University Press, 2014.

Vinogradoff, Paul. *The Growth of the Manor*. London: Swann Sonnenschein, 1905.

Vermeule, Blakey. *Why Do We Care About Literary Characters?* Baltimore, Md.: Johns Hopkins University Press, 2009.

Waddell, Brodie. "Governing England Through the Manor Courts, 1550–1850." *Historical Journal* 55, no. 2 (2012): 279–315.

Waldron, Jeremy. *God, Locke, and Equality*. Cambridge: Cambridge University Press, 2002.

Walpole, Horace. "Preface to the First Edition." In *The Castle of Otranto*, edited by W. S. Lewis. Oxford: Oxford University Press, 2008.

Walzer, Michael. "The Communitarian Critique of Liberalism." *Political Theory* 18 (1990): 6–23.

——. *The Revolution of the Saints: A Study in the Origins of Radical Politics*. Cambridge, Mass.: Harvard University Press, 1965.

Warner, Michael. *Publics and Counterpublics.* New York: Zone, 2005.

Watt, Ian. *The Rise of the Novel: Studies in Defoe, Richardson, and Fielding.* Berkeley: University of California Press, 2001.

Watt, James. *Contesting the Gothic: Fiction, Genre, and Cultural Conflict, 1764–1832.* Cambridge: Cambridge University Press, 1999.

Weber, Max. *The Protestant Ethic and the Spirit of Capitalism.* Translated by Talcott Parsons. New York: Charles Scribner's Sons, 1958.

Weisberg, Richard. *Poethics: And Other Strategies of Law and Literature.* New York: Columbia University Press, 1992.

Welsh, Alexander. *Strong Representations: Narrative and Circumstantial Evidence in England.* Baltimore, Md.: Johns Hopkins University Press, 1992.

West, Jane. *A Tale of the Times.* 3 vols. London: T. N. Longman and O. Rees, 1799.

Williams, Joan C. "The Invention of the Municipal Corporation: A Case Study in Legal Change." *American University Law Review* 34 (1985): 369–438.

Wolfe, Cary. *Animal Rites: American Culture, the Discourse of Species, and Posthumanist Theory.* Chicago: University of Chicago Press, 2003.

Woloch, Alex. *The One Versus the Many.* Princeton, N.J.: Princeton University Press, 2005.

Wordsworth, William. "Michael. A Pastoral Poem." In *The Poetical Works of William Wordsworth,* edited by E. de Selincourt and Helen Darbishire, 2nd ed., 5 vols. Oxford: Clarendon, 1954.

———. "Preface to *Lyrical Ballads*" (1802). In *Lyrical Ballads and Related Writings,* edited by William Richey and Daniel Robinson. Boston: Houghton Mifflin, 2002.

———. *The Thirteen Book Prelude of 1805.* In *The Prelude: The Four Texts (1798, 1799, 1805, 1850),* edited by Jonathan Wordsworth. London: Penguin, 1995.

———. "The World Is Too Much With Us." In *The Poetical Works of William Wordsworth,* edited by E. de Selincourt and Helen Darbishire, 5 vols., 2nd ed. Oxford: Clarendon, 1954.

Zelicovici, Dvora. "The Inefficacy of Lovers' Vows." *ELH* 50, no. 3 (1983): 531–540.

Žižek, Slavoj. "Robespierre; or, The 'Divine Violence' of Terror." In *Virtue and Terror,* edited by Jean Ducange and translated by John Howe. London: Verso, 2007.

Index

Sara Guyer and Brian McGrath, series editors